RUSSIA: THE 20th CENTURY

THE WORLD OF

ART MOVEMENT
IN EARLY 20th–CENTURY RUSSIA

AURORA ART PUBLISHERS • LENINGRAD

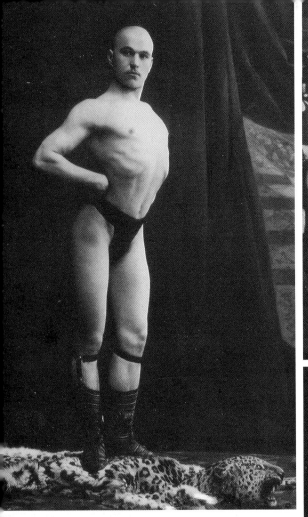

"Les Thérésanna's"

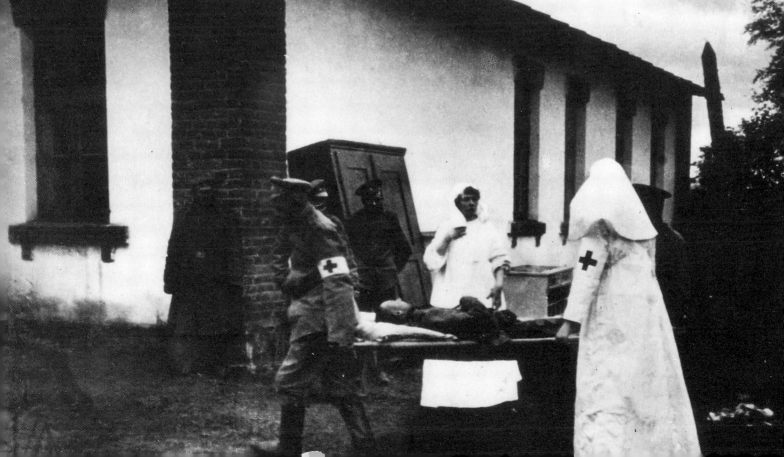

Introductory essays by **Vsevolod Petrov** and
Alexander Kamensky
Selection by **Alexander Kamensky**
Translated from the Russian by **Arthur Shkarovsky-Raffe**
Layout and design by **Sergei Dyachenko** and
Alexander Loshenkov
Managing editor **Irina Kharitonova**

© 1991: Aurora Art Publishers, Leningrad, and the contributors
Printed and bound in Finland

M $\frac{4903020000\text{-}931}{023(01)\text{-}91}$ 38-90

ISBN 5-7300-0215-7

VSEVOLOD PETROV'S ESSAY AND SOME ASPECTS OF THE WORLD OF ART MOVEMENT

Vsevolod Nikolayevich Petrov (1912–1978) was more than a profoundly erudite art historian and sensitive art critic. He is also remembered as a carrier of the Russian intelligentsia's finest traditions and a profound chronicler of St. Petersburg–Petrograd–Leningrad.

Whenener I think of this man, I first of all recall his astonishingly remarkable home on Mayakovsky Street, where he lived for several decades. Everything there bore the stamp of his personality, of his tastes and interests, whether the antique furniture, his collection of eighteenth- to twentieth-century engravings and paintings, his huge but affectionately chosen library, with its select art books and highly representative volumes of early twentieth-century Russian poets, and that enigmatic half-breed of baby grand and melodeon. I see in my mind's eye the winding corridors he so often paced in reflection and feel that special Petersburg atmosphere which evokes in every Russian shades of Dostoyevsky, Blok, and Bely. His apartment also conjures up memories of the fascinating people who often called upon Petrov, as he was an amiable friend of long standing with many illustrious names in Russian art and letters, including Anna Akhmatova, Mikhail Kuzmin, Vladimir Lebedev, Nikolai Tyrsa, Yuri Vasnetsov, Nikolai Punin, and Vladimir Orlov. Petrov recounted his meetings and conversations with all these men and women in his magnificently written *Book of Reminiscences*, from which only excerpts have been published so far. Finally, one must necessarily add that Vsevolod Petrov was the son of Academician Nikolai Nikolayevich Petrov, the founder of the Soviet school of oncology, for which reason he was very familiar with the city's academic community too.

Yet despite his close associations with the world of art and letters and his own literary talents, so manifest in the *Book of Reminiscences*, he was no rambling essayist inclined toward abstract metaphor and other literary niceties. On the contrary, in everything he penned that dealt with painters, sculptors, or graphic artists, he always supplied concise definition and factual accuracy. This he owed to his work at Leningrad's Russian Museum, where he worked as a researcher from 1934 through 1949 (except for the war years, when he served with the armed forces in the field). It is also possible that his ascetic explicitness bears the imprint of Kuzmin's style of writing and, more generally, of that "neo-classical" trend in twentieth-century Russian literature, associated above all, with the Acmeists, with whose protagonists, and, more specifically, Anna Akhmatova and Osip Mandelstam, he was such fast friends.

As for myself personally, Petrov's essays in the field of art history always evoke associations with his adored Petersburg architecture. Though he never produced a single monograph about these wonderful gems, he had every relevant fact at his fingertips. No wonder a stroll in his company down the streets of the city was a never-ending source of delight. Indeed, he knew the history of virtually every single old building, not only who designed and built it, but who lived in it, and what had happened there. His exhaustive account was lively and lucid, as if he were recounting episodes from his own life. He appreciated more than enything else the classical clarity and tectonic logic of Petersburg architecture, its harmonious proportions, what the poet termed its "austere and modest face." It is my conviction that he transferred all these properties to every thought he put down on paper, in everything he wrote as an art historian.

Petrov's essay on the World of Art movement – let alone his numerous researches concerned with Russian, mostly Petersburg sculpture – presents an apposite instance. In fact, it is largely "Petersburgian," as the author consistently emphasizes that this celebrated society of Russian artists was established on the shores of the Neva, that its founders were Petersburgians, and, finally, that Petersburg as such holds pride of place in their oeuvre. He affords ample proof that the vast cultural erudition of the *miriskusniki*, their infatuation with "the good old days," their constant "dialogues with history," their proclivity for the theater and the theatrical in art, derive, along with much else, from the fertile medium of the long-standing, stable traditions of the Petersburg intelligentsia, whose activities reflected the overall cultural, intellectual, and spiritual interests of Russia. Meanwhile the clarity of concept, the tactfully presented factual evidence, the firm sense of historical perspective, and – last, but not least – the logical and lucid exposition so characteristic of the essay in question, are quite obviously consistent with the strictly scientific principles of the Leningrad school of art history studies.

What is truly precious here is an inner quality that may be overlooked at a cursory glance. As an absolutely unbiassed, fastidious analyst and chronicler of the World of Art trend, Petrov speaks, in a certain sense, of himself when describing this movement. For he was not only personally acquainted with some of the younger *miriskusniki*, but was also nurtured to some extent by the specific cultural and artistic atmosphere which they generated. Though, as the years rolled by, he forged further ahead and adopted different positions in ideology and art history studies, he unquestionably benefited from the vast heritage of this largest association of early twentieth-century Russian artists, not only as an impartial observer, but also in his own intellectual evolution.

One must necessarily note that Petrov was the first to shoulder the laborious task of placing this movement in the proper historical perspective and objectively evaluating it. His essay, featured herein, precedes the chapter dealing with this trend that will be found in the first part of Volume 10 of *The History of Russian Art*. Other revelant essays written later cannot hold a candle to it conceptually. Petrov's innovative daring is especially appreciated when contrasted to the negative attitude toward the World of Art that persisted in Soviet art studies for years on end.

In his complete restoration of the objective picture, Petrov resolutely and clearly expounded his understanding of the creative principles of World of Art members. His effort – one for which he must be duly credited and from which other art historians proceeded later – should be viewed in the overall context of Russian art history. We can now discern more distinctly the deep-seated links between the style and imagery of the *miriskusniki* and the many trends and interests of Russian artists in the earlier decades. This impression of the organic place held by the *miriskusniki* in Russian culture as a whole is excellently conveyed. Petrov aptly links the creative endeavors of the World of Art members with what he terms their "educational" work. Again the author shows how profoundly this work reflected the basic interests of Russian society, inasmuch as their attraction for Russia's culture of the eighteenth and nineteenth centuries directly mirrored the growing national awareness characteristic of Russia at the turn of the twentieth century. One related aspect was the focus on folk art and mores – as evinced by Kustodiev, Sapunov, Roerich, and Serebryakova, to mention but four – that derived from the Abramtsevo Colony, a predecessor of the World of Art group. Then, the heightened interest in history typical of the World of Art was likewise a distinctive reflection of one of the most noteworthy of current tendencies, namely the urge to understand and see one's place in the context of the march of time and the scope of all of humanity. It was primarily these aspirations, not Russian "exoticism," that motivated the society's propagation of Russian art and culture abroad, through the medium of Sergei Diaghilev's celebrated Russian Seasons in Paris and other European capitals. Thanks to this man's volcanic energy and inexhaustible organizational gifts, the world learned of Russia's wealth of daring artistic talent and her cultural treasures. Diaghilev was deeply convinced that Russian culture held a special place of honor in the world. It was in this light that he viewed the "pagan" colorfulness and full-blooded imagery of Russian myths, legends, and fairy tales, the unusual resonance of the "Russian Muse" in the art galleries and opera and ballet houses of the globe. Against this background the "European standard" of Russian art and its exponents was seen as especially significant and historically conditioned. From the national to the global was the logic of the countless efforts undertaken by the World of Art group in the domains of art and "enlightenment."

By his essay Petrov has demonstrated this logic and its materialization. Reviewing the diverse approaches of the *miriskusniki*, he stresses the prevalence of the spectacular and the culturo-historical aspects in their works. The first was responsible for the magnificent scenic innovations of Alexander Benois, Léon Bakst, Alexander Golovin, Mstislav Dobuzhinsky, and others. The second was expressed in the plethora of subject matter derived from history, and also in book design and illustration; as Petrov so aptly notes, the *miriskusniki* effected a "breakthrough in the history of Russian book graphics – moreover, its revival and flowering."

Among the other genres which the artists of the World of Art society successfully developed, Petrov justly indicates the graphic easel portrait. As a matter of fact, he himself, if one may take the liberty of drawing such a parallel, has provided in his essay the "graphic profiles" of the exponents of the genre mentioned. In this sense, he has delineated Konstantin Somov and Mstislav Dobuzhinsky with particular aptitude.

While absolutely right in its basic aspects, at this time Petrov's overall assessment of the World of Art movement may stand in need of some corrections and amendments – of which further. Yet, this essay is still fully valid because, as was mentioned earlier, Petrov pioneered in art studies a new interpretation of the movement, and also because nothing has been published to this day which would have presented it from a different angle or in fuller detail and concept. Implied, of course, are only the efforts to attempt a general survey of the movement. As far as the various, separate aspects of it are concerned, numerous studies and researches (which have greatly changed matters) saw the light of day throughout the 1970s and the 1980s. In this respect, we could mention, firstly, the monographs, art books, and essays devoted to individual artists of the World of Art society, indeed, virtually all of them, with some publications coming out in several editions and reprints. Secondly, certain major aspects of the World of Art's history and stylistic and thematic evolution have been covered by D.V. Sarabyanov, G.Yu. Sternin, and A.A. Rusakova. Thirdly, a great contribution has been made through the medium of various exhibitions. Thus, the Abramyan collection shown at Yerevan's Museum of Russian Art in 1984 and the exciting exhibition of I.S. Silberstein's collection in Moscow in the following year presented so wonderfully diverse a panoramic survey of the World of Art movement, that they made for an entirely new understanding of the group's significance. Naturally, this was stimulated as well by the excellent individual shows of Mstislav Dobuzhinsky, Boris Kustodiev, Nicholas Roerich, Zinaida Serebryakova, and other artists. Finally, as the overall nature of assessments by Soviet art historians has largely changed over the last twenty to thirty years, that could not but affect the attitude toward the World of Art movement.

In this connection, what do we think needs to be done to complement and correct Petrov's essay?

No doubt, the modern art historian would find the trend's historical role still more significant and, at any rate, would regard as overly categorical the reproaches that the oeuvre of the World of Art group "was marked by sheer aestheticism" and was "divorced from the cardinal social issues of the time." Today we clearly realize that these artists have markedly modified both the range and level of Russian artistic culture, broadening horizons to encompass the heritage of Russian and European art – and not only art, may we add. They placed both art reviewing and art history on a professional level, raised to new pinnacles of achievement stage design and book illustration, both of which had previously eked out a dull, journeyman existence, and signally contributed to the applied arts, interior design, the synthesis of diverse decorative genres, sculpture, architecture, and, last but not least, art teaching and instruction – which was all of tremendous social significance.

Though this significance unquestionably derives from the actual works of the artists of the World of Art association, implied is more than the direct response to the events of the 1905 Revolution in Russia that Valentin Serov, Evgeny Lanceray, Mstislav Dobuzhinsky and Ivan Bilibin demonstrated in their political graphics. Earlier we indicated the profound social nature of the artists' keen interest in Russian history. Then, many vital signs of the times were reflected in their portrait painting as well.

However, it is rather the following problem, which the modern art historian would count of special import, precisely in connection with the social resonance of works by the group's members. Petrov did not overlook it; on the contrary, he quite justly noted that the "senior World of Art generation depicted, more often than not, festivities and carnivals." Yet how should we regard and construe this preference? Over the past fifteen – twenty years, students of literature and art have arrived at a theory, in line with which the festival would appear to comprise life's ideal model.[1]

The scenes of a happy and harmonious world, as presented on the stage of the "theater of the ideal," bring into focus the most cherished hopes of the time, the

[1] Major studies in this connection have been written by such Soviet scholars as A. Piotrovsky, V. Propp, M. Bakhtin, D. Likhachev, V. Shklovsky, Y. Bromlei, and A. Gurevich. A. Mazayev's highly appreciated *The Festival as a Socio-Artistic Phenomenon* came out in 1978. O. Nemiro's *The Decorative Artistic Design of Soviet Mass Festivals* (Leningrad, 1967) and A. Kamensky's articles "The Festival as the Theater of the Ideal," *Dekorativnoye iskusstvo*, 1978, No. 11, pp. 29–34 and "The Substance of the Festival," *Iskusstvo*, 1979, No. 3, pp. 70–71 are concerned with the same topic.

12

concepts of justice, beauty, and liberty nurtured in the heart. The long-standing tradition is complemented by the new civic and aesthetical experience. Against the background of Russian life at the turn of the century, marked by the dawning of revolution, these artistic solutions to the problem of the ideal comprised, in the final analysis, a response to the most vital issues of the country's social being.

Given this interpretation, the festive character of the works of the World of Art artists acquires a very special meaning and supreme designation. Naturally they constructed their ideal associative imagery with a dreaminess born of their own notions, more often than not detached from immediate observations. Indeed Benois' contemporaries already discerned in his pictures "the festivity of the royal West, which had gone never to return."[2] In Somov's compositions the action is always set in a cloudlessly idyllic Utopia, and in garb after the fashion of the eighteenth century, which is precisely where the scintillating, fun-provoking rainbows and fireworks displays accompany *fêtes galantes* and eccentric harlequinades. Lanceray was attracted to the pomp and glitter of the Russian court ritual in the times of the Empress Elizaveta. Bakst sought in some of his decorative panels to revive the spirits of the ennobled ancient idyll. Even the subject matter of his celebrated *Terror Antiquus* is presented as an awe-inspiring spectacle of cosmic scope, reflecting, in a certain sense, the festive "harmony of a placated spirit in the face of the spectacle of global disharmony."[3]

In all these and many other works by the society's leading artists, the festival appears as the sole worthwhile form of life.

Yet the works of this type reveal a decidedly ephemeral character. What we are treated to is a rather carefree, self-engrossing game, a virtuoso musical capriccio, wherein the elegant artistry of the author is blended with high culture and a subtle feeling for the artistic styles of previous epochs. Life is presented as a kaleidoscope of frivolous interludes, sparkling carnivals, and sarcastically pensive, sentimental episodes. The game principle is accentuated and made the key, with theatricalization of action set out as the program.

However, some leading World of Art exponents proceeded from other concepts in compositions of this order. Thus, toward the end of his life, Valentin Serov was concerned with the notion of the procession, which is linked to the festival tradition. He adapted his compositional arrangements to motifs of social advance, as in his *Peter the Great*, or of struggle, as in his *The Funeral of Baumann*, and, finally, to the romanticized imagery of a beautiful and happy world. The procession was made the dynamic pivot of festive dreams, couched in metaphor and symbol, or historicized, as, for instance, in his *Rape of Europa* and *Odysseus and Nausicaä*, wherein the ancient myths were construed in contemporary terms and reproduced as visions of a realm of bliss and liberty.[4]

The work of Boris Kustodiev occupies a special place in the World of Art heritage. His pictures of Shrovetide carnivals, bazaars, country reels, summer and winter festivals, and other festive occasions, as well as his colorful paraphrases of the peasant and merchant ideals of female beauty, like *La Belle* and *The Russian Venus*, all are done in a folk style to the very marrow. Most likely, this folk element, with its brimming vitality, eternal movement, and rainbow profusion of color, is the central "personage" of the artist's *festivities*. Though externally simple and artless, this is the quintessence of an integral, multifaceted philosophy of living that crowns with radiant joy every labor and day, every single human care, feeling, hope, and aspira-

[2] S. Makovsky, *Siluety russkikh khudozhnikov* (Silhouettes of Russian Artists), Prague, 1922, p. 90

[3] V. Ivanov, "Drevniy uzhas" (Terror Antiquus), in: *Po zviozdam* (Among the Stars), St. Petersburg, 1909, p. 403

[4] A. Bakushinsky, "Formalnoye razvitie motiva shestviya u Serova" (The Formal Development of the Procession Motif in Serov's Works), in: *Trudy sektsii iskusstvoznaniya Instituta arkheologii i iskusstvoznaniya*, Moscow, 2, 1928, pp. 128–213; A. Bakushinsky, "Monumentalno-dekorativnye iskaniya epokhi modern" (The Monumental-Decorative Searching in the Period of Art Nouveau), *Iskusstvo*, 1934, No. 4, pp. 160–167

tion. This folk element may seem sombrely mysterious, deceptive, frightening, but at heart it is kind and courteous, breathing that sensation of freedom gained, which, with its bright skies and romantic idea, comprises the core of every folk carnival and gala. Thus Kustodiev's "sempiternal" stories in pictures unexpectedly acquired an extreme topicality within the context of their time. Through the works of such masters as Kustodiev, with their vividly underivative fantasies, the World of Art directly, deeply, and organically merged with the crucial social and aesthetical issues of the day.

We observe the same, although in a totally different form, in the festive kingdom of Nikolai Sapunov's pictures. A virtuoso and refined master, with a subtle flair for color and wholeheartedly devoted to theatricalized convention, he is at total variance with the cold, contemplative, unruffled approach of the World of Art's founding members. His sense of popular merrymaking has naught of the pastoral idyll; it is as complex and confused as was Russia's life at the start of the century. His merry-go-rounds, masked balls, carnivals, and tavern carousals are throbbing pageants, offering a fanciful blend of self-absorbing infatuation and piercingly soulful perturbation. There is nothing here of the graphic severity and prim illusion of spatial perspective encountered in the works of Benois, Somov, and Lanceray. Thus, the first impression gained of the *Merry-go-round* of 1908, which is now in the Russian Museum, is of a riotous mixture of tints and hues much like a carnival fireworks display. Gradually there emerge from this glitter the outlines of figures and objects, phantomlike, as if ready to dissolve that very instant within the glowing motleyness of the fair-ground gaiety. No wonder the customary spatial structure has been discarded; it would overly regiment the colorful turbulence of the festival. Yet however brimmingly carefree this spectacle may seem, it is by no means chaotic, with the swirl of the merry-go-round distinctly delineated, serving as the dynamic pivot of the decorative unity of the color scheme with its dominant reds, greens, and cerulean blues, and thus organizing and directing the overall impression.

Sapunov breathes the very air of the festive sights which he reproduces and in which he directly participates. Here we encounter a characteristic paradox that I would term a "double–mirror system." After all, to a certain extent these pictures are self-descriptive, with reproduction and participation joining hands in a living, never-ending rhythm. In the artist's case, the logic of the imagery and the feeling for the festivity have led him through pastime and decorative arabesque to a somewhat blurred, yet deep and strong sensation of the drama characteristic of the national life of the time, whatever Commedia-dell'arte personages he may have portrayed. "Indeed, Sapunov," his contemporary exclaimed, "is both the song and the pain; his chaotic, excessively exuberant work…. is both the merry-go-round and Russia herself with the Red Flag."[5]

It would be quite appropriate to clarify the "Westernism" of the World of Art protagonists that is constantly mentioned in the relevant literature, and that we again find in Petrov's essay. They were doubtless keenly interested in Western culture, with which they were so familiar and maintained diverse links; they even borrowed subjects from European literature and art. But this on no account obscured the artists' invariable devotion to their homeland. With them the West was depicted more often than not from a Russian perspective and in a Russian manner, mirroring the new range of interests of Russia's intelligentsia, with its comprehensive contribution to worldwide intellectual and spiritual culture.

[5] N. Punin, "Tri khudozhnika…" (Three Artists: B. Grigoryev, Sapunov, Krymov), *Apollon*, 1915, No. 8–9, p. 8

Indeed, their dream of a free, happy life, the psychology of their imagery and, for that matter, their entire basic concept of style were Russian. For as we can now clearly see, all of this, in a definite sense, carried forward and rejuvenated the artistic quests of their predecessors in the domain of Russian culture. Further, with Bilibin, Dobuzhinsky, Kustodiev, Lanceray, Ostroumova-Lebedeva, Roerich, and Serebryakova, even the narrative aspect was Russian.

The latest studies offer new interpretations of some other aspects of art history that relate to the World of Art. Petrov's mention of Art Nouveau is primarily negative, synonymous with eclecticism and poor taste. However, since the publication of a whole series of papers, specifically those by such Soviet scholars as Rusakova, Sarabyanov, and Sternin, and earlier by A. Fyodorov-Davydov, the conviction has been gaining ground that this trend was an entirely logical chapter in art's evolution at the turn of the century, something which historians today regard as "a sweeping category deriving from the multitude of phenomena in *fin-de-siècle* art" and even as the "style of the epoch."[6] Though the knotty issue of the World of Art's approach toward Art Nouveau – the reciprocal borrowings, the Russian traditions retained and transformed, etc.– still calls for further detailed study, the related research has already started and proceeds from a completely different attitude than favored by art historians round the world, let alone in the USSR, between the 1940s and the 1960s.

Finally, still outstanding is the issue of the second phase of the World of Art movement following its revival in 1910. Should we restrict the creative range merely to the style of the founders and their direct successors? Should we maintain that, for instance, such constant exhibitors in the World of Art shows as Kuzma Petrov-Vodkin (who was represented at every single show from 1910 on), Martiros Saryan, Nathan Altman, Boris Grigoryev, Pavel Kuznetsov, Nikolai Krymov, and many others were not creatively kin and did not subscribe to its aesthetic principles? (Petrov writes: "artists, in effect far removed from the creative concepts of the World of Art, but seeking and finding moral backing within its highly cultured artistic milieu.") Had not these conceptions and this milieu changed by the 1910s? After all, in its final period, the World of Art trend had shelved factionalism, seeking rather to unite all that was most talented and promising in Russian painting and graphics – and, partly, in the realm of sculpture, too. Indeed, for significance, the abundance of talent, and the daring and power of artistic questing, no other trend in the pre-revolutionary art of Russia of the 1910s could hold a candle to the World of Art. It is high time to regard its activity then as a productive current in Russia's visual arts.

Future students of the problem will finalize the answers to all these knotty issues which the art historians of today have placed on the agenda. Whatever the case, Petrov's talented essay will continue to serve as the point of departure, as in his field he has indeed left an impressive landmark.

Alexander Kamensky

[6] D. Sarabyanov, "Russkiy variant stilia modern v zhivopisi kontsa XIX–nachala XX veka" (The Russian Version of Style Moderne in Turn-of-the-century Painting), in: *Russkaya zhivopis' XIX veka sredi evropeiskikh shkol* (19th-century Russian Painting among European Schools), Moscow, 1981, p. 182

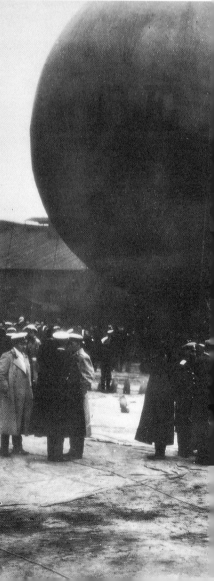

THE WORLD OF ART MOVEMENT

In the history of Russian art, the late nineteenth century was a period of creative innovation and a fundamental restructuring of form.

In the 1890s, a new chapter was opened in Russia's visual arts by a generation of artists who radically revised almost the entire range of established tradition. Authorities that had seemed immutable were suddenly toppled from their pedestals. The horizon of artistic creativity broadened, a new aesthetic emerged, and new art trends arose, all in striking contrast to what the earlier art movements of the nineteenth century had asserted. The re-evaluation of values led to cardinal changes in the interpretation and understanding of creative objectives and techniques.

THE WORLD OF ART: CHRONOLOGICAL REVIEW

The purpose of the Chronological Review herein presented is to furnish an annotated compendium of the documents and events associated with the history and creative practice of the World of Art movement. Since Vsevolod Petrov's essay is devoted almost exclusively to the "classical" period of the group's activities (1898–1910), commentaries are restricted, with its second phase presented solely by means of reference material. The compiler has addressed himself to most of the publications indicated in the bibliography, plus a range of archival documents and his own *card file*. Wherever use is made of quotations the source is necessarily indicated.

As for the biographical particulars of the different artists, information is provided from 1898 for founding members of the World of Art society, and for others, from the year in which the artist in question first exhibited in World of Art shows. Data have been borrowed from the reference material contained in catalogues of the Tretyakov Gallery in Moscow, the Russian Museum in Leningrad, other catalogues, mostly of one-man shows and museum collections, and also monographs devoted to individual artists of the association. Most valuable in this respect were such publications as A. Benois, *My Recollections* (prepared for press by N.I. Alexandrova, A.L. Grishunin, A.N. Savinov, L.V. Andreyeva, G.G. Pospelov, and G.Yu. Sternin); A. Benois, *The Emergence of the World of Art*; *Alexander Benois Meditates* (prepared for press, with an introduction and commentaries by I.S. Silberstein and A.N. Savinov); A.N. Benois, *Sergei Diaghilev and Russian Art* (compiled, introduced, and annotated by I.S. Silberstein and V.A. Samkov); *Valentin Serov in the Reminiscences, Diaries and*

Correspondence of Contemporaries (edited, compiled, introduced and annotated by I.S. Silberstein and V.A. Samkov); *Igor Grabar: Letters (1891–1912)* (edited and compiled by L.V. Andreyeva and T.P. Kazhdan); G.Yu. Sternin, *Turn-of-the-Century Russian Art*; G.Yu. Sternin, *Early 20th-Century Russian Art*; V.P. Lapshin, *The Union of Russian Artists* (all these publications are in Russian and duly listed in the bibliography).

The compiler is sincerely grateful to I.S. Silberstein, V.P. Lapshin, D.V. Sarabyanov, and G.Yu. Sternin for the valuable advice afforded when working on the Chronological Review, and also deeply appreciates the help given by the two art historians, T.G. Guryeva-Gurevich and M.K. Ivanova, in selecting and verifying the related factual data.

In this Chronological Review, the compiler has basically sought to provide a very general idea of the history of the World of Art movement from the perspective of its creative and organizational efforts. He by no means claims to have covered the entire range of problems tackled by the society, or more so, to have traced the evolution of each individual artist. He has merely endeavored to outline the vast, complex, and colorful phenomenon of early twentieth-century Russian culture known as the World of Art, and to furnish information concerning associated events in art serving to make comprehensible its creative directions and the part it played in the social and cultural affairs of the time. As for the lists of works by individual artists, only the most characteristic pieces are noted, in chronological order. The medium "oil" has been omitted; nor are the media used in stage design and book and magazine illustration indicated.

Before 1898
At the turn of the 1880s and 1890s, a group of secondary-school boys, subsequently university

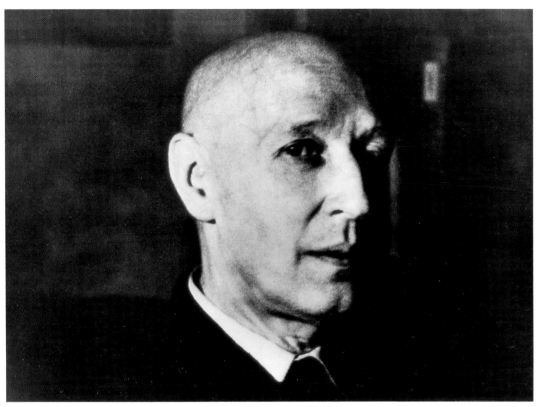

1. Vsevolod Petrov. Photograph. 1970s

students, gathered at the house of the architect Nikolai Benois, father of the two artists, Alexander and Albert Benois. It began as a club of several pupils studying at Karl Mai's Gymnasium in St. Petersburg – notably Alexander Benois, Walter Nouvel, Konstantin Somov, and Dmitry Filosofov. In 1890, Benois and his friends set up a Society for Self-Education which arranged regular lectures on various subjects, discussed the latest books and magazines, and held musical evenings. In his recollections Alexander Benois wrote: "Full members of this society – the actual cradle of the World of Art – included, besides myself, who was elected 'president,' Walter Fyodorovich Nouvel, Dmitry Vladimirovich Filosofov, Lev Samoilovich Rosenberg, who in the following year took his grandfather's name of Bakst, Grigory Yemelyanovich Kalin, Nikolai Vasilyevich Skalon....Present, but not always, as auditors and elected shortly afterwards as 'honorable members' were Konstantin Andreyevich Somov, my childhood chum Valentin Alexandrovich Brune de St. Hyppolite, who subsequently disappeared from the scene, Evgeny Nikolayevich Fenou, Yuri Anatolyevich Mamontov, Nikolai Petrovich Cherimisinov, Dmitry Alexandrovich Pypin, and Sergei Pavlovich Diaghilev...."[1]
The very name, World of Art, was devised by this group long before the journal and the related exhibitions began. The lectures read dealt with the history of the visual arts in the West and in Russia (Benois and Bakst), literary problems (Kalin), music (Nouvel, with Diaghilev providing illustrative accompaniment), history (Filosofov), and religion (Skalon). The "society" existed in this form till 1891. But when Evgeny Lanceray, who was to become an artist, and Alfred Nurok, the future writer and art critic, joined the group in 1891–93, the issues of the day began to crowd out the interest in history and

art. At the same time the idea arose of putting out a journal and arranging art shows, which, however, was not fated to be realized that soon.
In 1893, Benois made his literary debut with a chapter on Russian artists for Richard Muther's *Geschichte der Malerei im XIX. Jahrhundert*, while two years later Diaghilev published his first art reviews. In 1897, Diaghilev made his entrepreneurial debut, arranging an exhibition of English and German watercolorists, with one room devoted entirely to the portraits of the then highly popular German painter, Franz von Lenbach. He then organized an exhibition of Scandinavian art at which seventy odd artists of Sweden, Denmark, and Norway were represented. The success of these two shows, both of which were mounted in St. Petersburg, gave Diaghilev confidence and impelled him to undertake the daring initiatives that were to serve as the point of departure for the journal and exhibitions of the World of Art. It was this man who proved able to translate into practical organizational terms all the urges and desires of the society's members, that for years on end had gone no further than mere talk. "....What we lacked, though, was a 'leader.' Nothing would have come of it further, except a muddle, were everything confined to friendly chats, or even attempts to form a business-like association. Our personal qualities and temperaments were largely responsible. All we Petersburgians were spoilt, fastidious 'lordlings' or extremely impractical dreamers....It was then that Diaghilev ....newly accepted into our company as a full-fledged member, realized his real mission.
His creative energies, which had found no outlet in purely artistic 'production,' focused on a task, which though fully artistic, did not call for professional involvement. It was then that Diaghilev revealed himself as creator, determined to say 'so be

[1] A. Benois, *Vozniknoveniye Mira iskusstva* (The Emergence of the World of Art), Leningrad, 1928, pp. 8, 9. Further: Benois

In all these processes, a preeminent, if not definitive part was played by the artists and art critics grouped around the journal *Mir iskusstva* (The World of Art). However, in order to properly assess the historic significance of the artistic, educational, and organizational efforts of this group, one must at least briefly review the line-up in *fin-de-siècle* Russian art.

At that time academic painting was no longer the progressive factor it had once been. However, due to governmental backing it continued to thrive exclusively as a reactionary trend serving the purposes of official art. In truth, there were in the 1880s and 1890s some Academy painters of talent, but their works, though sometimes externally spectacular, were shallow and represented an eclectic salon-style modernization of the old-fashioned system of classicism.

A crucial role in the reshaping of Russian art during the last quarter of the nineteenth century was played by members of the Society of Traveling (or Wandering) Art Exhibitions, i.e. the Wanderers (the so-called *Peredvizhniki*). Having achieved remarkable results already in the 1870s, the Wanderers reached their peak in the 1880s. Genuine masterpieces appeared at practically each of the traveling exhibitions. At that time Vasily Surikov produced the *Morning of the Execution of the Streltsy, Menshikov in Beriozov*, and the *Boyarina Morozova*. Ilya Repin painted his *Religious Procession in the Province of Kursk, They Did Not Expect Him*, and many of his best portraits. A number of other well-known painters also took part in the Society's activities.

By the 1890s, having discharged their highly creditable social and historical mission of releasing progressive Russian painting from the shackles of the antiquated academic tradition and having developed a consistently realist method, the Wanderers had eventually ceased to be innovative and were about to come full circle.

[2] A.N. Benois, "O Diaghileve" (About Diaghilev), in: *Sergei Diaghilev i russkoye iskusstvo* (Sergei Diaghilev and Russian Art), 2 vols., Moscow, 1982, vol. 2. pp. 228, 229. Further: Diaghilev

it,' where we had merely said 'it would be a pretty good idea if.' "[2]

It would be absolutely wrong, though, to regard Diaghilev exclusively as a gifted, ingenious organizer and no more. He understood deeply the essence of the artistic and aesthetic quests of the members of the future World of Art society, knew how to expound them, and linked all of his many artistic enterprises with one definite program. This is also true of Diaghilev's literary activity, which was preceded by his circular letter of May 1897 – the first concrete project of future World of Art undertakings. The text which follows, was sent to Bakst, Benois, Fyodor Botkin, Apollinary Vasnetsov, Alexander Golovin, Konstantin Korovin, Lanceray, Isaac Levitan, Sergei Maliutin, Mikhail Nesterov, Vasily Perepletchikov, Elena Polenova, Serov, Somov, Maria Yakunchikova, and possibly, to some other would-be members of the "new society" described therein:

Dear Sir,   20th May, 1897
Russian art at the moment is in a state of transition. History places any emerging trend in this position when the principles of the older generation clash and struggle with the newly developing demands of youth. Each time, this phenomenon, which occurs so often in art history, impels young forces to resort to a united, concerted protest against the routine and views of the old, moribund authorities. This can be observed everywhere and finds expression in such brilliant, strong protests as the Munich Secession, the Paris Champs de Mars, the London New Gallery, etc. Everywhere talented youth have rallied together to initiate a new cause, on a new basis, with new programs and aims.
With us, 25 years ago, a group of artists branched off to form the new society of the Wanderers and 17 years ago a special society of watercolorists was set up. Neither group could bear so many years and still be sound. They have grown old, and if it weren't for a handful of young Wanderers, this exhibition, the best we have, would have depersonalized and collapsed like the shows of watercolors, academists, and all else.

2. Alexander Benois. Frontispiece for the book *My Recollections*

3. Boris Kustodiev. Group Portrait of the World of Art Artists. Sketch. 1916–20

Meanwhile, our art, far from having collapsed, may, on the contrary, be a cluster of young artists scattered throughout various cities and exhibitions, who, if brought together, could prove that Russian art exists, that it is fresh, original, and capable of contributing much novelty to the history of art. Why were our debuts in the West so ill-starred, while we as a school appear in Europe's eyes to be obsolete and asleep on a bed of long-moribund traditions? Precisely because our young trend, the only trend of interest to Europe, has not been singled out and integrated with sufficient brightness.

I think the moment ripe to unite and, as one, to take up our place in the life of European art.

Early this month I brought together several young Petersburg and Muscovite artists and explained to them my plan to found a new society to accomplish this goal. I proposed keeping to watercolors and pastels throughout the first year and only then proceeding to oils, so that the transition be not too abrupt. I also presented a tentative list of the society's founding members. This gathering, which was most sympathetic to my idea, only asked me that a start not be made by straightaway setting up the proposed society with a charter, the election of members and so forth, but by organizing exhibitions at my own discretion throughout the first year, the motive being that it would be easier for one person, by means of personal choice and observation, to impart a certain flavor and overall tone to the new cause. This exhibition should serve to bring the scattered forces together and pave the way for the establishment of the new society. Chosen as premise was a hall in Baron Stieglitz's museum, and as time, the month from January 15 to February 15, 1898. It was suggested that afterwards the exhibition travel to Moscow and thence, as a whole, to the Munich Secession, inasmuch I am currently negotiating the matter of its Russian section with its sponsor, Adolf Paulus.

So, having set out the above, I most sincerely request you, dear Sir, not to deny me assistance in my beginnings and to offer a response to this new cause of ours. The fate of the projected society largely hinges upon the results of this exhibition, as it will form and flourish only when the spirit of association is distinctly expressed and the strength of the communion of the like-minded is plain.

It would be desirable to keep to watercolors and pastels, but should there be oils at the studios which the artists would desire to exhibit, they, too, will be gratefully accepted. Should

4. Alexander Benois in his study in St. Petersburg. 1910s

Yet the creative potential that the Wanderers had introduced in their artistic approach was far from exhausted. In the 1890s, several of the younger painters represented at traveling exhibitions displayed superlative talent and signally contributed to the realist trend. One must necessarily mention Sergei Korovin's *Village Community Meeting* (1893), which was shown at the 22nd Traveling Exhibition, Nikolai Kasatkin's *Poor People Picking Up Coal at a Worked-Out Pit* and his study, *Woman Miner*, both done in 1894 and displayed at the 23rd Traveling Exhibition, and, finally, Sergei Ivanov's study of prisoner life that figured at the 28th Traveling Exhibition. Each of the artists named built on these pieces to initiate an extensive cycle of paintings.

Thus Sergei Korovin dedicated himself to the traditionally Wanderer theme of peasant life, furnishing a probing reflection of the Russian village with its acute social problems after the abolition of serfdom in 1861.

Like Korovin, Sergei Ivanov originally concentrated on the peasant theme. In the 1880s, he produced a series of pictures about migrant peasants who had abandoned their native lands and trekked out to Siberia in search of a better life. Later, in the 1890s, he embarked on a new cycle which portrayed life in prisons, stockades, and on the chain gang. Thematically, this cycle was particularly relevant during the period of reaction under Tsar Alexander III with its surging tide of popular unrest. As Ivanov's biographers most rightly noted, for him this cycle served as a source for that subject matter which was to gain prominence in his work at the time of the first Russian Revolution (1905–07).

Nikolai Kasatkin went even further than his fellow Wanderers. He was the first among Russian painters to derive his themes and images from the life of the newest and most advanced social class, the industrial proletariat that had emerged at the turn of the twentieth century. The artist's two abovementioned works marked the beginning of his extensive *Miners* cycle. The key painting of this cycle, *Coal-Miners on Shift* (1895), was shown at the 24th Traveling Exhibition. The entire cycle already had nothing of the Populist sentimentality so characteristic of the later genre paintings by the Wanderers. Kasatkin presents the proletariat as a mighty, formidable social force.

Be that as it may, such artists as Sergei Korovin, Sergei Ivanov, and Nikolai Kasatkin, while faithfully adhering to the democratic ideals of Russian critical realism, did not set the tone for the traveling exhibitions of the 1890s, either with regard to content or imagery. Among the later Wanderers the dominant role was played partly by landscape painters, who imitated Isaac Levitan and Arkhip Kuindzhi, and partly by genre painters unable to probe the grave social conflicts of reality. As the Soviet art historian R. Kaufman justly noted, "sentimentality and anecdotal episode more and more frequently replaced the austere authenticity of imagery."[1] While even in the 1890s, art critics observed that a "dull, routine reality, unmarked by highlights or powerful, captivating emotionality had become the constant overall theme of the traveling exhibitions."[2]

The art of the Wanderers declined at a very rapid pace. Their later works lacked content, social relevance, and artistic expressiveness. The traveling exhibitions arranged in the 1890s showed hardly anything comparable with the masterpieces of the previous decade. Now the epigones were in command.

In the 1880s, at a time when the Wanderers appeared to hold undivided sway, the earliest signs of the then barely noticeable revitalization of art were already evident. Mikhail Vrubel, a painter of genius, began his artistic career. Konstantin Korovin displayed his brilliant talents. Novel lyrical intonation sounded in Isaac Levitan's landscapes and in the pictures of the young Mikhail Nesterov. The twenty-year-old Valentin Serov painted his famous *Girl with Peaches (Vera Mamontova)*, the first gem in the output of the generation that had arrived to replace the Wanderers and that was to raise the traditions of Russian realist art to new heights.

These artists, with the exception of Vrubel, participated in the traveling exhibitions mounted in the 1880s and 1890s, even though they far from fully shared the ideological and aesthetic concepts of the Wanderers. Actually, they were alien to the Wanderers. Small wonder that in his reminiscences Nesterov labelled them the "stepchildren of the Wanderers."[3] They were becoming convinced that the day of the *Peredvizhniki* in Russian art was done and that it behooved the succeeding generation to search for new roads.

[1] R.S. Kaufman, "Bytovoi zhanr i istoricheskaya zhivopis" (Genre and History Painting), in: *Istoriya russkogo iskusstva* (History of Russian Art), 12 vols. Moscow, 1968, vol., 10, part 1, p. 44

[2] M. Komplevsky (M.S. Korelin), "21 peredviznaya vystavka" (The 21st Traveling Exhibition), in: *Russkaya mysl*, 1893

[3] M.B. Nesterov, *Davnie dni* (Bygone Days), Moscow, 1951, p. 123

5. Valentin Serov. Portrait of Alexander Pushkin. 1899

The Wanderer's philosophy was even more categorically rejected by the progressive younger generation of artists who made their appearance in the 1890s. Igor Grabar, a budding painter who developed into a prominent artist and art historian, thus noted in his *My Life: Automonograph*: "At first Korovin, Serov, Maliutin, Vrubel, Arkhipov, Ostroukhov and Levitan, and, after them, we the junior generation.... came to realize that the way of Miasoyedov, Volkov, Kiseliov, Bodarevsky, and Lemokh (Wanderer epigones – *V.P.*) was not our way, and that even the best Wanderers were fundamentally alien to us.... We accepted only Repin and Surikov as understandable and close ... We sought a greater dimension of truth, a more subtle understanding of nature, less convention, extemporization, less crudity, journeymanship, cliche...."[4]

[4] I.E. Grabar, *Moya zhizn: Avtomonografiya* (My Life: Automonograph), Moscow–Leningrad. 1937. pp. 125, 126

The younger generation's rebellion against the authority of their seniors, a typical 'fathers-and-sons' conflict, derived from the objective conditions within which Russian social thought evolved at the turn of the nineteenth and twentieth centuries and from the deep-seated historico-social processes peculiar to the Russian reality of the time. The Populist phase had given way to the new, proletarian period of the Russian liberation movement and the Wanderers' decline was a symptom of the hopeless crisis and degeneration of the Populist ideology. The onset of the twentieth century brought with it new social, moral, and aesthetic problems. In 1902, Lenin wrote: "We are living in stormy times, when Russian history is marching on with seven-league strides and every year sometimes signifies more than decades of tranquillity."[5] Anticipation of the impending revolution was the epoch's basic historical essence. It was in Russia that imperialism's most acute contradictions came into focus, and the Russian art of the period seethed in the crucible of boiling ideological wrangles.

[5] V.I. Lenin, *Collected Works*, vol. 6, Moscow, 1961, p. 186

Disillusionment with the Populist ideals of the nineteenth century resulted in unprecedented ideological confusion. Only a few artists and men of letters could achieve an awareness of socialism. These were, firstly, Maxim Gorky and, to some extent, several of the younger Wanderers, who responded, directly or indirectly, to the demands of progressive-minded Russians, furnishing a realistic reflection of life. However, for most Russian artists of the time, the process of creatively assessing its realities was an agonizing effort.

As Soviet art historians have rightly noted, in the period under review art's links with social life and the social struggle had changed in character. "Whereas in the preceding period art had followed the social and philosophical thought of the day, often directly expressing this thought – hence its strength – now the situation had changed. In the early twentieth-century artistic life grew most intense, and the links of poetry, drama, music, and painting with social movements were at times extremely involved and indirect. As a result, reactionary ideological and philosophical theories quite often penetrated into artistic creativity; however, the aesthetic meaning of certain art phenomena need not necessarily coincide with these theories.... Moreover, now art quite often reflected indirectly the progressive social movements in mood, passion, and emotion. All the greater, therefore, was the role of the aesthetic expressiveness of a work of art."[6]

[6] G.A. Nedoshivin, D.V. Sarabyanov, G.Yu. Sternin, "Vvedenie" (Introduction), in: *Istoriya russkogo iskusstva* (History of Russian Art), 12 vols., Moscow, 1968, vol. 10, p. 9

The increasingly complex conditions of the Russian art scene called for a new grouping of forces. One relevant manifestation was the appearance of the Abramtsevo Circle or Colony, artists who were drawn together by the well-known Moscow art patron and social figure Savva Mamontov. They included some of the major Wanderers, such as Ilya Repin, Vasily Polenov, and Victor Vasnetsov, who sympathized with the progressive-minded younger generation, but the dominant role in the circle was played by Konstantin Korovin, Valentin Serov, and Mikhail Vrubel. This young trio was instrumental in forming that creative milieu which largely rid itself of the superannuated Populist dogmas of the latter-day Wanderers. The work of the colony members mirrored certain substantial novel tendencies that were subsequently carried forward in early twentieth-century Russian art.

In 1885, Savva Mamontov established his private opera company in Moscow, enlisting many prominent artists to work as theatrical designers. This laid the foundation for a new type of stage decor having nothing in common with traditional stereotypes.

Likewise in Abramtsevo, Mamontov organized workshops to revive the techniques and forms of Russian folk arts and crafts. Artists such as Vrubel and Golovin worked there, realizing their innovative concepts.

6. Valentin Serov. Children. Sasha and Yura Serov. 1899

However, the Abramtsevo Colony was not to evolve those novel forms of artistic, educational, and exhibition activity which Russia's visual arts so badly needed.

Destined to achieve this objective at a somewhat later period was the group associated with the *World of Art* journal. By shaping new artistic forms, the members of this group brought to the Russian visual arts new ideas, aesthetic concepts, and creative principles. Though organizational problems seemed to them less important, such matters were also seen as urgent priorities.

The World of Art group, which gave rise to this forceful influential movement, was formed in St. Petersburg in the early 1890s. Its nucleus consisted of several young students, the former members of the Society for Self-Education. This small, select circle was dominated by Alexander Benois, to be famed subsequently as an artist, critic, and historian; Konstantin Somov, an Arts Academy student, a future painter and graphic artist; Dmitry Filosofov, who later developed into a writer; Sergei Diaghilev, a gifted musician, who achieved renown as an art critic and illustrious impresario; and Walter Nouvel, a budding music critic. They were soon joined by the two young artists, Lev Rosenberg, better known by his pseudonym, Léon Bakst, and Evgeny Lanceray. By virtue of their versatile talents and fine cultural standards, the group was soon engaged in extensive social activity that greatly affected the artistic life of the country.

The leading force behind many of the World of Art's activities was Sergei Diaghilev (1872–1929), who combined a sensitive understanding of art with an unquenchable energy and rare determination. In fact, he had a greater flair for assessing the artistic developments of the time than any of his colleagues. His basic motivations stemmed from the firm conviction that Russian art had a role of global significance to play. He set himself the goal of uniting the finest Russian artists, of helping them to make their way into the art arena of Europe, and, generally, as he himself put it, "of exalting Russian art in the eyes of the West." He dedicated himself wholeheartedly to this objective, advancing with persistence and fortitude, and capably surmounting every hurdle along the way.

In 1898, in St. Petersburg, Diaghilev organized an exhibition of Russian and Finnish artists, at which, for the first time, young Russian painters came out in a united front against the dreary traditions of the Academy and the epigones of obsolescent trends.

you consent to participate in the exhibition, allow me this autumn to call on your atelier and take what we would both believe appropriate for the purposes of the exhibition that is to be mounted.

I will shoulder all the preliminary related expenses, while the net income will be divided as dividends among all the exhibiting artists.

I would appreciate it if you, dear Sir, would answer this proposal at your earliest convenience.

Sincerely yours,
Sergei Diaghilev
45 Liteiny, St. Petersburg[3]

Apart from some details – the fact that mostly oils, not watercolors and pastels were shown at the 1898 exhibition and also that it did not travel to either Moscow or Munich – the letter quoted above set out a concise, concrete program for the first World of Art undertaking. True, though this is only a preliminary effort, it already furnishes a notion of the form the future association will take.

1898
The Exhibition of Russian and Finnish artists organized by Diaghilev was held in St. Petersburg in January – February.
Throughout the year he paved the way for the publication of the *World of Art* journal. In these efforts he was assisted by Benois and Filosofov. The trio persuaded Princess Maria Tenisheva, a

well-known, wealthy patroness of the arts, to agree to subsidize their venture. In this Benois played a special role, as from 1896 on he had served as "curator of the collection" that the princess owned. "I most insistently begged Maria Klavdievna to extend her patronage likewise to the publication of an art journal in Russia,"[4] he wrote. Also, at the outset, the still better-known Moscow art patron Savva Mamontov lent financial support. "The alliance of these two luminaries was marked by a banquet at Tenisheva's home, at which Jan Tsionglinsky delivered a most brilliant speech, and on March 18/30 the contract for the publication was signed."[5]
Diaghilev announced a contest for the journal cover, to which he invited ten members of the World of Art society. In the enclosed notice, he said that the "size of the cover should be 33 x 26 centimeters. The drawing should be done necessarily on tinted paper in no more than two colors of which one could be black. The artist should include in the drawing the inscription *Mir iskusstva* (The World of Art)."[6]
Korovin was placed first and designed the cover for the maiden issue. Shortly before publication Diaghilev gave an interview to *Peterburgskaya gazeta* (St. Petersburg Gazette) in which he set out the aims and purposes of the future journal. In this interview, published on May 25, 1898, under the heading "Arts and Crafts," he said: "At present Russian art is in that transitional state, in which

[3] Diaghilev, vol. 2, pp. 24, 25

[4] Benois, p. 20

[5] *Ibid.*, p. 31

[6] Diaghilev, vol. 2, p. 32

7. Valentin Serov. Bathing the Horse. 1905

8. Léon Bakst. Portrait of Isaac Levitan. 1899

9. Valentin Serov. Self-Portrait. 1901

10. Valentin Serov. First version of a curtain design for Rimsky-Korsakov's *Schéhérazade*. 1910

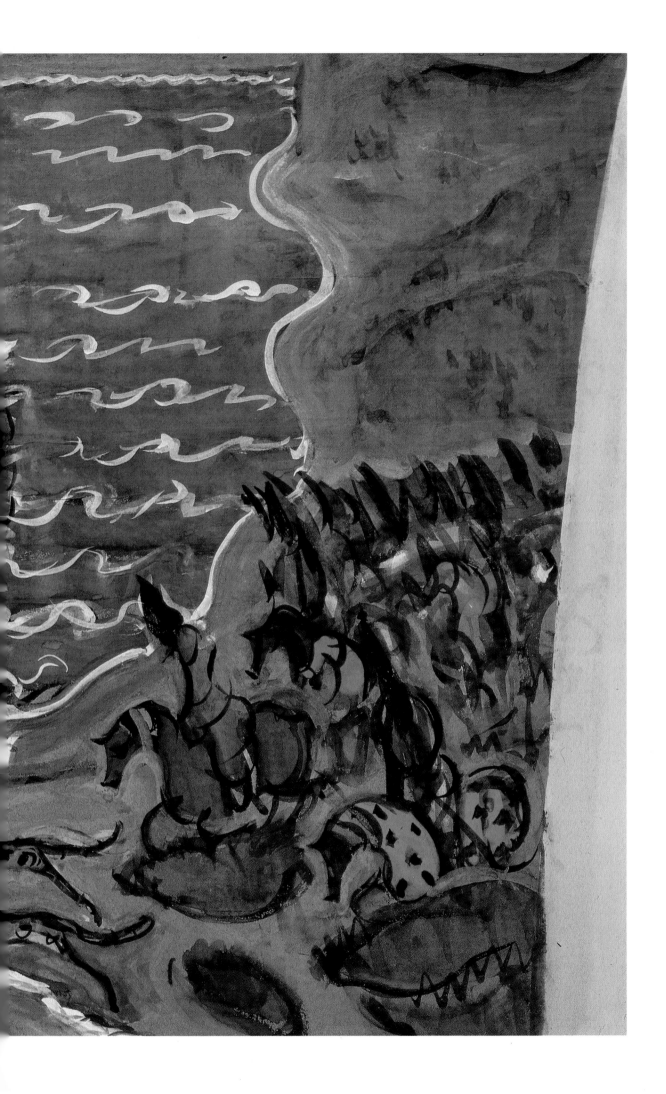

Diaghilev's Petersburg group of Somov, Bakst, Benois, and Lanceray formed a close-knit alliance with a number of prominent Muscovite painters, including Vrubel, Levitan, Serov, Konstantin Korovin, Nesterov, and Ryabushkin. The Finnish section of the exhibition was dominated by the works of Akseli Gallen-Kallela and Albert Edelfeldt. This broad association, immeasurably greater than Diaghilev's original circle, served as the point of departure from which Diaghilev could proceed to found the art journal which would become the ideological rallying center for early twentieth-century Russian art.

The *World of Art* journal came out for six years from 1899 through 1904. It was edited by Sergei Diaghilev, assisted by his entire Petersburg group. In 1901, Igor Grabar associated himself with the journal, eventually turning into one of the most industrious and influential art critics of the time. Diaghilev and his colleagues mounted annual exhibitions bearing the same name as the journal in which many progressive artists from both St. Petersburg and Moscow were invited to participate.

However, it was invariably Diaghilev's Petersburg group of Somov, Benois, and their closest companions whose paintings and graphic works formed the core of these exhibitions. They were responsible for shaping that original art movement which has long been known as the World of Art. In the following pages we shall attempt to describe the salient features of this movement, its aesthetic stance, creative problems, and pictorial principles. However, it must be most emphatically stressed that none of the exhibitions or educational activities of the group were confined to any single creative trend. The World of Art cannot be properly understood in isolation from the extensive range of diverse phenomena in early twentieth-century Russian art.

In other words, the history of the World of Art movement can be viewed from two separate, though interconnected, angles. On the one hand, this is the history of a creative trend evolved by the Petersburg group of artists under Benois and Somov. On the other hand, this is also the history of an intricate cultural and aesthetic movement that drew

11. Mikhail Vrubel. Portrait of Savva Mamontov. 1897

[7] Quoted from: Diaghilev, vol. 1, p. 76

[8] A. Benois, *Moi vospominaniya* (My Recollections), 5 books, 2 vols., Moscow, 1980, vol. 2, p. 230. Further: Benois. Recollections

[9] *Ibid.*

[10] *Ibid.*, vol. 2, p. 232

history places each emerging trend, when the principles of the older generation clash with newly developing demands ....For that reason it is essential to analyze these young forces and to enable our artists to state their views through the new journal and do useful work that will be all the greater as their craft allows them to come together."[7]

As one will gather, set out here were those selfsame ideas that Diaghilev propounded in his earlier quoted circular letter of May 20, 1897 to Russian artists. The interview's heading and its concluding remarks may produce the impression that the journal had been conceived as a publication devoted to the applied arts and crafts. However, its range proved to be far broader, although aspects of the applied arts and crafts always loomed large.

As Benois notes,[8] the first issue (a double number) came out in late October or early November 1898. But as it was dated 1899, this now and again causes confusion. In this issue the journal had not yet acquired either a final decorative and graphic aspect or a distinct trend. Incidentally, as Benois mentions, "this first issue was largely to be credited to Filosofov."[9] Subsequently Diaghilev ruled, yielding editorship to Benois only toward the close – especially as concerned the choice of illustrations and the trend of the art reviews – and leaving the literary side to Filosofov. As for the design, "only in 1901 did the journal's appearance satisfy the editors, hitherto each issue had evoked disappointment, if not despair."[10]

In 1898, another journal called *Iskusstvo i khudozhestvennaya promyshlennost* (Art and Art Industry) started publication. Guided by the critic Vladimir

12. Léon Bakst. Portrait of Alexander Benois. 1898

Stasov, it launched a constant diversified polemic with the *World of Art*, regarding it at the other end of the pole on all basic art issues. This continued up to 1902, when it folded.

However, it was in 1898 that Stasov and Diaghilev first "came to blows." In January, the former trenchantly assailed Diaghilev's show of Russian and Finnish artists in the St. Petersburg *Novosti i birzhevaya gazeta* (News and Stock Exchange Gazette). He most resolutely attacked Vrubel's decorative panel *Morning*. "Throughout there is nothing but total madness and ugliness, anti-artistic and repellent,"[11] he wrote. His evaluation of the well-known Finnish painter Akseli Gallen-Kallela was couched in a similar vein: "This artist's draftsmanship, line, color scheme, and composition are appalling."[12] Diaghilev produced a reply which, however, was not published despite his exertions thereto. While acknowledging Stasov's great services to Russian art ("You see how much both you and your time have done, how all that you sowed has taken root and has quietly and unshakably housed itself amongst museums and the programs and pages of history"[13]), Diaghilev regretted the unfairness of some of his assessments, more specifically his attacks against Vrubel and Gallen-Kallela: "Recall who damned these poor, utterly blameless artists earlier. Recall the castigations of those exposers of heretics in art who incarcerated Vrubel and pilloried Gallen-Kallela. Note with horror whose ranks you have joined, with whom you so peacefully and amicably walk hand in hand."[14]

Elena Polenova's death on November 19 was the first loss that the World of Art sustained.

13. Léon Bakst, Romulus Desmond and Konstantin Somov in Oranienbaum near St. Petersburg. 1908

[11] Quoted from: *V.V. Stasov. Izbrannye proizvedeniya* (Selected Writings), Moscow–Leningrad, 1950, vol. 1, pp. 335, 336. Further: Stasov

[12] *Ibid.*

[13] Diaghilev, vol. 1, p. 74

[14] *Ibid.*, p. 75

14. Léon Bakst. Portrait of Walter Nouvel. 1895   15. Konstantin Somov. Self-Portrait. 1898

1899
The International Exhibition of Paintings organized by the *World of Art* journal was opened in St. Petersburg for the duration of January. All Russian artists who had initiated the new tradition and alongside them, major painters of another trend, including Apollinary Vasnetsov and Ilya Repin, were represented. The group of foreign contributors was rather eclectic, but amazing by virtue of the celebrities invited. These included such names as Böcklin, Brangwyn, Degas, Carrière, Lenbach, Liebermann, Monet, Moreau, Puvis de Chavannes, Renoir, and Whistler. Diaghilev undoubtedly achieved his basic aim of demonstrating that Russian art stood on an equal footing with all of European art. At the same time, despite the eclecticism, he sought primarily to stress the significance of the new trends in the art of the period. It was this circumstance, along with the World of Art journal's stand, that provoked Stasov's anger. In his articles, "Beggars in Spirit" and "The House of Lepers," carried again in *Novosti i birzhevaya gazeta*, he accused the *miriskusniki* of decadence and branded their journal for its "dominant absurdity, vileness, and ugliness." Stigmatized as "lepers" were both Russian ("All those Baksts and Benoises, Botkins, Somovs, Maliutins, and Golovins with their disgraceful things are not worth dissecting") and foreign (Degas, de Chavannes, Gallen-Kallela, ets.) exhibitors.[15]
Though in 1898 Diaghilev had believed himself obliged to react, in the following year, as editor of the *World of Art*, he no longer thought that neces-

sary: his journal enjoyed a solid reputation, repelling charges by its very existence and publications. But when Repin assailed the *World of Art* in *Niva* (No. 15 for April of the same year), Diaghilev reprinted Repin's article and published his own reply in the *World of Art* (No. 10).
However, it was difficulties of quite another order that bedevilled the journal in 1899. Because of bankruptcy, Mamontov could no longer subsidize it, while Princess Tenisheva withdrew financial support out of a quarrel with Diaghilev. Yet, the journal continued to come out largely due to subscription and art patrons, plus backing of a totally unexpected kind. Benois wrote: "At the time, Serov, who was at the height of his fame, was painting a portrait of the tsar. He visited the Winter Palace daily. Availing himself of the liberal atmosphere prevalent at these sittings, he told the tsar of his worries (the journal's financial straits) and with straightforward conviction succeeded in getting the tsar to express, of his own volition, the desire to help the sinking ship. Though this assistance out of 'his own money chest' was no more than ten thousand roubles....that was enough to keep the journal afloat. The tsar's example was emulated by several private individuals (S. Botkin, I. Ostroukhov, one of the Morozovs, etc.) who contributed mites of no mean significance. The *World of Art* was saved."[16] Benois is not quite accurate when noting the sum received from the tsar. On June 6, 1900 Diaghilev telegraphed Benois that the journal had "received an annual subsidy of fifteen thousand per annum for three years."[17] Benois has also confused dates, inasmuch as the

[15] Stasov, vol. 1, p. 94

[16] Benois. Recollections, book 2, p. 290

[17] Diaghilev, vol. 2, p. 33

32

16. Léon Bakst. Portrait of Sergei Diaghilev with His Nurse. 1906

within its orbit a number of prominent Russian artists whose oeuvre developed independently of the aforementioned Petersburg group, and whose aesthetic concepts and pictorial language were at times miles apart. The World of Art movement extended not only to painting and graphic art, but also embraced several related fields, markedly affecting Russian architecture, sculpture, poetry, ballet and opera, and likewise art criticism and history.

The broad aesthetic views of the World of Art leaders, which were often eclectic, were especially manifest in their exhibitions. Diaghilev sought to bring under one roof outstanding Russian artists of diverse creative approaches. True, he failed to induct the major Wanderers, who were loath to break with their association. Only Repin agreed to participate once in the World of Art exhibition that Diaghilev mounted in 1899; afterwards he ruptured all ties with the World of Art, becoming its grim adversary – all because he took umbrage at a publication in Diaghilev's journal which was extremely disrespectful of Aivazovsky, Konstantin Flavitsky, Konstantin Makovsky, and several other academics. Likewise abortive was Diaghilev's short-lived infatuation with the painting of Victor Vasnetsov, to whom he devoted a special issue of the journal. On the other hand, Diaghilev ably enlisted a broad following among the younger generation of artists and thus gained the backing of the cream of contemporary Russian art.

17. Mikhail Vrubel. Morning. 1897

Tenisheva-Mamontov upset occurred in 1899, while the tsar's "charity" came in 1900. It is also unquestionable that the imperial "donation" was made exclusively due to Serov's charisma and prestige. The tsar frowned upon Diaghilev and quite in the spirit of the magazine *Novoye vremya* (New Times) regarded the World of Art artists as decadents. Indeed he entered in his diary for February 3, 1901 the note that he had visited a "show of paintings by decadents with Diaghilev at their head."[18] In 1899, though, a year before the tsar's contribution, Diaghilev was absolutely sure that the journal would continue. In retort to rumors that it had folded, he wrote to *New Times*, in a letter published on September 4, 1899, that the "publication of the

World of Art is by no means terminated, but will continue both this year and next, despite Princess Tenisheva's impending withdrawal from among its publishers. Nos. 16 and 17 will come out on September 10. Subscription for the second year will be announced in due course...."[19]

1900
The World of Art's Second Exhibition of Paintings was opened in St. Petersburg for the duration of January. This was the first show to have no foreign participants; by that time the journal's stance had become fairly firm and definite; moreover, it needed time to consolidate forces and gain an awareness of the established principles of style and poetics. The

[18] Quoted from: Diaghilev, vol. 2, p. 339

[19] Quoted from: Diaghilev, vol. 1, p. 94

18. Nicholas Roerich. The Ill-Omened. 1901

19. Arnold Böcklin. Spring (The Songs of Spring, Three Girls Singing)

20. Akseli Gallen-Kallela. Lamentation. 1897

show in question defined the main World of Art exponents over its initial period, notably, Bakst, Benois, Vrubel, Golovin, Korovin, Levitan, Maliavin, Maliutin, Nesterov, Polenova, Somov, Serov, Trubetskoi, Tsionglinsky, and Yakunchikova, who had been represented at the earlier shows in 1898 and 1899, plus such new exhibitors as Bilibin, Braz, Golubkina, Kardovsky, Kruglikova, Lanceray, and Ostroumova.

On February 24, 1900, a circular of the following content was mailed to World of Art exhibitors:

Dear Sir,
On February 24 inst., participants in the *World of Art* journal's exhibitions met at the editorial offices. The following artists were present: L. Bakst, Alexander Benois, I. Bilibin, I. Braz, I. Walter, Ap. Vasnetsov, N. Dosekin, E. Lanceray, I. Levitan, Ph. Maliavin, M. Nesterov, A. Ober, A. Ostroumova, V. Purvit, F. Rushchits, S. Svetoslavsky, K. Somov, V. Serov, J. Tsionglinsky, and S. Diaghilev, the publisher-editor of the *World of Art* journal.

This meeting drafted the basic principles for the arrangement of future exhibitions. An organizational committee for the next, third, exhibition in January – February 1901, was elected – namely, the artists V. Serov and Alexander Benois. Serving as the committee's third standing member, in keeping with the drafted rules, is the publisher-editor of the *World of Art* journal.

It was resolved to request you, dear Sir, to take part in the forthcoming exhibition by contributing your works. The terms of entry are enclosed herewith.

Still, many who took part in Diaghilev's exhibitions only provisionally associated themselves with the World of Art, as there was no positive platform upon which they could unite with the Petersburg group. According to Grabar's authoritative testimony, their alliance merely symbolized an "abhorrence of the monstrous vulgarity of the St. Petersburg exhibition groups (i.e. academic – V.P.) and a derision for the degenerate art of the one-time powerful Wanderers."[7] Though far from everything the World of Art had to offer was gratifying, it served as a valuable training-ground for many young artists.

[7] Grabar, op. cit., p. 180

This applies primarily to Mikhail Vrubel, the only painter who was to follow his own road throughout his life, a road totally unlike those of his contemporaries. However, he appreciated the World of Art's moral backing most deeply and to his dying day took part in all the exhibitions that Diaghilev organized. Nesterov, too, enthusiastically associated himself with the World of Art at the outset; however, he soon broke away, possibly revolted by the journal's overly pronounced pro-Western orientation. Finally, the many Moscow painters who temporarily allied themselves with the World of Art, notably Konstantin Korovin, Abram Arkhipov, Apollinary Vasnetsov, Sergei Maliutin, Svyatoslav Zhukovsky, and Sergei Vinogradov, subsequently organized, as a counterweight to the St. Petersburg group, their own Union of Russian Artists, with its headquarters in Moscow.

More dependable allies of the World of Art were Philipp Maliavin, who took part in all of Diaghilev's exhibitions, and Igor Grabar, who not only sent his paintings to these shows, but also contributed critical reviews and theoretical essays to the journal.

Special mention should be made of Valentin Serov, who not only collaborated with Diaghilev and Benois in mounting the World of Art exhibitions, but also participated in them. He was a member of the unofficial editorial board that shaped the journal's art policy. In fact, Serov's association with the World of Art may be regarded as a major achievement for Diaghilev's group. In fact, he was more than an ally; this great realist master, who was far superior to the World of Art artists in the power of his versatile talent, was aesthetically and, to some extent, creatively influenced by them, indeed becoming a full-fledged member of the "clan." Serov, in his turn, interpreted certain essential philosophical and artistic principles of the World of Art group in his painting and graphic art, exerting an impact of no mean magnitude on his colleagues.

The committee of the 1901 exhibition most humbly begs you to answer the proposal set forth and to transmit your answer to the committee at your earliest convenience.
The Organizing Committee for the *World of Art* journal 1901 Exhibition:

Artist V. Serov
Artist Alexander Benois
Publisher-editor of the *World of Art* journal S. Diaghilev.[20]

[20] Quoted from: Diaghilev, vol. 1, p. 49

The "terms of entry" were published in March 1900 in *Novosti i birzhevaya gazeta*, No. 72, for March 13, and in *Rossiya*, No. 321 for March 17. They were likewise carried in the *World of Art* journal itself (Nos. 5–6, 1900, pp. 113, 114) in a somewhat abbreviated form. Here is the text:
1. Exhibitions mounted by the *World of Art* journal comprise works by: a)artists who participated in previous shows or are newly invited, namely L. Bakst, Alexander Benois, I. Bilibin, I. Braz, I. Walter, Ap. Vasnetsov, N. Dosekin, E. Lanceray, I. Levitan, Ph. Maliavin, M. Nesterov, A. Ober, A. Ostroumova, V. Purvit, F. Rushchits, S. Svetoslavsky, K. Somov, V. Serov, J. Tsionglinsky, M. Vrubel, A. Golovin, K. Korovin, S. Korovin, M. Mamontov, P. Trubetskoi, M. Yakunchinkova, A. Arkhipov, V. Baksheyev, S. Vinogradov, A. Golubkina, I. Okolovich, L. Pasternak, V. Perepletchikov, N. Roerich, A. Rzhevskaya, A. Rylov, and A. Ryabushkin.
2. In charge of exhibition business is the three-member Organizing Committee. At their annual meeting the permanent participants in the *World of Art* journal's exhibitions elect from among themselves two of the committee members, one from among Petersburg, the other, Muscovite, artists. The committee's third standing member is the editor of the *World of Art* journal. At the February 24 meeting, V. Serov and Alexander Benois were elected to the said committee by secret ballot.
3. All contributed works of art are put before the committee which decides upon entry by a majority vote. The standing members are entitled to exhibit at their discretion, *hors de concours*, one work, of which the committee is notified concurrently with paintings entered. As for persons invited to exhibit, the committee pledges, whatever the case, to select at its own discretion one of the works each such person enters.
4. As concerns participation in other exhibitions, the meeting of February 24 resolved that in the next year of 1901 the artists in attendance, L. Bakst, Alexander Benois, I. Bilibin, I. Braz, I. Walter, N. Dosekin, E. Lanceray, I. Levitan, Ph. Maliavin, M. Nesterov, A.Ober, A. Ostroumova, V. Purvit, F. Rushchits, S. Svetoslavsky, K. Somov, V. Serov, and J. Tsionglinsky show all their works at the *World of Art* journal's exhibition, reserving the right to display at other shows only works which the committee of the *World of Art* journal's exhibition had not accepted.
5. The 1901 exhibition should not coincide with the show arranged by the Society of Traveling Art Exhibitions. The exhibiton's duration is to be of 4–6 weeks as the committee decides; the latter is also entitled to mount the works of art, etc. [....]7. It is proposed that the exhibition be held at Baron Stieglitz's museum in St. Petersburg. As for moving it to Moscow, that is seen as most desirable. The committee will duly announce the time limit for delivering paintings.
8. Every type of art work, such as oils, watercolors, pastels, drawings, original etchings and engravings, autolithographs, sculptures, and works of art industry will be accepted.

21. Alexander Benois. Feeding the Fish. From the *Last Walks of Louis XIV* series. 1897

9. New participants are invited by motion of the seven permanent participating members. The said invitation is extended to the newly invited in accordance with clause 3.

10. It has been decided that no foreign participants are to be invited. It is seen as desirable to invite only Finnish artists to participate in the exhibition on general terms.

The committee's address: the editorial offices of the *World of Art* journal, 45 Liteinaya St., St. Petersburg.[21]

The document cited above, along with the circular, quoted earlier, that Benois, Serov, and Diaghilev addressed to the participants in World of Art shows are of interest in many respects.

Firstly, one will realize how wrong is the fairly widespread view that the World of Art was a somewhat chaotic association with no hard-and-fast rules of organization, whose affairs and initiatives were implemented "in artistic disarray." Nothing of the sort! As the exhibition rules reveal, World of Art activities were strictly regulated. What we have is actually a variation on the association's charter, which prescribes the entry terms, the form of management, the principles for selecting entries, the range of participants, etc.

It should be noted though, that the organizational rules did not touch upon creative creeds. As the document indicates, from the very outset the World of Art sought to encompass the highly diverse forces active in Russian art of the time. The exhibition entry terms have nothing which would place the

World of Art in opposition to other trends; on the contrary, it was specially envisaged that shows not coincide with those of the Wanderers, manifestly to enable artists associated in one way or another with the Society of Traveling Exhibitions to participate in shows mounted by the *World of Art* journal, if desired.

Nonetheless, even the names of most of the "Muscovites" are listed separately. The organizing committee specially notes representation of artists from the two cities, a geographical aspect that discloses a deeper division on artistic principles. With the passage of time, this difference was to make itself felt in diverse ways, including organization.

The art show of the World Fair that opened in Paris in April 1900 was covered in detail by the *World of Art* journal. Among the artists represented were Golovin, Vrubel, Konstantin Korovin, Maliutin, Maliavin, Polenova, and Serov. A highlight was the Russian Handicrafts Section housed in a complex of pavilions designed by Korovin and Golovin. Korovin also executed, with the collaboration of Nikolai Klodt, 30 decorative panels for these pavilions; the panels were devoted to Northern Russia, Siberia, and Central Asia.

The World Fair jury panel awarded the Medal of Honor to Serov, gold medals to Korovin and Maliavin, and other medals to Vrubel, Golovin, Nesterov, Yakunchikova, and Trubetskoi. Though

[21] Quoted from: Diaghilev, vol. 1, pp. 370, 371

True, it would be a mistake or an exaggeration to fully associate everything Serov did in the final decade of his life with the World of Art movement. Serov never relinquished his bond to the traditional realist painting of the nineteenth century in his innovations. Yet, the intense experimentation characteristic of his late period was largely linked with the artistic issues that the Diaghilev group sought to elaborate. On the other hand, in their best works, Benois and other notable World of Art artists drew heavily on Serov's innovations.

World of Art philosophies also had a definitive impact on the creative efforts of Nicholas Roerich, who joined the group in 1902 and who played a significant part in its activities in the years preceding the First World War and the 1917 Revolution.

Apart from allies and temporary associates, the World of Art naturally had a faithful following, dedicated to its aesthetic to the end of their days. These were Alexander Golovin, who came to the Diaghilev group in 1899, Ivan Bilibin and Anna Ostroumova-Lebedeva, who joined in 1900, and, finally, Mstislav Dobuzhinsky, who began to contribute to its exhibitions in 1903. Absolutely independent in their reinterpretation of the World of Art concepts, these young artists subscribed to the movement as convinced partisans and continuers of the cause initiated by Diaghilev.

In their effort to gather and consolidate the vital forces of contemporary Russian art, Diaghilev and his associates demonstrated ample flexibility, fortitude, tact, and even perspicacity. True, they had their upsets. Thus, for a long time they ignored Victor Borisov-Musatov, though he could have been close kin in both technique and subject matter. Grabar tells us that none other than Serov advised Diaghilev not to invite Borisov-Musatov to the World of Art exhibitions, contemptuously styling the artist's works "cheap stuff."[8] By the time this attitude changed, it was too late. Borisov-Musatov had died without being acknowledged by the artists and critics who, one would have thought, should have accepted and supported him before all others. Only in 1906, when the journal had ceased publication and Borisov-Musatov was no longer alive, did Diaghilev include fifty of the artist's works in his last exhibition, thus paying a posthumous tribute to him. Among other blunders of the group was the underestimation of Andrei Ryabushkin and the slighting of the younger generation's Impressionist endeavors.

Nonetheless, the World of Art achieved its purposes at very short order and its activities had far-reaching consequences.

The World of Art exhibitions revolutionized the aesthetic outlook of most of Russia's intelligentsia, serving to enhance its cultural development and to cultivate new tastes, and a new concept of art in general. This could hardly have been attained without the contribution made by Diaghilev's journal.

The journal's art policy was not formulated by Diaghilev alone; one must necessarily mention the name of his collaborator Alexander Benois, the ideologue and theoretician of the World of Art trend. This highly talented man epitomized the new type of erudite artist – a rediscoverer and reinterpreter of forgotten aesthetic values – which evolved in the

[8] Grabar, op. cit., p. 169

[22] Benois. Recollections, vol. 2, p. 319

[23] Diaghilev (reprint), vol. 1, pp. 123–128

[24] A. Stasov, "Shakhmatny khod dekadentov" (Decadents' Chess Move), Novosti i birzhevaya gazeta, 25 November 1900. Reprint: Stasov, vol. 1, pp. 377–384

such distinction evoked sharp comment from both the Russian press and art circles, it definitely served to consolidate the prestige enjoyed by the artists of the World of Art group.
When Isaac Levitan, highly valued by the World of Art association, in whose first exhibitions he had participated, died on August 4, Diaghilev published an article in memoriam and sought to have a posthumous show mounted and publications devoted to the late artist.
"In the autumn of 1900, the editorial offices of the World of Art journal moved from Liteinaya St. to another, showier flat on the second floor at No. 11 Fontanka, whose windows opened onto the Sheremetev Palace."[22]

1901
In January – February the World of Art's Third Exhibition of Paintings was held in St. Petersburg. Feathers flew even before it opened. As the Stieglitz School, where the World of Art had arranged exhibitions in 1898–1900, refused to furnish premises any longer for this purpose, the organizing committee, in the person of Serov, asked the Academy of Arts to provide the necessary showrooms. This provoked heated discussion which Diaghilev was to describe in his article, "Exhibitions,"[23] and which was commented upon in the Russian press.[24]
This Third Exhibition was among the more significant in the history of the World of Art group. Presented there were such gems as Vrubel's Lilac

22. Valentin Serov. Peter II and Princess Elizaveta Riding to Hounds. 1900

and *Nightfall*, Serov's *Peter II and Princess Elizaveta Riding to Hounds* and portraits, Benois' series of Petersburg sketches that were sold out while the exhibition was still on, Korovin's panels, Somov's *Seaside Grove in Silamiagi*, *Island of Love*, and *Summer Evening*, Ryabushkin's *Seventeenth-Century Russian Women at Church*, Maliavin's portrait of Repin, Trubetskoi's portrait of Leo Tolstoy, Golubkina's "Fire" fireplace, graphics by Bilibin, Lanceray, and Ostroumova, and, finally, a posthumous retrospective show of Levitan's paintings, opened on the same premises and harmoniously linked with the World of Art exhibition.

This exhibition was crucial in the history of the World of Art group, and may serve all who argue how biassed it is to have viewed the association as a faction, inasmuch as not one show it mounted was confined exclusively either to the leanings and concepts of the handful of Petersburgians who had founded the society or to those of their disciples and younger followers. The movement was always much broader, as its aesthetic brought together under one roof certain fine traditions and all the talented and innovative work that the new times had produced. This logically brought together diverse artists who shared, above all, a common ability to express themselves through the medium of genuine art, to display a significant imagery and consummate style, and to generate a sense of beauty.

When the World of Art started out,

World of Art's milieu. Two other similiar figures, Igor Grabar and Stepan Yaremich, contributed critical essays to the journal, leaving a deep imprint on Russian art and, later, on Soviet art studies as well. On the other hand, Dmitry Filosofov, who headed the journal's literary desk, was far removed from the art scene. Incidentally, he and his staff were mainly concerned with religious and philosophical matters that had no relation to the range of problems tackled by the journal's art division. Indeed, this unbridgeable dichotomy of the journal's structure, which had been noted even by contemporaries, was one of the causes of its decline and eventual closure.

The journal's socio-piholosophical credo was none too original, at times even contradictory, and was extremely characteristic of the trends current among a large section of Russia's intelligentsia on the eve of the 1905 Revolution. The world outlook of its editors represented an eclectic blend of Kant's and Schopenhauer's aesthetics flavored by a Nietzschean individualism. Proceeding from idealistic notions of the unlimited freedom of the artist's creative personality and the equally unlimited freedom of art, which, in their view, was totally independent of any form of ideology, the World of Art theorists inevitably descended to advocating subjectivism, accentuating what, in a certain sense, was a programmatic apoliticalness, and, in the final analysis, the preaching of the theory of art for art's sake.

Yet one should base one's judgment of the World of Art not so much on the avowals of certain of its leaders as on an assessment of the results of the diversified and largely

23. Konstantin Somov. Portrait of Anna Ostroumova. 1901

24. Konstantin Somov. Portrait of Evgeny Lanceray. 1907

Vrubel, Levitan, Serov, Nesterov, the Vasnetsovs, Golubkina, Trubetskoi, and Konstantin Korovin associated themselves with it. Subsequently it allied itself, at least temporarily, with Muscovite artists seeking to rejuvenate the realistic tradition. After 1910, when the World of Art experienced a revival and again attained independence, diverse, yet mostly thought-provoking, talented artists of the younger generations rallied around its old nucleus. There is a definite logic to all this: a common intellectual culture and a sensitive feeling for the quality of art

enabled the *miriskusniki* to choose, at several stages, highlights of contemporary art. Their infatuation with olden times and their stylization never blinded them to surrounding realities, never prevented them from paying tribute to all artists capable of demonstrating these realities, however differently, yet with genuine power and conviction.

The Third Exhibition provoked conflicting comment and failed to receive any prestigious backing from the press – even though the reviews that Sergei Glagol and I. Gurland published in Moscow

25. Konstantin Somov. Promenade after Rain. 1896

newspapers were quite favorable. However, the trenchant attacks, including Suvorin's "Little Letters," in the February 4, 1901 issue of *Novoye vremya*, and Stasov's "Decadents at the Academy" in the February 2 issue of *Novosti i birzhevaya gazeta*,[25] appear anachronistic compared with the masterpieces shown and had no serious impact upon the *miriskusniki*. Shortly after it closed Diaghilev observed: "The World of Art Exhibition annually arouses endless interpretations and is vilified year after year; moreover lately, sundry means have been indiscriminately employed to fuel this unseemly abuse, including falsehood and that collection of blunt weaponry which is ever available to that envious milieu of countless art failures. Whatever modern art may be, whatever place it may occupy in history is of no import, as everything new, unhabitual, and strange is always entitled to express itself and demand an audience.... Living art is obstinate and stronger than its toothless enemies."[26] At this point it would be appropriate to note that Russia's turn-of-the-century art was far in advance of art criticism, which only by the mid-1900s really began to react to and reintepret the meaning of the changes in Russian artistic culture. The debut of the World of Art protagonists in art history and

[25] Stasov (reprint), vol. 1, pp. 385–389

[26] S. Diaghilev, "Vystavki" (Exhibitions), *Mir iskusstva*, 1901, No. 2–3, p. 106. Reprint: Diaghilev, vol. 1, pp. 123, 124

26. Valentin Serov. Portrait of Léon Bakst. 1900s   27. Léon Bakst. Portrait of Alexander Golovin. 1908   41

28. Konstantin Somov. The Ridiculed Kiss. 1908

productive creative efforts of the association. The journal's activity was by no means limited to mere declarations or a drive against the Academy of Arts and the Wanderers. Its program was more broadly conceived and was implemented with extreme vigor and persistence.

The educational activity that the journal pursued throughout all six years of its existence followed two basic lines. Firstly, it discussed the contemporary state of the visual arts in Russia and some countries of Western Europe. Secondly, it systematically rediscovered for the reader various forgotten or misunderstood values of the national artistic culture of the past.

Initially, the editorial members were concerned chiefly with the problems confronting contemporary painting. While furnishing an unbiassed picture of current Russian art and reproducing paintings shown at various exhibitions, even including those mounted by the Wanderers and the Academy, they devoted as much column space as possible to the newest trends in Western European art. Indeed, never before had the Russian public been offered so broad a panoramic survey of contemporary trends in German, British, Scandinavian, and progressive nineteenth-century French art, ranging from Ingres, Corot, and Daumier to the Impressionists, Cézanne, Van Gogh, and the then young Matisse. However, the emphasis was not on these great innovators, whose oeuvre paved the way for the evolution of twentieth-century world art, not even on the Impressionists, whom the journal's theorists were long inclined to underestimate, but on German and some British and Scandinavian exponents of Art Nouveau. During its initial period, the journal highly commended such Symbolists and stylizers as Arnold Böcklin, Max Klinger, Aubrey Beardsley, and Edvard Munch.

True, this infatuation with the *style moderne*, as Art Nouveau was called in Russia, had much that was casual and extraneous, perhaps even an element of the youthful craving to shock the public. With the passage of time, however, this craving gave way to other interests of a more serious nature that were more organically entwined with the demands of Russian culture. Indeed, the theme of Russian antiquity gained increasing significance, with the journal evolving from the *style moderne* to retrospectivism, in the process of which a range of crucial historico-artistic discoveries were made.

It was the World of Art that provided the basis for a systematic study of the already half-forgotten, if not misconstrued, artistic culture of eighteenth-century Russia. Diaghilev, Benois, Grabar and other critics revived the names of the painters Dmitry Levitsky and Vladimir Borovikovsky, as well as the splendid Russian Baroque and classical architects. They, too, were the first to explore the heritage of the Russian Romanticists and Sentimentalists, to analyze and reassess the work of Orest Kiprensky, Alexei Venetsianov, and Fyodor Tolstoy. The same critics are to be credited for having overhauled the established misconceptions as regards early Petersburg architecture, completely re-evaluating its artistic significance. The articles contributed by Benois, who adored the beauty of old-time St. Petersburg, came as a genuine revelation to the journal's readers... Profound historico-artistic studies markedly affected the subject matter and creative methods of the World of Art artists.

The editorial staff of the journal also rendered a crucial service to Russian culture by drawing attention to those fields of creative endeavor, which the preceding generation of artists had ignored. Russian book illustration and stage design were revived and innovated. All possible support was given to the decorative applied arts and to the artistic handicrafts. Finally, a new chapter was opened in Russian art criticism. Research into the visual arts of the past centuries disciplined the new generation of art historians, enabling them to better comprehend the specific aspects of various creative problems and evolve their own methodology.

Such was the fruit of the six-year-long life of Diaghilev's journal. Its organizational achievements gave Russian artists the incentive to form new exhibition groups and creative associations.

First to show the way were the Moscow participants of the World of Art exhibitions. As early as 1900, they called for limiting Diaghilev's "dictatorial" powers and by the next year were mounting their own exhibitions of the 36. Toward the close of 1903, they

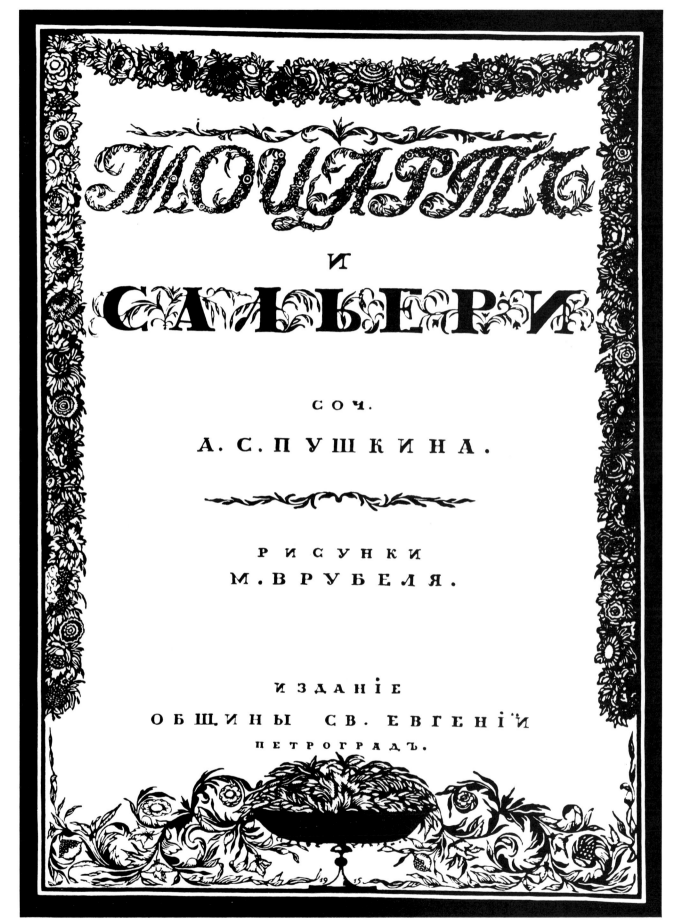

МОЦАРТ

И

САЛЬЕРИ

СОЧ.

А. С. ПУШКИНА.

РИСУНКИ
М. ВРУБЕЛЯ.

ИЗДАНІЕ
ОБЩИНЫ СВ. ЕВГЕНІИ
ПЕТРОГРАДЪ.

29. Sergei Chekhonin. Cover for Pushkin's *Mozart and Salieri*

established the Union of Russian Artists that incorporated both the 36 and the World of Art. Its emergence coincided with a period of trial and confusion within the World of Art ranks, whose leaders were increasingly convinced that it could no longer play a progressive role.

"It dawned upon us that we had said everything we wanted to say, that we were beginning to repeat ourselves, that what we had given would suffice Russian society for long," Benois recalled later.[9] Moreover, the contradictions between the literature and art divisions grew more acute and an unpleasant disagreement with Princess Maria Tenisheva, who subsidized the journal, also hastened its end. After the last issue in December 1904, the World of Art group discontinued activities, and its members joined the Union of Russian Artists.

Yet, as World of Art members themselves rightly observed, their journal "achieved what its founders, one may say, had never anticipated." They were able to state with pleasure that "not a single one of their initiatives had petered out.... and that all that was being done in a serious and talented manner in art of late, was in one way or another related to *Mir iskusstva*."[10]

To some extent the World of Art cause was taken up by the Moscow journals *Vesy* (The Scales) and *Zolotoye runo* (The Golden Fleece) and the Petersburg magazines *Starye gody* (Bygone Years) and *Apollon* (Apollo). Nor did Diaghilev end his organizational activities. Thus, in 1905, with the assistance of the former World of Art members, he mounted in the Tauride Palace a spectacular exhibition of Russian portraits, which contemporaries rightly regarded as an "event of epoch-making significance," for it "opened a new era in the study of Russian and European art of the eighteenth century and the first half of the nineteenth."[11] A year later, Diaghilev organized, in his "dictatorial" manner, his last exhibition in Russia, the seventh World of Art show, in which he presented, besides the works of the St. Petersburg group, those by Mikhail Vrubel, Konstantin Korovin, Mikhail Larionov, the two gifted young Moscow artists, Nikolai Sapunov and Pavel Kuznetsov, and, posthumously, Borisov-Musatov. Finally, after that year, he launched his unusually vigorous and persistent campaign to implement his cherished dream of "exalting Russian artists in the eyes of the West."

The opening salvo of Russian art's triumphal march through Western Europe was delivered by a retrospective display ranging from old icons to World of Art paintings, that

[9] A. Benois, *Vozniknoveniye Mira iskusstva* (The Emergence of the World of Art), Leningrad, 1928, p. 57

[10] D. Filosofov, "Tozhe tendentsiya" (Also a Tendency), *Zolotoye runo*, 1908, No. 1, pp. 71,72

[11] Grabar, *op. cit.*, p. 156

30. Aubrey Beardsley. Illustration for Oscar Wilde's *Salome*. 1894

31. Edvard Munch. Girls on the Bridge. 1910

32. Konstantin Somov. In the Bosquet. 1898–99

criticism (first of all Benois and Diaghilev) still seemed unusual and evoked certain mistrust. Shortly afterwards, however, Russian art criticism attained that professional standard which the World of Art propounded.

In 1901, a new art monthly called *Khudozhestvennye sokrovishcha Rossii* (Art Treasures of Russia) was launched, taking over from *Art and Art Industry* which, having lost its reputation, folded after its 38th issue in 1902. The founder and first editor of *Art Treasures* (up to early 1903) was Alexander Benois; after him, the art historian Adrian Prakhov took over until the journal folded in 1907. The basic purpose of this journal, initiated by the Society for the Encouragement of the Arts, was to study and propagate the art monuments of Russia. Assuming editorship, Benois emphasized that the new monthly should on no account conflict with the *World of Art*, but, must, on the contrary, pursue the same policy, only in respect to the history of Russian art.[27] Curiously enough, the abovementioned Society demanded of Benois that "everything needed for the publication be of Russian manufacture.... Even the paper had to be Russian.... Also the chromolithographs and the heliogravures had to be commissioned at home, mainly at A. Vilborg's zincography. The text meanwhile was printed at Golicke's."[28] The next issues for 1901 were of the order of monographs, devoted to one definite old building or collection, such as the Chinese Palace in Oranienbaum, Semyonov-Tien Shansky's collection of Dutch masters, or the Stroganov Palace in St. Petersburg. During this monthly's first year, practically the entire job fell to Benois: "As for my *Art Treasures*, my personal participation, in addition to the general editing, interminable proofs, etc., comprised composing at least three quarters of the printed text, covering the captions, news items, magazine reviews and bookvendor news...."[29]

In 1901, the Petersburgian members of the World of Art made the acquaintance of the painter, art historian, critic, and architect Igor Grabar, one of the most prominent representatives of the Moscow art world. Though Grabar had, at Diaghilev's suggestion, collaborated with the *World of Art* journal from its inception, he had never met his Petersburgian colleagues before. In spite of their becoming good friends after they met in 1901, there was for long, perhaps, even forever, definite divergencies of opinion between them. Several years later, in 1906, Grabar incisively commented upon this in a letter to Benois: ".... evidently there are two types of characters, you, Somov, and folk like you and Somov; such people, I have thought, always look back and always – note, always! – take a disdainful, condescending view of everything modern. You are too greatly enamored of the past to appreciate anything modern – well, I mean, not just appreciate,

[27] Benois. Recollections, vol. 2, p. 316

[28] *Ibid.*, p. 319

[29] *Ibid.*, p. 364

47

33. Léon Bakst. Cover for the *World of Art*. 1901

34. Léon Bakst. Costume design for the Tsarevna in Stravinsky's ballet *L'Oiseau de Feu*. 1910

opened in the Paris Salon d'Automne of 1906. It was organized according to Alexander Benois' historical concepts and emphasized the two pinnacles of Russian art, notably, the work of the great portrait painters of the eighteenth and early nineteenth centuries, and the new painting as represented by Vrubel, Konstantin Korovin, Serov, Borisov-Musatov, Somov, Benois, Bakst, Dobuzhinsky, and Lanceray. In his foreword to the catalogue Diaghilev emphasized that the show was intended not to embrace every chapter of Russian art history but to give an overview of Russian painting from the contemporary angle. "C'est une fidèle image de la Russie artistique de nos jours avec son entraînement sincère, sa respectueuse admiration pour le passé et sa foi ardente dans l'avenir."[12]

[12] *Exposition de l'art russe*, Paris, 1906, p. 7

The success of the exhibition exceeded all expectations. This was the first time that the Western European public could admire a strictly conceived survey of select periods in the development of Russian painting and the singular character of contemporary artists.

In 1907, Diaghilev arranged in Paris a series of Russian music recitals, and in the following year he produced Modest Mussorgsky's opera *Boris Godunov*, with Fyodor Chaliapin and other noted singers. The stage sets were designed by Golovin and Benois, while the costumes were sketched by Ivan Bilibin.

Yet however great the success enjoyed, however extensive the coverage in the world media, these events cannot compare with the spectacularly triumphant tours of the Ballets Russes that Diaghilev organized first in Paris, in 1909, and subsequently in London, Rome, Berlin, Vienna, and Madrid. The performances given by Anna Pavlova, Vaslav Nijinsky, Michel Fokine, Tamara Karsavina, and other splendid dancers comprised a highlight in European art and had a memorable impact on the history of culture in general. As profound and productive was the influence exerted by the Russian artists who executed the stage and costume designs for the ballet productions. Indeed, Bakst, Benois, Roerich, and later, Dobuzhinsky, Larionov and Goncharova, all revived and reformed world, let alone Russian, stage design.

Though the World of Art did not exist as an art group between 1904 and 1910, its former members continued to associate and were most active creatively, and some, socially as well.

During the period of the 1905 Russian Revolution with its short-lived freedom of the press, Serov, Lanceray, Dobuzhinsky, and Bilibin contributed to satirical magazines a number of political cartoons and drawings that figured prominently in the revolutionary graphic arts of the time. Thus, Serov executed a highly popular drawing, "*Soldiers, heroes everyone, where is all your glory?*," showing dragoons breaking up a defenceless demonstration. Though the other World of Art artists failed to produce anything comparable, such efforts as Dobuzhinsky's *October Idyll* and Lanceray's *Funeral Feast* received wide critical acclaim.

but assess very highly. I have thought that you at times take yourself in hand and appeal to the unprejudiced, closet art historian, and at such moments grudgingly speak of the beauties of today, while deep down seeing beauty only behind... On the other hand, there are people who most sensitively feel their bond with modernity, their oneness with it. This feeling has a bit of self-confidence and pride in it, for which reason, perhaps, nearly all those gravitating toward it and turning their backs on the old are such boors, even, at times, ruffians. I do not know whether I am boor or not, but I do know that our art is no whit inferior to the previous art, only that we do not see the whole picture yet. To tell the truth, it is a gigantic art, there's no getting away from that!"[30]

That, of course, is largely subjective, and as regards Benois a definition far removed from the truth – Grabar himself immediately made a reservation after what has just been cited: "Perhaps I am mistaken on your account."[31] However, he always experienced that feeling of being greatly at variance in views with Benois and the other Petersburgian members of the World of Art group. This, however, did not prevent him from counting himself and Benois as "like-minded in the struggle for the new art."[32] Hence, to the public eye, he and all his efforts, especially in the realm of art history, were initially associated with the World of Art. Grabar's initiatives in this field undoubtedly include the *History of Russian Art* that was put out under his direction and with his participation, plus a series of reputable monographs about various Russian artists.

Grabar as a painter was not quite as constant in his affiliation with the movement. Though he co-participated with its members in most of the exhibitions of the Society of Russian Artists, and in the special show arranged by Diaghilev in 1906, at first in St. Petersburg and then in Paris, he contributed to World of Art exhibitions as such only four times, in 1902, 1915, 1916, and 1922. Nonetheless, as an artist too, he was close to the World of Art trend. In short, Kustodiev was undoubtedly right when in his famous sketch for a group portrait of the "chief"

[30] I. Grabar, *Pis'ma 1891–1917* (Letters), Moscow, 1974, p. 183. Further: Grabar

[31] *Ibid.*

[32] I. Grabar, *Moya zhizn: Avtomonografiya* My Life: Automonograph), Moscow–Leningrad, 1937, p. 153. Further: Grabar. My Life

35. Alexander Golovin. Birches. 1908–10

members of the World of Art society, he depicted Grabar among them.

The Show of the 36 (actually 34) that opened in Moscow in late December included, among others, several artists who had taken part in all World of Art exhibitions, namely Benois, Braz, Vrubel, Golovin, Golubkina, Konstantin Korovin, Lanceray, Maliutin, Maliavin, Nesterov, Ostroumova, Serov, Somov, and Yakunchikova. Benois noted: "Though Diaghilev viewed this enterprise with suspicion, he nevertheless 'allowed' me to take part in this show."[33] Shortly afterwards, Diaghilev's "suspicion" developed into disfavor which openly manifested itself a year later. The show revealed that many of the creative principles espoused by Petersburgian *miriskusniki* differed from the aspirations of such Muscovite artists as Arkhipov, Vinogradov, Ivanov, Perepletchikov, and Stepanov. True, at the outset this difference was not so sharply in evidence, the more so as in Moscow, practically all the above artists enjoyed the reputation of radicals. Only

perspicacious Diaghilev discerned, with good reason, a menace to his own aesthetic leanings and stylistic tastes. Still for most of the public the show demonstrated the most innovative trends in Russian art.

1902
March–April
The World of Art's Fourth Exhibition of Paintings was mounted in St. Petersburg. Besides constant exhibitors there were several Muscovite artists who had participated in the Show of the 36, including Vinogradov, Sergei Korovin, Pasternak, Petrovichev, Perepletchikov, Svetoslavsky, and Shcherbov, as well as Grabar. For the young Pavel Kuznetsov and Nikolai Sapunov, this exhibit was their debut. Again the World of Art demonstrated the breadth of its aesthetic position, inviting Muscovite landscape and genre artists whose works represented an emotionally and painterly enriched version of Wanderer realism. At the other end of the pole was Vrubel's *Demon Downcast*, signifying the

[33] Benois. Recollections, book 2, p. 365

36. Alexander Golovin. Kashchei's Kingdom. Set design for Stravinsky's *The Firebird*. 1910

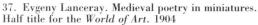

37. Evgeny Lanceray. Medieval poetry in miniatures.
Half title for the *World of Art*. 1904

38. Anna Ostroumova-Lebedeva. St. Petersburg.
The New Holland Arch. 1901

extreme of experimentation in which the World of
Art indulged, defying censure and vilification, to
which this work of Vrubel's was heavily subjected.
Incidentally, despite the picture's total non-acceptance by most reviewers, who gnashed their teeth in
rage, the persuasive power of Vrubel's great talent
and the prestige of the World of Art were so
impressive that in 1908 the board of the Tretyakov
Gallery acquired it from its first buyer, von Meck.
Indeed, the creative career of Vrubel toward the
close of his life was inextricably linked with the
activities of the World of Art.

A study of World of Art exhibitions, especially the
Fourth, necessitates amending the established notion
of this association's aesthetic during its classic
chapter of existence. As one will have gathered, it
did not at all shy away from the traditions of the
second half of the nineteenth century, provided they
were updated, and hence, did not appear shopworn
and lifeless. Indeed, one needs only mention the
innovative, daring transmutation of these traditions
by Levitan, Serov, Ryabushkin, and Nesterov,
whose works meant so much to the first World of
Art exhibitions.

At the same time, one could more and more distinctly observe the incorporation of Symbolist
tendencies, which, budding in the efforts of such
World of Art stalwarts as Bakst, Dobuzhinsky, and
Somov, burst into full flower in Vrubel's oeuvre.
Also highly symptomatic in this sense was the
appearance of the two future Blue Rose artists,
Kuznetsov and Sapunov, consistent Symbolists from
the very start, as was the publication in the *World
of Art* journal (No. 4 for 1902) of Valery Briusov's
article "Unwanted Truth," a programmatic declaration of Russian Symbolism.

In November–December, the *World of Art* journal
mounted one more showing of paintings in Moscow.
The circumstances attending the arrangement of this
exhibition reveal as just the assumption that it was
conceived as a "counterweight" to the activities of the
sponsors of the Show of the 36. It had been rumored
that the World of Art group was in the grip of a
crisis and was about to disintegrate – rumors that

were confirmed soon after. For a while Diaghilev
strove to keep things afloat. To begin with, he wrote
in an item in his journal: "When the Show of the 36
was initiated, genuine well-wishers spread rumors
alleging that many artists had broken away from
World of Art exhibitions and had formed their own
society. Such false rumors will be refuted by the fact
of the opening of a future World of Art exhibition,
where nearly all the more notable works currently
exhibited in Moscow will be shown."[34] Diaghilev
referred here to the works of World of Art artists
presented at the first Show of the 36, which indeed
figured later at the World of Art's Fourth Exhibition, and where as was noted, some paintings by
Muscovite artists from among the 36 were also
displayed. However, Diaghilev believed that inade-
quate, and so resolved to mount in Moscow itself the
first World of Art viewing to present the association's members in full brilliance and importance.
Or as he frankly intimated in a letter to Serov
dated October 15, 1902:

"They (i.e. several Muscovite artists – *A.K.*) must be
wrested free of the clutches of the Thirty-Six."[35]
The exhibition, which did take place, presented a
selection ranging over a number of years. The room
devoted to Vrubel, where hung, among other pieces,
his *Demon Seated*, *Spain*, *The Fortuneteller*, *Faust*,
Lilac, produced a memorable impression. Other
artists who were excellently represented included
Serov (some fifteen portraits), Golubkina ("Mist"
vase), Benois (Petersburg scenes), Roerich (the *Old
Russia* series), Somov (portrait of Ostroumova and
On the Balcony), Golovin, Lanceray, Trubetskoi,
Bakst, Konstantin Korovin, Sapunov, and Kuznetsov. Whatever had motivated Diaghilev when
putting together this somewhat improvised showing,
he definitely demonstrated that the World of Art
movement had attracted Russia's most eminent
artists of the period. It was a notable success, and
the association consolidated its reputation thereby.
Indeed, evidence of the success that this show
enjoyed was the Tretyakov Gallery's purchase of
four of the pictures (Bakst's portrait of Vasily
Rozanov, Vrubel's study for the *Demon*, Benois'

[34] *Mir iskusstva*, 1902,
No. 1, p. 13

[35] Diaghilev, vol. 2, p. 77

54

39. Ivan Bilibin. The Princess in the Tower. Illustration for the fairy tale *The Little White Duck*. 1902

Benois took no part in the satirical magazines of the period as he had gone abroad. Only later did he display his talents as critic and illustrator with extraordinary vigor. The articles he published between 1908 and 1917 in the Petersburgian newspaper *Rech* (Discourse) under the general title of *Art Letters* enjoyed a broad readership throughout the country, let alone the Russian capital. As a leading Russian critic, his views were heeded by both artists and the public at large.

During the same period most artists from Diaghilev's old group, who were now with the Union of Russian Artists, were able to bring their creative method to full fruition. Outstanding gems were produced by Somov, Benois, Bakst, Lanceray, Dobuzhinsky, and Ostroumova-Lebedeva. In fact, in the years following the 1905 Revolution, the bulk of Russian society drastically revised their attitude to contemporary art trends. The World of Art's educational activities bore fruit. Artists who but the day before had been unrecognized and ridiculed were now prized, with museums, collectors, and publishers demonstrating interest. World of Art achievements were acknowledged in diverse fields of artistic endeavour; its former members found themselves cramped within the Union of Russian Artists, which was quite foreign to them.

On March 19, 1910 Benois lambasted the Union's leading artists in a critical essay in *Rech*. In a categorical, authoritarian tone he attacked "superfluous and cumbersome, tasteless and dead" works. He even had no qualms about naming as the "ballast" certain well-known artists. The Union was furious, regarding this essay as a "violation of comradely ethics." A special deputation traveled to St. Petersburg to demand an explanation from Benois and present a note of collective protest that was signed by, among others, Konstantin Korovin and Sergei Maliutin, who had always been represented in Diaghilev's exhibitions.

Despite a demand from the Moscow artists for an apology, Benois maintained his appraisal – which he later termed "an overly unbiassed judgment" – preferring to withdraw from the Union. His example was followed by Serov, Somov, Bakst, Lanceray, Grabar, Dobuzhinsky, Yaremich, Ostroumova-Lebedeva, Bilibin, Roerich, as well as Kustodiev, who had long sought to join with the Petersburgians. In that same year of 1910 they founded their own, separate exhibition society called the World of Art, and demonstrated great vigor, mounting annual showings in both St. Petersburg and Moscow. Thus commenced the second chapter in the history of the World of Art.

Pavlovsk Palace, and Roerich's *Building a Town*). This purchase was effected by the representatives of the Gallery's board, namely Valentin Serov, Ilya Ostroukhov, and Alexandra Botkina, daughter of Pavel Tretyakov. Though the said acquisitions irked some conservatives, the tradition was launched and afterwards museums regularly bought works by World of Art artists for their collections – something which private individuals had long been doing! The elevation of World of Art paintings and graphics to the status of valuable museum acquisitions indirectly indicated their public prestige.

However, Diaghilev's hopes of undermining the second Show of the 36, which opened in late December 1902, did not materialize. Though most World of Art artists, including Benois, Golovin, Golubkina, Lanceray, Maliavin, Nesterov, Ostroumova, Serov, and Somov, did not participate this time, such reputable traditionalists as Arkhipov, Vasnetsov, Ivanov, Ostroukhov, and their younger colleague Yuon had their own admirers, who greatly appreciated their adherence to customary imagery, and this contributed to the éclat enjoyed. Generally speaking, the relationship between the two societies of St. Petersburg and Moscow was not one of conflict between "old" and "young," or between "advanced" and "backward," but rather one of two different forces equally entitled to exist within the context of the time. This factor was responsible for the provisional merger and coexistence of the World of Art group and the Thirty-Six within the Union of Russian Artists that was to form soon afterwards. Bearing on the preparations for the World of Art show in Moscow is another important document in this society's history, namely the *Minutes of the General Meeting of Participants in World of Art Exhibitions*, that was held on March 10, 1902. It reads as follows:

In attendance are the following constant exhibitors: 1) L. Bakst, 2) A. Benois, 3) I. Bilibin, 4) I. Braz, 5) M. Vrubel, 6) E. Lanceray, 7) Ph. Maliavin, 8) S. Maliutin, 9) A. Ostroumova, 10) F. Rushchits, 11) K. Somov, 12) V. Serov, and 13) J. Tsionglinsky.
Exponents: 1) I. Grabar, 2) V. Perepletchikov, and 3) S. Yaremich, and likewise S. Diaghilev, the publisher-editor of the *World of Art* journal.
Resolved:
1) To endorse without amendment for the next three years the statute as drafted at the Feb. 17, 1901 meeting of exhibitors.
2) To mount a World of Art show in Moscow, in January 1903, of works already exhibited in St. Petersburg.
3) To authorize V.V. von Meck, provided he kindly agrees, to organize and supervise the said exhibition in Moscow.
Next, the artists A. Benois and V. Serov were elected by secret ballot to the Organizing Committee for the exhibitions of 1903. Also elected by secret ballot as permanent exhibitors were I. Grabar, A. Rylov, and P. Shcherbov.

40. Alexander Benois. Anteroom of the Grand Palace in Pavlovsk. 1902

I. Braz and F. Rushchits were re-elected members of the auditing commission by an open show of hands.

The minutes were signed by: Alexander Benois, S. Diaghilev, Ph. Maliavin, M. Vrubel, F. Rushchits, I. Braz, L. Bakst, K. Somov, E. Lanceray, S. Maliutin, I. Bilibin, A. Ostroumova, J. Tsionglinsky, and V. Serov.

V. Purvit and K. Korovin have voiced assent with the resolution of the general meeting.[36]

This document again reveals how strictly and accurately the World of Art's organizational activity was arranged down to the slightest detail. One notable aspect is the mention of Vrubel, Maliutin, and Maliavin as full-fledged members ("permanent exhibitors"), inasmuch as they are not infrequently referred to as optional associates, which is wrong. Evidently more scrupulous efforts must be undertaken to trace and publish the group's archival documents, as that will largely clarify its membership, character of activity, and evolution....

On December 14, Maria Yakunchikova, who had taken part in all World of Art exhibitions, died.

The said year also saw the full publication of Benois' *History of Russian Painting in the Nineteenth Century*, which had evoked polemical comment even from intimate friends.[37] Despite its highly subjective qualities, it was the most comprehensive theoretical treatise reflecting the views of the *miriskusniki* on nineteenth-century Russian art.

1903
February–March

The World of Art's Fifth Exhibition was held in St. Petersburg. All the association's leading members were represented, plus Mstislav Dobuzhinsky, who was to become its leading exponent, and the eminent sculptor, Alexander Matveyev.

One essential feature of this exhibition was the participation of some Muscovite artists from among the 36. They included Aladzhalov, Arkhipov, Vinogradov, Dosekin, Zhukovsky, Ivanov, Pasternak, Perepletchikov, Petrovichev, Shcherbov, and Yuon. To a ceretain extent this resembled the first Show of the 36, the only difference being that then World of Art artists had gone to Moscow. Now, as some believed, the organic style and choice characteristic of previous World of Art shows had been upset and there was even talk of an inner crisis, to which the association's leaders reacted morbidly. Benois recollected later: "We began to think that we had already said all we could possibly say, that we were beginning to repeat ourselves, that we had gone so far forward, that what we had bestowed would suffice Russian society for long to come.... Incidentally, our very recent exhibition, mounted in the Great Hall of the Society for the Encouragement of the Arts, had been an unhappy one, from both the

[36] Quoted from: Diaghilev, vol. 2, p. 74

[37] S. Diaghilev, "Po povodu knigi A. Benua" (Re: A. Benois's Book), *Mir iskusstva*, 1902, No. 1

57

Gifted young artists at once flocked to the resurrected society. Though most, in effect, far from espoused World of Art concepts, they were eager to obtain moral backing. The most faithful of these new allies was Kuzma Petrov-Vodkin, who participated in every World of Art exhibition from 1912 through 1924. Likewise one must necessarily mention Martiros Saryan, Pavel Kuznetsov, Ilya Mashkov, Andrei Karev, and Nathan Altman. At the same time other younger artists, regarding themselves as disciples, followers, and direct heirs of the senior World of Art masters, joined the newly established society. Its very first show of 1911 attracted Kustodiev, Nikolai Sapunov, Sergei Sudeikin, Boris Anisfeld, Georgi Narbut, and Dmitry Mitrokhin. They, in turn, were joined by Zinaida Serebryakova in 1912 and Sergei Chekhonin in 1913. Characteristically, there were few easel painters among the new generation; most were stage designers and book illustrators.

The new World of Art society largely continued the policy pursued by Diaghilev's journal in the early years of the twentieth century. As before, its leaders sought to attract to their exhibitions all artists of talent, regardless of their creative stands. Whether Philipp Maliavin, Vladimir Tatlin, Arkady Rylov, Aristarkh Lentulov, Kustodiev or Marc Chagall, all were welcome. The only yardsticks were talent, professional skill and creative originality. However, considering the relentless rivalries between the various groupings and personalities representative of the most diverse trends throughout the 1910s, the World of Art shows were bound to be motley and eclectic, thus lacking the cohesion and consistency of the original group.

One must also note the essential difference between the two chapters of World of Art history. Whereas during the first, Diaghilev, period, the leading members strove to rejuvenate Russia's visual arts and marched in the vanguard of creative searchings, during the second phase – after academism had been put to rout and the Wanderers ousted, after leadership had been secured of all contemporary art groupings – the policy was largely one of safeguarding what had been achieved. Though some of the artists who joined from 1910 on were major innovative personalities – such as Petrov-Vodkin, Saryan, Mashkov, Karev, and Altman – they were but temporary associates. Unlike

[38] Benois, pp. 51, 53

[39] *Ibid.*, pp. 52, 53

[40] S. Diaghilev, "Vystavky" (Exhibitions), *Mir iskusstva*, 1903, No. 5, p. 45. Reprint: Diaghilev, vol. 1, p. 176

[41] Benois, p. 53

angle of selection and the angle of appearance."[38] Yet, to note a creative decline was totally groundless. The artists were in full flower. Having "gone so far forward," they were unable for a while to dredge up the proper organizational forms to promote their cause, which had already taken a distinct shape from the viewpoint of art history and had already acquired public acknowledgment in principle — however bitter the censure heaped by conservative critics. Certain personal motivations were also responsible. "Diaghilev," Benois subsequently recalled, "was already finding it hard to carry the burden. He realized that the artists he had introduced to the public already stood firmly on their own two feet. He grieved over all the 'betrayals' that were inevitable and gradually yielded to what was in fact the growth and cementation of the very organism. His stormy bursts of energy had infused our exhibitions with life, but they could not restrain themselves to statutes or obey definite rules, even though expressing the will of those very people he had brought together.... Moreover, his personal relations with some of them had become strained and unpleasant. For all these reasons the 1903 World of Art Exhibition was the last."[39] It was the "last" though, only as concerned the organizational tradition initiated in 1898, as concerned the old World of Art "firm". Already after the Fifth Exhibition had closed, and it was resolved to establish the Union of Russian Artists, Diaghilev observed: "I have no reason to speak of the World of Art Exhibition. Attempts were made to castigate it from every side, but one should not reply that it isn't worthwhile. One must not reply, because the answer to society's squeamish irritation over the new art is its far from ending, but broadly developing life. To reply isn't worthwhile because, despite society's protests, the young forces grouped around this exhibition will make headway and flourish, come what may, and, when the time arrives, will demonstrate to that selfsame society that at the given moment there is no other art in Russia save theirs."[40] In other words, Diaghilev believed that the creative flowering of the *miriskusniki* was obvious, that their standing in Russian art was firm, and that they were quite capable of evolving their own organizational forms for self-expression. That was actually to occur later.

The Fifth Exhibition, though, was indeed "last" of the series of shows launched in 1898. Even the planned Moscow tour, as noted in the *Minutes of the March 10, 1902 General Meeting*, was cancelled. "The death knell of the cause it had served was announced at the meeting of exhibition participants held on February 15, 1903 in the editorial offices of the *World of Art* journal."[41] On February 16, at a meeting in the Maly Yaroslavets Restaurant in St. Petersburg, World of Art artists Benois, Braz, Bilibin, Grabar, Lanceray, Maliavin, Roerich, Purvit, Trubetskoi, and Tsionglinsky, and also Arkhipov, Ivanov, Perepletchikov, Ostroukhov and Shcherbov, who represented the Muscovite 36, agreed to found, under the cognomen of the Union of Russian Artists, a new society that would bring

41. Nikolai Sapunov. The Masked Ball. 1907

together the diverse forces in Russian art and, henceforth, mount art shows "without Diaghilev's dictatorship." For the next several years, up to and through 1910, World of Art artists participated in the exhibitions which the Union mounted – with the exception of one of the farewell shows arranged by Diaghilev in Russia, notably the 1906 St. Petersburg exhibition, which was again held under the World of Art name, and the St. Petersburg Salon, which Sergei Makovsky organized in 1909. Nevertheless, at the Union's showings, World of Art artists stood out each time, often as a separate grouping.

At the Union's constituent assembly on December 16, 1903, it was resolved that in addition to the seventeen Muscovite founders, "proceeding from the contract that the participants in the 36 and World of Art shows had concluded on February 16, 1903, there were to be regarded as full members of the Union of Russian Artists: S.P. Diaghilev, A.Ya. Golovin, I.E. Grabar, E.E. Lanceray, Ph. A. Maliavin, Purvit, Rushchits, Prince P. Trubetskoi, J.F. Tsionglinsky, Ober, Nesterov, Golubkina,V .A. Serov, M.A. Durnov, N.V. Dosekin, M.A. Mamontov, P.G. Shcherbov, M.A. Vrubel, N.K. Roerich, S.A. Korovin, Ostroukhov, N.A. Tarkhov, and V.E. Borisov-Musatov" (Resolution taken by the constituent assembly on December 16, 1903).[42] Note that Vrubel, Dosekin, Sergei Korovin, Mamontov, Ostroukhov and Shcherbov were also listed as "founders" and thus, seemingly placed in opposition to the Petersburgians. However, for the previous five years, Vrubel had been most intimately associ-

ated with the World of Art, actually, was one of its founders. Other documents granted Union membership to Bakst, Benois, Braz, Konstantin Korovin, Maliutin, Ostroumova, and Somov. Consequently, all recent World of Art artists were organizationally inducted into the Union.

In operation at 33 Bolshaya Morskaya St. in St. Petersburg throughout 1903 was a singular enterprise known as "Contemporary Art," whose theory and practice were wholly associated with the World of Art movement. It should be pointed out that the *miriskusniki* took keen interest in the problems of applied art, the modern style of furnishing and interior design. As was noted earlier, the journal had originally been conceived as covering problems of the "applied genres and crafts." Though, subsequently, easel work unquestionably assumed priority, attention to applied art and its problems was as keen as ever, and this was expressed not only in the pages of the journal, but also in certain fields of the group's activity.

The Contemporary Art Enterprise was founded as an attempt to concretize the World of Art aesthetic in interior and furniture design, etc... The journal issue No. 9–10 for 1902 announced that Contemporary Art sought to extensively promote the applied arts and help artists work in this field "freely and quite independently." Moreover, its founders offered as relevant models "charming items in diverse fields of the art industry designed by Korovin, Maliutin, Golovina, Yakunchikova, and many others," which had been shown at World of Art exhibitions. The

[42] Quoted from: V.P. Lapshin, *Soyuz russkikh khudozhnikov* (The Union of Russian Artists), Moscow, 1974, pp. 39, 41. Further: Lapshin

the Diaghilev group, the World of Art's second generation did not come up with anything new; they merely elaborated upon the stylistic principles evolved toward the close of the nineteenth century. During the First World War the association ceased to play any progressive role and actually its day was done.

Though the society continued to exist even after the 1917 October Revolution in Russia, it did not contribute significantly to the development of the new Soviet art. Indeed, during the stormy period in Russian artistic life which followed immediately after the Revolution, it seemed to be a doomed throwback. In fact, the World of Art's historical objectives were of the past – they had been reached and surpassed. Participating in its final show in 1924 were – together for the last time – Benois, Somov, Dobuzhinsky, Golovin, Ostroumova-Lebedeva, Kustodiev, Serebryakova, and Chekhonin. After that the society broke up and its members went their various ways. True, some of the Russian artists who had emigrated did try once again to revive the society, inaugurating in Paris, in 1927, a World of Art exhibition chiefly represented by the former members and exponents of the Petersburg group, led by Dobuzhinsky. However, the show was ill-starred and with it the World of Art took its parting bow.

As one will have gathered, the World of Art played a preeminent educational and organizational role in early twentieth-century Russian culture. However, its historic significance goes much further. World of Art members were not only contributors to cultural advancement, organizers, critics, historians, and theorists; they were first and foremost gifted artists in their own right, each with his or her own vision, comprehension of reality, range of subject matter, imagery, and, last but not least, system of visual communication. As was noted earlier, the nucleus of the World of Art group evolved its own creative trend

42. Valentin Serov. "Soldiers, heroes everyone, where is all your glory?" 1905

43. Mstislav Dobuzhinsky. October Idyll. 1905

44. Mstislav Dobuzhinsky. Man with Spectacles. Portrait of the Art Critic and Poet Konstantin Sunnerberg. 1905–06

enterprise was subsidized by the two Muscovite art patrons, Prince Sergei Shcherbatov and the industrialist Vladimir von Meck. Igor Grabar was appointed art supervisor, while Alexander Benois was directly involved in the business. On display at the indicated address were Golovin's *terem*, Korovin's tearoom, Benois' dining room, Bakst's bedroom, and other designs, including some by Igor Grabar, Evgeny Lanceray, and the two art patrons named.

Despite the large funds afforded and the involvement of eminent artists, Contemporary Art enjoyed but a short-lived success with absolutely no commercial receipts, though it had been conceived as an art store and exhibition. Nothing was commissioned at all. It is hard to say why. Perhaps Diaghilev, who regarded the enterprise as a World of Art rival, failed to apply his organizing talents. Chiefly responsible, though, was the "utopian aesthetic" displayed by Grabar and his companions, who were unable to align their decorative fantasies with the vital needs of the time.[43]

The one-man shows of the French jeweler René Lalique and of the artists Roerich and Somov were also held on the Contemporary Art premises throughout the year. Later the Somov show traveled to Germany, where it enjoyed noteworthy acclaim. In addition to one-man shows, Contemporary Art also mounted two thematic exhibitions. One commemorated St. Petersburg's bicentenary and presented engravings, drawings, watercolors, and paintings depicting the city in the eighteenth century and the first half of the nineteenth. The other displayed Japanese engravings.[44]

[43] See: Benois. Recollections, vol. 2, ch. 45 and Grabar. My Life, pp. 184, 185

[44] *Mir iskusstva*, 1903, No. 8, pp. 82, 83

45. Osip (Iosif) Braz. Portrait of Mstislav Dobuzhinsky. 1922

46. Mstislav Dobuzhinsky. The City. 1904

that covered many aspects of painting and graphics, and that markedly affected the destiny of the new Russian art.

However, before probing its creative problems and salient features, one must first dwell on the traditions from which the aesthetic tastes and views of the World of Art protagonists stemmed. It must be stressed that their creative *Weltanschauung* formed totally aloof from the customary mainstream of *fin-de-siècle* Russian art. Neither academism nor the Wanderers had any effect on Benois and his associates, whose innovation began by revitalizing a range of topical art traditions.

Two sources which nourished the minds and imaginations of the future World of Art exponents were to serve as the basis for their aesthetic program: on the one hand, the contemporary art of Western Europe, chiefly Germany, Britain, and Scandinavia, where at the time Art Nouveau tendencies flourished and, on the other, their museum studies, primarily of eighteenth- and early nineteenth-century art.

One must necessarily name among those Western artists who strongly influenced the formative period of the World of Art movement the two British illustrators Aubrey Beardsley and Charles Conder, the German trio Thomas Theodor Heine, Heinrich Vogeler, and Julius Dietz; among seniors, Adolf von Menzel was revered not so much as a painter, but as the illustrator of Kugler's *History of Friedrich the Great* and an artful portrayer of eighteenth-century life in Germany. In their researches into old Western art Benois and his friends preferred to address themselves to eighteenth-century French and German painting, especially illustration and drawing; their favorite artists were Jean Honoré Fragonard, Gabriel de Saint-Aubin, Jean-Michel Moreau the Younger, and the Polish-born Daniel Nicholas Chodowiecki. As for national traditions, they skipped immediate predecessors and went back to the drawing and book illustration of the times of Alexander Pushkin, to the artists of the Venetsianov school, to Fyodor Tolstoy, and further back to portrait painters active in the reigns of Catherine the Great and Elizaveta Petrovna.

Worthy of note in this list is not so much the choice of names as the overall tendency. Priority is taken not by painters, but by illustrators, draftsmen, and engravers. Indeed, the marked proclivity for graphic art was in step with the quintessence of the pictorial concepts of the World of Art artists, who regarded line as the most expressive visual element; even in their paintings, line was the dominant force.

1904

December 1903 – January 1904. The First Exhibition of the Union of Russian Artists was held in Moscow. Of the 36 exhibitors, half were from among constant participants in the earlier World of Art shows. Nearly all the other Muscovite exhibitors had likewise taken part in World of Art shows at different times, but that had been rather casual and had not impelled them to share World of Art principles.

The difference in styles and imagery between the two groups was most pronounced. The *miriskusniki* preferred Art Nouveau and, at times, Symbolism, romanticized fantasies, historical retrospectivism, and decorative painterliness. The Muscovite artists, for the most part, entertained proclivities for the landscape and, at times, genre scenes, somewhat revitalizing the traditions of the second half of the nineteenth century emotionally and coloristically. No wonder Vrubel's *Valkyrie*, Somov's *Fireworks*, Maliavin's *Peasant Woman* and *Peasant Girl*, and Benois' *Parade in the Reign of Paul I* so greatly contrasted with Victor Vasnetsov's *Knight at the Crossroads*, Arkhipov's *Northern Village*, Korovin's genre pieces, and Apollinary Vasnetsov's *Bazaar* not only in the outlook on life, but also in the entire range of painterly means of expression. What was shared in common, though, was the prevalence of Russian themes, both modern and historical. For a certain period that could have served as the basis for a new organizational affiliation between the artists of Moscow and St. Petersburg and, also, of different trends. True, in his review of the exhibition Diaghilev acidly remarked that the "Muscovites were dominant, with the Petersburgians involuntarily appearing as invited guests."[45] Nonetheless, for the time being, this contrast, so natural and well founded in many respects, was still not viewed as a cause for confrontation.

In 1904, the *World of Art* journal folded for roughly the same reasons that brought about the closure of its exhibitions a year earlier. Benois wrote: "Right at that time (autumn of 1904 – *A.K.*), we resolved to end our offspring, the World of Art. The last attempt to prolong its existence came from outside, in the form of an offer from our previous benefactress Princess Maria Tenisheva to again shoulder the expense of publishing our journal. We could have agreed, as it was a pity to abandon so cherished a cause. But Tenisheva demanded that we accept N.K. Roerich as the third editor with equal powers, besides Diaghilev and myself. This, however, none of us liked, since despite our respect for Roerich's artistic talents, we did not quite trust him as man and comrade, did not believe in his sincerity and disposition toward us. May I add that the

[45] S. Diaghilev, "Vystavka Soyuza russkikh khudozhnikov v Moskve" (The Union of Russian Artists Show in Moscow), *Mir iskusstva*, 1904, No. 1, p. 6, Reprint: Diaghilev, vol. 1, p. 186

47. Konstantin Somov. Courtesans. 1903

48. Jean-Honoré Fragonard. The Stolen Kiss. 1780s

49. Daniel Chodowiecki. Jolly Company

50. Evgeny Lanceray. St. Petersburg. Cover for an edition marking the city's bicentennial. 1903

51. Alexander Benois. Frontispiece for Pushkin's *The Bronze Horseman*. 1905

But when discussing the sources of the World of Art movement, one should not restrict them exclusively to the visual arts. The basis was far broader. The impressions and emotions evoked by literature, music, and drama had a tremendous impact on the individuality of virtually every World of Art member. And again, as in the visual arts, devotion divided between Russia and the West, between contemporary times or the recent past and the beloved eighteenth and early nineteenth centuries. Idolized were Richard Wagner and Fyodor Dostoyevsky, and along with them, Henrik Ibsen and Pyotr Tchaikovsky. Yet the oeuvre of Somov, Benois, and their circle will not be properly appreciated outside the emotional and aesthical context of the romantic music of Mikhail Glinka, Frédéric Chopin, Georges Bizet, and Léo Delibes; the eighteenth-century French novel, such as *Manon Lescaut* and the *Liaisons dangereuses*; German Romantic prose, first of all Hoffmann, and particularly, the lyrics of Alexander Pushkin.

All World of Art members were strongly attracted to the theater. Much later, in his memoirs, Benois admitted that throughout his life he worshipped the theater, that in his mind the concept of "artistry" was always associated with the concept of "theatricality." The same is true of other World of Art masters who dedicated themselves to stage design and book illustration.

Still, there is no gainsaying the fact that the World of Art appreciably affected early twentieth-century easel painting by revitalizing its subject matter, forms, and techniques. The creative credo of the group is most distinctly manifest in history painting, with which its members occupied themselves to greater or lesser degree. Their originality in this respect becomes particularly obvious when compared with the mainstream of nineteenth-century Russian history painting.

It has to be noted that history painting had long dominated Russian art, with classical and romantic painters from Anton Losenko to Karl Briullov and the leaders of the academic school always asserting its priority. Indeed, in the eighteenth century the Academy of Arts developed a rigid concept of the historical picture as a conventional, highly solemn, histrionic act populated by classical, biblical and, now and again, old Russian heroes.

termination of the *World of Art* publication was not that much of a disappointement. All three, Diaghilev, Filosofov, and I were tired of the burden, and as it seemed to us that all that needed to be shown and said had been shown and said, anything more would be merely repetition and marking time."[46] For Diaghilev, the end of the journal spelled virtually the end of his career as art critic. True, later, he repeatedly gave interviews, contributed small essays and wrote "Letters to the editor," but these were almost exclusively related with theatrical and musical aspects of his enterprise. Benois, on the contrary, continued to write intensively, producing a plethora of essays and books devoted to art history and criticism. Diverse problems of the World of Art, now as an exhibiting association and as a definite trend in creative art and aesthetic theory, continued to be discussed in many Russian periodicals, such as the literary and art magazines *Vesy* (The Scales), *Zolotoye runo* (The Golden Fleece) and especially *Apollon* (1909–17). To a certain extent *Apollon* was the successor to the *World of Art*.
The Scales, which was founded in 1904, and published by S. Poliakov (with Valery Briusov actually in charge) was the main mouthpiece of Russian Symbolism. Among its art reviews, the journal featured comments on the activities of the artists in the World of Art movement.

1905
Most World of Art artists keenly responded to the events of the First Russian Revolution of 1905–07,

[46] Benois. Recollections, vol. 2, p. 414

especially the "Bloody Sunday" of January 9 and the December armed uprising. Valentin Serov, together with Vasily Polenov, resigned from the Academy of Arts because its president was Grand Duke Vladimir Alexandrovich, who had commanded the St. Petersburg garrison when the popular manifestation was gunned down on January 9. Meanwhile Anna Golubkina, who had been represented at World of Art shows, took a direct hand in revolutionary underground activity and was harrassed and repressed by the tsarist police.
Already in their capacity as members of the Union of Russian Artists, the leading *miriskusniki* signed a letter, adopted by the participants in the Union's Second Exhibition in St. Petersburg, which set out their attitude toward what was taking place in the country at the time. This letter, which the Petersburg newspaper *Russkiye vedomosti* (Russian Gazette) published on January 7, 1905, read: "Having assembled for a friendly dinner, the participants in the Union of Russian Artists exhibition cannot but respond to that call for deliverance which has rung out all over Russia, and have concluded that only free, creative work is viable, and that if our talent-rich country has not yet managed to have its decisive say in the domain of art and reveal its great latent artistic powers, if our art is deprived of a living link with the Russian people, then it is our deep conviction that chiefly responsible is the tutelary oppression of creative work, which kills not only Russian art, but likewise all other creative initiatives of Russian society. By virtue of

52. Konstantin Somov. Evening. 1900–02

which we cannot but feel our solidarity with those representatives of Russian society who are courageously and stalwartly struggling for Russia's deliverance and subscribe to the known zemstvo resolutions. I. Bilibin, Evgeny Lanceray, Vasily Milioti, Jan Tsionglinsky, L. Bakst, Igor Grabar, V. Perepletchikov, Alexander Benois, Valentin Serov, Konstantin Somov, Vic. Musatov, I. Braz, P. Shcherbakov, Konst. Pervukhin, Mstislav Dobuzhinsky."[47] A letter of similar content, written by Dobuzhinsky and cosigned by him, Benois, Somov, and Lanceray, was published on November 11, 1905 in the newspaper *Rus* under the heading "Voice of Artists."

During these stirring times many *miriskusniki*, such as Bilibin, Dobuzhinsky, Kustodiev, Lanceray, and Serov, drew caricature and satirical pieces reflecting highly topical political events. They included such gems as Serov's *"Soldiers, heroes every one, where is all your glory?"*, Dobuzhinsky's *October Idyll* and *As Our Brave General*, Lanceray's *The Fight, Funeral Feast* (Trizna) and *"Aye, Aye, Sir,"* Bilibin's *An Ass (Equus Asinus)* and *Tsar Dadon*, and Kustodiev's *After the Dispersal of a Demonstration*, *The Entrance*, and his caricatures of high tsarist officials. All these pieces were featured in the magazines *Zritel* (Spectator), *Zhupel* (Bugbear), *Pulemyot* (Machine-gun), and *Adskaya Pochta* (Hell's Mail).

Bugbear held a place of special prominence among these magazines. In a definite sense it was an offspring of the *World of Art*, whose ultimate issue

had come out but a little earlier. Grabar recollected later: "The revolutionary situation that existed in 1905 set the scene for the publication of a magazine of political satire. The indefatigable Zinovy Grzhebin was all afire with the idea. World of Art artists gathered now at one home, now at another's but mostly at Dobuzhinsky's; we discussed what the type should be like and what the magazine should look like. What racked our brains most was finding a lucky title for it. I don't remember now who first suggested *Bugbear*, which did not strike home at once, but which was eventually accepted. This all took place in April 1905.... Explaining the magazine's basic purpose, I said that we were to proceed from Social-Democratic principles, but we would have to camouflage that by employing an Aesopian language.... Serov took a most active part in all our discussions,"[48] The artists Grabar had had in mind included Anisfeld, Bakst, Benois, Bilibin, Braz, Grabar himself, Kustodiev, Lanceray, Ostroumova-Lebedeva, Somov, and Serov. Curiously enough, the new magazine employed the Elisabethan print-type which had been used but recently for the *World of Art* journal and which was available at the printshop of the Petersburg publishers Golicke and Wilborg. Though, to some extent, the famous German satirical journal *Simplicissimus* served as its model, from the point of view of its entire literary and pictorial content, the *Bugbear* dealt exclusively with events in Russian life at the time of the 1905 Revolution. However, after three issues, it was banned by the tsarist censors, and its editor Grzhebin was arrested.

[47] G. Yu. Sternin, *Khudozhestvennaya zhizn Rossii nachala XX veka* (Artistic Life in Early 20th-century Russia), Moscow, 1976, p. 65

[48] Quoted from: *Valentin Serov v vospominaniyakh, dnevnikakh i perepiske sovremennikov* (Valentin Serov in the Reminiscences, Diaries and Correspondance of Contemporaries), 2 vols., Leningrad, 1971, vol. 1, pp. 534, 535

The aim of such pictures was not to recreate the past but merely to convey, in allegorical form, a socio-political or moral message. In short, there was no historicism in academic history painting.

The Wanderers took an immeasurably deeper approach to historical subjects, striving to recreate the past as it had really been. They related the past to the topical social or psychological problems of the day. Such was Surikov, one of the nineteenth-century's greatest history painters, who attained pinnacles of authentic historical vision in his recreation of a world populated by truly Russian folk types.

The World of Art introduced into history painting innovations totally unlike anything produced before. Neither style, psychological probing, nor social problems played any essential part in the creative mentality of Somov, Benois, and their associates. Their objective was narrower, more intimate, yet, perhaps as complex. In their works on historical subjects, they sought to convey the elusive flavor and charm of bygone epochs, to express that disenchantment with reality, that nostalgic dream of the irretrievable past which assailed the minds and hearts of their milieu. This retrospective glance served as a romantic protest against the petty bourgeois prosaism of the time.

The Slavophile and Populist themes of nineteenth-century history painting were totally alien to the World of Art artists. Benois and his friends were, in effect, ignorant of old-

53. Konstantin Somov. Fireworks Display. 1922

54. Konstantin Somov. L'Echo du temps passé. 1903

55. Konstantin Somov. Harlequin and Lady. 1912

56. Konstantin Somov. Pierrot and Lady. 1910

time Russia and had no affection for it. They were attracted to the Versailles of Louis XIV, the sentimental Germany of Goethe, Hoffmann, and Chodowiecki, the personages of the Italian Commedia dell'Arte. Still, the mainspring of their works was Russian life, the times of Peter the Great, the eighteenth century, the Pushkin era, the St. Petersburg of Catherine the Great and Alexander I, the old Russian landed estate. There was a definite system, a definite consistency in the choice of historical subject. As champions of a Europeanized Russia, they adored Peter the Great as the founder of the new Europeanized Russian culture, St. Petersburg as the focal point of that culture, and Pushkin as the arch-important, arch-typical voice of Russian history's entire "Petersburg period."

Dmitry Filosofov, one of the founders of the World of Art, rightly observed that the artists of this group were interested chiefly in "the everyday life, intimacy and aesthetic of history."[13]

[13] N. Sokolova, *Mir iskusstva* (The World of Art), Moscow–Leningrad, 1934, p. 10

Indeed, they never sought to recreate past highlights or, at least, dramatic episodes, preferring festivities, carnivals, court ceremonies, or intimate genre scenes. Even so, within this restricted field they demonstrated so acute and accurate an intuition, so faithful and versatile a knowledge of history and archaeology as is rarely found in the preceding chapter of Russian painting. Never before had Russian art attained such finesse in reproducing the style of the past.

Like any other art trend, the World of Art embraced the creative discoveries and finds of all of its representatives. Naturally, their influence varied. The basic concepts and pictorial principles emerged and crystallized only in the work of the more gifted members. The first deserving of mention is Konstantin Andreyevich Somov (1869–1939), the leading authority and innovator at the initial stage of the movement. To elucidate the specific features of the World of Art's history painting, one must first analyze Somov's works.

Somov's salient feature was his precocity. He produced his finest works while still a young man, attaining full maturity when Benois and Bakst, who were of the same age, were only starting to grope for their own way in art. In his very first pieces, *The Letter*

He was released solely thanks to the intercession of Dobuzhinsky and Bilibin. The *Bugbear*'s follow-up was *Hell's Mail*, which after three issues in 1906 was likewise banned by the censors.

The Union of Russian Artists held its second show in St. Petersburg throughout the month of January. Before this exhibition opened, a large group of participants telegraphed Diaghilev; stressing the continuity between the World of Art and the Union, they noted:

The Union of Russian Artists, having unanimously elected you a permanent member, considers itself bound to express its profound amazement at that exceptional talent and that iron energy which enabled you in your ten years of unselfish, fervent effort to do so much for our deeply cherished Russian art. Having opened its first show in St. Petersburg this year, the Union is clearly aware of its duty to carry forward the cause that you initiated, and avails itself of the occasion to voice its hopes that the destinies of art in Russia will yet for long be associated with your valuable work. Please accept this as a token of our respect and sincere devotion. Somov, Perepletchikov, Musatov, Shcherbov, Serov, Tsionglinsky, Grabar, I. Bilibin, Dobuzhinsky, Lanceray, Pervukhin, Yuon, Bakst, Benois.[49]

[49] Quoted from: Diaghilev, vol. 2, p. 91

This notwithstanding, the Union could not be regarded as the World of Art's direct successor – as was also to be gleaned from its aforementioned second show in St. Petersburg. Thoug Arkhipov, Ivanov, Stepanov, Baksheyev, Vinogradov, the Vasnetsovs, and other leading lights of the Muscovite school were not represented, and, on the other hand, such classic World of Art pieces as Somov's *L'Echo du temps passé* and *Fireworks*, Benois'

[50] *Mir iskusstva*, 1904, No. 5, p. 113

illustrations to Pushkin's *The Bronze Horseman* and watercolors devoted to the history of St. Petersburg, and Dobuzhinsky's townscapes were shown there, still the real-life narrative landscapes and genre paintings presented by Muscovite artists dominated, thus making the exhibition a "double-decker" event. This stratification was just as distinctly manifest at the Moscow version of this showing, which was held over February–March and which, in composition and character, differed insignificantly from the preceding showing in St. Petersburg. True, critics active at the time scarcely spotted the difference between the various trends that the Union had brought under one roof and often accused of "decadence" both the dreamy romanticism and the dialogues with the past characteristic of the Petersburgians and that straightforward, emotionally packed interpretation of nature which was typical of the Muscovite landscapists and genre painters. Throughout 1904, Diaghilev, no longer preoccupied with preparation for new World of Art showings and journal issues, devoted his energies to organizing a stupendous Exhibition of Historic Russian Portraits, which opened at the Tauride Palace in St. Petersburg on March 6, 1905. This was beyond doubt one of the most precious, productive initiatives in keeping with the entire World of Art tradition. Diaghilev wholeheartedly threw himself into the preparatory work needed. Thus, he published an appeal to all owners of portraits of the Russian school including those painted in Russia by foreign artists to loan them for the exhibition.[50] To amass exhibits, he visited numerous old estates and cities in

57. Alexander Benois. Oranienbaum. 1901

Russia and borrowed from collections abroad. Some assistance was accorded by Benois, Dobuzhinsky, Bakst, Lanceray, and other World of Art colleagues. "We spent the last few months of 1904," Benois recalled, "making preparations for the Historic Show of Portraits. To this end, Diaghilev had obtained royal permission to use the vast premises of the Tauride Palace; now thought had to be given as to how to turn this to advantage.... It was most fascinating to sort out the pictures to study and compare them. Quite a few neglected and torn paintings had to be restored. New consignments arrived daily. As a result, many dramatic discoveries were made, and many obsolete mistakes and false 'traditions' were amended. The personalities of some of the top masters, with Levitsky at their head, became much better understood."[51]
Diaghilev prepared eight exhibition catalogue issues containing descriptions of 2,500 portraits as well as reference material about the artists included and the sitters portrayed. In the catalogue foreword, Diaghilev wrote: "The portraits shown are presented by reign, while within each reign they are grouped according to painter. True, this breakdown is tentative, in view of the extreme difficulty involved in thus grouping the artists concerned. Generally, it must be noted that given the breadth of said exhibition, its sponsors were obliged to ever bear in mind two angles – the artistic and the historical."[52]
The Tauride Palace exhibition was a great success and signally promoted Russian society's national awareness, including those cultural and artistic aspects that the cream of Russia's intelligentsia and,

more specifically, the World of Art association, had so vigorously sought to stimulate and encourage at the start of the century. The exhibition was likewise of significance for studies in Russian art history, for the material it furnished has been extensively drawn upon to this day by all writers of monographs and other books dealing with eighteenth- and nineteenth-century Russian art.
Fêting Diaghilev on March 24, Moscow artists and men of letters noted "his services as editor-publisher of the World of Art, whose closure had left an utterly unfilled hiatus in Russian journalism, and his grand feat, the creation of the Exhibition of Historic Portraits, that covered an entire epoch in the history of Russian art."[53] The banquet was attended by the artists Serov, Konstantin Korovin, Ostroukhov, Borisov-Musatov, Yuon, and Arkhipov, the writer Briusov, and also several art patrons and collectors, notably, Morozov, Mamontov, Shchukin, and Langovoi. In reply to the congratulations extended Diaghilev delivered a speech that was reprinted in The Scales under the heading "Hour of Summing-Up." The text ran as follows:[54]
"The honor you have accorded me with today's fête was for me as delightful as it was unexpected. When I learned yesterday of the coming assembly, I was extremely moved and felt totally unprepared to accept so touching a sign of regard for all that all of us had done and gained through anguish. Every fête is a symbol and every honoring of services, great or small, habitually extends from the person thus honored to the idea he expresses. Yet I would prefer not to speak now about the rightness of our convictions nor the reality of our efforts. We are used to thinking that we are right, and only the force of that conviction, of 'we or nobody,' could support us in our struggle

[51] Benois. Recollections, vol. 2, pp. 415, 516

[52] Quoted from: Diaghilev, vol. 1, p. 192

[53] Vesy (The Scales), 1905, No. 4, p. 45

[54] Reprint: Diaghilev, vol. 1, pp. 193, 194

(1896) and *In Confidence* (1897), Somov attempted to poeticize historical images, thus initiating and founding what we have termed "retrospectivism". He achieved the peak of his creative powers between the 1890s and 1900s.

Among Somov's best works from this period is *Evening* (1900–02), in which his lyricism, characteristic understanding of historical subject matter, and pictorial techniques are most fully manifest. In this painting Somov has depicted a nook in the park of a French palace that is sandwiched between columns of ornamentally pruned trees entwined in vines. Above, festoons of leaves and clusters of grapes resemble a raised drop curtain. In the background, clumps of pruned trees recede into the distance. Amidst this plethora of decorative ornamentation there step out, almost as if diffused, "shades of the past," in the person of a youth and two maidens garbed in sumptuous eighteenth-century costumes. The picture neither tells a story nor presents any dramatic action. The characters of this theatricalized scene are of no more significance in the artist's view than their accessories and surroundings. People and things are equally of interest, solely as means of conveying the spirit of a bygone age, its vanished beauties, its inner harmony and lyrical integrity, in short, everything so futilely sought in surrounding reality. In Somov's opinion, modernity is ugly, unaesthetic; only the past is beautiful.

Yet, despite his love for the old times, Somov was by no means a naive idealizer of the past. While admiring the aesthetic forms of eighteenth-century life, and reproducing this life in the forcefully authentic manner of an eyewitness and a highly intuitive erudite, he

58. Alexander Benois. The Kings's Walk. 1906

59. Alexander Benois. Fantasy on the Theme of Versailles. 1906

60. Alexander Benois. Water Parterre in Versailles. Autumn. 1905

was ever critical of the irretrievable past. His admiration of it combined with an acrid irony and scepticism. A most apposite case in question is his *L'Echo du temps passé* (1903). Again there is no story, as in *Evening* and most of Somov's other retrospective pieces. It portrays a girl in a white frock, seated in an armchair within a suite of rooms in an old country mansion. However, unlike the personages in *Evening*, she is no fleshless "shade of the past." She is a melancholic contemporary, a *fin-de-siècle* person with a morbid mentality, who like the artist himself heeds in profound torment "the echo of the bygone times." Somov seems to have invested her with his own sentiments, his own perturbed, dreamy nostalgia; the contrast between the stylized furnishings and the old-fashioned garments, on the one hand, and the girl's emphatically modern, "decadent" appearance, on the other, borders on the grotesque.

A few words about the salient features of Somov's pictorial arsenal are in order, since they markedly influenced almost all the artists of the group and, to a large extent, shaped their creative manner.

Despite his ability to fully and subtly sense the decorative harmony of color, Somov, essentially, was an artist of surface, not of volume and space. All his works rest on a strict and accurate line drawing, boldly reducing the object to a common denominator and sometimes transforming the visible form into an almost non-objective ornamental arabesque. Having defined the silhouette and inner shapes, the artist meticulously modeled the volumes, after which he colored the drawing, adding pools of color, sometimes localized, but more often than not integrated by one common tonality. His painting technique, with its small dabs forming an enamel-like surface, harks back to the eighteenth-century traditions in conformity with which the artist stylized his work.

As will have been gathered, Somov influenced not only history painting, but also all other fields practised by World of Art artists. In fact, all the artists developed and reinterpreted, in one way or another, the system Somov evolved.

The influence exerted by Alexander Nikolayevich Benois (1870–1960) was equally forceful. This artist's retrospective works derived from his extraordinary erudition. He was more than a scholarly historian familiar with cultural history and a peerless connoisseur of the art and life of his favorite epochs. Like Somov, Benois possessed the intuitive ability to "transport himself into the past," of viewing it as if through the eyes of a person on the spot; indeed, he admitted that he found it easier and simpler to draw a contemporary of Louis XIV than a contemporary of his own. "My attitude toward the past is more tender and affectionate than toward the present.... I understand the ideas, ideals, dreams and passions.... of that time better than I do these things on a contemporary level,"[14] he wrote. His retrospectivism is imbued with a spontaneous lyrical feeling.

[14] A. Benois, *Zhizn khudozhnika: Vospominaniya* (The Life of an Artist: Memoirs), 2 vols., New York, 1955, vol. 1, p. 262

Benois' creative principles have a direct link with Somov's stance. The two artists shared common tendencies in stylization and graphic decoration. In fact, in the case of Benois, the theatricality of the compositional and spatial structure is, perhaps, more distinctly manifest. Yet, at the same time he introduced into retrospective painting something innovative and completely independent, fathering a very specific genre which one could, perhaps, take the liberty of terming the "historical landscape." Indeed, landscapes comprise the bulk of his oeuvre, though he was drawn not so much to nature itself as to its associations with history. He mostly depicted historic sites, old cities, celebrated gems of architecture, and palatial parks adorned with statuary. He devoted extensive series not only to old-time St. Petersburg, but also to Pavlovsk, Peterhof (now Petrodvorets), Oranienbaum (now Lomonosov) and Tsarskoye Selo (now Pushkin)

His many paintings and watercolors always derive from faithfully done life studies, which, however, were seen only as preparatory material. When painting, Benois persistently emphasized the decorative aspects of a landscape motif, deliberately modifying the actual proportions, rearranging the compositional elements, and intensifying the color contrasts. Thus, his concrete observations were transmuted into the likeness of a stage setting with its flanking coulisses and backdrop.

Benois' favorite subject was the Versailles of Louis XIV, one to which he turned in 1897, 1905, 1906, 1914, and 1922. It is these works that best demonstrate his creative approach.

61. Alexander Benois. The Bath of the Marquise. 1906

His pictures lend themselves to an arrangement in series. Like the book illustrator or stage designer, he sequentially revealed in his cycles of studies and compositions the diverse aspects and facets of the conceived image, producing row upon row of seemingly alternating landscapes with architecture, which he from time to time populated with staffage figures garbed in antiquated costume. Note that the figures are staffage, nothing more; they merely enliven the view without introducing any dramatic action, without obliging the artist to engage in psychological characterization or tell a story. The miniature figures of the king and his entourage, dwarfed by the magnificent Versailles esplanades, are merely there to regenerate the bygone atmosphere and to theatricalize court etiquette. His "personages" are not people, but the works of art, the impressive statues and fountains of Versailles with the spectacular, stately mass of the royal palace. The artist seems to intimate that human beings are petty, negligible, and mortal, while art is great and eternal.

The subject matter of Benois' history paintings is not restricted by any means to the culture of Western Europe. Between 1907 and 1910, the Moscow publisher Iosif Knebel commissioned him to paint a large series of pictures illustrating eighteenth-century Russia to serve as aids to the study of history. Naturally, Benois, with his profound knowledge of the life and material culture of the past, was the most suitable choice in this connection. At any rate, the series of illustrations that he made well reproduced scenes from martial history and the life of the imperial court and landed gentry. They include two truly outstanding history paintings: *Parade in the Reign of Paul I* (1907) and *Peter I Walking in the Summer Gardens* (1910).

In comparison with his Versailles series, Benois' works devoted to Russian history display certain specific features. They are more realistic and are not as elegant in form, as greater attention is paid to genre detail and psychological characterization; the artist has provided an intimate glimpse of bygone life conveyed with historical authenticity. Though from the angle of concept the "Knebel series" may invoke reminiscences with Serov's history painting, Benois has retained his typical theatricalization of the past.

The retrospective paintings of Léon Bakst (1866–1924) betray a similar trend, though differing somewhat in detail. True, he too, emulating Benois and Somov, started out by

against the odds for such obvious truths. Allow me to interpet the meaning of tonight's fête from a somewhat different angle. Unquestionably every fête is a summing up, a conclusion.

"Of course, I am far from thinking that tonight's fête is in any respect the conclusion of those aspirations that have filled us thus far, but I think many will agree that the need to sum up and draw conclusions increasingly enters the mind these days. Of late I have unremittingly encountered this in my work. Do you not feel that the long gallery of portraits of people, great and small, with which I tried to populate the magnificent rooms of the Tauride Palace, is but a grand and convincing summing-up of a brilliant, but, alas, dead chapter of our history? With my aesthetic worldview, I delight in the theatrical glitter of eighteenth-century favoritism as much as in the fairy-tale prestige of the sultans.... But today, only elderly nannies remember those fairy tales, while the prolific Dowe suggests, with a tinge of elusive sarcasm, that we are unable to believe the romantic heroism of the fearful casques and the invincible gestures.

"I have earned the right to say this loudly and decisively, as with the last whiff of a summer breeze I ended my long travels around the length and breadth of boundless Russia. And it was precisely after these eager wanderings that I grew especially convinced that the time of summing-up had come. I observed this not only in the brilliant images of our forefathers so obviously distant, but mainly in their descendants eking out the rest of their days. The end of a way of life looms before us. Remote estates boarded up, palaces frightening in their dead splendor are strangely inhabited by today's nice, ordinary people unable to endure the gravity of past regalia. Here it is not people who are ending their days, but a way of life. And that is when I fully realized that we are living in a fearful time of change; we are doomed to die in order for a new culture to be erected, a culture which will take from us what is left of our weary wisdom. This is what history tells us, and what

62. Alexander Benois and Léon Bakst visiting Maria Tenisheva in Talashkino near Smolensk. 1895–96

63. Alexander Benois. Parade in the Reign of Paul I. 1907

64. Alexander Benois. Peter I Walking in the Summer Gardens. 1910

65. Léon Bakst. Vase (Self-Portrait). 1906

66. Léon Bakst. Terror Antiquus (decorative panel). 1908

aesthetics confirms. Now, plunged into the depths of the history of artistic images and thereby invulnerable to the reproaches of extreme artistic radicalism, I can state boldly and with conviction that he does not err who is assured that we are the witnesses to a great historical moment of summing-up and ending in the name of a new unknown culture – a culture which has arisen through us but which will sweep us away. Hence, without fear or unbelief, I raise my glass to the ruined walls of the beautiful palaces, as I do to the new behests of the new aesthetics. The sole wish that I, an incorrigible sensualist, can voice is that the impending struggle would not abuse the aesthetics of life and that death would be as beautiful and radiant as the Resurrection!"

Between 1900 and 1905, World of Art artists extensively worked for the Imperial Theaters. One can mention in this connection Golovin's decors for A. Koreshchenko's *The House of Ice* and Rimsky-Korsakov's *Maid of Pskov* at the Bolshoi Theater in 1900 and 1901 and for Glinka's *Ruslan and Ludmila* at the Mariinsky Theater in St. Petersburg in

67. Léon Bakst. Sergei Diaghilèv, and Vaslav Nijinsky in Venice. 1912

83

doing Versailles views and produced *Coppelius* after Hoffmann's tale. However, in effect, eighteenth-century reminiscences and the culture of the Russian landed gentry were alien to him. Bakst had other tendencies; he was the one and only World of Art artist to be literally enamored of antiquity. He visualized future art as embracing forms of a new classicism. In his graphic pieces, Bakst constantly drew upon Grecian mythology and the archaic art of Crete and Mycenae. He also used themes of antiquity in his easel painting.

In 1908, Bakst produced his *Terror Antiquus*, a symbolic piece, or rather, a decorative panel depicting the destruction of Atlantis. He conceived the idea after travels in Greece and Crete. In this panorama of a legendary state engulfed by the sea, we see rising out of the water the peaks of craggy mountains, several scattered buildings, temples, and an acropolis, which the surging seas are about to overrun. The tiny human figures scurry to and fro in horror, much like a disturbed anthill. Yet it is not the human tragedy in the sinking of Atlantis that engages the artist's attention. Again we are faced with a concept that reveals how puny man is when confronted with the immortal grandeur of art. Indeed, the chaotic destruction is dominated by an atmosphere of strange, imperturbable serenity. The land seems to be populated exclusively by huge statues that look on indifferently at the raging elements, and above it all towers the vast statue of an archaic, enigmatically smiling Aphrodite – a symbol of eternity.

One thus sees emerging in the work of the World of Art's leading exponents a new, singular, yet consistent concept of history painting. The oeuvre of Valentin Alexandrovich Serov (1865–1911) played a signal role in the evolution of this concept.

Serov was a fully mature, established artist when he joined the World of Art society. Yet, though he was older, far more experienced and gifted than the others, his association with Diaghilev's group was of great, if not vital, significance for certain of his activities, especially his history painting. Although art critics even before the 1917 Revolution had noted World of Art influences on Serov's outlook and work, it is definitely worthwhile elucidating the nature and extent of these influences.

Along with other World of Art members, Serov went through a period of intensive infatuation with eighteenth-century Russian art. He fully shared the interest evinced in the Europeanization of Russia and the worship of Peter the Great, the affection for old-time St. Petersburg and the enthusiasm for Pushkin and his world.

Serov had high praise for the historical intuition, versatile knowledge, and the methods and approaches employed by the World of Art artists when fathoming and reproducing the past. He was convinced that the "contemporaneousness" of their works was indisputably

68. Léon Bakst. 1900

1904, K. Korovin's decors for Puni's *Little Hump-backed Horse* and Minkus' *Don Quixote* at the Bolshoi Theater in 1902, and Bakst's set and costume designs for Euripides' *Hippolytus* and Sophocles' *Œdipus at Colonus* at the Alexandrinsky Theater in 1902 and 1904 and for Bayer's *Die Puppenfee* at the Mariinsky Theater in 1903. Besides the World of Art exhibition associations and journal, which enjoyed well-deserved popularity, there continued to exist a group of friends who had originally initiated the relevant tradition. With the passage of time, the group modified. "Throughout the 1900s our group of friends changed greatly," Benois recollected. "Filosofov completely broke with us, this process having begun yet when the *World of Art* journal was still afloat, as 'Dima's' interest in the plastic arts gradually waned.... So when the journal, having seen out 1904, folded, Filosofov comletely disappeared from view.... Neither did Nurok call on Diaghilev now.... Still keeping company with Seryozha (Diaghilev – *A.K.*) were, besides myself, Nouvel, and also Bakst and Prince Argutinsky. When talk about the Parisian Season was seriously resumed, Fokine and a total newcomer, the young Stravinsky, attended our gatherings."[55]

[55] Benois. Recollections, vol. 2, pp. 512, 513

69. Valentin Serov. Odysseus and Nausicaä. 1910

1906
**The World of Art show was held in St. Petersburg
in February–March.** It was due virtually to Diaghilev alone, however with the encouragement of most
of the *miriskusniki*.[56] As its chief sponsor, Diaghilev
demonstratively called it the World of Art show, a
name he so greatly cherished – although, *pro forma*,
the association as such no longer existed, having
merged with the Union of Russian Artists. Even
though he had been elected its honorary member on
December 16, 1903, and even though its leading
lights had assured him that they were merely
carrying forward the tradition, he could not yet
tolerate the organizational changes which had
resulted in the renunciation of the very name and
the erosion of its principles and traditions. The
purpose of his show was to emphasize the trend's
significance as a very special one in contemporary
art, along with its unquenchable vitality and ability
to evolve still further. This served as the point of
departure for selecting the exhibitors. The nucleus of
World of Art stalwarts was complemented by but two
Muscovite Union members, namely Vinogradov and
Yuon, plus several more Petersburgians, including

[56] See, for instance, Grabar, pp. 176–178

70. Valentin Serov. The Rape of Europa. 1910

71. Valentin Serov. Catherine II Setting Out to Hunt with Falcons. 1902

72. Valentin Serov. The Grand Eagle Cup. 1910

Rylov and a group of talented youngsters – which last is most characteristic and of special import. Indeed, by inviting the then virtually unknown but undoubtedly gifted young Anisfeld, Kuznetsov, Larionov, Vasily and Nikolai Milioti, Sapunov, Ulyanov, Feofilaktov, and Jawlensky, Diaghilev obviously sought to stress that the World of Art movement could renew itself by recruiting the young talents amongst whom it evoked response and understanding.

Nonetheless the focus was on the works of the leading World of Art figures. These included Serov's portraits of Chaliapin and Fedotova, Benois' illustrations to Pushkin's *The Queen of Spades* and *The Bronze Horseman* plus his Versailles motifs, Dobuzhinsky's *Man with Spectacles, Barbershop Window*, and Petersburg townscapes, Somov's *Fireworks, Lady in Pink*, and porcelain figurine *The Lovers*, Vrubel's *Six-winged Seraph, St. John the Baptist*, and *Portrait of Zabela-Vrubel against the Background of Birches*, Bakst's portraits of Bely, Diaghilev, and Gippius, Lanceray's *Empress Elizaveta in Tsarskoye Selo*, Grabar's *Balcony, Hoarfrost*, and *Frosty Morning*, and Golovin's triple portrait of theatrical personalities. These works set the tone for both the overall extremely high standard and the creative innovation that the younger exhibitors displayed in their searchings. Of special significance was the separate show of works by Victor Borisov-Musatov, who had died in 1905. This was more than a tribute to the memory of this fine artist. It was also an effort, even though a belated one, to remedy an earlier error, as at the outset, the World of Art group had underestimated the late artist and had barred him. Now the Saratov painter was fully accepted, the more so as he served as the ideal for a large group of young Muscovite artists led by Pavel Kuznetsov.

Again, as was his custom, Diaghilev took great care with the interior decoration and exposition as such.

73. Valentin Serov. Young Peter I Riding in the Chase. 1902

74. Valentin Serov. Peter the Great. 1907

an indication of the superiority of the new history painting. On the other hand, he was a realist possessing deeply rooted links with the humanitarian tradition of nineteenth-century art and, hence, could not be satisfied with the no-conflict nature of Somov's and Benois' retrospective pictures, their pronounced aestheticism, their neglect of social and psychological problems, their blindness to the human being. In his own history painting Serov sought, while borrowing World of Art stylistic achievements, to outdo his *confrères* in fathoming and reinterpreting the past.

In the early days of his collaboration with the World of Art group, Serov executed small tempera paintings illustrating N. Kutepov's book about the royal hunt in Russia. These included *Peter II and Princess Elizaveta Riding to Hounds* (1900), *Catherine II Setting Out to Hunt with Falcons*, and *Young Peter I Riding in the Chase* (both 1902). Though in their sense of style and their faithfully reproduced atmosphere, costume, and genre detail, these temperas are no whit inferior to similar pieces by other World of Art artists, they, in contrast, do tell a story, demonstrating well-worked-out action and deep psychological insight. In short, the characters depicted are no "shades of the past," no actors garbed in antiquated costume, but real, flesh-and-blood people, set in concrete, real-life situations.

Serov's historical interests were not limited to the "St. Petersburg period," or to Russia in general. In 1907, in the company of Bakst, he traveled to Greece and his impressions induced him to conceive several compositions on classical subjects of which, however, he realized only the *Rape of Europa* and *Odysseus and Nausicaä* (both 1910).

Art critics of pre-revolutionary times rightly ranked these pieces among Serov's finest creations, as revealing most forcefully his profound flair for decorativeness. Nikolai Punin observed that "Serov, like no one before him, felt the style, felt the rhythm, felt the epoch which he intended to recreate.... In his *Odysseus and Nausicaä*, Serov approached the archaic subject matter with amazing inspiration; he fathomed and reproduced it in extraordinary, highly artistic forms."[15] Here the artist was able to achieve what Bakst had not attained in his *Terror Antiquus*; in Serov's composition we perceive the living sensation of antiquity and a pungent, emotion-packed probing of the spirit of archaic art. While Bakst regarded antiquity merely as the pretext for stylization, Serov viewed it as the

[15] N. Punin, "V.A. Serov (Concerning a Posthumous Exhibitiion of His Works)," *Severnye zapiski*, 1914, No. 1, pp. 110, 111

[57] Grabar, p. 178

The architect F. Lidval was charged with the interior design and, as a matter of fact, the opening was delayed for almost a whole fortnight to have all the finishing touches put on.[57]

This brilliantly selected and arranged exposition contrasted greatly with the extremely uneven, heterogeneous displays characteristic of the exhibitions that the Union of Russian Artists mounted, a point most sensitively noted by contemporaries. As Benois recalled: "When designating as successor the well-organized Union, which was devoid of supreme idealistic motivations (the handiwork of the Muscovites with Perepletchikov at their head; within our group Serov dubbed him *Ganger*), Diaghilev's World of Art realized that its most vital, lovely fundamentals would go.... Yet, later, Diaghilev once again showed himself to the public as the same, sole master with the same knowledge. This occurred in the hard winter of 1906, when even the energies of the Union's bosses had weakened. The demoralization of the successors incited Diaghilev and as the final twist he gave a brilliant demonstration of the advantages of one-man command and likewise of the fact that difficulties were not for him and that he could do anything should he set his mind to it."[58]

[58] Benois, p. 54

In fact Diaghilev did more than that. His 1906 World of Art show revealed firstly the tremendous range and creative wealth of the "supreme idealistic motivations" of the artistic trend itself. Diaghilev

75. Valentin Serov. Portrait of Fyodor Chaliapin. 1905

76. Evgeny Lanceray. Ships in the Times of Peter I. 1911

himself was pleased. "It was a magnificent show, exceeding, as they say, all expectation,"[59] he wrote to Serov in March 1906. For the first time with respect to Diaghilev's undertakings, most of the newspaper reviews were likewise favorable. Only the sculptor Ilya Ginzburg came out in the newspaper *Rech* with the customary accusations, which this time were simply absurd; he claimed that the artists represented in the exhibition had supposedly borrowed "their revelations from the Parisian Salons des Refuses." In a terse retort, featured in the March 8 issue of the newspaper *Rus*, Diaghilev capped his argument, entitled, "In Defence of Art" with the ringing declaration: "Of course we seek recognition of 'our new art,' for the sole reason that outside of the artistic communion that emerged under the World of Art's banner, there is no other art in Russia today. All the present and the future are coming and will come from this, and will, in one way or another, feed on the behests that the World of Art derived from its attentive study of the great Russian masters since the times of Peter."[60] There was a certain amount of hyperbole in this categoric statement. Not all of Russia's important artists had affiliated themselves with the World of Art in the early years of the century. However, its mainstream had encompassed all leading productive art trends. Small wonder Diaghilev directly associated it with the more essential and characteristic

tradition in Russian art "since the times of Peter." Today it is absolutely clear that in the early twentieth century this tradition was carried forward by the artists of the World of Art group. Also note that by his 1906 show Diaghilev foresaw this movement's future as integrating its initial figurative and stylistic principles with creative innovation, inasmuch as that bond was characteristic of its revival, of the exhibitions it mounted from 1911 through 1917.

While arranging this "farewell" exhibition, Diaghilev was already planning to present to the West both the art and all that had preceded it. The initial attempt to achieve this was undertaken that same autumn. Meanwhile, the Union of Russian Artists mounted its Third Exhibition in April. To some degree it mirrored Diaghilev's show, presenting the same artists, with the exception of Larionov, Noakovsky, and Sapunov, while including Braz, Kustodiev, and a group of Muscovite Union members: Aladzhalov, Baksheyev, Dosekin, Durnov, Klodt, Sergei Korovin, Meshcherin, Pasternak, Perepletchikov, Petrovichev, and Turzhansky.

The artistic contrast between the works of the two trends, in evidence already at the Union's two previous exhibitions, was still greater. Yet at the same time, this Third Exhibition revealed in a new light – probably for the last time in a conciliatory manner, without any dichotomy between the two markedly dissimilar trends – the deep affinity

[59] Diaghilev, vol. 2, p. 96

[60] Reprint: Diaghilev, vol. 1, pp. 203, 204

source of novel, monumentally decorative solutions. Some of his compositions on antique themes were to serve as preliminary sketches for frescoes adorning a private mansion in Moscow.

Serov's *Peter the Great* (1907) occupies a very special place in the annals of twentieth-century Russian history painting. Grabar called it "Serov's most inspired creation" and a very significant phenomenon in the new Russian art.[16] Indeed, in this picture Serov was able to apply the merits of the World of Art's creative method and, at the same time, avoid its faults. Possibly, this work more vividly than any other displays World of Art influences. Its composition bears characteristic nuances of the theatricalization reminiscent of Benois' Versailles watercolors; the spatial planes are large, generalized, and simplified as would be for a monumental fresco; the rhythm is acutely asymmetrical; the line of horizon is low set while the near-grotesque, pointed silhouettes stand out against the gold-tinted, cloudy sky. However, besides an intuitive understanding of the past, the picture also reveals that profound historicity of concept and that verisimilitude which were so often lacking in the works of World of Art artists. Having subdued the illustrative features still observable in his earlier efforts, Serov has imparted a truly tragic note to the psychological characterization of the emperor, whose image develops into a full-fledged symbol of the Petrine era.

Peter the Great and his epoch continued to engage the artist's interest in the last years of his life. Serov conceived and began to paint three pictures, in which he showed his favorite personage in more intimate surroundings, notably *Peter I in Monplaisir* (1907–11), *The Grand Eagle Cup* (1910), and *Peter the Great at a Construction Site* (1911). All of them remained unfinished. Nevertheless, it was through his pictures devoted to the Petrine era that Serov particularly influenced World of Art history painting. This influence can be traced in Benois' later output, and especially in the works of the younger artists, first and foremost, Lanceray and Dobuzhinsky. No wonder that, for the World of Art group, Serov's early death came as an irreparable loss.

The creative principles and aesthetic credo of Evgeny Evgenyevich Lanceray (1875–1946) developed under Benois' direct guidance, from whom the artist assimilated the high

[16] I. Grabar, *Valentin Alexandrovich Serov*, Moscow, 1965, p. 208

between the creative endeavor of the two groups, who may be confidently classified as the cream of the Russian art of the period. Whereas at the earlier two shows the national thematic identity was characteristic of most paintings and drawings, now the feeling of life's lofty beauty – of man, nature, and the memory of past history – was more distinctly revealed. This feeling, quite often tinged with a festive romanticism, was in the nature of a philosophical *Weltanschauung*. Reviewers were not infrequently bewildered as to why artists were displaying works brimming with radiant hopes and dreams at such a turbulent, dramatic time in the nation's history (1905–06). This paradox received its explanation as time passed; it reflected a premonition of oncoming great changes, of new social and aesthetic vistas.

With his Russian art show at the Salon d'Automne in Paris in the autumn of 1906, Diaghilev launched his long-standing, fruitful attempts to popularize Russian art abroad. More than that, his "Seasons" developed into important vehicles for the promotion of many genres of national art. The show in question preceded and, to some extent, anticipated these seasons. Though with incredible vigor, Diaghilev had prepared it within but a few months and it was so immense that it occupied 12[61], if not 13[62], rooms in the Grand Palais, comprising a fully autonomous section of the Salon d'Automne.

Presented at this show, which opened on October 6, were 750 artworks from ancient till modern times, including "36 icons, 23 choice Levitskys, 6 Rokotovs, 20 Borovikovskys, 9 Kiprenskys, 14 Venetsianovs, 6 Sylvester Shchedrins, 12 Karl Briullovs, 18 Levitans, 19 Serovs, 33 K. Somovs, 9 I. Grabars, 12 Maliavins, 10 Yuons, 10 K. Korovins, 31 Baksts, and 23 Alexander Benois, the writer of these lines."[63] Also represented, besides the artists just mentioned, were Bogayevsky, Borisov-Musatov, Vrubel, Golovin, Dobuzhinsky, Kuznetsov, Lugovskaya-Diaghileva, Ostroumova-Lebedeva, Trubetskoi, Roerich, Sudeikin, and Yaremich. The icons were of the Novgorod, Moscow, and Stroganov schools. In addition, numerous pieces by other Russian painters and sculptors active in the eighteenth and first half of the nineteenth century were displayed. The art of the second half of the century was presented in a more modest and fragmentary manner than it really deserved.

The interior decoration was supervised by Bakst, who along with Benois assisted Diaghilev in his vast preparatory work.

In his foreword to the catalogue Diaghilev wrote: "The purpose of this exhibition is not to provide a full, scrupulously systematic survey of all of Russian art throughout the different phases of its evolution. The attainment of such a task would present insuperable difficulty and would be of doubtful value. Many previously famous names have by now lost their glory, some for a time, others forever. No small number of masters whose importance was exaggerated by their contemporaries are of no price

[61] Benois. Recollections, vol. 2, p. 454

[62] A. Shervashidze, "Vystavka russkogo khudozhestva v Parizhe" (Russian Art Show in Paris), *Zolotoye runo*, 1906, No. 11–12

[63] Benois. Recollections, vol. 2, p. 454

77. Evgeny Lanceray. The Empress Elizaveta Petrovna in Tsarskoye Selo. 1905

now and they had no impact whatever on present-day art. This explains the deliberate absence of works by many artists who for long had been regarded in the West as the sole representatives of Russian art and who for too long misrepresented in the eyes of the Western public the true character and real significance of national art.

The present exhibition furnishes a brief survey of the development of our art as seen from the modern angle. All elements that exerted a direct influence upon our country's contemporary character are represented.

This is a true image of the artistic Russia of our days, of its sincere inspiration, of its reverent admiration for the past, and of its fervent faith in the future. 1906."[64]

Diaghilev's "brief survey" of the history of Russian art mirrored, as it were, the World of Art's historico-artistic concepts with all its merits and faults. Indeed, the *miriskusniki* were, in effect, to visualize Russian art's evolution as an integral, continuous process. They interpreted it as part of world culture – which explains the Paris show. In their efforts they brought to light deep-seated, at times, half-forgotten chapters in the history of Russian art, seeking to reveal their importance anew. The presentation of early Russian painting affords a highly apposite instance which is all the more characteristic in that, as Benois recalls, "even in Russia in 1906 the public at large were only beginning to evince an interest in icons, and thus far no 'purely artistic approach' had

been evolved in that respect."[65] A still greater service was rendered by the *miriskusniki*, especially Diaghilev, by virtue of their rediscovery of the immense aesthetic value of the painting, sculpture and architecture of eighteenth-century Russia. On the other hand, the Paris show revealed the trend's characteristic underestimation of the genre-narrative, "literary" tendencies in Russian art of the second half of the nineteenth century, which in some degree was external and superficial, deriving primarily from the stylistic criticism of "dark" painting, the academic school, the sparse, restricted nature of the employed tradition, etc. Still, in their understanding of the human being, nature, and national history, in the severity of their draftsmanship, and lifelike representation, the *miriskusniki* did not, in effect, clash directly with the poetry and *Weltanschauung* of Russia's chief artworks of the second half of the nineteenth century.

At his Paris show, Diaghilev devoted six rooms to an extensive survey of World of Art artists as a young branch of the ages-old tree of the Russian creative tradition. He sought to prove that they were an inseparable part of contemporary world culture, occupying a very special niche in it. That was exactly how the exhibition was received by the public and the news media in France. "No success but rather a dream is this," Grabar wrote from Paris on October 4/17 1908. "I am bathing in a sea of admiration that has filled my ears. Everyone – artists, critics, collectors – burns incense (literally)

[64] Quoted from: Diaghilev, vol. 1, p. 204

[65] Benois. Recollections, vol. 2, p. 453

cultural standard, vast knowledge, and an acute sense of style. His easel painting, chiefly on old-time Petersburg subjects, almost fully corresponds to the retrospective landscape genre that Benois evolved and elaborated. The young Lanceray produced "historical landscapes," now and again enlivened by staffage, either figures or groups. His gifts were in no way inferior to Benois, and his enduring, invariably realistic tendency is distinctly manifest in his painting. Indeed, besides reproducing the decorative externals of episodes from history, he, like Serov, also sought to probe their inner, hidden meaning, without avoiding either psychological or social motives. Thus, among the staffage figures in such pieces as *St. Petersburg in the Eighteenth Century* (1903), *Walking along the Breakwater* (1908) or *Ships in the Times of Peter I* (1911), one will quite often spot characters drawn from the common Russian folk, needed to stress the social contrasts of the period. Meanwhile in such pictures as *Empress Elizaveta Petrovna in Tsarskoye Selo* (1905) and *Princess Elizaveta in the Guardhouse of the Winter Palace* (1910), Lanceray no longer depicted the figures as mere staffage, giving them most expressive and sarcastic characteristics.

The "historical landscape" was likewise the main genre practised by Anna Petrovna Ostroumova-Lebedeva (1871–1955). She revived to full artistic value the easel woodcut, which from the mid-nineteenth century had beed employed exclusively to copy in a semi-journeyman fashion, or more faithfully reproduce, various paintings and drawings. Besides engravings after her own sketches, she also produced large watercolors. These chiefly depicted the Baroque and classical architecture of St. Petersburg, in whose interpretation Ostroumova-Lebedeva followed in Benois' footsteps. She viewed the city's architecture as an outstanding artistic phenomenon of the past, totally disregarding its Art Nouveau railway stations, factories, and tenement houses. In her representation of the old buildings, whether individually or grouped, she too, like the adepts of retrospective painting, sought to convey the majesty and beauty of bygone times. Yet while accepting Benois' interpretation, she not infrequently excelled him in the lyrical power with which she invested her

[66] Grabar, p. 188

[67] Quoted from: *Valentin Serov v vospominaniyakh, dnevnikakh i perepiske sovremennikov* (Valentin Serov in the Reminiscences, Diaries and Correspondance of Contemporaries), vol. 2, Leningrad, 1972, p. 337

[68] "Vystavka kartin Soyuza russkikh khudozhnikov" (The Union of Russian Artists Exhibition of Paintings), *Vestnik zhizni*, 1907, No. 2, p. 100

[69] A. Lunacharsky, "Russkiye spektakli v Parizhe" (The Russian Performances in Paris), *Teatr i iskusstvo*, No, 23, 1913. Quoted from: *A.V. Lunacharsky. Ob iskusstve* (About Art), vol. 2, Moscow, 1982, p. 293

and courts us."[66] Featured in Russian periodicals were several reviews of Diaghilev's show, whose conclusions, considering the exhibition's success, were categoric and far-reaching. Thus, under the heading "Concerning Our Art", the critic Pavel Muratov observed in *Moskovsky yezhenedelnik* (Moscow Weekly), No. 38: "It is time, at last, to realize what has occurred over the past fifteen years. Russian painting has been fully rejuvenated. At the recent show in Paris, the entire cultural world discovered to its amazed delight the existence of a 'new Russian school.' In the West our artists of the written word have long been appreciated and now, at last, the turn has deservedly come for the artists of line and color. However, that evaluation of our painting now meted out to it by others, has still not been offered by its compatriots. It may be that the time is not far off when these years, the years of Serov, Korovin, Vrubel, Somov, Yakunchikova, and Musatov will be termed the radiant epoch of Russian painting."[67]

It should be pointed out that even with certain critical comment – the result of the absence in the display of painters of the second half of the nineteenth century, especially of the Wanderers – the significance of the Russian exhibits at the Paris Show of 1906 was noted in periodicals of diverse trends from *Novoye vremya* on the political right, to some featuring writers of Marxist views. Thus, Anatoly Lunacharsky, the most eminent of early twentieth-century Marxist critics, rebuked Diaghilev for having "dropped the entire Wanderer trend from his history of Russian painting"[68] at the 1906 Paris show. Yet, in 1913, he was to observe:

"It is now indubitably true that in some domains of art Russia is somewhere at the top of the table, affording Europe brilliant examples for emulation. Thus, the art show that Mr. Diaghilev mounted in Paris several years ago opened many an eye to the singular character and talent of our artists."[69]

The administration of the Salon d'Automne nominated Diaghilev, Benois, and Bakst for the Legion d'honneur, which decoration Diaghilev, incidentally, declined. After the exhibition its sponsor Diaghilev, and its patrons A. and S. Botkin, G. and V. Girshman, and I. Morozov were elected honorary members of the Salon, while Bakst, Benois, Bogayevsky, Vrubel, Grabar, Kuznetsov, Larionov, Lugovskaya-Diaghileva, Milioti, Ostroumova-Lebedeva, Roerich, and Yuon were elected Salon members for life. Diaghilev then took his show to Berlin and Venice.

A new journal, *Zolotoye runo* (The Golden Fleece), initiated publication, with the financial support of the major industrialist Pavel Ryabushinsky, who was its editor-publisher. Though primarily a literary journal associated with Russia's Symbolists, it also featured numerous reproductions and art reviews, extensively reflecting the work of World of Art artists.

1907

Another new publication was *Starye gody* (Bygone Years), a journal intended, as its subtitle implied, for "lovers of art and antiquity." Published by P. Veiner and edited by Vasily Vereshchagin, this journal had no relation to the World of Art from the

78. Anna Ostroumova-Lebedeva. The Admiralty Under Snow. 1901

formal angle; on the other hand, its entire activity undoubtedly derived from the interests, aesthetics, and proclivities of the *miriskusniki*. It paid special attention to the artistic culture and manorial mores of the eighteenth and early nineteenth centuries, as well as to the related architecture, painting, graphics, sculpture, and diverse applied arts and crafts. Intensively involved in this publication, which continued to come out up till 1918, were Benois and Grabar, and also such critics and museum curators and keepers as Muratov, Lukomsky, Kurbatov, Wrangel, and Troinitsky, who were closely associated with the World of Art....

The Union of Russian Artists held its Fourth Exhibition in St. Petersburg between December 1906 and January 1907 and in Moscow between February and March. Practically all the *miriskusniki* who had been represented earlier again participated. True, whereas Somov did not send his works to Moscow purely by chance, Grabar, on the other hand, exhibited only in Moscow, but this too was no matter of principle.

In both cities a special retrospective showing was devoted to the recently deceased Botkin. Among the exhibitors in St. Petersburg and Moscow were several young artists attracted to the new trends. They included D. and L. Burliuk, Krymov, Larionov, Milioti, Sudeikin, and Jawlensky. This generated a still motlier overall picture, since, besides the earlier contrast between the Petersburgians and the Muscovites (conventional definitions, as Vrubel, Serov, and Grabar also lived in Moscow), there was

now to be observed a dividing line between the traditionalists and the newest trends, against whose backround even the World of Art artists, so dazzlingly innovative recently, also appeared as traditionalists. However, this contrast emerged in full only several years later.

Thus far the critics discerned primarily the "old" stylistic divergencies, which was what Muratov had in mind when in his comments on the Union's Fourth Exhibition, he noted: "Time and again, one sees next to each other the works of artists who are profoundly different, sharply opposed, if not mutually exclusive."[70] These "tacit duels" presaged the Union's future split. Yet other aspects of the exhibition were responsible for the basic impression. In the first place, the exhibition presented works that stood outside, in effect, of every trend, such as the two brilliant portraits that Vrubel did of Briusov and Serov, of Yermolova, both of which displayed a probing characterization, a consummate perfection of form, and a sensitive eye for the times. It was scarcely thinkable to draw parallels or contrasts, as these two portraits ranked above hidebound schools and factional stylistic concepts. Note, though, that despite the concept of the World of Art as merely a "circle" which actually is long obsolete and unhistorical, portraiture directly adhered to that grand tradition which classical Russian art had generated, and which Vrubel and Serov so worthily emulated. Though the *miriskusniki* tended toward stylization, retrospectivism, decorativeness, and lush theatricalization, in their portraiture they were always up-to-date, strict, composed, perspicacious, and even "telling the story." Thus, one could also mention

[70] P. Muratov, "Vystavka Soyuza russkikh khudozhnikov" (The Union of Russian Artists Exhibition), *Russkoye slovo*, 16 February 1907. Quoted from: Lapshin, p. 63

79. Anna Ostroumova-Lebedeva. Amsterdam. The Iron Market. 1913

А. Остроумова

engravings, lithographs and watercolors. In truth, the St. Petersburg of the World of Art is above all the St. Petersburg of Ostroumova-Lebedeva.

The work of Mstislav Valerianovich Dobuzhinsky (1875–1957) was still more complex and diverse. Indeed, the artist played a leading role in the World of Art activities, even though he was not one of its founders, having associated himself with Diaghilev's group after it had already fully formulated its ideological and creative principles. However, having organically assimilated its artistic concepts, he elaborated them in a most original and productive manner.

Like Lanceray and Ostroumova-Lebedeva, he also started with the "historical landscape." The extensive series of drawings and watercolors that he produced depict the architecture of old-time St. Petersburg, romantic nooks in Gatchina and Tsarskoye Selo, the old quarters of London and Bruges, and the old streets of Vilna and other provincial Russian cities and towns. In fact he displayed as much an ability to immerse himself in the atmosphere of the past, as subtle a sense of style, and as refined a graphic elegance as Somov and Benois. His canvas, *The Provinces in the 1830s* (1907–09), which recreates with lyrical flair and romantic irony the bygone Russia of the times of Pushkin and Gogol, ranks among the most inspired and poetic achievements of World of Art retrospective painting. His later picture, *Peter the Great in Holland*, of which only the 1910 sketch survived, is more realistic and authentic, betraying the impact of Serov's history painting.

Dobuzhinsky, however, did not limit himself to retrospective themes alone; he evinced as keen an interest in the surrounding reality. Through the architectural view he attempted to convey the specific flavor of his own times.

The artist perceived St. Petersburg not only as a magnificent monument to the past. For him St. Petersburg was more than a cluster of Baroque and neo-classical masterpieces; he saw them as compressed within the new industrial metropolis that had arisen at the turn of the twentieth century; life in this appalling, bleak city seemed to him worthless and hopeless, crushed by the soulless masses of stone and brick. Dobuzhinsky stressed tha tragic aspect of the murky courtyards with their *brandmauer*-walls, the wastes and miserable streets on the factory outskirts. These scenes forcefully disclose the romantic dichotomy of the artist's mentality, his non-acceptance and negation of the ugliness of modern reality coupled with its poetization. There is something Hoffmannesque in his *Cottage in St. Petersburg* (1905) and his *Barbershop Window* (1906); in the same manner

Somov's portrait of Blok, Bakst's portrait of Diaghilev with his nurse and Dobuzhinsky's *Man with Spectacles*, and to continue, the portraits done by Golovin, Kustodiev, Serebryakova, Maliavin, Grabar, and other *miriskusniki*, who always faithfully complied with the artistic and psychological principles that their great predecessors had evolved.

The cream of the Union's Fourth Exhibition revealed an awareness of the times and a new interpretation of the features of the national character, especially in works by the artists of the World of Art society. This was noted even by reviewers who otherwise criticized the showing generally. Lunacharsky, for one, accused it of the "absence of an idea. to a point that was militant and fervent." Even so, there were some delightful aspects, in every case associated with World of Art artists. "We may take delight in Kustodiev," Lunacharsky commented. "He not only demonstrates a fine, healthy, distinct, and vibrant realism from the angle of technique; he is good because he evinces interest in life itself, in the living, effervescent, diversified, multicoloured life, in reality as such, not as the excuse for coloristic effects."[71] Lunacharsky also had high praise for Maliavin who, in his view,

"has created pictures – poems in color. His *Whirlwind* is a major poetic piece. Generally, Maliavin's 'baba' is wonderful for her crudity, fascinating for her elemental substance."[72] Lunacharsky paid special note to Dobuzhinsky, a World of Art classic, of whom he said: "Grand thoughts cross the mind when looking at Dobuzhinsky's drawings, grand hopes and joys are born, by the laws of contrast, of the social vista. Dobuzhinsky places us in the very heart of the times; he is able with triumphant power to bring home alive to our senses what the mind has theoretically recognized. 'I'm frightened when art approaches socialism so closely,' Vergezhsky (actually A. Verchezhinsky – A.K.) observed of Dobuzhinsky in the Constitutional Democrat paper *Rech*. Of course! But we are happy."[73]

On March 18, the *Golden Fleece* journal arranged the Blue Rose exhibition on factory-owner Kuznetsov's house at the corner of Myasnitskaya St. and Bolshoi Zlatoustinsky Lane in Moscow. Twelve of the sixteen artists represented, for the most part, disciples of Borisov-Musatov, addicted at the time to Symbolism – namely, Arapov, Krymov, Kuznetsov, Matveyev, V. and N. Milioti, Sapunov, Saryan, Sudeikin, Utkin, Feofilaktov, and Fonvizin – were

[71] A. Lunacharsky, "Vystavka kartin Soyuza russkikh khudozhnikov" (The Union of Russian Artists Exhibition of Paintings), *Vestnik zhizni*, 1907, No. 2. Quoted from: *A.V. Lunacharsky. Ob izobrazitelnom iskusstve* (On the Figurative Arts), Moscow, 1967, vol. 1, p. 386

[72] *Ibid.*, p. 391

[73] *Ibid.*, p. 392

80. Mstislav Dobuzhinsky. Peter the Great in Holland. Amsterdam, the Wharf of the East India Company. 1910

subsequently to participate in different World of Art
shows. Somewhat later, some of the exhibitors,
jointly with certain future members of the Jack of
Diamonds (Bubnovy valet) group – who were
likewise be represented subsequently in several
World of Art shows – mounted an exhibition known
as "Stephanos" (Wreath).
In May, Diaghilev launched his perennial drive to
promote Russian music, opera, ballet, and stage
design with a series of five historic recitals
of Russian music in Paris.
Throughout the second half of the first decade of the
century, World of Art artists and associated masters
continued to work for the Imperial Theaters. Thus,
Golovin designed the sets for Ibsen's drama
The Lady from the Sea at the Alexandrinsky
Theater in St. Petersburg in 1905, and the costumes
for Wagner's opera *Rheingold* that same year at the
Mariinsky Theater, also in St. Petersburg; in 1905,
Konstantin Korovin produced the sets for Minkus'
ballet *Don Quixote* and the costumes for Rimsky-
Korsakov's opera *The Tale of the Invisible City of
Kitezh* at the Mariinsky Theater. More instances
could be listed. At the same time the *miriskusniki*
established a closer relationship with the Symbolists,
with the more striking experiments undertaken at

Vera Komissarzhevskaya's Theater in St. Petersburg, where stage director Vsevolod Meyerhold
worked in 1906–07. Benois, Bakst, Dobuzhinsky
were involved, but more so were their juniors
Sapunov, Sudeikin and Anisfeld (with their friend
Denisov), who shortly became leading World of Art
figures. Thus, in 1906 Sapunov designed for this
theater the famous production of Blok's *Balaganchik* (The Fairground Booth); in the same year
he produced the decor for Ibsen's *Hedda Gabler*
there. Anisfeld made his debut as a stage designer
with Hoffmansthal's *Die Hochzeit der Sobeide*.
Meanwhile, Sudeikin, who in 1905 had cooperated
with Sapunov in designing the production of
Maeterlinck's *Death of Tintagilas*, directed by
Meyerhold at the Moscow Theater-Studio on
Povarskaya St., did the decor for Maeterlinck's
Sœur Beatrice at the Komissarzhevskaya Theater in
1906.
Practically all stage designers working for the
Antique Theater that opened in St. Petersburg in
1907 were World of Art artists – namely Benois, who
that same year designed the Theater's drop curtain,
Bilibin, and Lanceray, who with Benois created the
sets for Evreinov's production of *The Fair on
St. Denis' Day*, Dobuzhinsky, who did the decor for

as the great German Romantic author he has elevated the commonplace to almost fantastic heights.

Such, too, is the leitmotif of the numerous views that he painted on his frequent travels in Western Europe. In his cityscapes of London, The Hague, Amsterdam, and other European cities, Dobuzhinsky played up the industrial scene, depicting wharves, docks, railway bridges, building cranes, factory chimneys, and dreary plant structures. He distilled his observations and sketches into ominous urbanistic fantasies reflecting the sinister metropolises of the future.

Retrospective painting, with its stylized, decorative, graphic tendencies, had a marked impact upon many twentieth-century Russian artists. Among the masters who were the World of Art's first allies, perhaps only Vrubel, Konstantin Korovin, and Maliavin, plus artists of the younger generation, such as Petrov-Vodkin, Saryan, Kuznetsov, Mashkov, and Altman, were fully independent of the creative credo advocated by the nucleus of Diaghilev's group. All that the World of Art gave these men was moral support.

On the other hand, certain painters, who joined the group at its initial phase, or after the reorganization of 1910, established relations of a different order with it. Thus, the range of aesthetic concepts, which Diaghilev and his group espoused, appreciably influenced both Roerich and Kustodiev, two Art Academy graduates whose oeuvre forever bore the imprint of this schooling. Roerich was a pupil of Arkhip Kuindzhi's, Kustodiev, of Ilya Repin's. Yet their stylization, the distinct prevalence of the graphic over the painterly, the decorative approach to color, and the specific theatricalization of their spatial compositional arrangement definitely derived from the World of Art. Even so, their subject matter

81. Mstislav Dobuzhinsky. The Provinces in the 1830s. 1907–09

82. Mstislav Dobuzhinsky. City Types (City Grimaces). 1908

83. Mstislav Dobuzhinsky. Paris. 1914

[74] Benois. Recollections, vol. 2, p. 473

[75] K. Korovin. Zhizn i tvorchestvo. Pis'ma. Dokumenty. Vospominaniya (Life and Work. Letters. Documents. Reminiscences), Moscow, 1963, p. 276

[76] A. Benois, "Novye teatralnye postanovki" (New Theatrical Productions), Mir iskusstva, 1902, No. 2, p. 30

Adam de la Halle's pastorale *Le Jeu de Robin et de Marion*, and Roerich, who designed Evreinov's drama *The Three Magi*. They all exemplified subtle stylization and a very sensitive feeling for the spirit and externals of the past epochs, mostly the Middle Ages.

However, what had special import for the coming flourishing of the stage design of the *miriskusniki* was the decor that Benois created for Nikolai Tcherepnin's ballet *Le Pavillon d'Armide* at the Mariinsky Theater (choreography by Michel Fokine). "It was *Le Pavillon d'Armide* that initiated the subsequent worldwide acclaim enjoyed by the Ballets Russes,"[74] Benois commented. This romantic fantasy about the odd juxtaposition of the imaginary and the real, which is imbued with a nostalgic yearning for evanescent beauty, and that is set in the atmosphere of the seventeenth and eighteenth centuries, brought into focus the salient features of World of Art scenic design. It blended a picturesque glitter ("At the theater I created a feast for the eye,"[75] Korovin observed) with the consummate perfection of style ("Style, the ideal measure and proportions, the ideal convention"[76]) comprised the principles of stage

84. Konstantin Somov. Portrait of Mstislav Dobuzhinsky. 1910

85. Mstislav Dobuzhinsky. Barbershop Window. 1906

86. Mstislav Dobuzhinsky. A Cottage in St. Petersburg. 1905

design that Benois put forward. These were to pave the way for the flourishing triumph of World of Art scenic innovation on Europe's stages during Diaghilev's Russian Seasons.

In December, Tenisheva futilely sought to outvie Diaghilev with an exhibition in Paris of contemporary Russian art; shown there were works by the World of Art artists, Roerich and Bilibin, as well as some of the items produced at Tenisheva's workshop in Talashkino.

1908
The Union of Russian Artists staged its Fifth Exhibition between December 1907 and February 1908 in Moscow and between February and March of the year in St. Petersburg. There was little fundamental difference between the two expositions. Of substance for the World of Art trend was the debut of Sapunov, who at once rose to prominence within this movement. "Of the younger artists to have joined the Union," Vasily Milioti wrote of this latest exhibition, "Sapunov must necessarily be given top marks for freshness of interest. His coloristic temperament is truly wonderful…, in his theatrical searchings that are not devoid of Epicurism,

87. Léonide Massine, Natalia Goncharova, Mikhail Larionov, Igor Stravinsky, and Léon Bakst in Lausanne. 1915

is far removed from motif associated with the eighteenth century and the Petersburgian chapter of Russian history.

Nicholas Konstantinovich Roerich (1874–1947), a painter and a university educated historian, was basically interested in Slavonic paganism, Scandinavian sagas, and the religious myths of medieval Russia. His works are permeated with a singular, mystic pantheism, with the spirit of nature, upon which the artist has projected his understanding of history. His "landscapism" is a salient feature, inasmuch as human figures are often reduced to mere staffage; nature always dominates as the definitive element serving to convey the message and the emotional content of his pictures. Among his favorite media were tempera and pastel. By experimenting with colored backgrounds and extensively exploiting decorative lighting effects, Roerich achieved tones of particular depth and imparted a mysterious shimmer to the coloring of his paintings. In effect, this is the selfsame theatricalized "historical landscape" of Benois and other World of Art artists, however differently structured and construed in a typically Roerichean manner; in the compositional rhythms and color patterns of his landscapes, the artist sought to incarnate the spiritual world of the people of long, bygone ages, with their ability to be one with nature and imbue nature with all their emotions and feelings.

Roerich's closest affinity to World of Art concepts falls upon the period between 1902 and 1917, during which he was most active not only in the field of easel painting, but also in murals and stage design. The several noteworthy pieces he produced showed his historical intuition and sense of style. Among his first works to mirror World of Art ideas and creative principles was the painting *The Battle of Alexander Nevsky with Yarle Berger* (1904), which was skillfully stylized in the manner of a medieval miniature. The artistic solution rests on decorative contours and local pools of color. The same features are characteristic of the murals and mosaics that Roerich concurrently executed for several

88. Nicholas Roerich. Rostov the Great. 1903

he ably blends with it, by virtue of his own inner singular quality, the dramatism of emotional experience, which in *Wedekind* – a 1907 picture after Frank Wedekind's *Danse Macabre* – becomes well-nigh nightmarish. His roses and flowers – shown at the Union's Exhibition of 1907 was his *Blue Hydrangeas* – are virtually stories, told with passion and vibrant color. A master of the color patch, he, proceeding from that alone, constructs his composition, casual on the outside, but logical within. He subconsciously climbs to Symbolism: with him, the theater serves merely as a form whereby to speak of life's tears and laughter, while his flowers relate its joys."[77]

Most critics noted the heterogenous character of the Exhibition. Indeed that had become their customary remark, one that some critics believed justified and not without benefit. True, taken as the point of departure was that integral, organic impression which the World of Art shows usually produced. "Diaghilev will no doubt mount more than one World of Art show," Grabar surmised. "Yet why shouldn't the Union exist.... Its motley character in no way prevents one from singling out either whole groups or individual artists. I even think it absolutely essential to see Serov next to Sapunov and Sudeikin next to Benois at least once a year. I think that given that, it will be easier to assess what Serov and Sapunov and Benois and Sudeikin are really like. Far more distinct is what will probably survive this and dozens of future shows, while more observable is what will be forgotten the moment the exhibition closes."[78] True, Grabar's analysis is rather

[77] Mi[lio]ti, "O Soyuze russkikh khudozhnikov" (About the Union of Russian Artists), *Zolotoye runo*, 1908, No. 1

[78] I. Grabar, "Soyuz i Venok" (The Union and the Wreath), *Vesy*, 1908, No. 1, p. 137

89. Boris Kustodiev. A Moscow Tavern. 1916

90. Nicholas Roerich. The Slavs on the Dnieper. 1905

ecclesiastical and civil buildings. Standing out among these are the sketches for the panels of Moscow's Kazan Railway Station, notably *The Battle at Kerzhenets* and *The Conquest of Kazan* (1913, 1914), and likewise the wall painting in the apse of the church in the Talashkino village outside Smolensk (1911–14). In fact, Roerich was one of those pioneers in the new Russian art who strove to revive and assimilate the traditions of the old Russian icon and fresco, which, incidentally, he quite often reinterpreted in an Art Nouveau spirit. In short, his interest in ancient Russia, its artistic traditions and imagery, sets him poles apart from the marked pro-Western orientation of the World of Art nucleus.

However, toward the close of the period reviewed, especially during the years of the First World War, Roerich veered away into a somewhat different trend. Now the historical subject matter was almost completely absent, yielding pride of place to motif from fairy and folk tales and biblical legends. His Symbolist paintings, though to a certain degree still similar in style to the World of Art system, had nothing retrospectivist in them, as is illustrated by *Sword of Valor* (1912), *Cry of the Serpent* (1914), and *Doomed City* (1914). During the war he produced an extensive series of ardently patriotic pictures devoted to Russia, which, however, were imbued with Christian mysticism, for example, *St. Procopius the Righteous Averting a Cloud of Stone from Ustiug the Great* (1914) and *St. Pantaleon the Healer* and *The Three Joys* (both 1916).

The retrospectivism of Boris Mikhailovich Kustodiev (1878–1927) is of a very special kind, as the artist was not interested in history at all. He was concerned not with the remote, romanticized past, but with the living reality of his time, in which, however, he sought and found old-fashioned features – the static tradition of archaic customs, survivals of the doomed, provincial mode of life. He associated himself with the World of Art group at the time of the 1905 Russian Revolution, actively contributing, along with Serov, Lanceray, and Dobuzhinsky, to various satirical journals; thus, for *Zhupel* (The Bugbear) and *Adskaya Pochta* (Hell's Mail), he executed a number of superlative cartoons and pungent political drawings. He was by then a well-established, mature artist, enjoying a solid reputation as a portrait painter in the Repin tradition. Kustodiev had already begun work on a series of genre pictures in which his creative principles fully crystallized, making him kin with the World of Art group. Joining the society shortly after its 1910 reorganization, he soon rose to prominence as one of its leading lights.

Unlike the senior World of Art members with their deliberate, in a way programmatic, pro-Western orientation, Kustodiev was profoundly Russian, not only in motif and subject matter, but even from the angle of his entire mentality and world outlook; in his searchings, he proceeded from the national art tradition. His basic interest was "vanishing Russia," the patriarchal, provincial Russia of the peasantry and merchant lower-middle class, with their archaic mores, that continued to survive into the early twentieth century in the countryside and remote towns. In his portrayal of this living antiquity, the artist combined the grotesque with the lyrical, his irony coexisting with a sentimental affection for the beauties of this moribund way of life.

Kustoidiev consistently applied a bedrock World of Art principle, stylizing his works in the spirit of the artistic relics of the social strata whose life he depicted. He derived inspiration from old merchant portraits, signboards, rural arts and crafts and the *lubok*, the folk print similar to English chapbooks, with its motley, polychrome decorativeness, its sharply expressive narrative form, and its flat, conventional outline.

The artist's genre paintings fall into two basic cycles. One is purely lyrical, portraying the natural scenery and folk life of Russia. The other, in which the lyrical note is tinged with irony, deals with subject matter taken from the life and mores of the merchant class, echoing the images and characters described by Nikolai Leskov in his stories and by Alexander Ostrovsky in his plays, which the artist had reinterpreted time and again in book illustration and stage design.

In the first cycle of pictures, representations of fairs and folk festivities prevail. One of the finest and most characteristic in this respect is *Shrovetide* (1916), of which the artist produced three versions. In this colorful, decorative composition, the real-life genre episode of Shrovetide troika-sleigh rides has been transmuted into the veritable phantasmagoria of a fairy tale.

91. Nicholas Roerich. The Kiss to Earth. Set design for Stravinsky's *Le Sacre du Printemps*. 1912

92. Nicholas Roerich. Tristan's Ship. Set design for Act 1 of Wagner's *Tristan and Isolde*. 1912

Whereas the paintings of the first cycle are for the most part densely populated, the pictures in the second portray but one or two personages by means of which the artist has sought to depict a social and psychological type conveying the specific features of the Russian character and the national concept of beauty. Here Kustodiev has dedicated himself basically to portraying the Russian woman, as is illustrated by a whole row of pictures from *Merchant Woman* (1914–15), *La Belle* (1915), and *Girl on the Volga* (1915), to *Merchant Woman at Tea* (1918), *Merchant Woman with a Mirror* (1920) and, finally, *The Russian Venus* (1925–26).

In effect, the works of the second World of Art generation hardly ever displayed retrospectivism in that frank, pure way, as was the case with Somov, Benois, and Lanceray. Still, now directly, but most often indirectly, the influence of retrospectivist tendencies is distinctly observable in the easel painting of those notable artists who allied themselves with the World of Art society following its reorganization in 1910.

Thus the "retrospectivism" of Zinaida Evgenyevna Serebryakova (1884–1967) is of a complex, indirect nature. Like Kustodiev, she drew ispiration from her impressions of surrounding reality. She produced a series of genre paintings portraying the life and mores of the Russian peasantry of the time. These include *The Bathhouse* (1913), *Peasants* (1914), *Reaping* (1917), and *Bleaching Linen* (1917). She was never attracted to historical subject matter or exoticism and fantasy, with which her fellow artists were so greatly infatuated. Alexander Benois regarded her work as an expression of "sound and cheerful realism devoid of modernistic refinement."[17] Still, World of Art retrospectivism indirectly left its trace. Her imagery seems to be enveloped in the atmosphere of the past, while her technique is reminiscent of the Russian classical tradition and, at the same time, of Italian quattrocento art. Her genre compositions reflect Russian peasant life in a monumental, generalized manner that elevates the subject above the humdrum, run-of-the-mill reality, though the peaceful, patriarchal way of life, from which she borrowed inspiration, had long receded never to return. In her poetization of peasant toil, Serebryakova ignored both her contemporaries and the Wanderers, reviving the idyllic tradition of Venetsianov.

The retrospectivist tradition was manifest in an entirely different way in the easel painting of Nikolai Nikolayevich Sapunov (1880–1912). In his early, formative years he experienced the influences of Levitan, Konstantin Korovin, and Borisov-Musatov, but

[17] A. Benois, "Khudo-zhestvennye pis'ma: Vystavka Soyuza III" (Art Letters: 3rd Union Exhibition), *Rech*, 13 March 1910

[79] Lapshin, p. 69

lopsided, as he draws parallels solely between World of Art artists and totally ignores the Union's Muscovites. Meanwhile, the viewer presumably drew his own comparisons on a different, long-established basis, setting the World of Art artists against the other Union members from the angle of their characteristic tastes, interests, and traditions. Indeed, the exhibition presented such first-class works as Serov's *Peter the Great* and his portraits of Girshmann and Andreyeva, Dobuzhinsky's *Man with Spectacles*, Benois' *The Bath of the Marquise* and sketch for *Le Pavillon d'Armide*, Sapunov's aforementioned paintings, and Golovin's *Birches*, to mention but several. Meanwhile the Muscovites were represented, at any rate, by characteristic pieces of a good standard. Though there was no organic fusion between the two groups, indeed, could not be, the Union aroused interest as a venue for the coming together of the different forces in Russian art, and, no doubt, many could have echoed Grabar's "Why shouldn't the Union exist?"

In all likelihood the Union would have continued to exist in this form indefinitely, if not for the itch of the World of Art artists to continually recruit to its ranks those gifted younger brethren in whom they saw "kindred spirits." Meanwhile the Muscovites had no such urge, inasmuch as next to a new generation,

especially of questive contemporary, modern artists, they might well find themselves in a rather unenviable position. This situation provoked the first serious crisis within Union membership, especially when, in late 1908, the Petersburgians proposed inviting fifty odd young artists to take part in the Union's next exhibition.[79] In a blue funk, the Muscovites turned this down, demanding that no more than fifteen newcomers be invited. The Petersburgians countered by proposing that the Petersburg and Moscow variants of the exhibition differ. This proposal had, willy-nilly, to be accepted, as otherwise the Union would have collapsed at once. Even so, it was not destined to survive much longer in the form in which it had existed up till now, insofar as the Sixth Exhibition had different versions for St. Petersburg and Moscow, the two capitals of the Russian Empire, while the Seventh Exhibition was the Union's last.

On April 1, the maiden issue of a new magazine, *Satirikon*, a "weekly literary and art magazine of satire and humor," came out in St. Petersburg. Many World of Art artists were involved, among them Anisfeld, Bakst, Benois, Dobuzhinsky, Konstantin Korovin, Kustodiev, and their close associates Alexei Radakov, who edited the new publication, Nikolai Remizov, and others.

93. Boris Kustodiev. La Belle. 1915

During the year, Benois published a monograph on Goya and also accepted the position of art reviewer for the St. Petersburg newspaper *Rech* (Discourse). In the 230 odd articles that he produced for this newspaper between 1908 and 1917 under the "Art Letters" rubric, he commented upon the many developments in Russian and European art, analyzed diverse problems of a general nature, and assessed the efforts of individual artists, as well as exhibitions, books, theatrical productions, and catalogues. In toto, these lively, wise, brilliantly written essays comprise a classic gem of twentieth-century Russian art criticism.

In May, the Paris Opera presented seven performances of Mussorgsky's *Boris Godunov*, behind which Diaghilev was the moving spirit. They were hugely successful and served, as did Diaghilev's subsequent Russian Seasons, to further the World of Art's perennial effort to ensconce Russian art in a prestigious niche in world culture.

1909
Though all the leading World of Art lights were represented at both Moscow (from December 1908 through February 1909) and St. Petersburg (from February through April 1909) versions of the Union of Russian Artists' Sixth Exhibition, the *miriskus-*

niki gradually broke with the Union. Incidentally, the Muscovites displayed identical pieces in both cities, whereas the World of Art participants managed to include in the St. Petersburg showing such highly individual painters as Krymov, Larionov, Utkin, Yakovlev, Yakulov, and Čiurlionis, plus a large group of graphic artists fully within the mainstream of the World of Art trend such as Kruglikova, Levitsky, Mitrokhin, Narbut, and Chekhonin, who were soon destined to be known as the World of Art's "second generation."

It was precisely the "newcomers" who were responsible for the greatest novelties in the St. Petersburg Exhibition section devoted to World of Art artists. Their seniors displayed such characteristic pieces as Serov's psychologically probing portraits of Akimov, Mamontov, and Lensky with Yuzhin, Lanceray's watercolor fantasies on court life in the eighteenth century, Somov's elegant *Book of the Marquise* series of drawings, Dobuzhinsky's pungent and somewhat ironical townscapes and Benois' gloomy and habitually theatricalized series of visions, *Death*. Only Sapunov seemed "out of place," as his *Merry-go-round*, with its odd confusion of gaiety and apprehension steeped in the glow of vibrant hues, revealed a totally different world outlook, let alone a different style, than was characteristic of

94. Boris Kustodiev. Shrovetide. 1916

subsequently drifted into the World of Art movement from the Symbolist group *Golubaya rosa* (The Blue Rose). The artist died at an early age, and his oeuvre is relatively small. Even so, his work looms large in early twentieth-century Russian art, strongly differing from the efforts of World of Art artists above all in its painterly qualities, though it shares certain essential aesthetic principles.

Retrospective themes occur only in Sapunov's earliest work. Thus, his *Minuet* (1904?) and *Fancy-Dress Ball* (1907) are both stylized in the manner of eighteenth-century *fêtes galantes*. Later on he painted portraits, still lifes, and non-narrative compositions that could be conventionally termed genre scenes, such as *The Merry-go-round* (1908), *The Mummers* (1908), and *Tea-Drinking* (1912), as well as pictures after theater productions, such as *Balaganchik* (The Fairground Booth) of 1909, on a subject from Alexander Blok's lyrical drama; *The Scarf of Columbine* (1910), from an adaptation for the stage of an Arthur Schnitzler story; and *The Green Bull Hotel* (1910) after Mikhail Kuzmin's play, *The Dutch Girl Liza*.

Note that attempts to break down Sapunov's oeuvre by genre would only muddle this brief account. What must necessarily be emphasized are the features that all of his works share in common. Sapunov's painting conveys his understanding of life as theater. In his portraits the artist theatricalized his sitters, clothing them in fancy dress. His still lifes combine flowers with antique porcelain, while his genre scenes reflect galas, festivities, and round dances. In short, his work attests to the same theatricalization of life, which, as has been mentioned above, was so characteristic of World of Art painting.

Although the tastes nourished by the World of Art are responsible for Sapunov's fondness for antiques in his still lifes, this, actually, is the sum total of his retrospectivism. His

95. Boris Kustodiev. Shrovetide (Sleigh Riding). 1919

96. Boris Kustodiev. Portrait of Fyodor Chaliapin. 1921

[18] M.V. Alpatov, E.A. Gunst, *Nikolai Nikolayevich Sapunov*, Moscow, 1965, p. 11

subject matter has no links with history whatsoever; he recreates not the realities of bygone days, but merely his own romanticized dream of the past. He has nothing of the illustrativeness typical of Somov and Benois. As Mikhail Alpatov so aptly observed, "Sapunov's coloring bears the unique hallmark of a purely Russian notion of color. His paints are rainbow bright and resonant, as in the ancient icons of Novgorod and folk embroideries.... The language of color conveys not some complex emotional state, but, above all, joy and gaiety.... as do our folk songs and dances."[18]

The singular quality, which makes Sapunov so unlike his associates in the World of Art movement, derives from his way of thinking in the painterly categories of space and color, from his ability to achieve in his compositions a harmony of color of such consummate perfection as was seldom within reach of the founders and senior members of the World of Art society.

Another artist who allied himself with the society concurrently with Sapunov was Sergei Yuryevich Sudeikin (1884–1946). Chiefly famed as a stage designer, he also worked rather intensively in the realm of easel painting. As a member of the Blue Rose group in his salad days, he too did not escape the impact of Symbolism. True, his work displays an eclecticism, influenced, on the one hand, by such primitivist Russian arts and crafts as the folk toy and the hand-painted tray and signboard, and on the other, by the refined elegance of certain Russian and Western European artists, most prominently Somov, Borisov-Musatov, and Maurice Denis. His pastorales, ballet pageants, and *fêtes galantes*, themes to which he was particularly attracted, distinctly echo the favorite subject of Somov and his circle. In his creative approach Sudeikin realized, more brightly and fully than any other artist of his generation, the basic World of Art aesthetics of stylization, retrospectivism, and the interpretation of life as theater.

Still Sudeikin can be termed neither imitator, epigone, nor timid follower. He was absolutely independent in his handling of World of Art concepts, elaborating only those elements which harmonized with the nature of his own talent. Nor did he excel in line drawing, as did Somov and Dobuzhinsky, or possess so fine a sense of color as Sapunov. Finally, he had none of that historical erudition that was responsible for World of Art retrospectivism. Yet, all these shortcomings were compensated for by his forceful temperament and spontaneity of feeling. By comparison with the highly intellectualized reconstructions of the past characteristic of the senior members of the World of Art group, Sudeikin's retrospective pictures not infrequently seem naive. However, it is in this naivete that his charm lies. He was a born decorator, transmuting into decoration everything evoked by his flights of fancy – portrait, still life, pastoral, or theatrical extravaganza. His contemporary critics rightly observed that "Sudeikin thinks in terms of theatrical imagery; the theater has wholly absorbed his creative thinking."[19]

[19] V.N. Solovyov, "Sudeikin," *Apollon*, 1913, No. 4, p. 7

Though the historical genre dominated World of Art easel painting, its members were quite active in other fields as well. Thus, the landscapes of Benois, Lanceray, Ostroumova-Lebedeva, and Dobuzhinsky, as well as of Somov, Bakst, Golovin, Roerich, Serebryakova, and Kustodiev were not always devoted to retrospective themes. These artists evolved their own original concept independently of the landscape tradition of Levitan and the French Impressionists, a concept but remotely reminiscent of *fin-de-siècle* German painters.

World of Art landscapists always took for their point of departure the actual, concretely seen scenery, poeticizing it in an effort to distill the impressions gained. In this respect, the living beauty was not always definitive. Somov, Benois, and their followers depicted not only luxurious palatial parks or grand esplanades adorned with fountains and statuary, but also commonplace crannies of woods and country gardens. In attempting to reveal the landscape's inherent lyricism, they sought firstly to bring out the decorative potential.

One should regard Somov as the father of the new landscape concept; in the 1890s he painted a number of pictures far removed from the lyrical landscape, with a mood which Levitan adored, and which was further developed by his many followers. The subject matter of Somov's *Twilight in an Old Park* (1897) and *An Overgrown Pond* (1899) is, in effect, analogous with Levitan's, yet, though these pictures radiate a similar lyrical intimacy, they are theatricalized, as it were, with the actually observed scenery transmuted into a refined, well-harmonized decoration. However, there is something overly rationalized

97. Zinaida Serebryakova. Self-Portrait. 1922

98. Zinaida Serebryakova. Peasants at Dinner. 1914

99. Boris Kustodiev. The Fair. 1908

100. Zinaida Serebryakova. Bleaching Linen. 1917

101. Nikolai Sapunov. The Merry-go-round. 1908

102. The annual meeting of the *World of Art*. 1914

the classical World of Art artists. Actually, Sapunov was of a different generation than Benois or Lanceray, only having caught the public eye a little earlier than, for instance, Larionov, Yakulov, and the other "newcomers" to the St. Petersburg version of the Union's Sixth Exhibition, who, may we note, were a totally alien element for the Muscovites. Meanwhile, such draftsmen as Mitrokhin, Narbut, and Chekhonin, having assimilated the virtuoso graphics and book-illustration technique of the World of Art's founders, imparted to it a new brilliance and consummate perfection of their own; these artists are associated with a new chapter in the history of Russian book illustration, especially as concerns its ornamental and decorative aspects. No doubt the senior World of Art artists would have been in still fuller force at the Union's Sixth Exhibition, had they not been diverted to the St. Petersburg Salon which the writer-critic Sergei Makovsky arranged in early 1909. In effect, he attempted thereby to resuscitate the World of Art in its pure Diaghilevian shape, without, however, issuing any declarations or programmatic statements thereto. The entire pick of the World of Art was represented, including Bakst, Benois, Bilibin, Golovin, Dobuzhinsky, Kustodiev, Lanceray, Ostroumova-Lebedeva, Roerich, Sapunov, Serov, Somov, Stelletsky, and Sudeikin. This very fact was already a demonstration indicating that the Petersburgians were fully aware of the need for

103. Nikolai Sapunov. The Green Bull Hotel on the Canal Bank. Set design for Kuzmin's pastorale *The Dutch Girl Liza*. 1910

104. Nikolai Sapunov. Tea-Drinking. Sketch. 1912

105. Nikolai Sapunov. Spring. 1912

in the artist's keen perception, for despite the poetry, his landscapes not infrequently lack the living spontaneity of feeling.

The landscapes that Benois painted and drew – and here we do not mean his "historical landscapes" – followed a similar trend, as is well illustrated by the extensive series of watercolors and drawings done from life between 1908 and 1917. His portrayals of the scenic beauties of Italy and Switzerland, of the seashore in Brittany, of views in the Crimea, or of the rolling fields and woodlands of central European Russia have no historical associations whatever. On the contrary, the artist scrupulously sought to avoid such associations, depicting neither an old building nor a ruined castle. On the other hand, his landscapes are theatricalized compositionally. This applies first of all to his Swiss and Crimean views, in which the mountains in the background create the semblance of a backdrop, while the shapes in the foreground are arranged like coulisses enclosing a stage.

Benois likewise influenced the subtle decorative quality that Lanceray and Serebryakova imparted to their landscapes.

The landscape painting of Alexander Yakovlevich Golovin (1863–1930) is totally autonomous of Somov and Benois, even though its theatricalized aspect is perhaps even more pronounced. As early as 1913 one critic quite rightfully commented with respect to Golovin's landscapes, that "he observes nature as a realist.... but is always felt as romantic, fantast and visionary."[20] He transformed the realistic impression into a decoration wherein the form is subordinated to the organizing rhythm in order to integrate it into a complex ornamental design.

[20] S. Makovsky, "A.Ya. Golovin," *Apollon*, 1913, No. 4, p. 7

Incidentally, World of Art landscapes did not achieve great prominence in early-twentieth-century Russian easel painting, leaving a marked impact on stage design only. It was through their portraits, both painted and drawn, that members of the World of Art made a novel, important contribution to the artistic culture of the period.

In their early works, Somov and Bakst, who may be regarded as the founders of World of Art portraiture, still closely adhered to the creative concepts of the realistic art of the second half of the nineteenth century. Like Repin and the then youthful Serov, they saw the portrait painter's task as that of concretely depicting a real-life, contemporary character with his psychology and social background. Somov's early *Portrait of the Artist's Father* (1897) and Bakst's *Portrait of Alexander Benois* (1898) provide an immediate insight into the sitter's personality. Reproduced is, as it were, an arrested instant in the time flux, a most sensitively captured fragment of real life. The portrayed seem to have been caught unawares, with no thought of posing. The unconstrained casuality of pose and facial expression is thereby emphasized. Meanwhile the introduced interior and still-life elements serve to stress still more the social context.

Soon afterwards, however, World of Art portrait painting took quite a different turn. In their search for a "grand style" and novel means of expression, the artists addressed themselves to the great portrait painters of the eighteenth century. This was something more essential and deeper than stylization or imitation. The artists craved to bring back the integrity and poetic grandeur characteristic of the old masters, who had nothing of the tendency to detail the commonplace and who were as yet unspoiled by the hypertrophied psychologism that was the keynote, to a large extent, of the portrait painting of the second half of the nineteenth century. It was only much later that the World of Art portrait painters realized the tragic impossibility of evolving the "grand style" at a time of ideological confusion and implacable contradictions within the society. They were unable to rise above the individualistic absence of style, or even counter the Art Nouveau trends which so mightily affected their own creative development.

The first milestone along the new road was one of Somov's finest efforts, his portrait of the artist Elizaveta Martynova, better known as *Lady in Blue* (1897–1900). One must note that at no time before had the artist attained such consummate mastery, so penetrating a characterization, so powerful a lyrical revelation. The expressiveness of this masterpiece derives from the new approach, with the portrayal of a contemporary made retrospectivist. To poeticize the sitter, Somov extracted her from the real-life environment and transported her into an imaginary world conjured up by dreams of the past. The sitter is garbed in an old-time dress, and portrayed against a stylized, decorative park. Martynova's pose,

106. Sergei Sudeikin. Set design for Kuzmin's *Amusements for Virgins*. 1911

107. Alexander Benois. Italian Comedy: Billet doux. 1905

especially the position of her hands, is theatrically impressive; she seems to be posing for the viewer, who, nonetheless, will never mistake her for an eighteenth-century lady. The artist has invested the image with his own emotions and sensations, with his own dissatisfaction with life, with his own dreaminess, sadness, and tormenting dichotomy of consciousness that was so characteristic of the aesthetic intellectual élite at the turn of the nineteenth and twentieth centuries.

Similar tendencies, though in somewhat different forms, will be observed in Bakst's case – as is well illustrated by his *Portrait of Sergei Diaghilev* (1906). Here we have not the arrested instant in the flux of life, but a preconceived image of the sitter. Without abandoning the objective of probing the sitter's inner world in all its individual uniqueness, Bakst has deliberately accentuated in his representation of Diaghilev the typical traits of the members of the World of Art group. However, whereas Somov is retrospectivist, stylizing his portrait in the spirit of the eighteenth-century, Bakst seeks to be more in step with his own times, bringing his painterly devices closer to Art Nouveau. In his painterly, spatial construction, he stresses the imposing nature of the subject as the salient feature of the concept; the pose is spectacular, the gesture theatrical.

Thus, from the initial search for a real-life, psychological characterization, the leading exponents of World of Art portrait painting turned to a novel representational style that furnished a curious blend of the eighteenth-century tradition with Art Nouveau.

This novel concept was widely current among portrait painters of the World of Art group and those allied with it. A theatricality, for example, is characteristic of Mikhail Nesterov's celebrated *Portrait of the Artist's Daughter* (1905). The same holds true for Dobuzhinsky's *Man with Spectacles* (1905–06), depicting the critic and Symbolist poet Konstantin Sunnerberg. In an attempt to elevate his portrayal to the level of a symbol of the time, the artist has stressed the typical features of an early twentieth-century Russian intellectual, noting the tragic contrast between an inspired poet and the callous monotony of his environment.

In Golovin's portraits the Art Nouveau style and theatricality are still more pronounced. In his extensive series of portraits of writers and artists, including among others those of Mikhail Kuzmin (1910), Fyodor Chaliapin (1912), and Vsevolod Meyerhold (1917), Golovin often places the sitter on the stage, in front of footlights. Yet despite the lifelike characterization, these portraits are psychologically "faceless," as the artist sought to convey not so much the inner state of the sitters as the significance, power, and charm of their talent.

The World of Art portrait-painting concept was further elaborated by Serov toward the end of his life. Though his earliest representative portraits – of the Grand Duke Pavel Alexandrovich (1897), Sophia Botkina (1899), and Princess Zinaida Yusupova (1900–02)

108. Ida Rubinstein (seated center), Michel Fokine, Léon Bakst, and Olga Preobrajenska (standing at right) with Italian singers at La Scala, Milan. 1910s

autonomy, not only in the creative sense, but also organizationally.

True, Makovsky's Salon, which deliberately confined itself to the senior World of Art artists, with the exception of Sapunov and Sudeikin, did not yield any surprises; after all, its sole objective was to place before the public the World of Art style in its unadulterated form. Having been attained, this already presaged an early World of Art revival. Yet there was a sensation; shown for the first time in Russia was Bakst's *Terror Antiquus*, which hitherto had been displayed only at the Salon d'Automne in Paris in 1908. A whole body of literature has been devoted to its interpretation and to this day some aspects remain outstanding. What must be stressed at the given moment in time is that here Bakst had set himself the objective of raising problems common to all of humanity; he intricately interwove antique imagery with the concerns and anxieties of his contemporary world and reflected on the destinies of civilization, the laws that govern life, and the

109. Sergei Sudeikin. The Ballet. 1910

continuity of the concept and understanding of beauty. What critics and reviewers had noticed most in earlier World of Art efforts was a historico-cultural "pessimism," an infatuation with the externals of past centuries, especially the eighteenth, such as the mores, costumes, and pastimes, that were more often than not conveyed as an entertainment, fancy-dress ball, or carnival. Now, however, such gracious, erudite amusement had yielded to compositions of greater profundity and content. Thus, though born of World of Art elements, Serov's *Peter the Great* pictured with unexcelled pungency and symbolical meaning that epoch of grand reform in the nation's life. Somewhat later, Serov was, like Bakst, to borrow the material of antiquity to construct his philosophico-historical artistic concepts of that world of beauty wherein harmony and inner chastity reign supreme (*The Rape of Europa*, *Odysseus and Nausicaä*). In this manner the World of Art movement organically and logically paved the way for a new imagery and stylistic structure that

were to be elaborated upon by the younger Russian artists of the 1910s.

In May and June, the first ballet and operatic performances on the stage of the Théâtre du Châtelet in Paris comprised the first Russian Season. These productions, staged under Diaghilev's overall supervision, were truly Russian in every respect, that is, as concerned the music, the direction, the choreography, and stage design, while all actors, singers, dancers, and musicians were of Russian origin. The spectacular acclaim that this and all subsequent Seasons enjoyed welled up into a triumph for all the inner powers and traditions of Russian culture, let alone the performances as such. In the words of Benois, "Neither Borodin nor Rimsky, neither Chaliapin nor Golovin, neither Roerich nor Diaghilev were the triumphant in Paris; what triumphed was all of Russian culture, the entire originality of Russian art, with its power of conviction, its freshness and immediacy, and its wild force."[80] Moreover, it became clear that the Russian

[80] A. Benois, "Russkiye spektakli v Parizhe" (The Russian Performances in Paris), *Rech*, 19 June 1909

125

110. Sergei Sudeikin. Park. From the *Summer Gardens Studies* series. *C.* 1918

[21] I. Grabar, *Valentin Alexandrovich Serov*, p. 214

– coincided with the initial experimentation of Somov and Bakst, they have hardly any connection with the World of Art trend. Thus, according to Igor Grabar, it was only later on, after the historic 1905 exhibition in the Tauride Palace, that Serov fell under the sway of the great portrait painters of the eighteenth century and reached the conclusion that he "should undertake to seek the lost grand style."[21] Henceforth his portraits became more decorative, not infrequently acquiring that imposing theatricality which the World of Art painters so persistently tried to achieve. One could note a whole range of superb pieces reflecting this tendency, from his portrait of Elizaveta Karzinkina (1906), which he stylized in the eighteenth-century manner, to portraits of Henrietta Girshman (1907), portraits of Elena Oliv and Anna Pavlova (both 1909), and, finally, his masterpiece, a portrait of Princess Olga Orlova (1911). Despite their representative character and decorative, coloristic elegance, they are penetratingly psychological and acutely social.

[22] I. Grabar, "Boris Mikhailovich Kustodiev," *Krasnaya niva*, June 1927, p. 13

Between 1910 and 1916 Boris Kustodiev worked on a project that would implement all the basic principles of World of Art portrait painting. The large composition entitled *The Meeting of the World of Art Society* would include portraits of Grabar, Roerich, Lanceray, Bilibin, Benois, Narbut, Milioti, Somov, Dobuzhinsky, Petrov-Vodkin, Ostroumova-Lebedeva, and Kustodiev himself. Grabar recollected: "The picture was to be both decorative and realistic, monumental and true-to-life."[22] However, the artist was not up to his conception, and the project was not realized. Kustodiev produced only a sketch (1910–16), that was more in the nature of a genre piece, plus several studies which though of great iconographic interest, were not acknowledged by the leaders of the World of Art; Somov, for one, considered Kustodiev's efforts crude and caricaturish.

One very special sphere of portraiture, in which the chief World of Art artists were active, was easel portrait drawing. Again it was Somov who started this genre off and who excelled in it.

Between 1906 and 1914 Somov produced a number of pencil portraits slightly tinted with watercolors or red chalk. He chose his sitters from a small coterie of people associated with the World of Art group, namely the two artists Evgeny Lanceray (1907) and Mstislav Dobuzhinsky (1910), the Symbolist poet Vyacheslav Ivanov (1906), the collector Mefody Lukyanov (1911), and one of the society's founding members, Walter Nouvel (1914). At a cursory glance these intimate portraits of the artist's bosom friends, by no means ostentatious or theatrically imposing, may appear to negate those creative principles which Somov was first to assert in his portraiture. Nevertheless, they are in their own way both characteristic of the World of Art approach and fundamentally novel, compared with the drawn portrait of the second half of the nineteenth century. In form, Somov's graphic portraits proceed from a subtly conceived system of contrasts between an abstract, seemingly supraspatial background – devoid of the slightest hint of landscape or interior – and an emphatically concretized portrayal, now and again replete with well-nigh naturalistic detail, between the meticulously etched head and the sketchy lines of body and arms.

In these portraits Somov has extracted his sitters from their actual surroundings and deprived them of movement; despite the indisputable likeness (a point repeatedly confirmed by contemporaries), the sitters do not seem to be of flesh and blood, an aspect indicated by the more sensitive viewer. Thus the poet Georgi Chulkov, who was good friends with Alexander Blok and who often attended sittings, observed that "K.A. Somov's portrait, which is brilliant as a clever interpretation of the most essential, I would say, 'grave-like' feature of Blok, fails entirely to convey the other essential, notably the live rhythm of his face."[23] And further: "Alexander Blok's face on the portrait is overly tendentious and mask-like."[24] This petrified lifelessness of the Blok portrait is apparent in virtually all of Somov's drawings, indeed is the core of his concept. Despite their different appearances, destinies, and talents, he has imparted to all his sitters a common trait that serves to integrate them in one enclosed social and psychological category. In fact, these drawings have a certain tendency and hidden meaning, inasmuch as they express Somov's notion of the artists and poets of the pre-revolutionary period – people corroded by scepticism, completely out of joint with their time, and doomed to a tragic loneliness.

[23] G. Chulkov, "Gody stranstviy" (Years of Wandering), in: *Vospominaniya* (Recollections), Moscow, 1930, p. 124

[24] *Ibid.*, p. 200

Bakst addressed himself concurrently to the same subject matter as Somov. Thus, during the years of the first Russian revolution (1905–07) he drew portraits of writers and artists

111. Alexander Golovin. Self-Portrait. 1912

who were associated with the World of Art. They include portraits of Somov and the poet Andrei Bely, with a manner of depiction largely reminiscent of Somov's own style. Yet, though they are both lively and expressive, they lack Somov's forceful generalization and veiled meaning. As a graphic artist Bakst worked in a more traditional manner, adhering to the World of Art principles of portraiture. He was not indifferent to a representational and theatricalized portrayal.

It stands to reason that the World of Art's impact upon early twentieth-century Russian art far transcended the limitations of easel painting and graphics. Indeed, there was hardly any sphere of the spatial arts wherein the ideas, techniques, approaches, and traditions theoretically evolved in the aesthetics of the members of Diaghilev's group, or established through their creative practices, would have not taken effect. Of course, it must be noted that the degree of influence varied.

Thus in the domain of sculpture, the World of Art played but a limited role, which was rather more of an organizational, than creative, order. Diaghilev's journal supported and promoted all the advanced and progressive developments in contemporary Russian plastic art. Represented at the exhibitions which the journal's editorial board mounted were such diverse sculptors as Vrubel and Pavel Trubetskoi, and, later on, Anna Golubkina and Alexander Matveyev. However, these noted sculptors worked independently of the World of Art aesthetic; as for its core, it did not generate any productive ideas in the realm of the plastic arts, even though some members of the group, as well as those who allied with it, did make some essays at sculpture. Yet these efforts were episodic and none too professional. Thus, in 1905 Somov produced two porcelain figurines of a retrospectivist character. One, *The Lovers*, presented the fashions of the 1830, the other, *Lady Removing Her Mask*, was in eighteenth-century costume. Their elegance and expressiveness derive not so much from the decorative coloring and linear rhythm as from the plastic form and volume. Later on, in 1909–10, Kustodiev executed several portrait busts exclusively with the purpose of creating a faithful likeness.

More systematic and professional in this respect was the work of a representative of the second World of Art generation, the sculptor-painter Dmitry Semyonovich Stelletsky (1875–1947). Yet with him, too, the decorative and graphic aspect takes precedence over volume and plastic form. His oeuvre may be divided into two types of work, namely, the realistic portrait bust furnishing a penetrating psychological characterization, as is well illustrated by the posthumous bust of Valentin Serov (1912), and the historical genre piece stylized in the spirit of medieval Russian folk art, as is exemplified by the painted wooden statue *The Noblewoman* (1910).

The works named were created away from the mainstream of development in progressive Russian sculpture of the early twentieth century, and were merely episodic, even if conspicuous. On the other hand, the World of Arts's impact on Russian architecture of the time was far more fruitful, even though indirect. Indeed, among the members of the group only Grabar had the required professional training and could work as an architect.

[81] Benois. Recollections, vol. 2, p. 512

artists themselves were prone to underestimate their own powers and did not realize what sort of an appearance they would present on European stages. "Our Russian 'savage primitiveness,' our simplicity and naivete turned out in Paris – in the most cultured Paris – to be more subtle, more advanced and sensitive than what was generated locally,"[81] Benois recalled later on with acrid sarcasm. The Russian Seasons, so unexpected and underivative, finally showed and proved, not only by means of individual detail and the unanticipated discovery of brilliant talent, but, in toto, as the product of a profound and structurally concise overall concept, what so prominent and unique a figure in twentieth-century Russian and world art Sergei Diaghilev was. With full reason one may note the "phenomenon", if not the "paradox", of Diaghilev. Who was he,

really? He was no professional in any of the art genres. He wound up his art reviewing and editing long before the Seasons began. Nor can he be styled an art patron, as he had never had any worthwhile private means of his own. While to term him an administrator or manager is to say hardly anything, as this aspect was of secondary importance in his activities.

In its highest sense, Diaghilev was that concentrate of artistic resolve and determination, of that national artistic *Weltanschauung* which the creative atmosphere of the World of Art movement had nourished. The notion of "dilettante" or rather, a "well-educated dilettante" would seem to suggest itself. At times some of the members of the World of Art group would append that appelation to themselves. The World of Art never had any definite program,

112. Konstantin Somov. Lady in Blue. Portrait of the Artist Elizaveta Martynova. 1897–1900

Filosofov observed in an article headed "Also a Tendency." – "This was," he wrote, "the cult of dilettantism in its finest and truest sense. Professionalism was deeply alien to the World of Art. It had objectives of a generally cultural nature, for which reason it did not restrict itself to the purely practical arts, but also showed interest in literature, philosophy, and music."[82]

As concerns the artistic efforts of the *miriskusniki* in the narrow sense, that definition would sound unfounded, if not comical. After all, they cultivated professional mastery, even craftsmanship. In the domains of book illustration, easel drawing, and stage design, the legacy they bequeathed is to this day a genuine model in its execution, impeccable

virtuoso application and artistic form.

As for the overall aims, here the significance which can be attached to this definition is far greater. The World of Art founders were no consistent adherents to any theory in the arts, in the philosophical and aesthetic senses. More specifically, Diaghilev, for one, never pretended to be an adept of that order. However, that does not at all imply that he never professed any consistent conceptions, which from the present-day angle can be discerned with sufficient clarity. Diaghilev had a well-developed feeling for the national style which blended the spirit of ages-old tradition with a sensitive ear for the times; further, this was augmented by his go-getting energy and his flair for understanding what was needed

[82] *Zolotoye runo*, 1908, No. 1, pp. 71, 72

113. Alexander Golovin. Portrait of Fyodor Chaliapin as Holophernes in Serov's opera *Judith*. 1908

114. Léon Bakst. Cover for the journal *Comœdia Illustré*. 1910

to attain the perfect result from the artistic angle.

Can this be termed dilettantism? Only in the sense that all artistic creativity is dilettantism. After all, it can be stated with absolute conviction that the World of Art, and early twentieth-century Russian culture generally, manifested itself through Diaghilev in the same degree that it expressed itself via Serov, Vrubel, Benois, Somov, Bakst, and Dobuzhinsky....

The first issue of *Apollon* (Apollo), one of the leading Russian art journals of the early twentieth century, which actually folded in early 1918, although the last issue was dated 1917 – came out in October. Edited by Sergei Makovsky, it recruited top names in the world of Russian art reviewing and history. In its detailed coverage of artistic developments both in Russia and in Western Europe, it devoted much space to *miriskusniki* – including those who joined the group in the latter half of the 1910s – and dedicated monographic articles to all of them. Besides appreciations of various problems related to art history, museums, and private collections, and issues made moot by virtue of the creative practices of the day, it also mounted its own shows. Although it was independent and at times sharply critical of the World of Art, it was more in rapport with their

115. Alexander Golovin. Portrait of the Stage Director Vsevolod Meyerhold. 1917

Between 1909 and 1914, the Zakharyino hospital complex was built outside Moscow to his design in the Palladian classical style. However, this one and only structure does not loom large in twentieth-century Russian architecture, and as such, could hardly influence its development. What essentially did cause contemporary architecture to adopt a different trend was, instead, the overall intellectual atmosphere that the World of Art movement generated, as it served to revitalize the social aesthetic and bring home to the public a broad range of novel, or rather, forgotten, underrated artistic traditions.

As was noted earlier, at the outset, the World of Art group was vigorously influenced by Art Nouveau; however, later on its members did their best to overcome these influences. It was also pointed out that the movement had evolved from Art Nouveau to retrospectivism, and that in the process the staff of Diaghilev's journal had researched the Russian art of the past, which subsequently led to a cardinal reappraisal of certain highlights of national culture.

Toward the close of the 1890s Art Nouveau had infiltrated Russian architecture, causing several gifted architects to become infatuated with this trend. However, a mere five years or so passed before the internal contradictions and irremediable faults of the new style distinctly manifested themselves, and thus provoked sharp censure from the profession. Art Nouveau forms had no monumentality and the disparity between the structural basis and decorative embellishment disillusioned the fastidious critic. Progressive architects realized that they should follow a totally different course in the search for a modern style. The World of Art helped in this hour by stressing the promise inherent in the national tradition, of which modern architecture had thus far taken no notice.

In 1902, the *World of Art* journal published under the heading "Painterly Petersburg," a lavishly illustrated essay, in which the author, Benois, revealed for the first time the vast artistic value of the architecture of the Russian capital. Besides expressing his great appreciation of the architecture of the Petrine epoch and the gems of the style known as the Russian Baroque, he enthusiastically described classical architecture. Two years later the then young architect Ilya Fomin contributed to the journal an essay entitled *Muscovite Classicism: Moscow Architecture in the Reigns of Catherine II and Alexander I.* These two contributions served to initiate an in-depth study of the history of the new Russian architecture, a study undertaken by World of Art critics, especially Grabar, who between 1911 and 1914 put out the multi-volume *History of Russian Architecture,* written by a team of authors.

It should be noted, though, that the retrospectivist trend in Russian architecture emerged before the first volumes of the above publication came out. As early as 1905, the architect Alexander Dmitriyev designed the Peter the Great College in St. Petersburg. Built between 1909 and 1911, it now houses the Nakhimov Naval College. The façade of this building happily combines early eighteenth-century Russian architectural motifs with Baroque-style bas-reliefs designed by Benois. Several other buildings were put in the Russian capital early in the twentieth century and stylized in the spirit of the Petrine age. The least known of them, the Peter the Great Hospital complex (today the Mechnikov Hospital) was built to plans by Lev Ilyin, Roman Klein, and Alexander Rosenberg between 1910 and 1914. However, all these stylizations in the domain of architecture were episodic, inasmuch as the classical tradition continued to prevail throughout the period preceding the 1917 Revolution.

Russian neo-classicism, whose emergence was spurred by the World of Art, developed by the 1910s into a quite independent and productive trend that attracted many talented architects. It would be no exaggeration to state that the most exciting buildings erected in St. Petersburg and Moscow were designed in conformity with this trend. The theoreticians were convinced at the time that the traditional decorative form should not clash with the functional requirements and constructive possibilities. "We would very much desire," Benois wrote, "that St. Petersburg's lively, vivid style, which almost defies description, a style expressed in so unlike structures of the eighteenth and early nineteenth centuries, not disappear without trace, but, on the contrary, permeate every pore of our present-day life, all of our building art. We are of the view here that this style, far from conflicting with the demands of culture, is, as it were, specially designed to meet these demands. Far

116. Valentin Serov. Portrait of Princess Olga Orlova. 1911

[25] A. Benois, "Arkhitektura Peterburga" (Architecture of Petersburg), Mir iskusstva, 1902, vol. 8, p. 25

from striking a jarring note in St. Petersburg, the five-storey tenement house with its lift and electricity is this city's true child."[25]

To meet these desires, in 1912 Ilya Fomin built a five-storey residence on Golodai Island in the neo-classical style and produced the design for a huge complex in the New Petersburg area. In the same style Vladimir Shchuko constructed the Russian pavilions at the 1911 International Fairs in Rome and Turin, while Alexander Tamanyan erected the enormous Shcherbatov tenement (1911–13) in Moscow. They were subsequently emulated by many Russian architects.

However, one should classify as indisputable neo-classical achievements not so much the public buildings or large blocks of flats as the smaller private mansions and country villas. Possibly the shining example of pre-revolutionary architecture in this sense is the Polovtsev mansion (1911–13; now the Clinical Sanatorium) which was built by Fomin on Kamenny (Stone) Island in St. Petersburg.

Still, despite the isolated major achievements, Russia's architects were unable to revive the said style because of the capitalist realities of the period. There was plenty of talent, with architects of Fomin's calibre perhaps in no way inferior to the great architects of the past. However, a study of art history will reveal that only the very way of life of a period can serve as the medium for the birth of an organic style, and that the attempts at retrospectivism or restoration, made by any creative association in the conditions of individualism and ideological confusion, can only generate stylization attuned to Art Nouveau. In short, neither the architects, nor the artists grouped around the World of Art were able to shed its influences.

Some of the group's members contributed to architectural innovation as interior designers. In 1903, they showed their works at a specialized exhibition of the Contemporary Art Enterprise. The principal organizers were Prince Sergei Shcherbatov and Baron Vladimir von Meck, two art patrons both close to the World of Art. Benois and Lanceray designed the dining room embellished with bas-reliefs and decorative panels, Bakst, the boudoir, Konstantin Korovin decorated the tea room, and Golovin transformed one room into an old Russian *terem* (tower room). Although the artists endeavored to formulate new principles of furnishing and interior design, the objects displayed were eclectical, with the Russian classicist forms, or folk art forms, as was the case with Golovin, interpreted in *style moderne*. The exhibition was a complete failure. "Not a single commission was offered even for a chair, let alone the furnishings, or an entire room,"[26] Grabar recollected later. The sole exceptions were the dining room and boudoir designs, which were acquired by the exhibition's sponsors and subsequently used in the Shcherbatov house built by Alexander Tamanyan.

[26] Grabar, Moya zhizn, p. 187

Shortly before the outbreak of the First World War, several members of the World of Art group were commissioned to decorate the interior of Moscow's Kazan Railway Station, built by Alexander Shchusev. General supervision was entrusted to Benois, with Lanceray as his assistant. Roerich, Dobuzhinsky, Kustodiev, and Serebryakova were invited to participate. By its impressive scale this concept had no equal in early twentieth-century Russian art. It now seemed as if the World of Art would make a signal contribution to monumental painting. However, the concept was only partly implemented and even then, only much later. All the artists mentioned produced designs based on diverse allegorical or historical themes. But the war intervened and part of the effort was discarded altogether; only the decoration for the restaurant, which Benois and Lanceray had designed, was realized by the latter in 1944, toward the close of the Second World War.

From interior design it is only natural to proceed to the decorative applied arts as such. The contribution that the World of Art movement made in this field was significant, though, perhaps, not as great as would have been desired by the relevant artists. At the outset, they had evinced keen interest in the diverse crafts and had vigorously promoted and backed all the progressive initiatives displayed at the Abramtsevo and Talashkino workshops and studios, where Vrubel, Golovin, Konstantin Korovin, and other outstanding artists worked at the time. As was observed earlier, in 1903 some members of the World of Art nucleus tried their hand at the decorative applied arts. However, the Contemporary Art exhibition's lack of success convinced them that Russian society still had no feeling

117. Konstantin Somov. Portrait of the Poet Alexander Blok. 1907

118. Ivan Bilibin. Chernomor's Gardens. Set design for Scene 1 of Glinka's *Ruslan and Ludmila*. 1913

views and convictions that with any other trend. The maiden issue led with Alexander Benois' program statement "In Anticipation of a Hymn to Apollo."

Some of the exhibitions that were held in provincial Russia served as noteworthy commentaries to artistic life in St. Petersburg and Moscow. Thus, the Odessa Salon organized by the sculptor V. Izdebsky invited artists of diverse trends, which the sponsor believed were "the new and the newest." Works by both young and acknowledged artists, including members of the World of Art group, were shown. There was also a small but rather representative collection of foreign artists, among them Georges Braque, Maurice Denis, Félix Vallotton, André Derain, Henri Matisse, Albert Marquet, Henri Rousseau, Georges Rouault, and Paul Signac. Indeed, the tendency to analyze the new developments in Russian art within the context of the world art process had been initiated by the first World of Art shows up to and inclusive of Diaghilev's Historical exhibition and carried forward by the Golden Fleece Salons (1907–09), and similar enterprises in some of Russia's larger cities. Thus, the Izdebsky Salon was later taken on tour to Kiev, Riga, and eventually St. Petersburg.

1910

On April 1, Mikhail Vrubel, a constant World of Art member and the greatest of its artists, passed away.

The first issues of the *History of Russian art*, edited by Igor Grabar, came out. Three of the five volumes published between 1910 and 1916 were devoted to architecture (1910–12), one to sculpture (1911), and one to painting (1916). The first volume included Grabar's extensive "Introduction to the History of Russian Art." Although due to the First World

119. Ivan Bilibin in a Russian costume made after his design for Igor Stravinsky's *The Firebird*, Paris

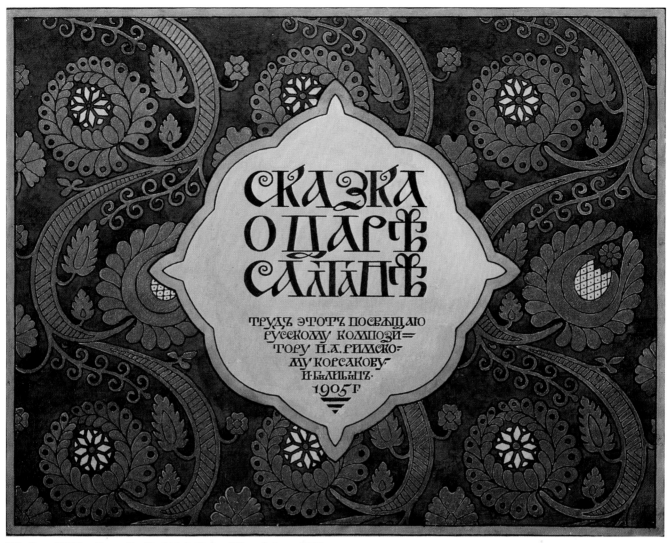

120. Ivan Bilibin. Cover for Pushkin's *Tale of Tsar Saltan*. 1905

121. Ivan Bilibin. The Chambers of the Novgorod Fraternity. Set design for Scene 1 of Rimsky-Korsakov's *Sadko*. 1913

for the aesthetic they sought to propagate. That came later, indeed, too late for most of the senior World of Art generation.

Bakst was able to apply his talent and fantasy in this area only after leaving Russia and settling in Paris in 1912. In the same year, Lanceray was enlisted as art director of the Imperial Porcelain Factory; however, few members of even the younger World of Art generation responded to his invitation to collaborate. He himself did not contribute much; deserving of mention is the *Reapers* vase sculpted after his design in 1915 by Natalia Yakovlevna Dan'ko (1892–1942), who soon also won acclaim as the most gifted sculptor in the later World of Art circle. Her best works, in only the first few years after the 1917 Revolution, include *The Decembrists* bas-relief (1918, biscuit) and a number of exquisitely molded decorative china statuettes on revolutionary and everyday themes.

A more versatile artist in this field was Sergei Vasilyevich Chekhonin (1878–1936). He originally associated himself with the World of Art group in 1903, at the aforementioned 1903 exhibition, to which he contributed as decorator and woodcarver, executing the *terem* that Golovin had designed. Subsequently he developed into a notable book illustrator and a full-fledged member of the society. According to Nikolai Punin, who wrote the first ever monograph about Chekhonin, "he is familiar not only with graphics, which is usually considered his basic field, but likewise with all the related crafts, wherever the brush is applied, be this painting on porcelain and enamel, enameling as such, the miniature, also jewelry and cabinetmaking, majolica, glass-cutting, textile manufacture, etc."[27] This diverse technical grounding was responsible for his high professional standard; in Chekhonin's hands, the crafts developed into an art in its own right. But, like other members of the World of Art group he was only a stylizer and retrospectivist. In the monograph cited above, Punin termed the artistic life of the first two decades of the twentieth century the "afterglow of the grand epoch of Russian classicism; the unappreciated service that the artists of these two decades rendered is that they induced one more – this time, a farewell retrospective – glance; but that may be their greatest weakness."[28]

The essays of World of Art artists in diverse spheres of the visual arts, their persistent attempts to master all the decorative and applied arts should not be taken to signify the random, haphazard gropings of gifted but undisciplined artistic personalities. Behind all these attempts was a consistent *Weltanschauung*, based on the integrated concept of style and the synthesis of arts as the supreme objective. The World of Art artists sought an organic style, originally seen as an imported yet Russified Art Nouveau, and subsequently as a new classicism. But, as has been noted, all these attempts were fatefully abortive. Neither architecture, nor the crafts were able to entrench themselves along the course that the World of Art movement paved, while the conceived synthesis of the arts disintegrated under the pressure of insuperable forces generated by the egoistic trends of bourgeois society. Any tangible synthesis of architecture, sculpture, and monumental painting proved unattainable within the context of early twentieth-century bourgeois reality. The two World of Art generations were fated to achieve but an illusory synthesis in stage design.

The World of Art group played a preeminent role in twentieth-century stage design, whose significance transcends national boundaries. Indeed, it is of world stature. Implied is not only the extensive acknowledgment throughout Europe of Russian stage designers, but also their direct impact upon scene-painting the world over. However, it should be emphasized that the *miriskusniki* did not initiate those changes that were to be observed in stage design in the first quarter of the twentieth century. They merely continued the innovations introduced much earlier by the Abramtsevo Colony and the Mamontov Private Opera founded in 1885.

By that year Russian stage design, which had once flourished, had become degraded to the point where it had largely lost its links with everything progressive in contemporary national art. No longer did notable artists, but "professionals," mostly of journeyman calibre, rule the roost, plunging this field into a stereotype hardly witnessed in any other domain of the visual arts. As a result, the stage designer's role was reduced merely to the creation of a cliche-ridden backdrop, either conventional or narrative, and the same sets were often used for the most varied productions.

[27] N. Punin, "O masterstve S.V. Chekhonina" (The Mastery of S.V. Chekhonin), in: A. Efros and N. Punin, *S. Chekhonin*, Moscow–Petrograd, 1924, p. 26

[28] *Ibid.*, p. 38

122. Sergei Chekhonin. Frontispiece for the journal *Apollon*. 1917

Mamontov's pritave company did away with this practice. Eminent painters again turned to design decoration. At first these were the Wanderers, Victor Vasnetsov and Vasily Polenov, later – their juniors, Mikhail Vrubel and Konstantin Korovin. Enhancing the role of the stage designer, they maintained a firm conviction in the essential role of the sets and costumes in the entire theatrical production. Further, by ousting the "narrativeness" of standard settings, Vrubel, Konstantin Korovin and, later, Golovin created an atmosphere of poeticized "theatrical reality."

Some World of Art members had already undertaken stage design after such memorable productions as Rimsky-Korsakov's operas *The Tale of Tsar Saltan* (1900, stage sets by Vrubel) and *The Maid of Pskov* (1901, with decor by Golovin) and the ballet, *The Little Humpbacked Horse* (1901, with decor by Konstantin Korovin).

A new chapter in Russian stage design had begun.

Earlier in these pages we stressed time and again the immense role which the initial theatrical impressions gained by the members of Diaghilev's group played in the development of the World of Art aesthetic. Hence, it was only natural for them to turn to stage design. However, their initial attempts were abortive.

In the autumn of 1899, Diaghilev was made "Official for Special Commissions" under Prince Sergei Volkonsky, Director of the Imperial Theaters. Taking charge of the production of the Delibes' ballet, *Sylvia*, he invited Benois, Lanceray, Bakst, Konstantin Korovin, and Serov to do the sets and costumes. However, the appearance of such a massive group of advanced artists scared the conservatives and the production was called off. Diaghilev himself was dismissed from his post and, in solidarity with him, the artists mentioned decided never to work for the Imperial Theaters again. However, not for long, Russia had too few private companies at the time, and this decision was tantamount to abandoning the very idea of engaging in stage design altogether. In 1902, Benois executed the decors for the Mariinsky Theater production of Wagners's *Götterdämmerung*. Between 1902 and

123. Sergei Chekhonin. Cover for the journal *Mysl* (Thought). 1918

124. Sergei Chekhonin. Cover for Averchenko's book *The Bengal Lights*. 1914

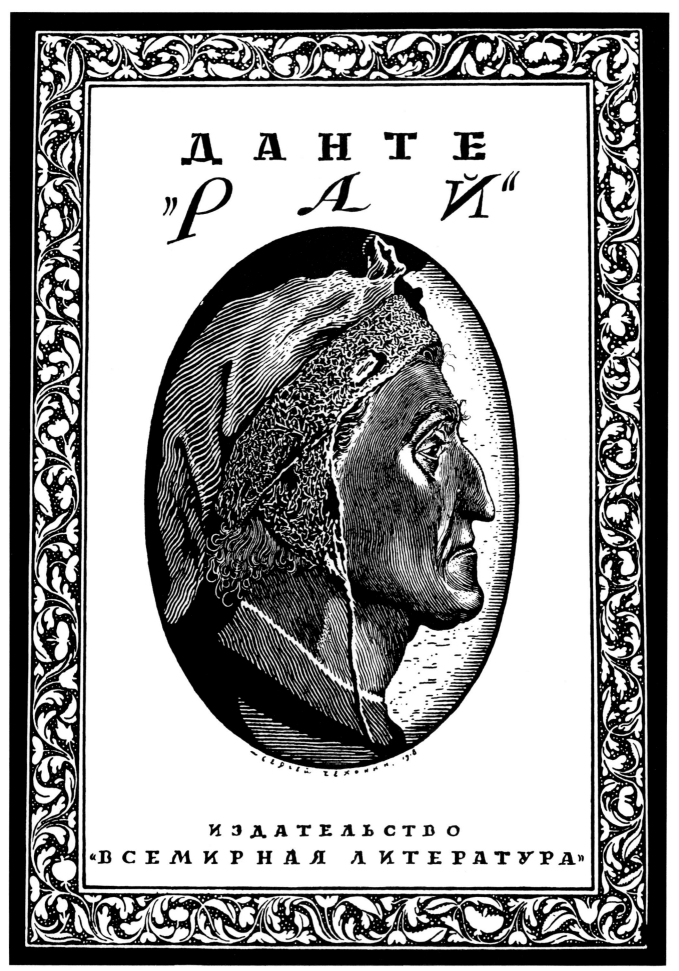

125. Sergei Chekhonin. Cover for Dante's *Paradise*. 1918

1904, Bakst did the sets and costumes for productions at the Alexandrinsky Theater, also in St. Petersburg, of Euripides' tragedy *Hippolytus* and Sophocles' *Œdipus at Colonus*. Diaghilev criticized Benois for his "inappropriate realism," a rebuke he could not present to Bakst, who had stylized his sets in the spirit of Greek antiquity. With these pieces, the two artists initiated what was to become the characteristic World of Art style of stage design – the decorative, flat style that, despite the highly intensive color scheme, was nonetheless more in the nature of a drawing than a painting.

Toward the close of 1907, a theatrical enterprise conceived by a circle of enthusiasts in the vein of the World of Art aesthetic was established in St. Petersburg. Called the Antique Theater, its basic goal was to restore the forms and methods of the ancient European theater, especially that of the Middle Ages and the fifteenth and sixteenth centuries, and consequently, to focus attention on the eleventh-century liturgical play, the miracle play and pastorale of the thirteenth century, the fifteenth-century morality play, and the street farces of the sixteenth century.

Most of the World of Art members worked for this theater; Dobuzhinsky and Benois, who had helped found it, acted as artistic and historical consultants. Benois designed the theater's drop curtain. Dobuzhinsky executed the superb stage design for Adam de la Halle's *Jeu de Robin et Marion*. Collaborating with them at the Antique Theater were also Lanceray, Bilibin, Roerich, the young graphic artist Chembers, and the architect Shchuko.

The intensive, though short-lived, work for the Antique Theater essentially contributed to the development of the World of Art style of stage design. This group of artists, with their vast historical erudition and fine feeling for the past, was in an excellent position to accomplish the objective of restoration and stylization that faced the Theater. In fact, they dominated the Theater's work and are to be credited for the success it enjoyed. The stage designer was at the same time creator of the production's overall style, while the "ethnographical" accuracy sought was no aim in itself, but a means to achieving artistic authenticity. Soon, however, the artists were confronted with different, still thornier tasks of a creative and ideological order.

The same year of 1907 saw the beginning of the World of Art's close association with the Moscow Art Theater. Konstantin Stanislavsky came specially to St. Petersburg to see for himself of what the members of this still progressive group were capable.

It should be noted that prior to this the directors of the Moscow Art Theater had not attached any particular significance to the stage designer; they merely required verisimilitude and to a certain extent ignored the decor's aesthetic value as such. It remained for the artists of the World of Art society to introduce genuine stage design. On the other hand, the Theater itself influenced these artists in a most productive manner, promoting a psychological realism that was most sensitively attuned to the social environment.

Between 1909 and 1915 Benois, Dobuzhinsky, and Kustodiev designed an extensive range of productions in the classical repertoire at the Moscow Art Theater. Benois did the sets and costumes for the comedies of Molière and Goldoni, as well as for three "little tragedies" by Pushkin; Dobuzhinsky executed the decors for the plays of Turgenev, Griboyedov, and Blok, as well as for *Nikolai Stavrogin* (an adaptation of Dostoyevsky's novel, *The Demons*), and Kustodiev, for Saltykov-Shchedrin's drama, *The Death of Pazukhin*.

Though some of these productions were highlights for the time, collaboration between the realistic theater and the Petersburg stylizers was often marred by conflict. Thus the theater's directors took care to prevent "domination by the artists," so as not to subordinate the idea-content to them. Differing with Dobuzhinsky as to the interpretation of one of the personages in Turgenev's play, Stanislavsky sharply rebuked him, saying: "You need the frame of the theater to show your pictures. You need our body to garb it in your costumes, you need our face to paint it as in a picture."[29] These words reflect the anxiety felt not only due to the presumed "non-scenic character" of the artist's concept, but also the far-going divergency of views between a stage director of the realist mold and a stage designer proceeding from motivations of retrospectivism and stylization. Yet, Dobuzhinsky understood the creative approach of the Moscow Art Theater better than all the other

[29] K. Stanislavsky. *Stat'i, rechi, besedy, pis'ma* (Essays, Speeches, Conversations and Letters), Moscow, 1953, p. 485

126. Valentin Serov. Anna Pavlova in *Les Sylphides*. 1909

127. Nikolai Sapunov. The Turkish Ceremony. Set design for Act 4 of Molière's *Le Bourgeois Gentilhomme*

artists of the World of Art group, and was much more willing than the others to strike a balance between his own concepts and those of the director.

As will be gathered, Dobuzhinsky was not only an excellent stylizer and erudite connoisseur of-past history, but likewise a keenly perceptive artist, capable of profoundly sensing and energetically expressing psychological problems of a social order. Never pleased with the pro-forma aspect of stage design, he was able, in a range of productions, to bring across the idea-content. Thus, when working on the stage ensemble for Stanislavsky's production of Turgenev's *A Month in the Country* (1909), he, according to his own words, sought to have the "decor correspond to the spirit and meaning of the play as a reflection of cosy, tranquil life on a landed estate, where.... everything is stable, and into which a storm bursts – however, after it dies down, everything remains as it was, and life again follows the same old tenor."[30] The artist subordinated to this concept the entire pattern of the ensemble with its gently flowing symmetrical rhythms and subtle, well-harmonized color scheme of reds, greens, and blacks.

Dobuzhinsky's stage design for *Nikolai Stavrogin* (1913), possibly his finest, is totally different. The Art Theater directors interpreted this play as an acute tragedy and the artist's highly ingenious and expressive decor, constructed of asymmetrical rhythms and intensive color contrasts, conveys a spirit of profound tragedy, that at times reaches the heights of a psychological grotesque.

Benois was less amenable, and when working for the Moscow Art Theater insisted upon his own creative concepts, which not infrequently clashed with the director's ideas. Still, he commanded such indisputable authority that in 1913 the Art Theater directorate invited him to join as the member in charge of stage design, and for the next three years (1913–15), he supervised the work of all invited stage designers as the theater's artistic director. The decors he provided for the 1913 productions of Molière's *Le Mariage forcé* and *Le Malade imaginaire* and Goldoni's *La Locandiera* (The Mistress of the Inn) served

[30] M.V. Dobuzhinsky, *Vospominaniya o Moskovskom Khudozhestvennom teatre* (Reminiscences of the Moscow Art Theater). An unpublished manuscript from the collection of G.I. Chugunov, to whom the author is gratefully obliged for permission to quote.

War, this undertaking remained unfinished, it was of immense historico-cultural significance. Along with the series of fine monographs on such Russian artists as Vrubel, Levitan, Serov, Nesterov, and Ryabushkin that were put out between 1911 and 1916 by Knebel's publishing house, again under Grabar's editorship, this *History* served as the crowning success of the enormous work undertaken by the *miriskusniki* to research, reinterpret, and promote the national school of art in the process of its centuries-old evolution.

The Union of Russian Artists' Seventh Exhibition came as the death knell of this organization, which had sought to fuse together the two diverse groups of Muscovite and Petersburgian artists. Unlike previous shows, it had not two, but three different versions. The first was opened in December 1910 in Moscow and continued through February 1910. Represented at the second showing, held in St. Petersburg in February–March, were, along with the World of Art stalwarts, a large group of young followers and adherents of novel trends, whom the Petersburgians had invited to take part. Practically all these entrants were presented at the third showing in Kiev in April–May.

The situation that had developed was a singular one. At the Moscow show the confrontation followed the "beaten track." However, at the showing in St. Petersburg this confrontation was intensified by the addition of such novel, questive artists as Aristarch Lentulov, Kuzma Petrov-Vodkin, and Georgi Yakulov, plus gifted followers of the World of Art tradition, especially Zinaida Serebryakova, who made a spectacular debut, and the already more or less well-known Dmitry Mitrokhin, Georgi Narbut,

and Sergei Chekhonin. Incidentally, it should be noted that the confrontation was not quite of the order as is at times presented, that is between "retrospective dreamers," as Sergei Makovsky once dubbed the World of Art artists, and modernists, implying authors of landscapes, and less often, genre pieces of a modern mood....

In the first place this "modernity" was rather limited in scope. True, the Russian landscapes which Vinogradov, Zhukovsky, Stepanov, and other typical Union artists created year after year abounded in sincere feeling and displayed an affection for their native lands and other fine qualities; the only difference from nineteenth-century landscapes was, perhaps, that there was more of *plein-airism*, a greater assortment of tints and a more intensive play of color. However, these artists seemed completely oblivious of the dramatic collisions of the world around them, of the dynamic intensity with which it was perceived within the context of the spiritual life of the time, for which reason Dobuzhinsky's dramatic townscapes appear far more consonant with the spirit of the age.

On the other hand, even the senior World of Art members did not at all confine themselves to dreamy stylizations at this Seventh Exhibition. Earlier we mentioned Bakst's *Terror Antiquus*, which was transferred to this showing from the St. Petersburg Salon of 1909, a piece that is totally at variance with any sentimentalizing over the past. Though Dobuzhinsky's designs for the Moscow Art Theater production of Turgenev's *A Month in the Country* may have seemed more closely related to such moods, even they, as Yakov Tugendhold aptly observed, displayed "that dead squireachy in a

128. Leon Bakst. Costume designs for Sophocles' tragedy *Œdipus at Colonus*. 1904

restored, shining, radiant today." Moreover, that critic added: "We never saw on the stage before such colorful, purely visual delights."[83] There unquestionably exists a profound, logical link between the "modern" view of the olden times which Tugendhold notes in Dobuzhinsky's case, and his ability to give the contemporary spectator a living delight by virtue of the consummate perfection of artistic form. Any epigonistic stylization is always completely denuded of such qualities! Similar notions come to mind again when evaluating other decor designs created by World of Art artists and shown at the aforesaid exhibition. An apposite instance is more specifically afforded by Roerich's suite for *Prince Igor* and *The Maid of Pskov*, wherein the feeling for national history is permeated with an acute sense of drama and spiritual force, which is best manifest in the severe and energetic color scheme. Finally, what could be more modern than the fine portraits executed by *miriskusniki*, including such gems as Serov's *Elena Oliv* and *Anna Pavlova*, Somov's *Mikhail Kuzmin*, and Kustodiev's *Portrait of the Artist's Wife*.

The list could be continued with similar instances culled not only from the aforesaid exhibition but also from earlier efforts by *miriskusniki*. That will only throw into greater relief the point that to reduce the entire oeuvre of this group of illustrious Russian artists to no more than elegant stylization and a dreamy infatuation with past history is nothing but a trite platitude. The said features were characteristic primarily of the initial phase of the World of Art

129. Scene from *Œdipus at Colonus*

movement. With the passage of time the content of the creative efforts of the relevant artists grew increasingly richer to encompass a considerable proportion of the aesthetic of their day and age. Hence, in the final analysis, the power of their mastery and that quality of contemporary vision which keynoted the works of most of the *miriskusniki* in question. No wonder the landscapes of the Union Moscovites seem archaic by comparison. And

[83] Ya. Tugendhold, "Moskovskiye vystavki" (Moscow Exhibitions), *Apollon*, 1910, No. 4, pp. 53, 54

149

to introduce the atmosphere of historical stylization in the Moscow Art Theater; still, according to Grabar, the "center of gravity and basic interest is not historical, but the inner authenticity of the production.... In works dealing with archaeology and art, one will look in vain for these capitals, with such ornamental scrolls or such charming landscapes, as they are not reproductions of originals, but inventions of a contemporary artist, however so admirably conceived that they well substitute for the most authentic of realities."[31] True, some critics then had already indicated, not without good reason, that the productions which Benois designed lacked authentic artistic integrity, inasmuch as the purely visual aspect was overly obvious, thereby obscuring the actors and depreciating their acting. The same shortcoming is evident in the production of Pushkin's three "little tragedies", including *Mozart and Salieri*, *The Stone Guest*, and *The Feast in Time of Plague*. The settings were inordinately sumptuous and cumbersome. "The background absorbed the action," critics noted. This failure led to Benois' complete break shortly afterwards with the Moscow Art Theater. Thereafter, most of his stage sets were executed abroad, primarily for Diaghilev's ballet company.

Only Kustodiev did not conflict with the Moscow Art Theater directors. His flair for genre detail was in harmony with their creative concepts. Thus, the 1914 production of *The Death of Pazukhin*, for which he executed the decor, and which was staged by Vasily Luzhsky, in collaboration with Ivan Moskvin and Vladimir Nemirovich-Danchenko, was an important event in the life of the Russian theater. Yet the Art Theater failed to make full use of Kustodiev's potential. In that same year he furnished the stage design for *Autumn Violins*, a trifle by the contemporary dramatist Ilya Surguchev, which he found of little interest, while the sets he made in 1915 for Ostrovsky's comedy *Wolves and Sheep*, a play he admired, were never used. The alliance between the World of Art designers and the Moscow Art Theater disintegrated without yielding the desired results.

However, in 1908–09 Diaghilev started a new theatrical enterprise outside Russia. After an initial series of Russian music recitals in Paris, he produced *Boris Godunov* and, eventually, from 1909 on, an impressive range of Russian operas and ballets. We have already dwelt on the immense success that Diaghilev's enterprise enjoyed and the outstanding contribution it made to European artistic life prior to the First World War. This is not surprising, since between 1908 and 1914 Diaghilev produced in Paris ten operas and twenty-two ballets, all of which were designed by artists of the World of Art society.

The key figure here, moreover at once, was Léon Bakst, though he had not worked for either the Antique Theater of St. Petersburg or the Art Theater of Moscow. This

[31] I. Grabar, "O postanovke *Khoziaiki gostinitsy*" (On the Production of *La Locandiera*), in: *Russkie vedomosti*, 1914

no wonder, too, that the *miriskusniki* were able to rear a new, gifted generation of disciples and followers – that the Union Muscovites did not have! – and enlist as adherents young people of other, different artistic outlooks.

True, somewhat later on, the World of Art's leading figures reviewed these differences in the cold light of the day, and far from approved or backed every aspect of them. In the meantime, they sought to invite these younger artists to exhibit everything genuinely professional and capable of attracting interest, even if totally unlike their own efforts. The Union Muscovites could not agree with that principle, and this explains the essential divergence between the showings in Moscow and St. Petersburg. This circumstance was likewise responsible for bringing to a head the conflict that had erupted between the Union's two main groups of artists. What triggered the conflict was a series of four "Art Letters" that Benois published in *Rech* in February–March 1910, in which, reviewing the Seventh Exhibition, the author noted with uncompromising candor the crisis that had emerged in Russian art by the start of the 1910s. He presented what he himself

termed "a bird's-eye view" of every flank of national artistic life. What he detected were "faded, dried, dusty old schools" on the right, the Union of Russian Artists in the middle, and budding tendencies on the left. Further he indicated the pronounced stratification within the Union itself. He continued to heap praise upon the World of Art's leading figures, such as Bakst, Dobuzhinsky, Kustodiev, Somov, and Roerich, whom he complemented with Yuon and Čiurlionis, and the younger Serebryakova and Petrov-Vodkin whose painting *Dream* was displayed at the Seventh Exhibition, provoked an acute, even scandalous polemic, all because of the furious give-and-take between Repin and his opponents.

At the same time Benois mentioned the "rearguard" and "ballast" within the Union. Incidentally, the said epithet "ballast" had been applied with respect to the "traditionalists" still earlier on the pages of the new journal *Apollon*. "One is willy-nilly amazed," Georgi Lukomsky observed in that portion of "Moscow Artistic Life" devoted to the Seventh Exhibition, "why there is so much ballast in the form of the works on the 'right' of the Muscovite landscapists, except for Krymov, who depicts again

130. Mstislav Dobuzhinsky. Birdhouses (after *Nikolai Stavrogin*). 1913

and again hillocks and woods."[84] A little later Sergei Makovsky employed the same castigating epithet with respect to Union Muscovites on the pages of the same journal: "The Union's topheavy ballast imparts to the exhibition the stamp of backwardness and boring (partly Wanderer-like) stereotype."[85]

Benois, speaking of the "ballast", ranked in the "rearguard" a large group of Muscovites, including such notables as Arkhipov, Vasnetsov, Stepanov, Perepletchikov, Vinogradov, and Zhukovsky. This was taken as an affront. The further existence within one Union of two groups of artists so categorically, and now quite frankly, opposed both in their views on art and in concrete creative practices, was out of question.

In their collective letter of April 8, 1910, addressed to Benois, the Union Muscovites declared that they counted "awkward and against the corporation's ethical requirements, such pronouncements in the press by a member of the corporation."[86] Benois, and in his wake the Petersburgian World of Art artists, who were joined by the Muscovites Grabar, Sapunov, and, naturally, that staunch *miriskusnik* Serov, resigned from the Union. This was followed

by the World of Art's organizational renaissance. The related, purely technical aspect may be deduced from the letter that Dobuzhinsky dispatched to Maliavin on October 17, 1910;

Dear Sir,
Philipp Andreyevich!
At their meeting on October 6, the former members of the Union of Russian Artists Alexander Benois, I. Bilibin, I. Braz, M. Dobuzhinsky, B. Kustodiev, A. Ostroumova, N. Roerich, K. Somov, J. Tsionglinsky, and S. Yaremich resolved to constitute a new art association, which it is proposed to name the World of Art. Incorporated thus in it as founding members are also L. Bakst, I. Grabar, E. Lanceray, A. Ober, V. Serov, N. Tarkhov, and K. Yuon, who also resigned from the Union. In view of the extreme desirability of having you as a founding member of the new association, the Committee hereby requests you to notify us of your assent to become one such member.
       M. Dobuzhinsky, Committee member, Secretary of the association, Oct. 17, '910.[87]

The new association's tentative membership may suggest that on the agenda was resurrection of the previous World of Art society seven years after its last exhibition had closed. However, this was different. Though most of the "old" *miriskusniki* still had a long life to live and though they were still to

[84] *Apollon*, 1910, No. 4, p. 62

[85] S. Makovsky, "Khudozhestvennye itogi" (Artistic Results), *Apollon*, 1910, No. 7, p. 33

[86] Russian Museum MSS Department, col. 137, dep. unit 2092, f. 1

[87] Tretyakov Gallery MSS Department, col. 41, dep. unit 9

splendid artist's talents flourished under Diaghilev. Within the period mentioned he designed the sets and costumes for as many as a dozen ballets. The contribution of Benois, who not only executed stage designs, but also acted as director and wrote the libretti for several ballets, was almost equal in importance. Working side by side with these leaders were Golovin, Bilibin, Roerich, Dobuzhinsky, Anisfeld, and Sudeikin. Under Diaghilev, they at last had every opportunity to elaborate upon the principles of stage design that they had evolved, and to implement their creative concept of theater as a synthetic art, integrating music, painting, and choreography into one composite artistic image.

Indeed, despite the artists' remarkable individuality, their stage designs all display one definite style, a style reflecting the basic aesthetic principles common to the entire World of Art group. Though Bakst was unlike Dobuzhinsky, and while Roerich would appear to have little in common with either Sudeikin or Golovin, they all shared a common understanding of their task, which could be defined, on the one hand, as the attainment of an organic artistic unity of all the components of the production, and on the other, as the creation of a strikingly magnificent spectacle, capable of transporting the viewer into the irreal, romanticized world of a theater totally at variance with the commonplace of everyday life.

This was innovative for the Western European, let alone Russian, theater. Describing the impact that the scenic innovations of the Ballets Russes had on world stage design in general, French art critics persistently stressed that prior to Diaghilev's Seasons, a drab illusiuonistic naturalism had prevailed in the theaters of Paris, the decor was of deliberately pale tones so as to be barely noticeable, for the concept usually allotted to it was the most insignificant; in effect, it played an auxiliary role.[32]

The Russian ballet stage designers dealt this superannuated convention its *coup de grace*, reinterpreting the designer's role in the theater in a totally new sense and creating

[32] Wernod, "Les peintres et les Ballets Russes," *La Revue musicale*, December 1930, pp. 79, 80

131. Alexander Golovin. The Ballroom. Set design for Scene 2 of Lermontov's *The Masquerade*. 1917

132. Nicholas Roerich. St. Pantaleon the Healer. 1916

133. Mstislav Dobuzhinsky. The Blue Lounge. Set design for Act 1 of Turgenev's *A Month in the Country*. 1909

a range of exemplary shows which left an indelible imprint upon European art. In part, the reader should already be familiar with the approaches and techniques that secured so dazzling a result, insofar as they derived from the easel painting of the artists named.

Even though the artists of the World of Art group did not lean toward painting by virtue of their specific gifts, they did possess a sensitive eye for the decorative potential of color. They were, instead, draftsmen, who excelled in line drawing. Hence, they transferred to stage design the same decorative and graphic principles as used in line drawing, contouring each form and shape by means of a firmly stenciled line, and dividing them into a number of juxtaposed planes that not infrequently transformed objects into components of an ornamental design. Inasmuch as the stage designer tinted each plane with pure, bright and resonant pools of color, the scenic ensemble came to possess a color scheme of particular intensity.

World of Art retrospectivism was most forcefully manifest in the ballets and operas that Diaghilev produced abroad. The imagery of the romanticized part was recreated on the stage, thus enabling each designer to address himself to that chapter of history with which he was most fascinated and familiar.

Of all stage designers Bakst proved to be the most ingenious and versatile. In the productions of the ballets *Schéhérazade* (1910) and *Le Dieu Bleu* (1911), he created a world of fantasy out of an oriental fairy tale stylized in the manner of the Persian miniature. In *Narcisse* (1911), *Daphnis et Chloë* (1912) and *L'Apres-midi d'un Faune* (1912), he revived the atmosphere of Ancient Hellas by borrowing from the motifs of Grecian sculpture and painted vases. Finally, in *Le Carnaval* (1910) and *Le Spectre de la Rose* (1911), he gave his own original interpretation of the Romantic Age. Benois' vast historical erudition enabled him to resurrect imagery from the most diverse cultures, ranging from his favorite times of Louis XIV in the ballet *Le Pavilion d'Armide* (1909) to the romantic 1830s in *Chopiniana* (1909) and *Giselle* (1910), from the Petersburg fair-booth show of the Punch and Judy type that Igor Stravinsky recreated in his ballet *Petrouchka* (1911) to Andersen's fairy tale about China, stylized in the manner of the eighteenth-century chinoiserie, in his design for Stravinsky's opera *Le Rossignol* (1914).

Roerich's designs for the opera *The Maid of Pskov* (1909), for the Polovtsian Dances from the opera *Prince Igor* (1909 and 1910) and especially for Stravinsky's ballet *Le Sacre du Printemps* (1912) took West European audiences by storm, for this was the first time they were offered a glimpse of the unknown poetic world of medieval Russia and the enigmatic paganism of ancient Slavs. True success and world acclaim attended the efforts of all Russian artists designing productions for Diaghilev's company. The names of Bakst, Benois, Roerich, Dobuzhinsky, Golovin, Konstantin Korovin, Stelletsky, Bibilin, Anisfeld, and Sudeikin are inscribed forever in the annals of the European theater.

The basic creative approach responsible for the acclaim was the artful stylization which these artists had so well developed in their easel painting, and which ranged from the strictly historical stylization of Benois and Dobuzhinsky to the freer interpretation characteristic of Bakst, Golovin, and the others. However, it invariably derived from vast, diversified knowledge and, above all, from sensitive historical intuition.

The outbreak of the First World War put an end to the World of Art's brilliant endeavors in stage design, as subsequently the artists of this group seldom, only episodically, contributed to the Diaghilev productions. Between 1914 and 1916, their place was taken by representatives of a younger generation, notably Mikhail Larionov and Natalia Goncharova. Later on Diaghilev invited leading painters from France and Western Europe in general, some of whom had not engaged in stage design before, to furnish the settings and costumes for his Ballets Russes. Among them were Pablo Picasso, André Derain, Georges Braque, Henri Matisse, Georges Rouault, Maurice Utrillo, Juan Gris, Joan Miró, and Max Ernst.

Besides stage design the World of Art also left a marked impact on book illustration. In fact, the artists effected a notable turn of the tide in the history of Russian book graphics, bringing about its revival and flowering. It was in this field that the artists grouped around Diaghilev's journal most strikingly manifested their innovative designs. Indeed, thanks to their concerted efforts, Russian book illustration was eventually

134. Alexander Benois. Set design for Pushkin's tragedy *The Feast in Time of Plague*. 1914

135. Alexander Benois. Set design for the inn room in Goldoni's *La Locandiera*. 1913

136. Léon Bakst. Costume design for a Bœotian in Tcherepnin's ballet *Narcisse*. 1911

137. Léon Bakst. Costume designs for the Bœotian girls in Tcherepnin's ballet *Narcisse*. 1911

extracted from its *fin-de-siècle* stagnation. By revising and revitalizing the traditions of book graphics and reconstruing the artistic approach and the specific logic of this form of art, they evolved a well-conceived, consistent system based on the concept of the book as one integral decorative and graphic entity, whose every component was linked in overall style and rhythm.

Since the World of Art group saw the book as an object for embellishment, they regarded decorative designs as the basic aim. Yet the embellishment could not be casual, arbitrary. When preparing his illustration the artist had to reckon with the page, prove capable of duly resorting to its size and format, stress its two-dimensional character, and relate the picture to the graphic effect of the type of print used. Inasmuch as the illustrator is called upon to work with the flat plane of the page, then the picture as such must also necessarily be flat and conventional, wherein the chief visual components would be the line and a patch either of one tone or color, which would be strictly contoured and subordinated to the linear rhythm.

The system was fathered by Somov, Benois, Bakst, and the then youthful Lanceray. Proceeding from the experience of contemporary Western European, primarily English and German, graphics, they originally ventured into what was pure decoration, notably covers, vignettes, initials, head- and tailpieces, and other decorative elements used in the World of Art and other magazines and journals. According to Lanceray, at the outset the artists had followed the "modernist trend which made extensive use of floral motifs for ornamentation, and the historical trend, in which they proceeded from studies of the eighteenth century."[33] The approach developed into an amalgam of the present and the past. They brought to book illustration Gothic, Petrine Baroque, and Russian classicist motifs, however quite independently worked, with close notice paid to the specific structural features of the book and the compositional rhythm of the book page, coupled with a most sensitive feel for the right proportions and tasteful execution.

At the very start of the 1900s, two talented book illustrators, Bilibin and Dobuzhinsky, joined the World of Art group. Both unreservedly accepted the system evolved and both

[33] Quoted after O. Podobedova: *Evgeny Evgenyevich Lanceray. 1875–1946,* Moscow, 1961, p. 45

138. Ivan Bilibin. Title page for Uspensky's article "Early Russian Painting (15th–18th Centuries)," *The Golden Fleece,* 1906, No. 7–9

139. Dmitry Mitrokhin. Cover for Zamyatin's *Provincial Tales.* 1915

140. **Mstislav Dobuzhinsky.** Sketch-version of the title page for Hans Christian Andersen's *The Swineherd*. 1917

contributed much to its elaboration and entrenchment. Bilibin, for one, initiated a new tradition derived from medieval Russian art and the peasant crafts, delighting in the decoration of Russian *bylinas* (folk sagas) and fairy tales. Dobuzhinsky, on the other hand, was more versatile, producing hundreds of covers and other embellishments and illustrations for diverse publications, including not only magazines, but, especially so, the works of contemporary writers and Symbolist poets, as well as monographs on art history. In fact, more than any other of his *confrères*, Dobuzhinsky helped to enhance the standard of book illustration and influenced the development of Russian graphics in the first quarter of the twentieth century.

The second World of Art generation also brought to the fore notable book illustrators who joined the group after 1910. Two virtuoso masters were the earlier mentioned Chekhonin and Georgi Ivanovich Narbut (1886–1920), who, while they added nothing new to the World of Art system, amplified and enhanced it. Though they offered much in the way of brilliant technique, they were distinct imitators, manifesting the system's most salient shortcomings – its eclecticism, its proclivity for decorative embellishment, and its tendency to transform a living object into an elegant ornamental arabesque.

Another virtuoso artist, but of greater power and originality, was Dmitry Isidorovich Mitrokhin (1883–1973), who later became a guiding light in Soviet book illustration.

Graphic designs always dominated the work of Somov and Bakst as book illustrators, and almost completely absorbed the creative ventures of the younger generation of artists. However, the World of Art group gave rise to brilliant, thoughtful illustrators, who rose above the purely decorative embellishment to reveal and interpret the literary imagery in a most profound and original manner.

Here pride of place must go to Benois, who transmuted book graphics into a narrative, rather than purely decorative art. Far from overcharging the book with ornamental motifs, he, on the contrary, sought to invest his graphic embellishments with a definite narrative sense. One of the milestones in Benois' career was his cycle of drawings for Pushkin's poem *The Bronze Horseman*, which took him about twenty years to produce (1903–29). In fact, in none of his easel works will one encounter such powerful emotionality, such sensitive thought, such confident, consummate mastery. In these illustrations Pushkin's Petersburg imagery is imbued, as it were, with the reflections and emotions of a man of

141. Evgeny Lanceray. Road to Tsarskoye Selo in Anna Ioannovna's time. Headpiece for Benois' *Tsarskoye Selo in the Reign of Empress Elizaveta Petrovna*. 1904–12

142. Evgeny Lanceray. The taking of the Swedish grange. Headpiece for Benois' *Tsarskoye Selo in the Reign of Empress Elizaveta Petrovna*. 1904–10

enjoy success time and again, they had already rendered their basic service and were not destined, in principle, to make any new creative discoveries of importance. Further, their relationship with the new generation would be complex. In his articles about the Seventh Exhibition that had prodded the Union of Russian Artists to divide, Benois assailed not only the "rearguard" but also the youthful "vanguard." The World of Art's theoretical leader, who took a cautious and, on some matters, an irreconcilable stand, regarded the youth's searchings and uncertainties as symptoms of crisis. On the other hand, the younger artists whom Benois sincerely welcomed, such as, for instance, Petrov-Vodkin, or Saryan and Kuznetsov, who displayed their efforts at other shows, employed a different imagery and style than their seniors in the World of Art movement. Hence, when the works of these artists of different generations and trends were hung side by side at the shows mounted by the resurrected World of Art, stratification – though of a totally different order than in the Union – again became inevitable. Consequently, these shows were no longer integral, but grew more and more contradictory and motley with every

143. Evgeny Lanceray. Hadji Murat coming down the mountain. Illustration for Leo Tolstoy's *Hadji Murat*. 1913

161

the twentieth century. From the artist's point of view, the twists and turns of Pushkin's tale and the psychology of its chief character are of secondary significanse, as he attaches particular priority to the socio-historical motifs, conveying the poem's inner drama with a penetrating insight.

One more instance of an artist's inspired probing of the text is afforded by Lanceray's drawings, done between 1912 and 1915, for Leo Tolstoy's story *Hadji Murat*. In contrast to his earlier illustrations, often construed as ornamental vignettes, all the decorative elements in the Tolstoy book are of a narrative order following the plot of the story. To compete with the writer's expressive technique, Lanceray artfully varied his pictures, alternating a multifigured composition with an unpretentious landscape and a symbolical vignette with a socio-psychologically delineated portrait, all ingeniously depicted by sundry graphic means ranging from a lightly tinted pen-and-ink drawing to a dense, vivid watercolor.

The climaxing masterpiece of World of Art book graphics was Dobuzhinsky's cycle of illustrations for Dostoyevsky's *White Nights*, done in 1922. This work demonstrated a remarkable harmony of intentions between the writer and the artist, a harmony still closer to Dostoyevsky's concept than Lanceray's illustrations for the Tolstoy story. The illustrations present no episodes and hardly any concrete genre details; they rather convey a sensitive inspired understanding of the atmosphere which the writer sought to generate; the poetry is expressed throught cityscapes of St. Petersburg, which, as was noted earlier, was Dobuzhinsky's favorite subject matter.

Having completed our survey of the wide-ranging activities of the World of Art group, we may now attempt to summarize and assess its creative efforts and works of cultural enlightenment. In what way did the World of Art influence Russian art generally? Why do we today, at the close of the twentieth century, so greatly prize its artists? Wherein lies the historic significance of their experience?

Earlier we said that this historic significance should be viewed from two different, though interconnected, angles.

It so happened that at the turn of the nineteenth and twentieth centuries the World of Art group stood at the head of a broad cultural and aesthetical movement that reevaluated all the established values in Russia's visual arts, revised their creative problems, revitalized their principles, and outlined new pathways. Its influence was felt at the time in diverse realms of national culture. Our foregoing analysis demonstrated how the creative credo of the World of Art, initially developed in the fields of easel painting and graphics, gradually penetrated the decorative and applied arts, sculpture, and architecture, and also how vigorously it served to promote art criticism and art history.

We could even note the impact on early twentieth-century Russian literature and trace World of Art motifs in the poetry of Andrei Bely and Vyacheslav Ivanov, the story-telling of Fyodor Sologub and Zinaida Gippius, the verse and art criticism of Maximilian Voloshin, and especially so, in the poetry, prose, and plays of Mikhail Kuzmin. However, that would lead us far astray from our overall theme – the problems of the visual arts and how they were affected and resolved by the artists of the World of Art society.... Those intensive searches for a modern style so characteristic of the World of Art comprised a whole epoch in areas of culture that would appear far apart.

Note that the World of Art was but one very specific movement among several to be observed in the domain of Russian painting and graphics between the late 1890s and the early 1920s.

The artists allied with this movement introduced to Russian art an innovative, highly original method for creatively interpreting and typifying reality. In our analysis we endeavored to trace the evolution of a new concept of history painting. That was followed by innovation in landscape painting, and next, in portraiture. Noteworthy results were achieved in all these fields, as is well illustrated by the history paintings of Serov, Somov, Lanceray, Roerich, and Dobuzhinsky, by the watercolor landscapes of Benois and the engravings of Ostroumova-Lebedeva, by the portraits that Serov produced toward the end of his life, and by Somov's splendid graphic portraits. Works by these artists comprise part of the treasure-trove of pre-revolutionary Russian art. It would be only fair to likewise

144–147. Mstislav Dobuzhinsky. Illustrations for Dostoyevsky's *White Nights*. 1922

148. Alexander Benois. "Where lonely waters, struggling sought to reach the sea." Illustration for Pushkin's *The Bronze Horseman*. 1916–22

149. Alexander Benois. "The wide, majestic Neva labors, in granite clad." Illustration for Pushkin's *The Bronze Horseman*. 1916–22

150. Alexander Benois. "November's breath of autumn cold." Illustration for Pushkin's *The Bronze Horseman*. 1916–22

passing year, although placing before the eyes of the Russian spectator a plethora of fascinating artistic phenomena.

Yet, despite these conflicts and the future lot of the World of Art association, it had rendered a fine service to contemporary Russian art and had paved the way for the emergence on the art scene of the cream of the new generations, a point that Petrov-Vodkin most aptly and sincerely noted decades later (in the second half of the 1930s), in what was already a different age:

"The World of Art consummated its historic mission. We, its participants and contemporaries, can criticize it from various sides.... But whenever we recall how twenty years earlier, amidst the miasma of decadence, amidst the historical insipidity, blackness, and muddiness of painting, Sergei Diaghilev and his comrades equipped their ship, and how we, young fellows, choking in the obscurantism around us, felt wings sprout along with them, when we recall all that, we'll say: Yes, you chaps were fine fellows, you carried us on your shoulders up to the present."[88]

Alexander Kamensky

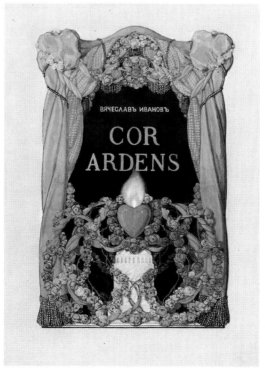

[88] Quoted from: *Valentin Serov in the Reminiscences....*, vol. 1, p. 514

151. Konstantin Somov. Frontispiece for Ivanov's *Cor Ardens*. 1907

place Kustodiev, Serebriakova, Sudeikin, and Sapunov on the list of oustanding painters and graphic artists of the period.

Yet it was not in the areas of easel painting and drawing that the artists of the World Art movement scored their greatest achievements. By their efforts, Bakst, Golovin, Benois, Roerich, Dobuzhinsky, Lanceray, Kustodiev, Sapunov, and Sudeikin caused the world to sit up and take notice of the pinnacles reached in Russian stage design.

And a signal contribution was made to Russian book illustration. Somov, Benois, Lanceray, and Dobuzhinsky, along with their juniors Narbut, Chekhonin, and Mitrokhin, revived book illustration and design in Russia, creating not only a range of exemplary works, but also a well-conceived, consistent system in this area.

Do not take all our praise to imply an apology for the World of Art movement. The worldview and artistic method of its members was limited by an inborn, one might say, fateful ceiling, above which they were not able to rise. Their entire oeuvre, so greatly divorced from the cardinal social issues of the time, was marked by sheer aestheticism. This, one feels, was responsible for the movement's short-lived history, and likewise for its non-recognition, until lately, by many Soviet art historians.

By now, though, the World of Art is a thing of the past, the distant past event, and the controversies that once raged around it have died down. From time's plateau one realizes more distinctly that the artists associated with this movement discharged a definite historical mission, and having exited from the stage, bequeathed a vast heritage that continues to remain of undisputed artistic importance.

Vsevolod Petrov

152. The annual meeting of the *World of Art*. Petrograd, 1914

153. Konstantin Somov. Harlequin and Death. 1907

OUTLINE BIOGRAPHIES OF ARTISTS WITH THEIR WORKS LISTED IN CHRONOLOGICAL ORDER

Léon Bakst

Born Lev Samoilovich Rosenberg on April 27 O.S. (May 9), 1866 in Grodno. His father was a merchant, his grandfather, who originally hailed from Paris, had been a fashionable tailor. In the 1870s, the family moved to St. Petersburg, where Lev spent his boyhood and youth. Between 1883 and 1887, he studied as an auditor at the Academy of Arts where his teachers were Isaac Asknazi, Karl Wenig, and Pavel Chistyakov. Between 1893 and 1896, he attended art classes in Paris at Jean-Leon Gérôme's studio and at Rodophe Julian's Academy. In 1890, he met Alexander Benois, with whose companions Konstantin Somov, Sergei Diaghilev, Walter Nouvel, Dmitry Filosofov, and Alfred Nurok he soon established a close relationship, joining their "Society for Self-Education." In 1891, he traveled to Germany, Belgium, France, Spain, and Italy. In 1897, he journeyed to North Africa and in 1907 to Greece with Valentin Serov. In 1906, he was elected a full member of the St. Petersburg Academy of Arts.

Bakst was a founding member of the World of Art association and took an active part in many of its initiatives. He contributed to numerous exhibitions from 1889 on, including the Exhibition of Russian and Finnish Watercolorists that Diaghilev mounted in 1898, and in all World of Art shows, from the first one in 1899.

---

* The medium of each work is indicated in parentheses, except in the case of oil paintings, set designs, and book illustrations.

1899 *Mountain Lake.** *Girl with a Doll*: Design for a poster (pastel). *Portrait of the Actress Maria Savina* (black chalk). *Portrait of Isaac Levitan* (lithograph). *Portrait of the Painter Philipp Maliavin* (lithograph).

1900 *Paris Welcomes Admiral Avellane. Portrait of the Poetess Zinaida Gippius* (lithograph). *Portrait of Anna Benois* (lithograph). Cover for Richard Muther's *History of Painting in the 19th Century*.

1901 *Siamese Ritual Dance* (watercolor). *Portrait of the Writer Vasily Rozanov* (pastel and gouache). Set (2nd Scene) and costume designs for an unrealized production of Delibes' ballet *Sylvia*. Half titles, head- and tailpieces for the *World of Art* and *Art Treasures of Russia* journals.

1902 *The Supper. Empress Elizaveta Petrovna and Catherine II Alexeyevna* (India ink). *Elizaveta Petrovna Hunting* (gouache). Design for the boudoir at the Contemporary Art Store and Exhibition. Costume designs for the pantomime *Le Cœur de la Marquise* to music by G. Guiraud at the St. Petersburg Hermitage Theater. Set and costume designs for Euripides' tragedy *Hippolytus* at the Mariinsky Theater, St. Petersburg.

1903 *Portrait of Lubov Gritsenko. Quay in Menton. View of Ventimiglia.* Set and costume designs for Josef Bayer's *Die Puppenfee* (The Fairy Doll) at the St. Petersburg Hermitage Theater. Design of the costume of Wilhelm Meister for Leonid Sobinov in Ambroise Thomas' opera *Mignon*. Covers for *Vesy* (Scales), Nos. 1–3, 1904 and the almanac *Severnye tsvety* (Northern Flowers)

1904 *Village Church. A Rainy Day in the Alps.* Set and costume designs for Sophocles' tragedy *Œdipus at Colonus* at the Alexandrinsky Theater and for Ida Rubinstein's debut in Sophocles' *Antigone* at the New Theater in St. Petersburg. Illustrations for Gogol's novella *The Nose*.

1905 *Portrait of Marina Gritsenko, the Artist's Stepdaughter. Portrait of Andrei Bely* (crayons and chalk). *Ida Rubinstein as Antigone* (watercolor). Cover for the *Northern Flowers* almanac.

1906 *Portrait of Sergei Diaghilev with His Nurse. Vase: Self-Portrait* (gouache). *Self-Portrait* (charcoal, red chalk and crayons). *The Downpour* (gouache and India ink). *Portrait of the Poetess Zinaida Gippius* (pencil, chalk, and red chalk). *Portrait of Konstantin Somov* (charcoal, crayons, and chalk). The *Elysium* decorative panel (watercolour and gouache). *The Elysium* curtain for Vera Komissarzhevskaya's Theater.

1907 *Delphi* (gouache). *Corfu. Knossos Port* (pencil). Drawings from life (lead pencil and watercolor) done while traveling in Greece. *Morning*

172

154. Léon Bakst. Elysium (decorative panel). 1906

155. Léon Bakst. Frontispiece for Blok's *Snow Mask* volume of verse. 1907

Nijinsky in the Diaghilev Company's production of Tchaikovsky's ballet *The Sleeping Beauty*.

1910 *The Red Sultana* (gouache and gold paint). *The Pink Sultana* (watercolor). Set and costume designs for the Diaghilev Company's productions of Robert Schumann's *Le Carnaval* and Nikolai Rimsky-Korsakov's *Schéhérazade*. Costume designs for the Firebird and the Tsarevna in the Diaghilev Company's production of Igor Stravinsky's ballet *L'Oiseau de Feu*. Costume designs for Anna Pavlova and Laurent Novikoff in Glazunov's *Bacchanale* at the Nobility Assembly in St. Petersburg, and for Vaslav Nijinsky in the Diaghilev Company's production of *Les Orientales* to the music of Edvard Grieg and Christian Sinding.

1911 *Portrait of Jean Cocteau* (pencil). Set and costume designs for the Diaghilev Company's productions of *Le Spectre de la Rose* (to the music of Weber's *Invitation to the Dance*) and Nikolai Tcherepnin's *Narcisse* as well as for the Ida Rubinstein Company's production of Claude Debussy's *Le Martyre de St. Sébastien* at the Théâtre du Chatêlet, Paris. Costume designs for Natasha Trukhanova and Vaslav Nijinsky in the Diaghilev Company's unrealized production of Paul Dukas' *La Peri*. Set designs for Arrigo Boito's *Mephistopheles* at the Royal Opera House, Covent Garden, London.

Toilette (watercolor and gouache). *Isadora Duncan Dancing* (India ink). Costume designs for Anna Pavlova in Camille Saint-Saëns' *Dying Swan*, Tamara Karsavina in Anton Arensky's *Torch Dance*, Anna Pavlova and Mikhail Obukov in *Chopiniana*, and Mathilda Kshessinska in Andrei Shcherbachov's *Eunice*, all at the Mariinsky Theater, St. Petersburg.

1908 *Terror Antiquus* (decorative panel). *Bacchanalia* (watercolor). *Portrait of Isadora Duncan* (pencil). *Portrait of Andriusha Bakst* (watercolor and India ink heightened with white). *Portrait of Anna Pavlova* (pencil). Costume designs for an unrealized production of Oscar Wilde's *Salome* at the Mikhailovsky Theater, St. Petersburg. Drawings for the journal *Satiricon*.

1909 *At the Beach. Portrait of Princess Olga Orlova* (pencil). *Portrait of the Writer Alexei Tolstoy* (lithograph). Set and costume designs for the Diaghilev Company's production of *Cléopâtre*. Costume designs for Act 3 of the Diaghilev Company's production of Alexander Serov's opera *Judith*. Costume designs for Tamara Karsavina and Vaslav

156. Léon Bakst. Costume design for Orpheus in an unrealized production of Roger-Ducasse's ballet. 1915

174

157. Léon Bakst. Costume design for Florestan in Schumann's *Le Carnaval*. 1910

158. Léon Bakst. Costume design for the dancer Tamara Karsavina. 1907

159. Léon Bakst. Costume design for the Blue God in Hahn's *Le Dieu Bleu*. 1912

160. Léon Bakst. Costume design for Richard Strauss' *Le Légende de Joseph*. 1914

161. Léon Bakst. The Supper. 1902

1912 *Portrait of the Marchesa Casati* (pencil). Set and costume designs for the Diaghilev Company's productions of Maurice Ravel's *Daphnis and Chloë*, Mily Balakirev's *Thamar*, and Claude Debussy's *L'Apres-midi d'un Faun* as well as for the Ida Rubinstein Company's productions of Oscar Wilde's *Salome* and Emile Verhaeren's *Helen of Sparta* at the Théatre du Châtelet, Paris. Costume designs for the Diaghilev Company's production of Reynaldo Hahn's *Le Dieu Bleu* at the Mariinsky Theater, St. Petersburg. Costume designs for the singer Maria Kuznetsova-Benois.

1913 Set designs for the Diaghilev Company's production of Debussy's ballet *Les Jeux*. *Self-Portrait* (pencil). Set and costume designs for the Ida Rubinstein Company's production of Gabriele d'Annunzio's *La Pisanella* at the Théâtre du Châtelet, Paris.

1914 *Portrait of Léonide Massine* (pencil). Costume designs for the Diaghilev Company's production of Richard Strauss' *Le Légende de Joseph*.

1915 Set and costume designs for an unrealized production of Roger-Ducasse's *Orpheus*, and for the Diaghilev Company's revised productions of Tchaikovsky's ballet *The Sleeping Beauty* and Rimsky-Korsakov's *Schéhérazade*.

1916 *The Yellow Sultana* (watercolor, pencil, gold and silver paint).

1917 *Pablo Picasso, a Caricature* (pencil). *Portrait of Virginia Zucchi*. Costume designs for the Diaghilev Company's production of Domenico Scarlatti's *Les Femmes de Bonne Humeur* and an unrealized production of Rimsky-Korsakov's opera *Sadko*.

1918 Costume designs for the Diaghilev Company's production of *La Boutique Fantasque* to the music of Gioacchino Rossini.

1919 Costume designs for Anna Pavlova in Gino Marinuzzi's *Old-Style Minuet* and M. Padilla's *Mexican Dance*.

1920 *Portrait of the Ballerina Anna Pavlova* (crayons).

1921 *Portrait of Ida Rubinstein* (watercolor, charcoal, and gouache). *Portrait of the Writer Ivan Bunin* (pencil). Set and costume designs for the Diaghilev Company's revised production of *The Sleeping Beauty*.

1922 *Judith with the Head of Holofernes* (watercolor). *The Moscow Kremlin* (watercolor). Costume designs for *Artémis Troublée* at the Paris Opera.

1923 Set and costume designs for Gabriele d'Annunzio's *Phèdre* and for the ballet *The Magic Night* (to the music of Chopin) at the Paris Opera. Set designs for Racine's *Phèdre* at the Théâtre de la Renaissance, Paris.

1924 Costume designs for the ballet *Istar* to the music of Vincent d'Indy at the Paris Opera. Bakst died in Paris on December 27, 1924.

162. Léon Bakst. Portrait of the Poetess Zinaida Gippius. 1906

163. Léon Bakst. Illustration for Gogol's novella *The Nose*. 1904

Alexander Benois

Alexander Nikolayevich Benois was born on April 25 O.S. (May 3), 1870 in St. Petersburg. His father, Prof. Nikolai Leontyevich Benois, was an academician and architect, President of the St. Petersburg Society of Architects. His mother, Kamilla Albertovna, was the daughter of the architect Kavos. Between 1885 and 1890s, he attended Karl Mai's gymnasium where he befriended his classmates Walter Nouvel, Dmitry Filosofov, and Konstantin Somov. A little later, this group was joined by Sergei Diaghilev, Léon Bakst, Alfred Nurok, and Evgeny Lanceray.

In the autumn of 1887, aspired to become a stage designer, he entered the Academy of Arts, but disillusioned, dropped out a mere four months later. Between 1890 and 1894, he studied law with Filosofov, Nouvel, and Diaghilev at the University of St. Petersburg. He made his debut in the realm of literature with an essay on nineteenth-century Russian painting to supplement Richard Muther's *History of Painting in the 19th Century* (his main writings are listed in the bibliographical section). In 1890, he visited Germany for the first time, then revisited it in 1894, in which year he also traveled to Switzerland and Italy. In late 1896, he went with Somov and Bakst to Paris where he stayed until the autumn of 1899. He co-drafted the program for the *World of Art* journal, of which he became editor and a regular contributor. He exhibited from 1892, and participated in most of the World of Art shows.

1897 *The Last Walks of Louis XIV* series (watercolor, gouache, charcoal, and gold paint.

1898 *"The King Takes His Walk in Every Weather..."* (watercolor). *Masquerade in the Reign of Louis XIV* (pastel). Illustrations and headpiece for Pushkin's *The Queen of Spades*.

1899 *The Chornaya River* (three verions, watercolor). *The Country House of Albert Benois and Evgeny Lanceray* (watercolor). *Portrait of the Artist Valentin Serov* (pencil). Illustrations for Hoffmann's *Der Goldene Topf* (The Golden Pot).

1900 *Peterhof. The Left-Hand Pond in Front of the Grand Palace* (watercolor and pencil heightened with white). *Monplaisir. The Dining Room* (watercolor and pencil). *Monplaisir* (gouache, pencil, and charcoal). *The Dining Room in Marly* (watercolor, pastel, and pencil). *Marly* (gouache). *Marly. The Garden* (watercolor). *Marly. The Pond* (watercolor). *Marly* (gouache). *Peterhof* (watercolor). *Peterhof Park* (watercolor). *Fountain in Peterhof* (watercolor). *The English Palace* (watercolor). *The Pond in Front of the Grand Palace in Peterhof* (watercolor). *The Hermitage in Peterhof* (watercolor). *Portrait of Walter Nouvel* (pencil). *View onto the Terrace of the Grand Palace* (pencil). Set and costume designs for Alexander Taneyev's *Cupid's Revenge* at the Hermitage Theater, St. Petersburg, performed in 1902.

1901 *Avenue in Autumn. Oranienbaum* (tempera). *Oranienbaum. The Monkey Cabinet in the Tobogganing Hill Pavilion* (pastel). *Oranienbaum. The Great Hall in the Tobogganing Hill Pavilion* (pastel). *Park at Oranienbaum* (tempera, pastel, gouache, and pencil). *Oranienbaum* (gouache). *Woods*: set design for an unrealized production of Scene 1 of Delibes' *Sylvia*. Illustrations (in collaboration with Lanceray) for Nikolai Kutepov's *The Tsarist and Imperial Hunt in Russia. Late 17th and 18th Centuries*.

1902 *The Temple of Friendship in Winter. Anteroom of the Grand Palace in Pavlovsk* (pastel, charcoal, and gouache). *The Pavlovsk Palace* (watercolor). *The Grand Circles. Pavlovsk* (watercolor and pencil). *The Bip Fortress* (watercolor). *Peterhof in the Eighteenth Century*: Half-title drawing (India ink heightened with white). *The Gardens of Diana*: Sketches of a panel for a dining room at the Contemporary Art Store and Exhibition in St. Petersburg (watercolor and gouache). Set and

164. Alexander Benois. Set design for the seashore in Stravinsky's *Le Rossignol*. 1914

costume designs for Richard Wagner's *Götterdämmerung* at the Mariinsky Theater in St. Petersburg produced in 1903.

1903 *Villa d'Este in Tivoli* (watercolor and pencil). *Evening in Rome* (watercolor). *St. Dominic's Stairs* (watercolor and pencil). *Villa Borghese* (watercolor). *Villa Médicis* (watercolor). *Landscape at Albano* (watercolor). *Anzio Harbor* (watercolor). *The Neva Embankment by the Senate* (charcoal). *The Fontanka in the Days of Catherine II* (watercolor). *Empress Elizaveta Petrovna Taking a Walk through the Streets of St. Petersburg* (watercolor). *The Changing of the Guard in Front of the Winter Palace in the Reign of Paul I* (watercolor). Illustrations for Pushkin's *The Bronze Horseman*.

1904 *Toys* series of drawings (pencil and watercolor). *A Nook in St. Petersburg* (watercolor).

Petrouchka Street Show (pencil). *Stepan Yaremich at a Recital of Modern Music* (pencil). *Anna Ostroumova-Lebedeva and the Artist's Daughter in Gorki* (pencil and India ink). *Paris Boulevard* (watercolor). Designs for the interior decoration of the exhibition at the Tauride Palace (India ink and pencil; watercolor and pencil). Illustrations for Pushkin's *The Captain's Daughter* and Fenimore Cooper's *The Last of the Mohicans*. Cover, title page, and illustrations for an ABC book.

1905 *Seashore: Primel. Rural Landscape: Primel. Versailles: The Palace. Versailles. Fountain. In the Park at Versailles. Autumn in Versailles. Cliffs* (watercolor). *Sunset in Primel* (watercolor). *Primel. The Valley* (watercolor). *Water Parterre in Versailles* (watercolor and gouache). *Autumn Evening in Versailles* (gouache). *Allegory of the River. Versailles* (watercolor). Frontispiece and illustrations for

179

165. Alexander Benois. The Gambling House. Illustration for Pushkin's *The Queen of Spades*. 1905

166. Alexander Benois. Costume design
for Truffaldino in Goldoni's *The Servant
of Two Masters*. 1920

Pushkin's *The Bronze Horseman*. Illustrations for
Pushkin's *The Queen of Spades*.

1906 *Italian Comedy: The Indiscreet Punchinello.
Landscape in Brittany. Evening in Brittany.
Brittany. Breton Dances. The Bath of the Marquise*
(gouache, pen and ink). *The King's Walk* (gouache,
watercolor, gold and silver paint, pen and ink,
pencil). *The Chinese Pavilion. The Jealous Man*
(gouache, pen and ink). *The Pyramid Fountain in
May* (gouache, watercolor, and pencil). *Le Trianon.
The Ponds* (watercolor). *Versailles* (gouache). *Old
Man in an Armchair* (India ink heightened with
white). *Self-Portrait* (pencil). *Konstantin Balmont in
Primel* (pencil). Head- and tailpieces for *The Golden
Fleece* journal.

1907 *Death* series (India ink and watercolor). *Paul
I and His Retinue Walking in the Menagerie at
Gatchina. Nikolai Pavlovich Walking with Alexandra Fyodorovna in Gatchina* (watercolor and
gouache). *Parade in the Reign of Paul I* (gouache).
Harlequinade (tempera). *Perseus Fountain* (watercol-
or). *Portrait of Sergei Diaghilev* (red chalk). Set
and costume designs for Tcherepnin's *Le Pavillon
d'Armide* produced at the Mariinsky Theater, St.
Petersburg. Curtain design for the Antique Theater
in St. Petersburg. Costume designs for Evreinov's
Fair on St. Denis' Day at the Antique Theater, St.
Petersburg. Frontispiece for *The Theater. A Book
About the New Theater*. Illustrations for Kutepov's

The Tsarist and Imperial Hunt in Russia. Late 17th and 18th Centuries. Covers, illustrations and headpieces for Dmitry Merezhkovsky's *Paul I.*

1908 *Alexander I Feeding Birds in the Aviary at Tsarskoye Selo* (watercolor and gouache). *The Kiss* (gouache). *Apollo and Daphne* (watercolor and pencil). Portraits of the artists Bakst, Somov, and Yaremich, the singer Sobinov, and the composer Tcherepnin (pencil). *Self-Portrait* (pencil). Sketches for a bust of Peter the Great and the statuary for embellishing the façade of the Peter the Great School in St. Petersburg (watercolor). Design of a panel for the pediment of the Architectural and Industrial Fair Building in St. Petersburg (watercolor). Set and costume designs for the production, by Benois and Komissarzhevsky, of Franz Grillparzer's *Die Ahnfrau* (The Ancestress) at Vera Komissarzhevskaya's Theater, St. Petersburg. Illustrations for Kutepov's *The Tsarist and Imperial Hunt in Russia. Late 17th and 18th Centuries.*

1909 *Village Landlord* (gouache). *Our Dacha in Oranienbaum* (watercolor). *Portrait of the Artist Stepan Yaremich* (red chalk). Set and costume designs for the productions by Diaghilev's Company of Tcherepnin's *Le Pavillon d'Armide* and Chopin's *Sylphides (Chopiniana).* Frontispiece and illustrations for H. de Régnier's *Contes de Marquise d'Amercoeur. The Gardens at Tsarskoye Selo in the Times of Elizaveta Petrovna:* headpiece for Benois' *Tsarskoye Selo.*

1910 *Suvorov's Camp* (gouache). *A Street in St. Petersburg in the Times of Peter I* (gouache). *Peter I Walking in the Summer Gardens* (gouache). *Versailles* (gouache and watercolor). *Peterhof* (watercolor). *Winter in Finland* (watercolor). *Mountain Hamlet* (India ink). *A Venetian Garden* (gouache). Set and costume designs for the production by Diaghilev's Company of Adam's *Giselle.* Frontispiece, half titles, illustrations, head- and tailpieces for Pushkin's *The Queen of Spades.*

1911 *Mountain Lake. Lugano* (watercolor). *Landscape near Bologna* (gouache and watercolor). *The Church of Santa Maria di Torello. Interior* (watercolor). *Mountain Landscape. Monte Generoso* (watercolor). *A Church in the Mountains* (watercolor). *A Street in Montagnola* (pencil). Portraits of the artists Boris Anisfeld and Mstislav Dobuzhinsky (pencil). *Michel Fokine Teaching Antique Pas for the Ballet "Narcisse"* (pencil). Set and costume designs for the production by Diaghilev's Company of Igor Stravinsky's *Petrouchka.*

1912 *Pink Cottage in Cresogno* (watercolor). *Venice. The Doge's Palace* (watercolor). *Canal in Venice* (pencil, watercolor, and gouache). *Pavilion in Vicenza* (watercolor). *Path in Belvedere* (watercolor). *Church of San Pietro in Bambio* (watercolor and pencil). *Venetian Fête in the Sixteenth Century.* Set designs for an unrealized production of Debussy's *Les Jeux* (Festivities). Set and costume designs for an unrealized production of Molière's *Tartuffe,* a production of Molière's *Le Malade imaginaire* at the Art Theater of Moscow, and the Molière Show of 1913.

1913 *Mountain Lake. Lugano* (watercolor). *View of the Bay* (watercolor). *Embankment in Anzio* (watercolor). *Lake at the Foot of the Mountains* (pencil and sepia). *The Simplon Pass* (gouache). *Self-Portrait* (watercolor and pencil heghtenend with white). *Nikolai Remizov at a "Satiricon" Meeting*

167. Alexander Benois. Costume design for the dancing girl in Stravinsky's *Petrouchka.* 1911

168. Alexander Benois. Costume design for Stravinsky's *Le Rossignol.* 1914

181

169. Alexander Benois. Hermann in the House of the Countess.
Illustration for Pushkin's *The Queen of Spades*. 1905

170. Alexander Benois. Set design for Scene 2 of Tcherepnin's
Le Pavillon d'Armide. 1907

171. Alexander Benois. Venetian Fête in the Sixteenth Century. Set design
for an unrealized production of Debussy's *Les Jeux* (Festivities). 1912

(pencil). *Portrait of the Artist Nicholas Roerich*
(pencil). *The Artist Anna Ostroumova-Lebedeva with
Benois' Wife and Son* (crayons). *Portrait of Sergei
Diaghilev* (pencil). *Portrait of the Actress Maria
Lilina* (pencil). Set and costume designs for the
Moscow Art Theater's productions of Molière's *Le
Mariage forcé* in the Molière Show and of Goldoni's
La Locandiera.

1914 *Bay* (watercolor). *Falesi* (watercolor). *Saint-
Jean-de-Luz* (watercolor). *Landscape with a
Belltower* (watercolor and India ink heightened with
white). Designs for an unrealized panel at Moscow's
Kazan Railway Station (oil, gouache, tempera, and
watercolor heightened with white). Set and costume
designs for the production by Diaghilev's Company
of Stravinsky's *Le Rossignol* and for the Moscow Art
Theater's Pushkin Show (1915).

1915 *The Tarakhtash Valley. Soudak* (watercolor).
The Soudak Fort (watercolor). *Terrace of the
Baidaké Countryhouse in Soudak. Early Morning*
(pastel). *Novy Svet* (Crimea). *Bay Between Cliffs*
(watercolor). *Self-Portrait* (crayons). Portraits of the
artists Stepan Yaremich, Anna Ostroumova-Lebedeva, Dmitry Mitrokhin, and Georgi Narbut (pencil).
Portrait of Anna Benois, the Artist's Wife (red chalk
and blue pencil).

1916 *Mountain Landscape* (watercolor). *Kapsel.
Shore* (watercolor). *Seashore* (watercolor). Set and
costume designs for Chopin's *Les Sylphides* (*Chopiniana*) and sets for Stravinsky's *Petrouchka* at the
Royal Theater in Madrid.

1917 *Peterhof Fountains* (gouache). *The Village of
Puzyryovo* (watercolor). *Puzyryovo. House in the
Woods* (watercolor). *Peter I on the Shore of the Gulf
of Finland* (gouache). *The Neptune Fountain in
Peterhof* (watercolor). *Sergei Prokofiev at the Piano*
(pencil). Colophon for the *Raduga* (Rainbow)
Publishing House. Illustrations for the fairy tale
Tom Thumb.

1918 *Peterhof* (watercolor). *The Artist's Studio*
(India ink). *The Grand Canal in Peterhof*
(pencil and India ink). Covers for *The Palace
Museum of Tsarskoye Selo* (Part I: *The Alexander
Palace*).

1919 *Statues Outside the Gatchina Palace. Sunset*
(watercolor). *In the Gardens of the Villa Borghese*
(watercolor and India ink). *Fireworks in the Park*
(pastel). Set and costume designs for the renewed
1907 production of Tcherepnin's *Le Pavillon
d'Armide*. Cover and illustrations for Pushkin's *The
Captain's Daughter*.

1920 *Oscar Waldhauer in Gatchina* (pencil). Set
designs for Stravinsky's *Petrouchka* at the Bolshoi
Theater, Moscow. Set and costume designs for
Merezhkovsky's *The Tsarevich Alexis*, Shakespeare's
The Merchant of Venice, and Goldoni's *The Servant
of Two Masters* at the Bolshoi Drama Theater,
Petrograd.

1921 *The Temple of Friendship in Pavlovsk*
(watercolor). *View of the Moika* (watercolor and
pencil). *Portrait of Sergei Ernst* (pencil). Set and
costume designs for his own productions of Tchaikovsky's *The Queen of Spades* at the Opera and
Ballet Theater, Petrograd, and of the Molière Show
at the Bolshoi Drama Theater, Petrograd.

172. Alexander Benois. Lake Primel. Brittany. 1905

1922 *Belltower of the St. Nicholas Cathedral* (watercolor and pencil). *Versailles Park* (watercolor). *The Artist's Study* (watercolor).Set and prop designs for Shakespeare's *Julius Caesar* at the Bolshoi Drama Theater, Petrograd. Set and costume designs for the Diaghilev Company's production of Tchaikovsky's *The Marriage of Aurora*. The ornamentation and illustration of Pushkin's *The Bronze Horseman* (Completion of work started in 1916).

1923 *Seine Embankment* (watercolor). *Moika Embankment* (watercolor and pencil). *Les Tuileries* (gouache and watercolor). Portraits of the artists Vladimir Tatlin and Pavel Filonov, and of the art historians Abram Efros, Oscar Waldhauer, and Igor Grabar (pencil). Set and costume designs for Henri Meilhac and L. Halevy's *Warming Pan* and Molière's *Le Bourgeois Gentilhomme* at the Bolshoi Drama Theater, Petrograd, and for the Ida Rubinstein Company's production of Alexandre Dumas' *La Dame aux camélias* at the Sarah Bernhard Théâtre, Paris.

1924 *The Grand Palace in Peterhof* (watercolor). *Versailles Palace on a Winter Evening* (watercolor). *Houses at Versailles* (watercolor). *The Artists Albert Benois and Zinaida Serebryakova* (pencil). *Portrait of the Artist Alexander Shervashidze* (pencil). Set and costume designs for an unrealized production of Goldoni's *The Fan* and Adam's *Giselle* at the Paris Opera, and for the Diaghilev Company's productions of Gounod's *Philémon and Baucis* and *Le Médicin malgré lui.*
Throughout his life Benois also staged various theatrical productions. Together with other directors, he produced Grilparzer's *Die Ahnfrau* at Vera Komissarzhevskaya's Theater in St. Petersburg, The Pushkin Show at the Art Theater in Moscow, Merezhkovskys's *The Tsarevich Alexis* at the Bolshoi

173. Alexander Benois. Frontispiece for *The Theater. A Book About the New Theater.* 1907

Drama Theater in Petrograd, Tchaikovsky's *The Queen of Spades* at the Opera and Ballet Theater in Petrograd, and Molière's *Le Bourgeois Gentilhomme* at the Drama Theater, Petrograd.
From 1918 till 1926, Benois was Keeper of the Hermitage Department of French and English Paintings. From 1926, he lived in France where he continued to work as a stage designer, painter, graphic artist, and art critic.
Benois died in Paris on February 9, 1960.

Ivan Bilibin

Ivan Yakovlevich Bilibin was born on August 4 O.S. (16), 1876 into the family of a naval doctor in Tarkhovka, near Sestroretsk, outside St. Petersburg. Between 1895 and 1898, he attended classes at the School of the Society for the Encouragement of the Arts. Part of 1898 was spent at Anton Ažbè's studio in Munich. Later in the year and up to 1900 he took courses under Ilya Repin at the private school run by Princess Tenisheva. Simultaneously, between 1896 and 1900, he studied law at the University of St. Petersburg. In 1898, he traveled in Switzerland and Italy. Between 1902 and 1904, he audited Ilya Repin's studio at the Academy of Arts' Higher Art School. Summers between 1902 and 1904 were spent in field expeditions to Vologda, Arkhangelsk, and Olonets provinces, which gathered works of folk arts and crafts and photographed old wooden buildings for the Ethnography Department of the Russian Museum. He took part in World of Art shows from 1900 on.

1900 Design for the first page, headpiece on the second page, and picture for the riddle "Not of princely breed, but wears a crown" in the *Russian Reader* published in 1901.

1901 *Peasant* (lead pencil and watercolor). *Young Peasant Woman, At the Well, Easter Morning,* and *Christ Hath Arisen* (picture postcards for the Society of St. Eugenia). *Prince Vladimir Gives a Feast* and *The Siege of the Trinity-St. Sergius Lavra* for the *Russian Folk Pictures* (art book).

1902 *Thomas' Village. Kem Cathedral. Volgá with His Troops,* a version of an illustration for the heroic poem *Volgá* (watercolor and India ink). *Prince Vladimir Gives a Feast, Ilya of Murom, Dobrynia Nikitich, Alyosha Popovich, Mikhailo Potyk,* and *Churilo Plenkovich* (picture postcards for the Society of St. Eugenia). Covers for Arthur Schnitzler's *The Wise Man's Wife* and *Living Hours* and for E. Steinger's *The New Drama. Ibsen, Hauptmann, Maeterlinck, Sudermann.*

1903 *Evening.* Covers for the journals *Zhurnal dlya vsekh* (Everyman's Magazine, No. 1–5, 1904), *Pechatnoye iskusstvo* (Printer's Art, April 1903), and *Rossiya v kartinkakh* (Russia in Pictures, issues 1–8).

1904 Set and costume designs for Rimsky-Korsakov's *The Snow Maiden* at the Prague National Theater. Covers, tailpieces, half titles, illustrations, and headpieces for *The Bylina of Dobrynia Nikitich, The Bylina of Ilya of Murom (Everyman's Magazine,* Nos. 4–11, 1904 and No. 5, 1905), Mikhail Lermontov's *Song of the Tsar Ivan Vasilyevich, the Young Oprichnik and the Brave Merchant Kalashni-*

kov, *Letopis voiny s Yaponiyei* (Chronicle of the War with Japan, Nos. 1–40, 1904 and Nos. 41–84, 1905), and the *World of Art* journal (1904, No. 11).

1904–06 Design and illustrations for Pushkin's *Tale of Tsar Saltan.*

1905 *Tsar Dadon* cartoon (cover) and *Sic Transit* cartoon for *Zhupel* (Bugbear, No. 2). *Alkonost and Sirin, Birds of Paradise* (picture postcards for the Society of St. Eugenia). *A Married Woman from Olonets Province, A Young Vologda Peasant Woman in Festive Dress,* and *A Vologda Maiden in Holiday Attire* (picture postcards for the same society).

1906 Covers, title pages, and tailpieces for A. Amfiteatrov's *Modern Fairy Tales,* Benois' *Russian School of Painting* (vol. 1–2, issues 1–2), George Kennan's *Siberia and Exile* (vol. 1), Fyodor Sologub's *Political Tittle-Tales,* Alexei Tolstoy's *Complete Works* (4 volumes) and his *Torches* (book 1). The cartoon *An Ass (Equus Asinus) 1/20 Natural Size* for *Zhupel* (No. 3). Cover, title page, headpieces and half titles for the *Golden Fleece* (No. 7–9). Cover and title page for *Polarnaya zvezda* (The North Star, No. 12–14).

1906–07, 1910 Designs and illustrations for Pushkin's *The Tale of the Golden Cockerel.*

1907 Set and costume designs for Ruteboeuf's *Le Miracle de Théophile* at the Antique Theater. Covers and title pages for Konstantin Balmont's *Birds of the Air, The Living Word Reader,* A. Kamensky's *Short Stories,* and *Beneath Vaulted Ceilings, a Collection of Tales, Poems, and Reminiscences by Inmates of the Old Schlüsselburg Fortress.* Headpieces for

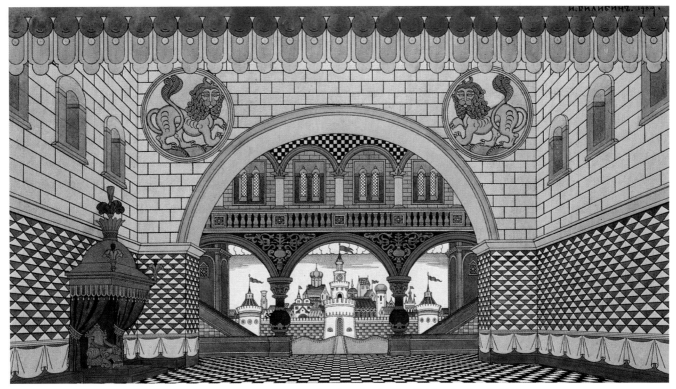

174. Ivan Bilibin. Dadon's Palace. Set design for Act 1 of Rimsky-Korsakov's *The Golden Cockerel*. 1909

A. Uspensky's "Devil in Old Russian Representations" (*The Golden Fleece*, No. 1) and for Balmont's "October" (*The Golden Fleece*, No. 11–12).

1908 *Winter. Learning Is Light* (panel). *Building Adorns Towns* (panel). *Cornwall Study* (lead pencil, watercolor, and gouache). Russian costume designs for the Diaghilev Company's production of Mussorgsky's *Boris Godunov* at the Paris Opera. Set and costume designs for the production of Fyodor Sologub's' *Honor and Vengeance* at the Lukomorye Theater, St. Petersburg. Covers, title pages, and tailpieces for Vol. 5 of Mikhail Artsybashev's *Collected Works*, Konstantin Balmont's *The Green Garden*, Frank Wedekind's *Plays*, Rudyard Kipling's *Selected Stories*, Alexander Kuprin's *Stories for Children*, Sergei Makovsky's *Pages of Art Criticism* (book 2), Octave Mirbeau's *Travels in a Motorcar*, and Sergei Sergeyev-Tsensky's *Death*.

1908–09 Set and costume designs for the production of Rimsky-Korsakov's *The Golden Cockerel* by S. Zimin's Opera Company, Moscow.

1909 Costume designs for the production by the Diaghilev Company of *Le Festin* (The Feast) at the Théâtre du Châtelet, Paris. Covers and headpieces for Vol. 1 of Grabar's *History of Russian Art*, Part 3 of *The Living Word Reader*, Book 9 of *The Almanac of Literature and Art*, V. Lukomsky's *Historico-Archeological Congress in Kostroma*, Friedrich Nietzsche's *Complete Works*, Herbert Wells' *Complete Works*, and Alexander Ertel's *Collected Works*.

1910 *Cottage* (watercolor). *Winter: The Crimea. Paths to Uzunju*. Costume designs for *Russian Dances* as performed by Anna Pavlova and Mikhail Mordkin. Covers for Gabriele d'Annunzio's *Col-*

lected Works, Herzyg's *Poems*, Zachinyayev's *Little Primer*, and Fyodorov's *Surf* and *Harvest*.

1911 *Moonlit Stream. Yaman-Kola: Sunset.* Costume designs for Lope de Vega's *Fuente ovejuna* and Pedro Calderon's *The Purgatory of St. Patrick* at the Antique Theater, St. Petersburg, and for the production of Alexei Verstovsky's *Tomb of Askold* by S. Zimin's Opera Company, Moscow. *The Glorious City of Ledenets, The Marvelous Paladin Bova the Prince, Easter-Cake Town*, and *The Dragon Gorynych* (picture postcards for the Society of St. Eugenia).

1912 Set and costume designs for S. Zimin's Opera Company's production of Verstovsky's *Tomb of Askold. The Last Bulwark* cartoon for the cover of the *Satirikon* (No. 47, 1912) and the *Austrian Tactic* cartoon for the cover of *Solntse Rossii* (The Sun of Russia, No. 5, 1912).

1913–14 Designs for the decoration of halls in the State Bank in Nizhny Novgorod (watercolor and gold paint). Set and costume designs for Glinka's *Ruslan and Ludmila* at the People's House Theater, St. Petersburg. Designs and illustrations for Vol. 6 of Grabar's *History of Russian Art, Kostroma, a Historical Outline* by V. Lukomsky and *Description of Old Art Monuments* by G. Lukomsky, and *Moscow and Village in Engravings and Lithographs. 1800–1850.*
Set and costume designs for Rimsky-Korsakov's *Sadko* at the People's House Theater, Petrograd.

1915 *Fir Trees: Study. Stream.* Designs for the ceiling painting of Moscow's Kazan Railway Station.

1916 *The Crimea. Mountain Peaks* (watercolor).

175. Ivan Bilibin. Tailpiece for Benois' *Russian School of Painting*. 1906

176. Ivan Bilibin. Bill: Historical Exhibition of Artworks. 1904

1917 *Batiliman. Mt. Kalanykh-Kaya* (watercolor). *December in Batiliman. Whirling Snow* (lead pencil and watercolor). *The Crimea. Batiliman. A Juniper Tree* (watercolor). *The Crimea. Mt. Kush-Kaya* (watercolor). *Brook* (lead pencil and watercolor). *Sugarloaf Cliffs. Laspi* (watercolor). *Poplars. The Baidar Valley* (watercolor). Designs for the new state seal of Russia (lead pencil). Design for the new Russian coat of arms (lead pencil and watercolor).

1918 *The Baidar Valley* (watercolor). *The Baidar Valley. The Crimea* (watercolor). *The Crimea. An Old Juniper Tree* (charcoal). *Portrait of N. Chiriko-va. Old Walnut Trees: The Crimea* (watercolor). *Chernomor Carrying Ruslan through the Air*: Illustration for Pushkin's, *Ruslan and Ludmila* (India ink).

1919 *Crimean Landscape. Portrait of Ludmila Chirikova. Pine Trees and Cliffs. Mountain Path.* Illustrations for the Russian folktale *Go There I Know Not Where.*

1920 Panel: *Worship of the Byzantine Emperor and Empress. Portrait of Groppi.*

1921 Iconostasis of the Greek Hospital church in Cairo. *Cairo. The Citadel* (watercolor). *Portrait of an Old Arab. A Little Street in Cairo* (watercolor). The initial *A* (India ink).

1922 Panel: *St. Boris and St. Gleb Aboard a Ship.* Panel: *Yaroslavna's Lament. Portrait of a Little Girl with a Dog. Portrait of an Old Arab* (lead pencil). *Portrait of Ludmila Chirikova* (black

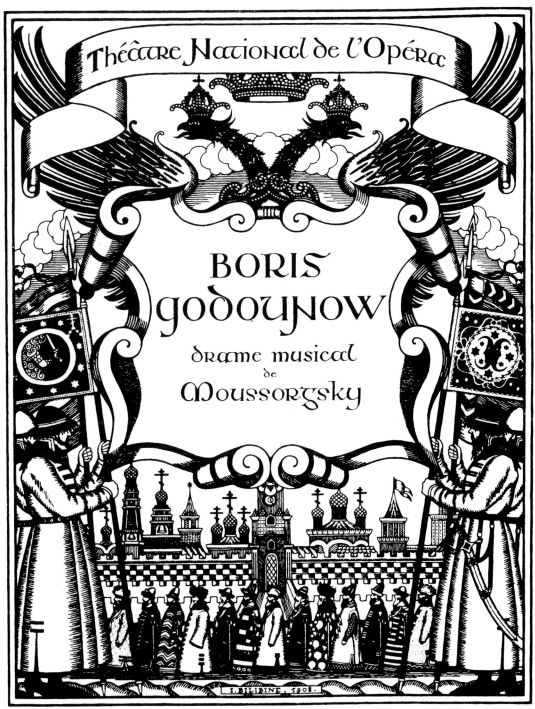

Théâtre National de l'Opéra

BORIS GODOUNOW drame musical de Moussorgsky

I. BILIBINE. 1908.

177. Ivan Bilibin. Program cover for Mussorgsky's *Boris Godunov*. 1908

chalk). *Rose* (lead pencil). *Fellah* (lead pencil). The initials *Z* and *O* (India ink). Colophon for E. Mpenaki.

1923 Panel: *Horseman* (watercolor). *Boy Fellah* (lead pencil). Set and costume designs for the Pavlova Company's production of Tcherepnin's *Russian Fairy Tale*. Illustrations for the Russian folktale *The Two Old Men*.

1924 Sketches (lead pencil). Panel: *St. Boris and St. Gleb* (watercolor). *Egypt. The Pyramids* (watercolor and lead pencil). *Monastery of St. George. Palestine* (watercolor). *Monastery of St. Sabas* (watercolor). *Palestine. Lake Tiberias* (watercolor). *Old Olive Trees. Lebanon* (watercolor).

In 1920, Bilibin settled in Cairo and then moved to Alexandria. Between 1925 and 1936, he lived in Paris where he designed productions of Rimsky-Korsakov's operas *The Tale of Tsar Saltan* and *The Tale of the Invisible City of Kitezh and the Maid Fevronia*, Borodin's *Prince Igor*, and Mussorgsky's *Boris Godunov*. He also designed sets and costumes for Stravinsky's ballet *The Firebird*.

In 1936, Bilibin returned to Russia, where until his death he headed the Graphic Art Studio at the Leningrad Institute of Painting, Sculpture and Architecture of the All-Russia Academy of Arts. He likewise took part in the decoration of the Palace of Soviets.

Bilibin died in besieged Leningrad on February 7, 1942.

Alexander Golovin

Alexander Yakovlevich Golovin was born on February 17 O.S. (March 1), 1863 in Moscow into the family of an instructor at the Peter the Great Agricultural Academy. From 1881 to 1889, he attended the Moscow School of Painting, Sculpture and Architecture where he studied architecture and later took up painting under Vladimir Makovsky and Illarion Prianishnikov. In 1889, he went to Paris where he enrolled in the Academie Colarossi and, in 1897, took courses at the private school of Witti, under Raphael Colin. In 1899–1900, he worked at Abramtsevo and executed settings for Savva Mamontov's Russian Private Opera. He lived in Moscow until 1901, then moved to St. Petersburg where he worked as stage designer for the Imperial Theaters. He frequently traveled abroad, to France, Germany, Italy, and Spain. He first exhibited in 1893, participating in World of Art shows from 1899 on.

1898 *Portrait of Maria Golovina* (pastel). *Portrait of Egishe Tatevosyan* (charcoal).

1899 Covers for the *World of Art* journal. Applied artworks at the Abramtsevo Colony. With K. Korovin designed the interior of the handicrafts sections of the Russian Pavilion at the Paris World Fair.

1900 *In the Garden. Rivulet* (tempera). Sets (Acts 2 and 3) and costumes designed for Alexander Dargomyzhsky's *The Rusalka* (Mermaid) and sets for A. Koreshchenko's *The House of Ice* at the Bolshoi Theater, Moscow. Set designs for Scenes 1 and 6 and costume designs for Minkus' *Don Quixote* at the Bolshoi Theater, Moscow. Design for the *Floating Swans* majolica frieze on the Hotel Metropole, Moscow (watercolor).

1901 Set designs for Acts 1 and 3 of Tchaikovsky's *Swan Lake* and Rimsky-Korsakov's *Maid of Pskov* at the Bolshoi Theater, Moscow. The last-named sets were transferred to the Mariinsky Theater in St. Petersburg in 1904. Costume of Mephistopheles for Fyodor Chaliapin in Boito's opera on his La Scala tour in Milan. Set and costume design for César Cui's *The Mandarin's Son* at the New Theater, Moscow.

1902 *Spanish Girl* (watercolor and India ink, heightened with white). Set designs for Act 3 of Tchaikovsky's *Swan Lake* at the Chinese Theater, Tsarskoye Selo. Set designs for Rimsky-Korsakov's *Mozart and Salieri* at the Mariinsky Theater, St. Petersburg; reused at the same theater in 1904. Set designs for the Mariinsky Theater's production of Anton Rubinstein's *Demon*.

1903 Set designs for A. Koreshchenko's ballet *Magic Mirror* at the Mariinsky Theater in St. Petersburg; reused for the Moscow Bolshoi Theater's production of the ballet in 1905. Sets, costumes, and props designed for Act 3 of Gounod's *Faust* at the Hermitage Theater, St. Petersburg.

1904 *Portrait of S. Feleizen* (pastel). Set and costume designs for Glinka's *Ruslan and Ludmila* at the Mariinsky Theater, St. Petersburg.

1905 *Portrait of Fyodor Chaliapin as Mephistopheles. Portrait of Maria Voyeikova.* Set designs for Ibsen's *Lady from the Sea* at the Alexandrinsky Theater and Wagner's *Rheingold* at the Mariinsky Theater in St. Petersburg.

1906 *Portrait of Nicholas Roerich* (pastel). *Portrait of Fyodor Chaliapin as the Demon* (tempera). *Group Portrait of Staff Members of the Imperial Theaters* (tempera and pastel). Set and costume designs for Sophocles' *Antigone* at the Alexandrinsky Theater, St. Petersburg. Costume designs for Tchaikovsky's *The Awakening of Flora* at the Mariinsky Theater, St. Petersburg.

1907 *Spanish Girl* (tempera, pastel, and charcoal). *Portrait of Fyodor Chaliapin as Farlaf* (tempera). Costume designs for Glazunov's *The Seasons* at the Mariinsky Theater, St. Petersburg. Set designs for Ibsen's *Little Eyolf* at the Alexandrinsky Theater and Rimsky-Korsakov's *Tale of Tsar Saltan* at the Mariinsky Theater, St. Petersburg.

1908 *Portrait of Fyodor Chaliapin as Holophernes* (tempera, gouache, and pastel). *Spanish Girl in a Black Shawl* (tempera, pastel, and charcoal).

178. Alexander Golovin. Spanish Girl in a Black Shawl. 1908

179. Alexander Golovin. Children on the Balcony. Spain

180. Alexander Golovin. Spanish Woman on the Balcony. 1911

181. Alexander Golovin. Roses and China. 1920s

Moonlit Night in Pavlovsk (tempera). *The Marquese* (gouache). Set and costume designs for Bizet's *Carmen* at the Mariinsky Theater, St. Petersburg, for Diaghilev's production of Mussorgsky's *Boris Godunov* and the St. Petersburg Alexandrinsky Theater's production of Knut Hamsun's *At the Gate of the Kingdom.*

1909 *Portrait of Fyodor Chaliapin as Mephistopheles* (tempera). *Portrait of Dmitry Smirnov as de Grieux* (tempera). *Portrait of Count Vladimir Kankrin* (tempera and pastel). *The Silver Willows* (tempera). *Portrait of the Poet Maximilian Voloshin* (red chalk).

1910 *Portrait of the Ballerina Elena Smirnova* (tempera and pastel). *Portrait of the Poet Mikhail Kuzmin* (tempera and pastel). Set designs for d'Annunzio's *La Città Morta* (The Dead City) at the Alexandrinsky Theater, St. Petersburg. Set and costume designs for the Diaghilev Company's production of Stravinsky's *The Firebird* and of the Alexandrinsky Theater's production of Molière's *Don Juan.*

1911 *Portrait of the Artist Dmitry Stelletsky* (tempera and pastel). *Spanish Woman on the Balcony* (tempera and pastel). *Phloxes* (tempera). Set designs for Christoph Gluck's *Orpheus and Eurydice*

182. Alexander Golovin. Neskuchny Garden in Moscow. 1920s

183. Alexander Golovin. Spanish Girl. 1900s

184. Alexander Golovin. Still Life with Flowers

185. Alexander Golovin. The Volga Bank. Set design for Act 1 of Ostrovsky's drama *The Thunderstorm*. 1916

186. Alexander Golovin. Careno's Room. Set design for Hamsun's play *At the Gate of the Kingdom*. 1908

and Mussorgsky's *Boris Godunov* (Scenes: Kremlin Square, The Tavern, and At Marina's) at the Mariinsky Theater, St. Petersburg.

1912 *Self-Portrait* (tempera). *Portrait of Marina Makovskaya* (tempera). *Portrait of the Actor Vasily Dalmatov* (tempera). *Portrait of Fyodor Chaliapin as Boris Godunov* (tempera, gouache, size paint, chalk, gold paint and tinfoil). Decorative panel: *The Appian Way in Rome* (tempera).

1913 *Portrait of Mikhail Tereshchenko* (tempera). *Portrait ot the Actress Alexandra Sadovskaya.* Set, costume, and props designs for Richard Strauss' *Elektra* at the Mariinsky Theater, St. Petersburg.

1914 *Portrait of the Actor Konstantin Varlamov* (tempera). *Portrait of the Composer Alexander Scryabin* (tempera and pastel). *Portrait of Alexandra Suvchinskaya* (tempera and pastel).

1915 *Portrait of Natalya Vysotskaya* (tempera, pastel, and charcoal). *Portrait of Pyotr Suvchinsky* (tempera). *Still Life with China and Flowers* (tempera and pastel). Set and costume designs for the Literary Fund Benefit Performance of Lermontov's *Two Brothers* at the Mariinsky Theater, Petrograd, and for Calderon's *El principe constante* (The Constant Prince) at the Alexandrinsky Theater, Petrograd. Cover for *Love for Three Oranges.* Set and costume designs for Glinka's *Jota Aragonese* at the Mariinsky Theater, Petrograd.

1916 *Portrait of Evfimia Nosova* (tempera and gouache). *The Little Girl Frosya and Chinaware* (tempera). *Portrait of Sergei Bakhrushin* (tempera). *Portrait of Anna Golovina. Portrait of Maria Troyanova* (tempera). Set and costume designs for Ostrovsky's *Thunderstorm* at the Alexandrinsky Theater, Petrograd.

1917 *Self-Portrait* (tempera). *Portrait of the Stage Director Vsevolod Meyerhold* (tempera). Set, curtains, and costumes for Dargomyzhsky's *The Stone Guest* at the Mariinsky Theater and Lermontov's *Masquerade* at the Alexandrinsky Theater, Petrograd.

1918 Set designs for Leo Tolstoy's *Pyotr Khlebnik* at the Alexandrinsky Theater, Petrograd.

1919 *Self-Portrait Against the Background of a Red Kerchief* (tempera and pastel). *Portrait of the Conductor Emile Cooper* (tempera). Set and costume designs for Gluck's *Queen of May* and Stravinsky's *Le Rossignol* at the Mariinsky Theater, Petrograd. Covers for the *Notes of Dreamers* anthology.

1920 *Self-Portrait Against the Background of a Golden Shawl* (tempera). *Portrait of Nadezhda Dobychina* (tempera). *Portrait of Sophia Alyanskaya* (tempera). *Portrait of Friedrich Krimmer* (tempera). *Spanish Peasant Woman* (tempera).

1921 *Spanish Dance: Jota Aragonese* (tempera and gouache). *Portrait of Nikolai Efimov* (tempera). Sets, costumes and props for Stravinsky's *The*

187. Alexander Golovin. Portrait of Count Vladimir Kankrin, an Official of the Imperial Theatres. 1909

Firebird at the Opera and Ballet Theater, Petrograd. Cover for Mikhail Kuzmin's *Echo.*

1922 *Portrait of Ivan Ekskuzovich* (tempera). *Dance in the Tavern* (tempera). Sets, costumes, and props for Grieg's *Solveig* at the Opera and Ballet Theater, Petrograd. Illustration for Leconte de Lisle's *Les Erinnyes.*

1923 *Portrait of Eric Gollerbakh* (tempera). *Portrait of the Actor Yuri Yuryev* (tempera, pastel). Portrait of *Lydia Rybakova with Her Daughter* (tempera). Set designs for an unrealized production of Wagner's *Tannhäuser.* Cover and illustrations for Knut Hamsun's *Growth of the Soil* and Vladimir Doroshevich's *Old-Time Theatrical Moscow.*

1924 *Portrait of the Actress Evgenia Chudovskaya* (tempera and gouache). *Portrait of Mikhail Sergeyev* (tempera). Set and costume designs for Gioacchino Rossini's *The Barber of Seville* at the Opera and Ballet Theater, Leningrad.
The more significant works done in Golovin's later years include set and costume designs for the Moscow Art Theater productions of Beaumarchais' *The Marriage of Figaro* and Shakespeare's *Othello.*
In 1928, he was the first Soviet stage designer to be awarded the title of People's Artist of the Russian Federation.
Golovin died on April 17, 1930 in Detskoye Selo (formerly Tsarskoye Selo, now the town of Pushkin).

Mstislav Dobuzhinsky

Mstislav Valerianovich Dobuzhinsky was born on August 2. O.S. (14), 1875 in Novgorod into the family of an army officer. From 1885 to 1887, he attended the Drawing School of the Society for the Encouragement of the Arts. Between 1895 and 1899, he studied law at the University of St. Petersburg. From 1899 to 1901, he was trained under Anton Ažbè in Munich and under Simon Hollósy in Nagybánya (Austria-Hungary). He first collaborated with the World of Art as illustrator of books and magazines. From 1903, he took part in World of Art shows. From 1910 he traveled annually abroad, visiting Britain, France, Italy, Germany, and Holland.

1903 *Evening* (pastel and gouache). *View of a House in St. Petersburg* (India ink heightened with white). *The Courtyard* (pastel, gouache, and pencil). *Landscape* (gouache and pencil, heightened with white). *Pskov. Shopping Arcade* (watercolor). *Semyonovka* (gouache). *St. Petersburg: The New Admiralty, St. Petersburg: The Trinity Bridge, Tsarskoye Selo: The Gate to the Cameron Gallery,* and *Tsarskoye Selo: The Ceilings of the Hanging Gardens* (picture postcards for the Society of St. Eugenia). Head- and tailpieces, vignettes, headings, captions and half titles for the Nos. 2, 3, 9 and 12 issues of the *World of Art* and the No. 1 issue of the *Art Treasures of Russia*. Frontispiece, headings, and borders for Benois' *The Russian School of Painting*.

1904 *A Nighttime View of St. Petersburg* (pastel). *Company Barracks: Winter in Town* (watercolor and pencil, heightened with white). *In the Thirties* (watercolor). *View of the Chinese Village in Tsarskoye Selo* (pastel). *Novgorod* (watercolor and pencil). *A Nook in St. Petersburg* (pastel and pencil). *The Fontanka in Winter* (watercolor). *Tsarskoye Selo. The Ceilings of the Hanging Gardens* (gouache). Half titles, head- and tailpieces, borders, and frontispieces for Nos. 11 and 12 issues of the *World of Art* and for F. Wolf's *The Imperial Porcelain Factory*.

1905 *A Cottage in St. Petersburg* (pastel, gouache, and pencil). *The Doll* (watercolor, charcoal, and pencil, heightened with white). *An Old Cottage* (watercolor and gouache). *The Cathedral of Our Lady of Kazan* (crayon, sauce, sepia, and pencil). *In the Company Barracks of the Izmailovsky Regiment* (watercolor). Illustrations for Pushkin's *The Station Inspector*. Cartoons for the Nos. 1 and 2 issues of the *Bugbear*.

1905–06 *Man with Spectacles. Portrait of the Art Critic and Poet Konstantin Sunnerberg* (charcoal and watercolor heightened with white).

1906 *The Daily Grind* (India ink, touched up with gold paint). *Glassmakers' Street in Vilna* (lead pencil and watercolor). *The Devil* (watercolor). *Caricature of Nicholas II* (pencil). *Barbershop Window* (watercolor and gouache). *A Parisian Cityscape* (watercolor and gouache). *London. An Old Jetty* (pencil and gouache). Covers, title pages, half titles, vignettes, head- and tailpieces for F. Sologub's *Political Tittle-Tales*, the first book of B. Zaitsev's *Torches* and his *Short Stories*, G. Chulkov's *Mystic Anarchism*, and Dostoyevsky's *Poor Folk*. Cover for the No. 3 issue of the *Bugbear*. Title heading, head- and tailpieces, and vignettes for Nos. 1 and 2 of the *Hell's Mail*. Headings, vignette, half title, and tailpieces for Nos. 1, 2, 4, 6, 10, and 11–12 of the *Golden Fleece*.

1907 *Vilna. The University Quadrangle* (gouache). *Vilna. Bazaar by the Wall* (gouache and watercolor). *A Country Cottage* (watercolor). *Porch of the Church of St. Nicholas in Vilna* (watercolor and pencil). *The Provinces in the 1830s* (1907–09, watercolor and pencil, heightened with white). Set and costume designs for A. Remizov's *A Devilish Act on a Certain Husband*, and also *Life's Disputes with Death* at Vera Komissarzhevskaya's Theater, St. Petersburg. Covers, title pages, illustrations, and tailpieces for F. Sologub's *Little Imp* and *White Nights. The St. Petersburg Almanac*, A. Remizov's *The Wrinkle*, L. Zinovyeva-Annibal's *The Tragic Menagerie*, A. Blok's *Snow Mask* (cover jointly with Bakst), and V. Ivanov's *Golden Behests, By the Stars, The Or Flowerbed, The Taiga,* and P. Verlaine's *Poemse*.

1908 *Embankment in St. Petersburg* (watercolor and India ink heightened with white). *Model* (pencil and chalk). *Perugia* (watercolor and India ink). *The Organ Grinder* in the *City Types (City Grimaces)* series (watercolor and gouache). Set and costume designs for d'Annunzio's *Francesca da Rimini* at Vera Komissarzhevskaya's Theater, St. Petersburg, and for P. Potyomkin's *Petrouchka* and a scenic

188. Mstislav Dobuzhinsky. Vilna. Nocturnal Scene. 1910s

adaptation of Edgar Allan Poe's *Fall of the House of Usher* at the Lukomorye Theater, St. Petersburg. Covers and half titles for F. Sologub's *Heavy Dreams*, Benois' *Goya*, K. Balmont's *The Calls of Antiquity*, and A. Remizov's *Pond*.

1909 *Winter* (gouache and watercolor). *The City Types (City Grimaces)* series: *The Legless Cripple* (watercolor and gouache) and *The Hunchback* (watercolor). Set and costume designs for Turgenev's *A Month in the Country* at the Moscow Art Theater. Covers, half titles, and tailpieces for the No. 1 issue of *Apollon*. Covers, illustrations, and endpiece for S. Ausländer's *Prince of Night*. Prospectus for I. Grabar's *History of Russian Art*. Cover for F. Sologub's *Collected Works*.

1910 *Peter the Great in Holland* (sketch). *Exercises of Army Recruits in the Times of Nicholas I* (tempera). *Self-Portrait by Bookshelves* (gouache and watercolor). *Bruges* (watercolor). *Vilna* (gouache, watercolor, and pencil). *Canal in Haarlem* (watercolor and pencil). *Improvisation* (pencil). *Portrait of Lydia Koreneva* (watercolor and pencil). *Portrait of Rostislav Dobuzhinsky* (pencil). *The Artist's Sons* (watercolor). *Drozhki Drivers, Drayman, Wetnurse,* and *Vendors of Hot Mead* in the St. Petersburg Types

series (watercolor). Set and costume designs for an unrealized Moscow Art Theater production of Turgenev's *Lunch with the Marshal of Nobility*. Illustrations for Turgenev's *A Month in the Country*. Covers and half titles for Sasha Chorny's *Satires* and V. Svetlov's *Modern Ballet*.

1911 *In the Rhône Valley* (tempera). *Vilna at Night* (pastel). *Army Encampment* (gouache). *Italy. Rome. The Thermae of Caracalla* (pencil). *Naples* (crayons). *Switzerland. Matialiola* (watercolor and pencil). Set and costume designs for M. Zagoskin's *A Lesson for Fond Mothers* at Countess Shuvalova's residence, St. Petersburg. Set and costume designs for Shakespeare's *Hamlet* and an unrealized production of Turgenev's *Evening in Sorrento* at the Moscow Art Theater. Covers for R. Wagner's *My Life* and *The Alkonost* (book 1). Illustrations for an unpublished ABC of the *World of Art* and *Steve and Doddy's Primer*.

1912 *In Denmark* (tempera). *Denmark. A Small Theater* (gouache and pencil). *Denmark. A Street in Oyensee. Voronezh. The Outskirts* (watercolor). *Kiev. The Bell Tower of the Monastery of St. Michael* (gouache, India ink, and chalk). *Nezhin.*

195

189. Mstislav Dobuzhinsky. Exercises of Army Recruits in the Times of Nicholas I. 1910

Churches (watercolor). *Portrait of Valgren* (crayon). *Chernigov. Street* (watercolor). *Chernigov. Photograph* (watercolor). Set and costume designs for Moscow Art Theater productions of Ivan Turgenev's *Where It's Thin, It Breaks, The Provincial Lady,* and *The Parasite,* and for a perfomance of K. Vatace's *The Hut a Cossack Saved, or Gratitude* at Countess Shuvalova's residence, St. Petersburg. Covers, tailpieces and title pages for *One Hundred Portraits of Russian Art Personalities* and Benois' *Monuments of Western European Painting.*

1913 *Still Life. Portrait of the Artist's Wife. Alexei Tolstoy, Alexander Benois, and Konstantin Stanislavsky* (pencil). *St. Petersburg: The Pryazhka* (pencil). *Portrait of Alexander Sakharov* (pencil). *Portrait of Ivan Bersenev as Pyotr Verkhovensky in "Nikolai Stavrogin"* (pencil). Set designs for an unrealized Moscow Art Theater production of Anton Chekhov's *The Seagull.* Set and costume designs for an unrealized Moscow Art Theater production of Friedrich Schiller's *Kabale und Liebe* and for the same theater's production of *Nikolai Stavrogin* after Dostoyevsky's novel *The Demons.* Covers, title pages and tailpiece for S. Makovsky's *Pages of Art Criticism,* K. Erberg's *The Purpose of Creativity,* N. Krandievskaya's *Poems,* R. de Gourmont's *Book of Masks,* and M. Lermontov's *The Treasurer's Wife.*

1914 *City Outskirts: The Pryazhka Embankment. St. Petersburg. Little Wooden Old Men. Portrait of*

the Artist's Children. Portrait of Elizaveta Dobuzhinskaya. Vilna: The Ostrobram Gates (watercolor, pencil, and pastel). *Cubist Studies* (charcoal). *London. Cranes* (pencil). *Portrait of Valerian Dobuzhinsky* (pencil). *A Group Portrait of Stepan Yaremich, Alexander Benois, and Nikolai Lanceray* (pencil). *Portrait of Georgi Narbut* (pencil). *Portrait of the Artist's Daughter Verochka* (pencil). *Portrait of Tamara Karsavina as the Danseuse in "Petrouchka"* (pencil). Frontline sketches (pencil and watercolor). Set designs for the Diaghilev Company's productions of Schumann's *Les Papillons* and M. Steinberg's *Midas.* Set and costume designs for J. Bayer's *Die Puppenfee* for Anna Pavlova's tour.

1915 *Vishenki: Trees. Bridge. Portrait of Olga Korovina. Evening Landscape* (watercolor). *Vishenki: Hall* (watercolor). *City of the Future* (pencil). *Composition* (watercolor). *Viaduct in London* (lithograph). *Galician Types* series (lithograph). *Portrait of a Woman* (pencil). *Portrait of Anna Benois* (charcoal). *Portrait of Tamara Karsavina* (pencil). Set and costume designs for an unrealized production of Brueys J. Palaprat's *Maître Pathelin* at the Marionettes Theater, Petrograd. Costume designs for Tamara Karsavina in P. Hertel's *La Fille mal gardée* at the Mariinsky Theater, Petrograd.

1916 *City: Iron City. Room* (tempera). *Street in Lovice* (pencil). *Village Street* (pencil). *St. Petersburg.*

190. Mstislav Dobuzhinsky. Canal in Haarlem. 1910

192. Mstislav Dobuzhinsky. Night in St. Petersburg. 1924

191. Mstislav Dobuzhinsky. Glassmakers'
Street in Vilna. 1906

197

193. Mstislav Dobuzhinsky. Scene from the Life of Petrograd in 1920. 1920

194. Mstislav Dobuzhinsky. Denmark. A Small Theater. 1912

195. Mstislav Dobuzhinsky. The Kiss. 1916

196. Mstislav Dobuzhinsky. Curtain design for Lunacharsky's drama *Oliver Cromwell*. 1920–21

198. Mstislav Dobuzhinsky. By Izora's Window. Set design for Blok's *The Rose and the Cross*. 1916–17

197. Mstislav Dobuzhinsky. Set design for the prologue to Remizov's mystery-play *A Devilish Act on a Certain Husband, and also Life's Disputes with Death*. 1907

Rooftops under Snow (charcoal and watercolor heightened with white). *Portrait ot the Artist's Son* (India ink). *The Kiss* (lead pencil and red chalk).

1916–17 Set and costume designs for an unrealized Moscow Art Theater production of Alexander Blok's *The Rose and the Cross*.

1917 *St. Petersburg Study. Interior with a Female Figure* (pencil). *Moscow. Funeral of the Victims of the Revolution* (pencil). *Portrait of Grandi* (pencil). *Portrait of Maxim Gorky* (pencil). *Urban Dreams* (pencil). Set and costume designs for a Moscow Art

Theater production of *The Village of Stepanchikovo* after Dostoyevsky's novella. Illustrations for Hans Christian Andersen's fairy tale *The Swineherd*.

1918 *Vitebsk. Street* (pencil and crayons). *Urban Visions* series (pencil, and charcoal). *Portrait of Valerian Dobuzhinky* (pencil). *Portrait of Gennady Michurin as Banco* (pencil). *Portrait of Mikhail Babenchikov* (pencil). *Portrait of Maria Andreyeva as Lady Macbeth* (pencil). Costume designs for Œdipus in Sophocles's *Œdipus Rex* at the Petrograd Theater of Tragedies (the former Cinizelli Circus). Set and costume designs for the Petrograd Art Drama Theater's production of Tirso de Molina's *Seducer from Seville* and the production of M. Kuzmin's *The Supper* at the Comedians Halt cabaret, Petrograd. Covers, head- and tailpieces for Maxim Gorky's *Articles. 1905–16*, K. Erberg's *Captivity*, L. Zinovyeva-Annibal's *No!* Hans Christian Andersen's *The Princess and the Pea*, and M. Kuzmin's *The New Plutarch (Cagliostro)*.

1919 Set and costume designs for *The Fairy Tales* by Hans Christian Andersen at the Comedians Halt cabaret, Gounod's *Faust* at the Bolshoi Opera Theater (the former People's House), Schiller's *Die Räuber* and M. Levberg's *Danton* at the Bolshoi Drama Theater, and K. Gutzkow's *Uriel Acosta* at the Jewish Theater (all in Petrograd). Covers, headpieces, and illustrations for Pushkin's *La Demoiselle paysanne*, N. Sukhanov's *Notes about the Revolution*, and M. Kuzmin's *Parabolas*.

1920 *The Yard of the Arts House* (pencil). *Glimpses of Life in Petrograd in 1920* (watercolor, gouache, and pencil). *The Summer Garden in the Hermitage* (pencil). *Grove* (pencil). *Portrait of Dmitry Mitrokhin* (pencil). Designs for the album *The Second Congress of the Communist International*. Set and costume designs for Shakespeare's *King Lear* at the Bolshoi Drama Theater, Petrograd. Decoration for the theatricalized show *Hymn to Liberated Labor (The Mystery Play of Liberated Labor)*, presented in the portico of the Stock Exchange, Petrograd. Cover and drawings for *Dom iskusstv* (Arts House), No. 1.

1921 *In the Room. The Felled Forest. The Gold Room. Vladimir Milashevsky, a Humorous Sketch* (pencil). *Urban Visions. Work* (India and plain ink). *Pskov in Winter* (gouache and watercolor). *The Factory* (pencil and pastel). *A Village Hut* (pencil), *Portrait of Georgi Vereisky* (pencil), *Urban Visions* series (lithographs). Set and costume designs for the Moscow Maly Theater's production of A. Lunacharsky's *Oliver Cromwell*. Design and illustrations for N. Karamzin's *Poor Liza*, Pushkin's *The Covetous Knight*, and N. Leskov's *The Toupee Artist*. Covers for A. Akhmatova's *Plantain*, M. Kuzmin's *Mary's Tuesday* and *Evenings in Another Place*.

1922 *Pskov: Fish Market. St. Petersburg: A Courtyard* (pencil). *St. Petersburg: The Lithuanian Castle and Market* (watercolor, India ink, and crayon). *Interior with a Bull's Skull* (India ink). *Portrait of Olga Knipper* (pencil). *Portrait of Leonid Leonidov* (pencil). *St. Petersburg in 1912* (lithographs). Design and illustrations for Dostoyevsky's *White Nights*, Blok's *The Rose and the Cross* (unpublished), and Schiller's *Die Räuber* (unpublished). Design and illustrations for M. Kuzmin's *Thicket* and his own *Recollections of Italy*. Covers and headpieces for Verhaeren's *Complete Works*, and for *Orpheus*. *Book About Music* (book 1) and G. Spet's *Aesthetic Fragments*.

199. Mstislav Dobuzhinsky. *The Opening of the Congress.* In the album *The Second Congress of the Communist International.* 1920

1923 *St. Petersburg: Courtyards. Portrait of Bellin, Secretary of the American Embassy. White Night: St. Petersburg* (gouache). *Vilna. The Yard of the Artist's House* (gouache, India ink, and pencil). *Paris. Arc de Triomphe du Carrousel* (gouache). *Portrait of A. Ziloti* (pencil). *Portrait of the Artist Alexander Yakovlev* (pencil). *Portrait of D. Rochas* (pencil). *Portrait of Ludwig Gira* (pencil). *Portrait of Troinitsky* (pencil). *The Viaduct* (woodcut). *Vitebsk. Steps* (autolithograph). *Lithuania. Kovno* (autolithograph). Set designs for an unrealized production of Leo Tolstoy's *The Fruits of Enlightenment* at the Moscow Art Theater and a production of *The Prayer of the Virgin* at the Berlin "Golden Cockerel" Miniatures Theater. Covers, headpieces, tailpiece, and illustrations for E. Gollerbach's *Dobuzhinsky's Drawings*, A. Lunacharsky's *Oliver Cromwell*, E. Zamyatin's *St. Dominic's Lights*, and N. Antsiferov's *The St. Petersburg of Dostoyevsky*.

1924 *Self-Portrait with One Eye* (pencil). Cityscapes of Dresden, Moscow, Nezhin, Pskov, Riga, and provincial Russian towns (watercolor and gouache). *Portrait of Ilya Dobrovein* (pencil). *Night in St. Petersburg* (gouache). *Pushkin in Kamenka* (India ink heightened with white). *Self-Portrait* (lithograph). *Ways* (woodcut). Set and costume designs for the Dresden Opera production of Tchaikovsky's opera *Eugene Onegin*. Design and illustrations for O. Mandelstam's *The Primus*, K. Chukovsky's *Barmaley*, and S. Makovsky's *The Graphic Art of M. Dobuzhinsky*.

During the First World War Dobuzhinsky went with Evgeny Lanceray to the front lines to sketch. Later, he took part in the Second Congress of the Communist International. In 1918, he supervised the theatrical workshop at the State Educational Workshops of the Decorative Arts (the former Stieglitz School of Technical Drawing). In 1923–24, he went abroad to study developments in European art and to arrange one-man shows. In 1924, he moved to Lithuania, and in 1939, to the USA, working primarily as a stage designer. He died in New York on November 20, 1957.

200. Sergei Diaghilev. Photograph

Sergei Diaghilev

Sergei Pavlovich Diaghilev was born on March 19 O.S. (31), 1872 in the vicinity of Novgorod on the estate of his father, a career army officer, with the rank of General. As a youth, he received a solid academic training in music, was fluent in several European languages, and while studying law — from 1890 through 1896 at the University of St. Petersburg — also audited singing classes at the city's conservatoire. In the early 1890s, his cousin, Dmitry Filosofov, who subsequently developed into a professional writer and critic, introduced him to Alexander Benois, Léon Bakst, Konstantin Somov, and other future members of the World of Art group. Between 1890 and 1895, he traveled widely in Western Europe. From 1896, he began to contribute critical essays to the Russian periodical press. In 1896–97, he published, in *Novosti i Birzhevaya gazeta* (News and Stock Exchange Gazette), the following articles: "Exhibition of Watercolors," "The Finnish Artist Edelfeldt," "European Exhibitions and Russian Artists," "Concerning the Dutch Exhibition," "An Exhibition of English and German Watercolorists," "Concerning Two Exhibitions of Watercolors," "A Traveling Exhibition," and "An Academy Show."

1898 Mounted an Exhibition of Russian and Finnish Artists. Was the driving spirit behind the organization of the *World of Art* journal. Became its editor. Found patrons in the person of Princess Maria Tenisheva and Savva Mamontov, who bankrolled the publication at the outset. Published in the journal's maiden issue the first part of his program statement "Complex Questions" and also an analysis of trends in *fin-de-siècle* Finnish painting, under the heading "Exhibition in Helsingfors." The article concluded thus: "By uniting the power of our national character with the high cultural standard of our neighbors, we could lay the foundations for a new flourishing of art and for our joint, triumphal march on the West." Evidently this was the underlying motivation for the aforementioned show of Russian and Finnish artists.

1899 *World of Art* contributions: "Exhibitions" with subheads "Belgian Show" and "Apprentice Show" in No. 3–4; "Concerning the Exhibition of Victor Vasnetsov" in No. 7–8; "Concerning Exhibitions" (analyzing the controversies over the 27th Traveling Show and the latest Academy show) in No. 9; "A Letter Addressed to I. Repin" (taking issue with Repin's letter addressed to the *World of Art* that was featured in the literary supplement to the magazine *Niva* (No. 15, 1899) in No. 10; "Illustrations to Pushkin" (in connection with illustrated editions of

the poet's works marking his birth centenary) in No. 16–17. Made "Official for Special Commissions" under the Director of the Imperial Theaters and edited the *Annual of the Imperial Theaters*. Organized an international show of World of Art paintings.

1900 *World of Art* contributions: "Exhibitions" (dealing with the shows of the Society of St. Petersburg Artists and of the Wanderers as well as with the related polemics and problems) in No. 5–6; "Art Critics" (notes on the state of art criticism in Russian periodicals) in No. 7–8; "Levitan: In Memoriam" in No. 15–16. Mounted the Second World of Art Exhibition which presented for the first time exclusively Russian artists grouped around the journal, plus pieces from the Abramtsevo workshops.

1901 Helped to mount the Third World of Art Exhibition in the rooms of the Academy of Arts in St. Petersburg, which provoked furious comment. However, surmounting every difficulty, he was able to install within the Academy building a "Trojan Horse" — an innovative trend in Russian art. A posthumous Levitan show was held conjointly within the framework of the Third Exhibition. *World of Art* contributions: "Exhibitions" (the first part noting the troubles associated with the efforts to

arrange the Third Show, and the second part, criticizing the 29th Traveling Show) in No. 2–3; "Paris Shows" (a critique of the three shows of modern art in Paris) in No. 7; "Russian Museums" (reflections concerned with the display, system of collecting, and other activities of the Tretyakov Gallery in Moscow and the Russian Museum and the Hermitage in St. Petersburg) in No. 10; "Exhibitions in Germany" (critical comments on shows of modern art in Darmstadt, Dresden, and Berlin) in No. 8–9.
Diaghilev's attempt to produce Delibes' *Sylvia*, to which he invited Benois, Somov, Lanceray, and Serov as stage designers, culminated in conflict with the Ministry of the Court, after which he was dismissed from his post with the Directorate of the Imperial Theaters.

1902 *World of Art* contributions: "Exhibition of Historic Russian Portraits" in No. 2; "Theater. I. Delibes' Ballets" in No. 9–10; "Concerning Benois' *History of Russian Painting in the Nineteenth Century*. Part II" in No. 11; "Theater. II. Operatic Reforms" and "M. Yakunchikova (an obituary)" in No. 12.
Wrote "Concerning the Biography of the Artist V. Borovikovsky" for the journal *Russky arkhiv* (Russian Archives, No. 6). Published a comprehensive monograph about Dmitry Levitsky conceived as the first in a series of editions dedicated to the history of eighteenth-century Russian painting. Helped to mount the Fourth World of Art Exhibition in St. Petersburg and a World of Art showing in Moscow.

1903 *World of Art* contributions: "Moscow News. Exhibition of Architecture and the 36" in No. 1; "Contemporary Art" (about the Art Store and Exhibition prepared by World of Art artists that opened in St. Petersburg on January 26) in No. 3; "Götterdämmerung" (about the Wagner production at the Mariinsky Theater in St. Petersburg) in No. 3; "Some Words about S. Maliutin" (about the artist's work in Talashkino) in No. 4; "Exhibitions" (responding to criticism of the Fifth World of Art Exhibition and also commenting on the latest Wanderers, Academy, and St. Petersburg Artists exhibitions) in No. 5; "M. Morozov" (an obituary devoted to this celebrated collector of Russian and French masters) in No. 9; "Blanc et Noir Show" (commenting on the exhibition of drawings and engravings that Vasily Mathé mounted in St. Petersburg) and "More About *Julius Caesar*" (reviewing on the Moscow Art Theater production of Shakespeare's tragedy). Helped to mount the Fifth World of Art Exhibition, the last in the initial period of this association's history.

1904 *World of Art* contributions: "The Union of Russian Artists Show in Moscow" (at which the recent World of Art artists exhibited for the first time within the framework of this new association) in No. 1; "Portraitist Shibanov" in No. 3; "New Developments at the Moscow Art Theater" (concerned with its Maeterlinck productions) in No. 8–9.

1905 Mounted a spectacular historico-artistic show of Russian portraits in the Tauride Palace, St. Petersburg. As its Commissioner-General had spent

almost two years preparing for it. Supervised the compilation of a scholarly exhibition catalogue in eight separate books, to which he wrote the foreword. Also devoted to this show an article in the newspaper *Rus* issue for September 17, under the heading "The Tauride Palace." In a contribution to the same newspaper two days earlier lambasted the Directorate of the Imperial Theaters, especially for slighting Russian art, under the heading "Program of the Theater Director."

1906 Organized an exhibition under the old World of Art name, which opened in February. A brilliant, though somewhat demonstrative affair, it climaxed Diaghilev's activities as art critic and organizer of exhibitions in Russia. All his subsequent projects were realized abroad where he made his debut with the historic Russian art show at the Paris Salon d'Automne.

1907 Organized in Paris five Russian music recitals that were an enormous success, causing Russian periodicals to carry not only comment but also an interview with Diaghilev.

1908 Supervised the production of Mussorgsky's *Boris Godunov* at the Paris Opera, inviting Golovin, Benois, and Bilibin to design, and Anisfeld, Yuon, and Lokkenberg, to execute the decor. The seven performances of the opera with Chaliapin in the title role created a furore, thus paving the way for the *Saisons Russes* which started the following year.

1909 The first *Saison Russe* organized by Diaghilev at the Théâtre du Châtelet. Seven operas and ballets were staged to the music of Tcherepnin, Glinka, Glazunov, Rimsky-Korsakov, Tchaikovsky, Chopin, Arensky, and Mussorgsky, with set and costume designs by Benois, Konstantin Korovin, Bakst, and Bilibin. All subsequent *Saisons Russes* represented, apart from everything else, a topflight achievement in scenic design for the World of Art artists.

1910 This *Saison Russe* billed five ballets — in Berlin and Rome, besides Paris — to the music of Schumann, Rimsky-Korsakov, Adam, Stravinsky, Glazunov, Sinding, Arensky, Grieg, and Borodin, with scenic designs by Bakst, Benois, Golovin, and Korovin.

1911 The *Saisons Russes* served to establish the permanent company known as the *Ballets Russes de Serge Diaghileff* which gave in Paris, London, and Monte Carlo performances of five ballets to the music of Weber, Tcherepnin, Rimsky-Korsakov, Stravinsky, and Tchaikovsky, with designs by Bakst, Anisfeld, Benois, Korovin, and Golovin.

1912 The Diaghilev Company gave at the Théâtre du Châtelet, Paris, performances of four ballets to the music of Hahn, Balakirev, Debussy, and Ravel, all designed by Bakst.

1913 Besides ballets, Diaghilev produced operas with Russian performers. During this season his troupe gave performances in Paris and London of five ballets to the music of Tchaikovsky, Stravinsky,

Debussy, and Schmitt, as well as of Mussorgsky's *Boris Godunov* and *Khovanshchina* with Chaliapin. Billed during the London Season were *Boris Godunov*, *Petrouchka*, *Le Dieu Bleu*, and other new productions. The Company also toured Vienna, Berlin, and South America.

1914 Seven ballet and operatic productions to the music of Schumann, Richard Strauss, Rimsky-Korsakov, Stravinsky, Steinberg, and Borodin, with scenic designs by Bakst, Goncharova, Dobuzhinsky, Roerich, and Fyodorovsky.

1915–17 With Diaghilev trapped outside Russia by the war, his Company almost disintegrated, recruiting but few performers for the rare productions. Among the Russian artists who continued to collaborate with Diaghilev at this time were Bakst, Goncharova, and Larionov.

Throughout the 1920s, detached from Russia, the Diaghilev Company became cosmopolitan, with the World of Art traditions muted and fragmented. Of Russian artists, only Bakst, Goncharova, Larionov, and Benois designed decors for the Company, with Diaghilev now inviting such notable Western European artists as Picasso, Matisse, Braque, Gris, and Derain, among others. Nonetheless, the Company still retained much of its Russian flavor in the eyes of European audiences.

Diaghilev died in Venice on August 19, 1929.

Boris Kustodiev

Boris Mikhailovich Kustodiev was born in Astrakhan on February 23 O.S. (March 7), 1878. His father taught philology, the history of literature, and logic at the local theological seminary. Between 1893 and 1896, he took private lessons in Astrakhan from Pavel Vlasov, a pupil of Vasily Perov. Subsequently, from 1896 to 1903, he attended Ilya Repin's studio at the Higher Art School of the Academy of Arts in St. Petersburg. Concurrently he took classes in sculpture under Dmitry Stelletsky and in etching under Vasily Mathé. He first exhibited in 1896. In 1904, he attended the private studio of René Ménard in Paris. In 1904, he traveled to Spain, in 1907 to Italy, and in 1909 visited Austria, France, and Germany, and again Italy. During these years he painted portraits and genre pieces. In 1905–06, he contributed to the satirical journals *Zhupel* (Bugbear) and *Adskaya Pochta* (Hell's Mail), and he first met the World of Art artists, whose Society he joined in 1910. Earlier, in 1909, he was made an Academician of Painting. In 1911, he was elected a World of Art Committee member from St. Petersburg. From 1911 on, he took part in the World of Art shows.

In 1909, Kustodiev developed the initial symptoms of the grave illness that in 1916 paralyzed the lower part of his body, thus confining him to his studio where he continued to paint, relying on boyhood and youth memories.

1910 *Festivities. On the Volga. Village Fête* (tempera). *At the Fair* (tempera). *Portrait of the Collector Vladimir Argutinsky-Dolgorukov* (tempera). *Motherhood: L. Kustodieva with Her Daughter Iya* (plaster). *Portrait of the Writer Alexei Remizov* (tinted plaster bust). *Portrait of the Sculptor Nikolai Danko* (tinted plaster bust). *Portrait of Vsevolod Meyerhold* (plasticine bust, lost). Illustrations for the writings of Ivan Krylov and Nikolai Nekrasov.

1910–16 Studies for *Group Portrait of the World of Art Artists.*

1911 *Irina Kustodieva in Leysin* (tempera).

1912 *Merchant Women* (tempera). *The Trinity - St. Sergius Lavra* (tempera). *Portrait of N. Zelenskaya. Self-Portrait* (tempera). *Portrait of E. Botkina* (watercolor and lead pencil). Set and costume designs for Ostrovsky's *The Ardent Heart* at the K. Nezlobin Theater, Moscow.

1913 *A Frosty Day. Drinking Tea. Bathing. Portrait of Nikolai von Meck. Portrait of V. Tuzhsky, Actor of the Moscow Art Theater* (gouache and pastel).

1914 *Harvesting. Summer. Rural Festival in Autumn. Still Life with a Pheasant. Portrait of R. Notgaft. Portrait of N. Alexandrov, Actor of the Moscow Art Theater* (pencil). *Portrait of Ivan Moskvin, Actor of the Moscow Art Theater* (pencil). *Portrait of the Writer Fyodor Sologub* (marble bust). Set and costume designs for Mikhail Saltykov-Schedrin's *The Death of Pazukhin* at the Moscow Art Theater.

1915 *Merchant Woman. La Belle. Girl on the Volga. Religious Procession. Riding Out. Toy-Balloon Vendor* (watercolor). *Reclining Model* (red chalk and charcoal). *Portrait of E. Kustodieva, the Artist's Mother* (red chalk and charcoal). *K. Kustodiev on a Sofa* (lead pencil and crayons). *Portrait of Yu. Kustodieva, the Artist's Wife* (lead pencil). Set and costume designs for an unrealized Moscow Art Theater production of Ostrovsky's *Wolves and Sheep.* Set designs for the Moscow Art Theater production of I. Surguchov's *Autumn Violins.*

1916 *Shrovetide* series. *Moscow Tavern. Winter. Bonfire (Night Watch). On the Fontanka. Apple. Easter: Exchanging a Triple Kiss* (tempera).

1917–27 *February 1917. Fairbooths. Palm Sunday. Market by the Redeemer Gates in Moscow. Merchant Wedding (Wedding Feast). Hoarfrost. Portrait of the Architect Alexei Shchusev. Portrait of the Artist Georgi Vereisky* (lead pencil and red chalk).

201. Boris Kustodiev. Merchant Woman at Tea. 1918

202. Boris Kustodiev. Cover for *Six Poems by Nikolai Nekrasov*. 1921

203. Boris Kustodiev. Cover for Ostrovsky's *The Thunderstorm*. 1920

204. Boris Kustodiev. "In the distance, heavens knows where, a light twinkled in a watch house." Illustration for Gogol's *The Greatcoat*. 1905

205. Boris Kustodiev. Merchant Women. 1912

206. Boris Kustodiev. Tula. Sketch for a production of *The Flea*. 1924

207. Boris Kustodiev. Portrait of Prof. Pyotr Kapitsa and
Prof. Nikolai Semyonov. 1921

208. Boris Kustodiev. Portrait of the Art Historian A. Anisimov. 1919

Set and costume designs for an unrealized Moscow
Maly Theater production of Ostrovsky's *From Rags
to Riches*.

1918 *Merchant Woman at Tea. Merchant Woman
Drinking Tea* (tempera). *Merchant (Old Man Counting His Money). Xmas Tree Market. Summer. Stepan Razin. Autumn (Over the City). Chest Vendor*
(lead pencil, watercolor, and gouache). *Self-Portrait*
(lead pencil and red chalk). *Self-Portrait with Wife
(In a Sleigh)* (lead pencil). *Portrait of the Art
Historian and Collector Fyodor Notgaft* (watercolor,
lead pencil, and crayons). *Portrait of the Art Historian S. Ernst* (lead pencil and crayons). Designs
of panels for decorating Petrograd's Ruzheinaya
Square during the Celebration of the First Anniversary of the October Revolution (watercolor). Set
designs started in 1917 and now completed for an
unrealized production of Ostrovsky's play *The
Thunderstorm*.

1919 *Shrovetide. Winter. Shrovetide Festivities.
Village Fête. Skiers. On Vorobyov Hills. Portrait of
Maria Chaliapina. Portrait of the Art Historian A.
Anisimov. Girl in a Chequered Kerchief. Portrait of
Mitya Shostakovich* (red chalk and charcoal). *Por-
trait of the Artist Victor Zamirailo* (lead pencil, pas-
tel, and red chalk). *Yu. Kustodieva, the Artist's
Wife, on a Sofa* (lead pencil). Set and costume designs
for Gogol's *The Inspector-General* at the Maly
Theater, Petrograd. Cover for the No. 1 issue of the
Kommunistichesky International (The Communist
International). Illustrations for *Works of Pushkin* in
the *People's Library* series.

1920 *The Bolshevik. Shrovetide. Merchant Woman
with a Mirror. Merchant Woman on a Balcony* (tempera). *Merchant Woman with Purchases. Autumn.
The Blue Cottage. Trinity Sunday. Portrait of Yu.
Kustodieva. Portrait of Olga Shimanovskaya.* Study
(begun in 1916) for the *Group Portrait of the World
of Art Artists. Portrait of Isaac Brodsky* (watercol-
or). *Dmitry Shostakovich at the Piano* (lead pencil).
Russian Types series of watercolors. Set and costume
designs for A. Serov's *The Power of Evil* at the
Opera and Ballet Theater, Petrograd, for Rimsky-
Korsakov's *The Tsar's Bride* at the Bolshoi Opera
Theater of the People's House, Petrograd, and for
an unrealized production of Ostrovsky's *The Thunderstorm* at the Pskov Municipal Theater. Cover,
decoration, and illustrations for an unrealized
edition of Ostrovsky's play *The Thunderstorm*.

1921 *Festivities on Uritsky Square Marking the
Opening of the Second Congress of the Third International. After the Storm. Spring. Winter Consecra-
tion of the Water on Epiphany. Bathing. Girl Bathing. Portrait of Fyodor Chaliapin. Portrait of
Prof. Pyotr Kapitsa and Prof. Nikolai Semyonov.*
Lithographs for the artbook *Sixteen Autolithographs
by Boris Kustodiev.* Set designs for an unrealized
production of Ostrovsky's *From Rags to Riches* at
the Drama Theater, Petrograd. Set and costume
designs for A. Neverov's *Peasant Women* at the
Smolny Theater, Petrograd. Decoration and illustrations for *Six Poems by Nikolai Nekrasov.*

1922 *Summer. The Provinces. Autumn Festivities.
Portrait of the Architect I. Zolotarevsky. Portrait of
Ivan Yershov, Singer of the Mariinsky Theater* (pencil and red chalk). *Thunderstorm* (lithograph). Set
and costume designs for Alexei Tolstoy's *The Mayor*
at the Drama Theater, Petrograd. Illustrations for
Six Poems by Nikolai Nekrasov. Decoration and
illustrations for Nikolai Leskov's *The Darner.*

209. Boris Kustodiev. Night Gala on the Neva. 1923

1923 *Night Gala on the Neva. Merchant Woman at Tea. The Coachman. Autumn: Farewells. Portrait of the Pianist Konstantin Igumnov* (lead pencil and red chalk). *Portrait of the Pianist P. Semyonov* (lead pencil and red chalk). Twin porcelain figurines: *Concertina Player* and *Girl*. Set and make-up designs for Ostrovsky's *Between Ourselves We'll Come to Terms* at the Drama Theater, Petrograd. Decoration of Leskov's *Lady Macbeth of Mtsensk*. Cover and illustrations for V. Voinov's book *B. Kustodiev*.

1924 *Portrait of the Poet Maximilian Voloshin. Irina Kustodieva on a Sofa* (watercolor). *Portrait of the Artist Georgi Vereisky* (lead pencil). *Portrait of N.S. and G.A. Kuk* (crayons heightened with white). *Portrait of the Artist Victor Zamirailo* (plaster bust). Set and costume designs for Evgeny Zamyatin's *The Flea* at the Moscow Art Theater-II. Decoration and illustrations for Samuel Marshak's *Lenin and the Young Leninists* and for *The Adventures of the Table and Chair. The Nonsense Rhymes after Edward Lear*.

In 1923, Kustodiev joined the Association of Artists of Revolutionary Russia and up to his death on May 26, 1927 in Leningrad he continued to paint, make engravings, illustrate books and design productions.

210. Boris Kustodiev. The Bolshevik. 1919–20

Evgeny Lanceray

Evgeny Evgenyevich Lanceray was born in Pavlovsk near St. Petersburg on August 23 O.S. (September 4), 1875. His father was a sculptor, his grandfather Nikolai Leontyevich Benois, an architect. From the age of eleven upon the death of his father Lanceray was brought up in the Benois family. From 1892 to 1895, he attended classes under Jan Tsionglinsky at the School of the Society for the Encouragement of the Arts. From 1895 to 1898, he studied at the private academies of Colarossi and Julian in Paris. In 1898, he traveled in Germany, France, and Italy. From 1900 on, he exhibited in World of Art shows.

1898 Illustrations for E. Balabanova's *Legends About the Old Castles of Brittany*.

1899 Headpieces and illustrations for Pushkin's *The Shot* and *Dubrovsky* and Lermontov's *Bela*. Initials and headpieces for the *World of Art* journal.

1900 Vignettes, head- and tailpieces for the *World of Art journal*.

1901 *The Old St. Nicholas Market in St. Petersburg* (gouache, charcoal, and crayon). Set and costume designs for Delibes' *Sylvia*. Headpieces for the *World of Art* journal.

1902 *Kalinkin Bridge* (watercolor). *The Kazan Cathedral* (watercolor). *The Old Winter Palace in the Mid 18th Century* (watercolor and crayon, heightened with white). Cover for R. Muther's *History of Painting*. Vignettes, head- and tailpieces, and autolithographs on the theme of Petersburg architecture for the *World of Art* journal.

1902–05 Head- and tailpieces and initials for N. Kutepov's *The Tsarist and Imperial Hunt in Russia. Late 17th and 18th Centuries*. Vol. 3.

1903 *St. Petersburg in the Eighteenth Century. The Twelve Collegia Building* (tempera). Covers, head- and tailpieces, title pages, and illustrations for the *World of Art*. Covers for *Portraits of Russian Writers, St. Petersburg*, and I. Bozheryanov's *Nevsky Prospekt*.

1904 Vignettes, headpieces, title pages, initials, tailpieces, and illustrations for the *World of Art*. Covers for the catalogues: *Exhibition of Russian Portraits* and *The Russian Museum in St. Petersburg*, and for Benois' *Russian School of Painting*.

1904–10 Headpieces and title-page vignettes for Benois' *Tsarskoye Selo in the Reign of Empress Elizaveta Petrovna*.

1905 *Empress Elizaveta Petrovna in Tsarskoye Selo* (gouache). Covers for D. Merezhkovsky's *Christ and Antichrist* and (with decoration) for S. Makovsky's *Poems*.

1905–06 Satirical cartoons for *Zhupel* (Bugbear) and *Adskaya Pochta* (Hell's Mail).

1906 *Peter the Great's Boat* (gouache, watercolor, and India ink). Sketch of a panel for the Grand Moscow Hotel. Design for the decoration of the building of the *Rossiya* Insurance Society. Cover for the *Annual of the Society of Architect-Artists*.

1907 Sketch of a panel for the Café de France. Frontispiece for the *Calendar of the Russian Revolution*. *June (The Mutiny aboard the Potemkin Cruiser)*. Headpiece for the *Golden Fleece*. Decoration of *The Enchantments of the Moon*. Title page for *Torches*. Poster for the Russian Historical Music Recitals in Paris.

1907–08 Set designs (jointly with Benois) for the St. Petersburg Antique Theater's production of N. Evreinov's *Fair on St. Denis' Day*.

1908 *Walking along the Breakwater* (tempera). *Senate Square* (watercolor and India ink). Covers for the *Golden Fleece* and A. Blok's *Snowbound Soil*. Decoration of L. Andreyev's *King Hunger* and S. Kondurushkin's *Syrian Stories*.

1909 Decorative panel: *Relaxations* and three smaller panels for Ya. Zhukovsky's dacha in the Crimea. *Ships in the Times of Peter I* (tempera, first version). Covers for the *Annual of the Imperial Theaters* and the *Jubilee Collection of Drawings by Eminent Artists for the Works of N. Gogol*. Vignettes

211. Evgeny Lanceray. Cathedral of Our Lady of Kazan in St. Petersburg. 1897

212. Evgeny Lanceray. The Old St. Nicholas Market in St. Petersburg. 1901

for the *Russian Cities and Towns* and *Russian Artists* series.

1909–10 Set designs for an unrealized Moscow Maly Theater production of Schiller's *Kabale und Liebe*.

1910 *Princess Elizaveta in the Guardhouse of the Winter Palace* (tempera). *Portrait of the Writer Georgi Chulkov* (pencil). Cover for Book 12 of the *Dog Rose* almanac. Illustrations for Cerubina de Gabriac's poems in the No. 10 issue of *Apollon*.

1910–12 Sketches for the decoration of the Tarasovs' residence in Moscow.

1911 *Ships in the Times of Peter I* (tempera, second version). Sketch of a ceiling design for the Nosovs' residence in Moscow. Sketches for the monumental panels *The Rape of Deianeira* and *Hercules and Nessus*. Set designs (jointly with Benois) for the St. Petersburg Antique Theater production of Calderon's *The Purgatory of St. Patrick*.

1912 *The Hemp Jetty in St. Petersburg*. Covers for the catalogues to the *World of Art Exhibition* and *The Russian Museum in St. Petersburg*.

1912–15 Illustrations for Leo Tolstoy's *Hadji Murat*. Decoration of Benois' *History of Painting in the 19th Century*.

1913 *The Hemp Jetty in St. Petersburg* (gouache).

1914 Illustrations for Lermontov's *Ashik-Kerib*.

1915 Drawings and watercolors inspired by a visit to the Caucasian Front. Decoration of the Library Room of the Academy of Arts, St. Petersburg. Title page and cover for V. Kurbatov's *Gardens and Parks*.

1916 Sketches for the unrealized decoration of a ceiling at Moscow's Kazan Railway Station on the theme of *Russia Uniting Europe with Asia*. Decoration of *A Wreath for Wrangel*.

1917 Sketch for the unrealized decoration of the *Marine Commerce* canteen. Eleven panels for embellishing the ceiling of the head office of Moscow's Kazan Railway Station.

1918–46 Lived in the Caucasus twice, between 1915

213. Evgeny Lanceray. Shamil with his lieutenants. Illustration for Leo Tolstoy's *Hadji Murat*. 1914

and 1927 and between 1932 and 1934, in Paris on assignment between 1927 and 1931, and in Moscow from 1934 to 1946. Major works done over this period include illustrations for Leo Tolstoy's stories *The Cossacks* (1917–37) and *Hadji Murat* (with the second version in 1937, and the third in 1941), set designs for Shakespeare's *Julius Caesar* (1923) and *Macbeth* (1928), Alexander Griboyedov's *Woe from Wit* (1938), Schiller's *Kabale und Liebe* and Sergei Prokofiev's opera *The Duenna*, sketches for the decoration of the restaurant of Moscow's Kazan Railway Station (1933–34), of the ceiling of the Hotel Moskva restaurant in Moscow (1937), and of the vestibule of Moscow's Kazan Railway Station (1940 and 1946), and also easel paintings and graphics. In 1943, Lanceray was awarded a State Prize for his outstanding services in the domain of art, and in 1945 the title of People's Artist of the Russian Federation. He died in Moscow on September 13, 1946.

214. Evgeny Lanceray. Nicholas I. Illustration for Leo Tolstoy's *Hadji Murat*. 1914

Dmitry Mitrokhin

Dmitry Isidorovich Mitrokhin was born into the family of a commercial clerk on May 15 O.S. (27), 1883 in the Azov seaside town of Yeisk. Between 1902 and 1904, he studied at the Moscow School of Painting, Sculpture and Architecture under Apollinary Vasnetsov and Alexei Stepanov, and from 1904 to 1905, at the Stroganov School of Art and Industry under Stanislav Noakovsky, while simultaneously working for the Murava artel of pottery artists, also in Moscow. In 1905 and 1906, he lived in Paris where he perfected his skills at sundry schools of art. He first exhibited in 1905 and took part in World of Art shows from 1911 on, though earlier, in 1909 and 1910 he had participated with members of the World of Art in Union of Russian Artists shows.

1904 Headpieces for *Vesy* (Scales) and *Pravda* (Truth).

1905 Illustrations for Pushkin's *The Tale of the Priest and His Servant Blockhead*. Vignettes for *Zritel* (The Spectator).

1906 *In a Café* (lithograph). *In the Luxembourg Gardens* (lithograph).

1907 Cover for N. Poyarkov's *Short Stories*. Vignettes and drawings for *Yunost* (Youth).

1908 Vignettes for *Zritel* and *Satiricon*. Cover for the almanac *Crystal*.

1909 Title page and illustrations for the *Pervotsvet* (Primrose) collection. Vignettes for *Satiricon* and the *Journal of the Theater of the Literature and Arts Society*.

1910 *Women* (colored linocut). *Flowers* (colored linocut). *Cupids* (linocut). Binding for Benois' *Tsarskoye Selo in the Reign of Empress Elizaveta Petrovna*. Covers for L. Andreyev's *Anfisa* and *The Black Masks*. Illustrations, vignettes, and titles for *Apollon*.

1911 *The Ballerina* (colored linocut). *The Warrior* (colored linocut). *Woman with an Apple* (colored linocut). *Horn of Plenty* (colored linocut). Cover for D. Merezhkovsky's *Collected Poems*. Cover, frontispiece, initials, head- and tailpieces, and illustrations for I. Hemnitzer's *Fables*.

1912 Cover for Valery Briusov's *Mirror of Shadows*. Cover and vignettes for *Exhibition Commemorating the War of 1812*. Covers, illustrations, vignettes, and initials for Wilhelm Hauff's *The Life of Almansore*, *Little Muck*, and *The Phantom Ship*.

Vignettes for *Leo Tolstoy. His Life and Work*. Cover for the *Countries, Centuries, and Nations* series.

1913 Cover, frontispiece, vignettes, and drawings for Mikhail Lermontov's *The Dispute*. Covers, drawings, vignettes, and initials for Vasily Zhukovsky's *The Goblet* and *Roland the Squire*. Cover for *Japanese Folktales* and V. Rozanov's *Fallen Leaves*. *The Second and Last Basket*. Vignettes for *Satiricon* and *New Satiricon*. Cover, initials, vignettes, and drawings for R. Gustafson's *The Barge*.

1914 Cover, title page, and decoration for *Fairy Tales for Leisure*. Cover for the *Monuments of World Literature* series. Vignettes, headpieces, and decorative elements for *Lukomorye* (The Seashore), *Satiricon*, *New Satiricon*, *The Monthly of Literature, Science and Social Affairs*, *Golos zhizhi* (Voice of Life), and *Vershiny* (Peaks). Cover and title page for *A. Rodin. Art*. Cover and drawings for *The Goldfish, a Folk Tale*.

1915 Covers for Konstantin Aksakov's *Poems*, S. Ausländer's *Heart of a Warrior*, M. Vlagin's *Russia, the Slavs and Tsargrad*, M. Vund's *The Greek Weltanschauung*, V. Voinov's *Strong in Spirit*, E. Zamyatin's *Provincial Tales*, D. Krachkovsky's *Humility*, S. Gorodetsky's *The Year 1914*, B. Lazarevsky's *The Eternal* and *The Family*, E. Levy's *Greek Sculpture*, O'Henry's *The Heart of the Mid-West*, O. Ozarovskaya's *Grannie's Oldtime Tales*, D. Zensor's *Slighted Love*, A. Roslavlev's *Through Colored Glass*, I. Severianin's *Collected Verse*, B. Sadovsky's *Noon*, and Yu. Slyozkin's *Silly Heart*. Covers and title pages for *Russian Propylaea. Materials on the History of Russian Thought and Literature* and Leo Tolstoy's *Complete Works*. Covers, vignettes, and initials for *Vershiny*, *Golos zhizni*, *Lukomorye*, and *New Satiricon*.

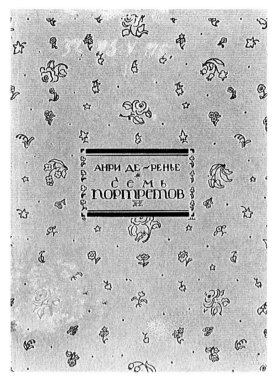

215. Dmitry Mitrokhin. Cover for Régnier's *Seven Portraits*. 1921

216. Dmitry Mitrokhin. Cover for Konradi's *Among the Paintings of the Hermitage*. 1917

1916 Covers for K. Balmont's *Collected Lyrics* and *Sun, Honey and Moon Sonnets. Song of the Worlds*, A. Bely's *Collected Works*, E.T.A. Hoffmann's *Collected Works*, *A Critique of I. Severianin's Œuvre*, B. Lazarevsky's *Favorites*, and V. Rozanov's *In the Sahara Desert*. Covers and title pages for V. Denisov's *War and the Lubok*, D. Merezhkovsky's *There Will Be Joy* and G. Chulkov's *Satan*. Covers for *Lukomorye*, *The Year 1914*, and the *Little Library* series. Cover and title page for *Tolstoy Collection*.

1917 Covers and title pages for *Eighty-Eight Modern Poems Selected by Z. Gippius*, G. Vyatkin's *Saddened Joy*, V. Konradi's *Among the Paintings of the Hermitage*, and M. Cervantes' *Novellas*. Cover and frontispiece for I. Severianin's *Behind the Lyre's Fence of Strings*. Covers for the *People's Cheap Library* series, *The Military Political* series, and the *Creators of Eternal Beauty* series. Vignettes, covers, and drawings for *Lukomorye*, *Luch zhizni* (Beam of Life), *New Satiricon* and *The Free Journal*. Cover and fly-leaf for the *Spruce Almanac for Children*.

1918 Cover for the *Socio-Historical Novels and Dramas* series. Covers, vignettes, drawings, and headings for *Sirena* and the *Stremniny* (Rapids) almanac.

1919 Covers for V. Voinov's *First Volume of Verse*, *Annual of the Russian Institute of Arts History*, V. Kliuchevsky's *Course of Russian History*, V. Knyazev's *First Volume of Verse*, *New Russian Folktales*, Chekhov's *In the Ravine. Peasant Women* and *Slavish Souls*, and Schiller's *Don Carlos*. Cover for *World Literature. Popular Series*. Covers and headpieces for Lermontov's *Collected Works*, *Ballads*, and *Bela*. Vignettes for I. Annensky's *Thamyris*.

1920 Covers for A. Altayev's *A. Felice. From Chains to Glory*, Balmont's *Song of the Worker's*

217. Dmitry Mitrokhin. Cover for Zhukovsky's *The Goblet, a Ballad*. 1913

218. Dmitry Mitrokhin. Illustration for Hauff's *The Life of Almansore*. 1912

Hammer, The Second Congress of the Communist International, Ben Johnson's *Epicene, or the Taciturn Woman, New Russian Folktales*, J.H. Rosny's *The Red Room*, P. Stolpyansky's *Revolutionary Petersburg. The Cradle of Russia's Liberty*, and Walt Whitman's *Poems*. Drawings for N. Gumilev's *In China*. Cover, frontispiece, title page, and vignettes for H. de Régnier's *Portraits and Souvenirs*. Covers for the *Historico-Revolutionary Library* and the *World of Books* series.

1921 Covers for V. Voinov's *The Ex-libri of D. Mitrokhin*, M. Kuzmin's *Nets, Catalogue of 13 Petersburg Publishing Houses* and V. Rozhdestvensky's *Gold Spindle*. Cover, title page, frontispiece, illustrations, head- and tailpieces for S. Coleridge's

Christabel. Covers, vignettes, head- and tailpieces for *House of Arts, The Red Baltic Seaman*, and *The Young Proletarian*.

1922 Covers for Bernhard Kellermann's *The Sea*, M. Kovalensky's *Russian History*, P. Kogan's *Essays on the History of Western European Literature*, Jack London's *White Fang*, N. Piksanov's *Griboyedov and Molière. The Reassessment of a Tradition*, Upton Sinclair's *Sylvia*, K. Staniukovich's *Sea Stories*, and *The Russian Museum. A Catalogue of the Exhibition of Pomor Arts*. Cover, title page, frontispiece, drawings, headings, and initials for Edgar Allan Poe's *The Gold Bug*. Cover and title page for *D. Mitrokhin* by M. Kuzmin and V. Voinov. Cover, title and half-title pages, head- and tailpieces for M. Tsvetayeva's *The Tsar Maid*.

1923 *Girl Friends* (woodcut). *By the Sea* (woodcut).
Covers for A. Blok's *The Twelve* and *The Scythians*,
O. Voltsenburg's *Bibliography of the Visual Arts*,
L. Grossman's *The Theater of Turgenev*, Karl Kaut-
sky's *The Origins of Christianity*, A. Kugel's *Theat-
rical Portraits*, V. Margerit's *Comrade*, Octave Mir-
beau's *La Vache Tachetee*, V. Muizhel's *Journey on
Rafts. Short Stories*, A. Neverov's *Plays*, H. de Ré-
gnier's *Romaine Mirmault*, Upton Sinclair's *Christ
in Western City*, Herbert George Wells's *The War in
the Air*, and *A Short History of the World*, Anatole
France's *The Revolt of the Angels*, *The Antique
Theater in Russia*, and the *Memoirs Library*,
Library of Fiction, and *Science for Everyone* series.
Cover, title page, head- and tailpieces, and initials
for B. Pilnyak's *Plain Stories*. Cover, title page,
head- and tailpieces for Rabindranath's Tagore's
Birds of Passage. Covers and drawings for the
journals *Atelye*, *Vremya* (Time), *Drezina* (Trolley),
Iskra (The Spark), *Krasnaya Niva* (Red Field),
Masterskaya (Workshop), and *Chelovek i priroda*
(Man and Nature).

1924 *Woman with a Cigarette* (woodcut). *Mother*
(woodcut). *Ruins* (woodcut). *The Kitchen
Garden* (woodcut). *Storm Clouds* (woodcut). Covers
for E. Bertels's *The Persian Theater*, Jean-Jacques
Brousson, and *Anatole France in Slippers and Dressing Gown*, F. Werfel's *Not Killer But Killed Is To
Blame*, Bernhard Kellermann's *Land of Chrysanthe-
mums* and *The Tunnel*, M. Kuzmin's *The New Gull*,
André Maurois's *Ariel ou la Vie de Shelley*, *Roman
de la Vie de Shelley et Byron*, M. Pokrovsky's *Russian History*, H. de Régnier's *The Living Past*, A.
Strug's *People of the Underground*, I. Ehrenburg's
The Jack of Diamonds & Co., and the *Land and
Factory*, *Foreign Literature Library* and *Discoveries, Conquests, and Adventures* series. Covers,
headpieces and drawings for *Vestnik profsoyuzov*

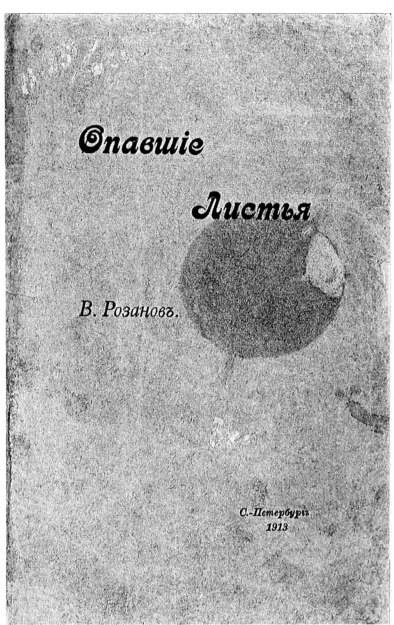

220. Dmitry Mitrokhin. Cover for Rozanov's *Fallen Leaves. The Second
and Last Basket.* 1913

(Trade Unions Herald), *Kinonedelya* (Film Weekly),
Novy Robinzon (The New Robinson), *Promyshlennost i torgovlia* (Industry and Commerce), *Khochu
vsyo znat'* (Want to Know All), and *Man and
Nature*.
Between 1925 and 1973, Mitrokhin lived alternately
in Leningrad (till 1942), in Alma Ata (1942–44) and
in Moscow (1944–73), working as etcher, lithograph-
er and book designer and illustrator. He died in
Moscow on November 7, 1973.

219. Dmitry Mitrokhin. Cover for Schiller's
Don Carlos. 1919

Georgi Narbut

Georgi Ivanovich Narbut was born into the family of a petty landowner on February 14 O.S. (26), 1886 in the hamlet of Narbutovka near the town of Glukhov (which is today in the Sumy Region of the Ukraine). In 1906–07, he studied philology at St. Petersburg University, where he simultaneously took advice in drawing from artists of the World of Art group. During the winter of 1907–08 he attended Elizaveta Zvantseva's studio in St. Petersburg. He spent 1909 and 1910 gaining greater artistic proficiency at Simon Hollósy's studio in Munich. His artistic leanings were heavily influenced by Ivan Bilibin. From 1911 he took part in World of Art shows.

1903 Illustrations for *The Song of Roland*.

1904 Illustrations for *Yegor the Brave*.

1905 *Tsar Koshchei*, an illustration for Pushkin's *Ruslan and Ludmila*.

1906 Illustrations for *The War of the Mushrooms* and *The Snow Maiden*.

1907 Illustrations for *The Crane and the Stork* and *The Bear*.

1908 Cover and illustrations for *Teremok. Misgir*. Illustrations for L. Ostrogorsky's *The Living Word*.

1909 Illustrations for *The War of the Mushrooms*.

1910 Cover and illustrations for *Dance Matvei and Spare Not Your Lapti!* Illustrations for *Teremok. Misgir*.

1911 Cover and illustrations for the *Toys*. Illustrations for Krylov's *Fables*.

1912 *Street in Chernigov. Skarzhinskaya's House in Lubny. Lockers. The Church in the Village of Khokhlovka. Drip* (pencil). Cover for *The Castle of Vyshnevets* by V. and G. Lukomsky. Frontispiece and illustrations for Hans Christian Andersen's *The Nightingale* and *The Year of 1812* in Krylov's *Fables*.

1913 Silhouetted portraits (pen and ink). Decoration and illustrations for *The Rescued Russian* in Krylov's *Fables*. Title page and headpieces for the *Connoisseur of Arms*. Cover and illustrations for *The Fairy Tales* of Hans Christian Andersen. Cover for A. Sacchetti's *The History of the Music of All Ages and Nations*.

1914 *Lubok* pictures on World War themes (watercolor, pen and ink). Allegories of the World War (watercolor and gouache). Decoration (jointly with S. Chekhonin) of *Contemporary Russian Graphic Arts* by S. Makovsky and N. Radlov. Initials and illustrations for Lermontov's poetry. Title pages for *Hellenistic Culture* by F. Baumgarten, F. Poland, and R. Wagner.

1915 *Lubok* pictures on World War themes (watercolor, pen and ink). *Roses in a Goblet* (watercolor). *Night on a Landed Estate* (watercolor). Decoration of T. Shchepkina-Kupernik's *Song of the Brussels Lace-Makers*. Cover for G. Lukomsky's *The Old Architecture of Galicia*.

1916 Allegorical representations on war themes (watercolor and gouache). *A Moonlit Night* (gouache and India ink). Illustrations and headpieces for S. Repin's *The Tale of the Love of the Beautiful Queen and the Devoted Prince*. Cover for vol. 3 of V. Vereshchagin's *Russian Caricature. A.O. Orlovsky*. Frontispiece for *Apollon*.

1917 Decoration of Part 1 of G. Lukomsky's *Old Landed Estates in Kharkov Province*. Cover, initials, and drawings for the *Ukrainian ABC*.

1918 Decoration of the family *Akta Narbutorum* archives (pen and ink, gouache). Silhouetted portraits (pen and ink). Cover for *Our Past*. Decoration of P. Zaitsev's *Oxana, Shevchenko's First Love*.

1919 Silhouetted portraits (pen and ink). *Architectural Fantasy* (watercolour and gouache). *Ruins and Windmill on a Moonlit Night* (gouache, pen, and India ink). Sheets for the first three letters of the Ukrainian alphabet in the *Ukrainian ABC. The Cur, a Soulless Creature*, a caricature dealing with the installation of a Directory in the Ukraine in place of Hetman rule. *Æneas and His Troops* (an illustration for I. Kotlyarevsky's *Æneid*). Cover and frontispiece for V. Narbut's *Hallelujah*. Covers for the journals *Zori* (Dawns), *Narodnoye khozyaistvo Ukrainy* (The Economy of the Ukraine), and *Solntse truda* (The Sun of Labor). Frontispiece for *Mistetsvo* (Art). Cover for *Revolutsionnoye iskusstvo* (Revolutionary Art).

1920 Covers for *Mistetsvo* and M. Zernov's *Anthology*. Narbut died in Kiev on May 23, 1920.

221. Georgi Narbut. Illustration for Hans Christian Andersen's tale *The Intrepid Tin Soldier*. 1913

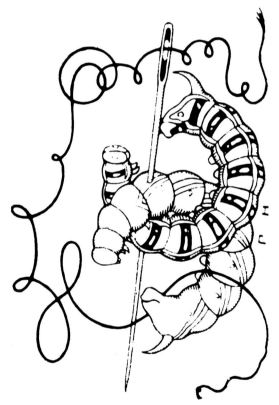

222. Georgi Narbut. Tailpiece for *Teremok. Misgir*
(Moscow, 1910)

223. Georgi Narbut. Illustration for Zhukovsky's tale *How the Mice Buried the Cat*. 1910

Anna Ostroumova-Lebedeva

Anna Petrovna Ostroumova was born in St. Petersburg on May 5 O.S.(17), 1871 into the family of an official who subsequently rose to senatorial rank. Between 1889 and 1892, she studied at the Stieglitz School of Technical Drawing under Prof. Vasily Mathé. In 1892, she entered the Academy of Arts, at first attending the general classes, but later, between 1896 and 1898, taking instruction from Ilya Repin. While in Paris, in 1898 and 1899, she worked at the studio of the American painter James Whistler. Also in Paris she first took up engraving in earnest, continuing her studies in 1899 and 1900, upon her return to St. Petersburg, at the Academy of Arts under Mathé. Between 1899 and 1903, she traveled to Italy. After her marriage to the chemist Sergei Lebedev in 1905, they visited France, Holland, Belgium, and Spain. Toward the close of the 1900s, she perfected her skills in the technique of the watercolor under Léon Bakst at Elizaveta Zvantseva's school in St. Petersburg. She first exhibited in 1898 and participated in World of Art shows from 1900 on.

1898 *Portrait of N. Smirnov. Perseus and Andromeda*, a hand-colored woodcut copy of Rubens. *Boy with a Dog* (colored woodcut).

1899 *Versailles. Genoa. Hadrian's Villa in Tivoli. Model.*

1900 *Finnish Lakes* (colored woodcut). *Finland Beneath Blue Skies* (colored woodcut). *The Moon* (colored woodcut). *Three Lakes* (colored woodcut). *Winter* (woodcut).

1901 *Cypresses in the Sunshine: The Crimea. Pavlovsk: Park. Pavlovsk: Cupids and Bench* (watercolor). *St. Petersburg: The Chain Bridge* (woodcut). *St. Petersburg: The New Holland Arch* (woodcut). *The Moika at Night* (woodcut). *Neva Embankment* (woodcut). *View of the Stock Exchange* (woodcut). *The Rostral Column* (woodcut). *The Ferry at Smolny* (woodcut).

1902 *Yard of the Vorontsov Palace in Alupka* (watercolor). *St. Petersburg. The Summer Gardens* (colored woodcut). *A Broken Spruce* (woodcut). *Winter under a Yellow Sky* (colored woodcut).

1903 *Fountain at the Mandragone Villa. Villa d'Este. Villa Falconiere* (watercolor). *Pool and Statues* (watercolor). *The Coliseum* (watercolor). *Statue of Athena and the She-Wolf* (watercolor). *Gates to the Pavlovsk Park* (colored woodcut). *The Columns of the Kazan Cathedral* (colored woodcut). *The Chain Bridge* (colored woodcut). *Salny Buyan (Lard Depot)* (colored woodcut). *The Bronze Horseman* (colored woodcut after a drawing by Benois). *Gates to the Tomb of Paul I* (colored woodcut).

1904 *White Night in Tsarskoye Selo* (watercolor). *Peterhof. The Samson Statue* (watercolor). *Avenue in Tsarskoye Selo* (watercolor). *Pavlovsk. Psyche's Pavilion* (watercolor). *The Admiralty Glimpsed through Branches* (watercolor). *Fiesole* (colored woodcut). *Tivoli* (colored woodcut). *Tsarskoye Selo. Perspective* (colored woodcut). *Villa Borghese* (colored woodcut).

1905 *The Old Church in Nadendal* (watercolor). *Cherries at Sunset* (watercolor). *View of Åbo* (watercolor). *View of Helsingfors* (watercolor). *Flowers* (colored woodcut).

1906 *Paris. Notre Dame* (watercolor). *Paris. St. Severins* (watercolor and lead pencil). *Paris. The Garlands Avenue in the Luxembourg Gardens* (red chalk). *Paris. The Seine at Night* (lead pencil). *A St. Petersburg Garden in Winter* (lead pencil). *Tyrol* (watercolor and lead pencil). A series of illustrations for the works of Fenimore Cooper (colored woodcuts).

1907 *Grapes: The Crimea. St. Petersburg: The Admiralty and the Senate* (watercolor). *View of the Old Gostiny Dvor* (lead pencil). *Versailles* (colored woodcut).

1908 *The Neva Seen through the Columns of the Stock Exchange* (watercolor). *The Rostral Column and the Customs* (watercolor). *The Neva in Perspective* (watercolor). *The Kriukov Canal* (watercolor). *The Columns of the Stock Exchange and the Fortress* (watercolor). *Punkaharju* (watercolor). *The*

224. Anna Ostroumova-Lebedeva. St. Petersburg. The Summer Gardens. 1929

Railings of the Summer Gardens (watercolor). *Fireworks in Paris* (colored woodcut).

1909 *In the Woods. Bouquet of Nasturtiums. White Night on the Neva* (watercolor). *The Rostral Column in Winter* (watercolor). *The Columns of the Exchange* (colored woodcut). *Bonfires* (gouache). *The Lithuanian Castle in St. Petersburg* (watercolor). *The Senate under Snow* (colored woodcut). *The Mining Institute* (colored woodcut). *Fireworks in Paris* (colored woodcut).

1910 *Nasturtium* (pastel). *White Night in St. Petersburg* (watercolor). *The Crimea. The Artek Gardens* (watercolor). *Bakhchisarai. The Cemetery of the Khans* (watercolor). *Oreanda* (watercolor). *The Catherine Canal* (colored woodcut). *Sunrise* (colored woodcut).

1911 *St. Petersburg. Lions and the Fortress* (watercolor). *St. Isaac's on Easter Night* (watercolor). *Rome. The Colonnade of St. Peter's* (watercolor and gouache). *Venice. The Grand Canal* (watercolor). *The Trevi Fountain in Rome* (watercolor). *The Coliseum* (watercolor). *Venice by Night* (watercolor). *A Street in Perugia* (watercolor).

1912 *The Neva and a Fortress Bastion on a Foggy Day* (gouache). *St. Petersburg. The Biron Palace and Barques* (watercolor and lead pencil). *The Smolny Cathedral and Breaking Ice* (watercolor).

St. Petersburg. The Egyptian Bridge (watercolor). *The Moika near the Round Market* (watercolor). *St. Petersburg. The Academy of Arts and the Sphinxes* (watercolor). *The Bronze Horseman and the Academy of Arts* (woodcut). *The Winter Canal* (woodcut). *The New Holland* (woodcut). *The Yelagin Palace* (woodcut). *Cycle of illustrations for V. Kurbatov's St. Petersburg.*

1913 *Lugano: Blue Landscape. St. Petersburg: View of the Winter Palace in Early Spring* (watercolor). *Amsterdam. The Iron Market. Amsterdam: Canal and Church* (watercolor). *Bruges. The Old Gates* (watercolor). *Pavlovsk. Rain and Rainbow* (watercolor). *Carcassonne. Evening* (watercolor). *Antwerp. Old Houses* (lead pencil). *Simplon* (lead pencil). *Rostov the Great* (woodcut). *Kostroma* (woodcut). *Yaroslavl* (woodcut).

1914 *The Biron Palace and Arch* (watercolor). *Segovia. Square and Stairs* (watercolor). *Carcassonne. Ruins of a Castle* (watercolor). *The Environs of Toledo at Noon* (watercolor). *Paris. The Seine and the Louvre* (lead pencil). *An Angel Flew through the Midnight Sky*, an illustration for Lermontov's poem *The Angel*.

1915 *Portrait of Alexandra Verkhovskaya. The Tajo River in Toledo* (tempera). *St. Petersburg. A Foggy Day with a View of the Admiralty and St.*

223

225. Anna Ostroumova-Lebedeva. The Biron Palace and Barques. 1916

226. Anna Ostroumova-Lebedeva. The Chain Bridge. 1903

227. Anna Ostroumova-Lebedeva. Venice at Night. 1914

228. Anna Ostroumova-Lebedeva. Petrograd. Red Pillars. 1922

229. Anna Ostroumova-Lebedeva. Venice. The Grand Canal. 1911

Isaac's (watercolor). *Portrait of the Chemist Sergei Lebedev, the Artist's Husband* (watercolor). *St. Petersburg. View from the Petrovsky Park of Vasilyevsky Island* (watercolor). *Kislovodsk. View from the Park* (watercolor).

1916 *Baku. The Square in Winter* (watercolor). *Baku. Bibi-Eibat and Old Oil Derricks* (watercolor and lead pencil). *Baku. Twilight* (watercolor). *Venice. The Grand Canal* (woodcut). *The Biron Palace and Barques* (colored woodcut).

1917 *St. Petersburg. Sails. Sailing Boats by the Tuchkov Quay. Unloading Firewood at the Tuchkov Quay. St. Petersburg. The Day of the Funeral of the Victims of the Revolution: March 23, 1917* (watercolor). *Mayday 1917. Sketch* (watercolor). *View from the Laboratory Window in Winter* (watercolor and lead pencil). *Tackle* (colored woodcut).

1918 *St. Petersburg. Ice Breaking in the Evening* (watercolor). *St. Petersburg. A Windy Evening* (watercolor). *St. Petersburg. Breaking Ice from the Windows of the Winter Palace* (watercolor). *St. Petersburg. The Kazan Cathedral* (watercolor). *St. Petersburg. View of the Petrograd Side* (watercolor). *St. Petersburg. Shafts of Smoke on a Frosty Day* (watercolor). *St. Petersburg. The Field of Mars and the Suvorov Monument* (colored woodcut).

1919 *Interior with a Dog. Tree under Snow* (watercolor). *Millionnaya Street* (watercolor). *St. Petersburg. A Rainy Day from a Hermitage Balcony* (watercolor). *View of the Chernyshov Bridge* (watercolor). *View from the Summer Gardens of the Saltykova Residence* (watercolor). *Building the Palace Bridge* (woodcut). *The Moika* (woodcut).

1920 *St. Petersburg. The Fontanka by the Summer Gardens* (watercolor). *St. Petersburg. The Field of Mars* (watercolor). *St. Petersburg. Broken-up Barques by the Cottage of Peter I* (watercolor). *St. Petersburg. Kamenny (Stone) Island and Barques* (watercolor). *Pskov. The Tower of the Intercession of the Holy Virgin* (watercolor). *Pskov. The Gremyachaya (Thunderer) Tower and Church* (watercolor). *View of the Stock Exchange* (woodcut). *The Catherine Canal* (woodcut). *The New Holland* (woodcut).

1921 *St. Petersburg. Bell Above the Neva* (watercolor). *Pavlovsk. Yellow Birches by the Constantin Bridge* (watercolor). *Pavlovsk. An Autumn Landscape and the Temple of Friendship* (watercolor). *St. Petersburg. The French Quay from the Pirogov Bridge* (watercolor). *Pavlovsk. The Apollo Cascade* (drawing).

1922 *Caucasian Valley in the Evening* (tempera). *Petrograd. Red Pillars* (watercolor). *Pavlovsk. The New Sylvia Bridge* (watercolor). *Pavlovsk. The Small Iron Bridge* (watercolor). *The Stock Exchange* in the *St. Petersburg* album (lithograph). *The Island of Love* (woodcut). *The Round Pond* (woodcut). *Peterhof. The Samson Fountain* (woodcut).

1923 *Portrait of M. Filonenko. Portrait of Sergei Lebedev. Portrait of the Actor Ivan Yershov. Pavlovsk. Pussy Willows by the New Sylvia Bridge* (woodcut). *Pavlovsk. The Slavyanka River Valley* (woodcut).

1924 *Koktebel. The Saddle Mountain* (watercolor). *Smolny* (woodcut).
Anna Ostroumova-Lebedeva died in Leningrad on May 5, 1955.

Nicholas Roerich

Nicholas Konstantinovich Roerich was born into the family of a well-known lawyer in St. Petersburg on September 27 (October 9), 1874. After finishing Karl Mai's gymnasium, he entered the Academy of Arts in 1893, where he worked with Pavel Chistyakov and Arkhip Kuinji till 1897, simultaneously studying law at St. Petersburg University. In 1900, he took a course in painting at Fernand Cormon's studio in Paris. In 1901, he was appointed Secretary of the Society for the Encouragement of the Arts, and in 1906 director of its school of drawing. In 1909, he was elected a Fellow of the Russian Academy of Arts, and in the following year, Chairman of the revived World of Art society. In 1903 and 1904, he made an extensive tour of old Russian towns, and in 1906 traveled to Germany, Italy, France, and Sweden to familiarize himself with foreign experience in the sphere of artistic education. In 1916, he moved to Karelia. He first exhibited in 1900, participating in World of Art shows from 1902 on.

1902 *Building a Town. A Sacred Place. Guests from Overseas. Combat* (pastel).

1903 *Building the Boats. Monastery. Siberian Frieze.* Studies done during the journey to the old Russian towns of Bogoliubovo, Vladimir, Grodno, Izborsk, Kostroma, Pskov, Pechora, Rostov the Great, Smolensk, Suzdal, Yuriev-Podolsky, Yaroslavl, etc.

1904 *St. Boris and St. Gleb.* Studies done while visiting the old Russian towns of Valdai, Zvenigorod, Kalyazin, Pskov, Tver, and Uglich. *The Battle of Alexander Nevsky with Yarle Berger:* Sketch for a mosaic (gouache). *Ancient Life.* Sketch (pastel). *Nomads* (pastel). *Round Dances* (gouache). *The Stone Age* (majolica). Sketches for the Talashkino workshops.

1905 *The Treasure of the Angels. Birches* (tempera and pastel). *The Patrol. Sorcerers* (gouache and pastel). *Pskov. The Slavs on the Dnieper* (tempera). *The North. The Valkyries in Flight:* Sketch for the *Battle* composition (pencil). Cartoons for majolica friezes and pediments of the house of the former *Rossiya* Insurance Society (gouache). Illustrations for the works of Maeterlinck.

1906 *Self-Portrait* (sketch). *The Pomors. Daybreak. Battle. The Serpent Woman. Sorcerer. Bear Hunt.* Studies done while traveling in Italy and Switzerland (pastel, tempera, and gouache). Sketches for mosaics in the Parkhomovka village church near Kiev (tempera). *Head of the Saviour. The Intercession of the Virgin.* Sketches for mosaics in the Church-at-the-Gunpowder-Factories (now the village of Morozovka) (tempera). Illustrations for Pushkin's *Ruslan and Ludmila.*

1907 *The Otherworld Lords. The Stone Age* (frieze for majolica). Iconostasis for the Kamensky family's chapel in the Perm Convent. *Town* (tempera). *The Earthly Conjuration* (tempera). *The Prophet Elijah* (tempera and pastel). *Three Young Hebrews in the Blazing Furnace* (tempera and gouache). *The Song of the Viking* (tempera). *The Pskov-Pechorsky Monastery* (tempera and pastel). *The Seven Shivery Sisters* (two versions, one tempera, the other, pastel). Set designs for *The Three Magi* at St. Petersburg's Antique Theater and for Wagner's *The Valkyrie.* Finnish sketchbook. *Raven Perched on a Dead Horse,* an illustration for I. Nikitin's *Neither Cloud Nor Wind* (India ink and pencil).

1908 *White Birds* (begun in 1905). *St. George and the Dragon. Gathering Tribute* (pastel). *The Archers* (pastel). Set designs for the Paris Opera Comique production of Rimsky-Korsakov's *The Snow Maiden* and the Diaghilev Company's production of Borodin's *Prince Igor.*

1909 *The Town by the Sea* (tempera). *Heavenly Battle* (tempera and pastel). *God's Acre. The Girl Captive. The Rhine: Heinersheim. A Varangian Motif* (pastel). *The Hillfort* (pastel). *The Sorcerer* (gouache and pastel). *The Lone Ship* (tempera). *Christ the Pantocrator* (gouache and gold paint). *By the Monastery Walls* (gouache). *The Bell Tower* (crayon, sauce, and wash). *Our Saviour:* Cartoon for a mosaic over the entrance to the Talashkino church (gouache). Set and costume designs for the Diaghilev Company's productions of Borodin's

230. Nicholas Roerich. Guests from Overseas. 1902

Prince Igor and Rimsky-Korsakov's *The Maid of Pskov*, and for an unrealized production of A. Remizov's *The Tragedy of Judas, Prince Iscariot.*

1910 *The Varangian Sea* (tempera). *Great Lands Beyond the Seas* (tempera and gouache). *The Korsun Campaign* (gouache and India ink). *Holy Princes*: Sketch of a mosaic for the Pochaevs Lavra (tempera). *The Paladins*: A decorative panel for the dining room in the Bazhanov residence in St. Petersburg. Set designs for the Diaghilev Company's production of Stravinsky's *Le Sacre de Printemps.*

1911 *The Hillfort* (tempera). *The Dove's Book* (tempera). *Father of the Human Race* (tempera). *The Battle at Kerzhenets*: A decorative panel accompanying the performance of the musical entracte in Rimsky-Korsakov's opera *The Tale of the Invisible City of Kitezh and the Maid Fevronia.* Set designs for the Moscow Art Theater's 1912 production of Ibsen's *Peer Gynt* and the St. Petersburg Antique Theater's 1912 production of Lope de Vega's *Fuente ovejuna.*

1912 *Sword of Valor* (tempera). *Subterranean Fires* (tempera). *Combat with the Serpent* (tempera). *Star Runes* (tempera). *The City Chaste Infuriates the Foe*

(tempera). Set and costume designs for unrealized productions of Ostrovsky's *The Snow Maiden* at the Reinecke Drama Theater, St. Petersburg, and of Wagner's *Tristan and Isolde* at the S. Zimin Opera House, Moscow, and for the Diaghilev Company's 1913 production of Stravinsky's *Le Sacre du Printemps.*

1913 *Standards. Caucasian Studies* (tempera). *Monastery* (tempera). Sketches for decoration of a Pskov chapel (tempera). Sketch of a mosaic for a monument to Arkhip Kuindzhi (gouache and bronze paint). *The Battle at Kerzhenets*: Sketch of a panel for Moscow's Kazan Railway Station (tempera). Set and costume designs for an unrealized production of Maeterlinck's *La Princesse Maleine* at the Free Theater, Moscow.

1914 *The Seat of Holiness* (tempera). *The Lord* (tempera). *The Magician. Red Skies* (tempera). *Cry of the Serpent* (tempera). *St. Procopius the Righteous Praying for the Unknown at Sea* (tempera). *St. Procopius the Righteous Averting a Cloud of Stone from Ustiug the Great* (tempera). *The Doomed City* (tempera). *The Messenger* (charcoal and pastel). *The Conquest of Kazan*: Sketch of a panel for Moscow's

229

231. Nicholas Roerich. Ancient Life. Sketch. 1904

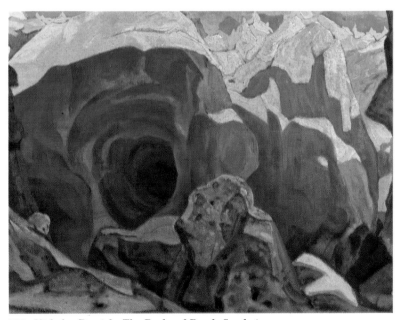

232. Nicholas Roerich. The Rocks of Rond. Set design
for Ibsen's *Peer Gynt*. 1912

Kazan Railway Station. Set and costume designs for
the Petrograd Music Drama Theater's production of
Maeterlinck's *Sœur Beatrice* and the London Covent
Garden's production of Borodin's *Prince Igor*.

1915 *The Giant's Grave* (begun in 1910). *The
Command of the Heavens* (tempera). *Overland
Haulage* (tempera). *Mehesky — The Moon People*
(tempera). *The Arrows of Heaven, the Spears of the
Earth* (tempera). *The Enemy of the Human Race.*
Poster (chromolithograph).

1916 *The Flying Carpet. St. Nicholas* (tempera).
St. Pantaleon the Healer. The Three Joys (tempera).
The Laws of Manu. Old Vilna (charcoal). *La
Princesse Maleine* series of drawings. Set designs
for Mussorgsky's *Night on the Bare Mountain*.

1917 *Endless Steps. Flaming Stones.* The *Heroic*
series (tempera). *The Flaming Heart* (tempera).
Lake (tempera). *Castle Hill* (tempera).

1918 *The Gold Mist. The Incantation. The Sea
Marvel. The Pipe of Peace. The Eternal Riders*

series (pastel and tempera). *Lake Ladoga* (tempera).
Cloud (pastel). *The Fog Thickens* (pastel).
St. Mercury of Smolensk (pencil).

1919 *The Treasure. The White Lady* (tempera).
The Legend of the Conqueror (tempera). *The Tsar
Saltan* suite (tempera). *The Sons of the Heavens*
(tempera). *St. Boris and St. Gleb* (tempera). *Solar
Eclipse* (pastel).

1920 *Message from the Orient* (tempera). The
Dreams of Wisdom suite (tempera). *The Dream of
the Orient* (tempera). *The Camp* (tempera). *The
Guardians of the Gate* (tempera). *The Song of the
Morning* (tempera). *St. George Slaying the Dragon*
(tempera). *The Prophetess* (pastel). Set designs for
the London Covent Garden's production of Rimsky-
Korsakov's *Sadko*.

1921 *Arizona. The Grand Canyon* (tempera). *The
White Stone* (tempera). *The Cloud No Bigger Than
a Man's Hand* (tempera). *Tristan's Palace* (tempera). *The Crown of Peace* (tempera). *Message from
the Heavens* (tempera). *The Patriarchs* (tempera).
The Desert (tempera). *Santa Fe. The Red Hills*
(tempera). *The Holy Hunters* (tempera).

1922 *The White Cloud* (tempera). *The Boyarina*
(pastel). *The Dove's Book* (tempera). *The Messenger*
(tempera). *The Incantation* (tempera). *The Land's
Prayer: Rostov the Great* (tempera). *The Show
Sentinels* (tempera). *St. Sergius* (tempera). *The Last
King (The Empty Throne)* (tempera). *Berendei Girl*
(pastel).

1923 The *Messiah* series. *Reflections* (tempera).
The Vision (tempera). *The Legend* (tempera). *The
Miracle* (tempera). *The Holy Visitors* (tempera). *The
Solovki Monastery* (tempera). *The Three Arrows*
(tempera). *Bridge of Glory* (tempera).

1924 *White Steeds* (tempera). *Mountain Monastery*
(tempera). *Mountain Town* (tempera). *Guru
Shambhala* (tempera). *The Road to Tibet* (tempera).
The Source of the Indus (tempera). *And We Open
the Gates* (tempera). *Where the Ways of Christ and
Buddha Cross* (tempera). The *Himalayas, Sikkim,
Standards of the Orient*, and *Tibetan Road* series
(all tempera).
In 1919, Roerich met Rabindranath Tagore in
London. In 1920–22, while traveling in the United
States, he exhibited his works and engaged in
enlightening activities. In May 1923, he left for India
via Europe as leader of scientific expeditions to
Sikkim and Bhutan in 1924. Between 1925 and 1936,
besides artistic work he carried on intensive
researches. In 1929, he published his project for
a Roerich Pact to safeguard cultural treasures. He
lived in India (Kulu) from 1936 until his death on
December 13, 1947. During the Second World War
he organized exhibition-sales of paintings for the
benefit of the Red Army.

233. Nicholas Roerich. The Idols. Sketch. 1901

234. Nicholas Roerich. The Polovtsy's Camp. Set design for Act 2
of Borodin's *Prince Igor*. 1908

235. Nicholas Roerich. Heavenly Battle. Version of the 1909 picture. 1912

Nikolai Sapunov

Nikolai Nikolayevich Sapunov was born into a Moscow merchant's family of modest means on December 17 O.S. (29), 1880. Between 1893 and 1904, he studied under Isaac Levitan, Valentin Serov, and Konstantin Korovin at the Moscow School of Painting, Sculpture and Architecture, and from 1904 to 1911 under Alexander Kiseliov at the St. Petersburg Academy of Arts. In 1900, he worked at the theatrical workshops of the Moscow Art Theater under the supervision of Victor Simov and between 1901 and 1902 at the Bolshoi Theater in Moscow where he made settings after Konstantin Korovin's designs. In 1902, he traveled to Italy. In 1908, he settled in St. Petersburg, where he was a co-founder and member of the Artistic Council of Vsevolod Meyerhold's House of Interludes. He exhibited from 1900 on, taking part in the famous Blue Rose show of 1907, from which year he co-participated with World of Art artists in various exhibitions. He was represented at World of Art shows between 1910 and 1913.

1900 *Winter. Blossoming Apple Trees* (c. 1900, tempera).

1902–03 Set designs for the Moscow Hermitage Theater's production of E. Esposito's *Camorra*.

1903 Set designs for unrealized productions of Gluck's *Orpheus and Eurydice* and Bizet's *Carmen*.

1904 (?) *Minuet* (tempera). *Ballet* (tempera and charcoal, touched with silver paint and tinted bronze). *Roses. Nighttime Gala.* Set designs for an unrealized production of E. Humperdinck's *Hänsel and Gretel* and for Tchaikovsky's *Romeo and Juliet*.

1905 *Still Life. Roses* (gouache and tempera). Set designs for the Moscow Opera Studio's production of Rossini's *The Barber of Seville* and for Acts 4 and 5 of Maeterlinck's *Death of Tintagiles* at the Theatrical Studio on Povarskaya St., Moscow.

1906 Set designs for Ibsen's *Hedda Gabbler* and sets and the costume of Pierrot for Blok's *Balaganchik* (Fairground Booth) at Vera Komissarzhevskaya's Theater, St. Petersburg.

1907 *Still Life with Self-Portrait* (tempera). *Blue Hydrangeas* (tempera). *Fancy-Dress Ball* (silver and gold paint with tinted bronze). *Danse Macabre* after F. Wedekind's play (tempera, sized paint, oil, gold paint, India ink, charcoal, and pastel). Set designs for Maeterlinck's *Pelléas et Mélisande*, produced presumably in the same year at Vera Komissarzhevskaya's Theater, St. Petersburg.

1908 *Portrait of the Artist Nikolai Milioti. The Merry-go-round* (tempera). *The Merry-go-round* (tempera). *The Dog Rose* (tempera). *Peonies* (tempera). *The Mummers* (1908 ?, watercolor). Set designs for a production of Chekhov's *Uncle Vanya* at Vera Komissarzhevskaya's Theater, St. Petersburg.

1909 *The Mystic Gathering* after Blok's *Balaganchik* (gouache and charcoal, with gold, silver, and bronze paint). *Night* (tempera). Set designs for Shaw's *Caesar and Cleopatra*. Vignettes for *Vesy* (Scales).

1910 *Still Life with Vase and Flowers* (tempera). *The Tavern. The Green Bull Hotel on the Canal Bank*, after M. Kuzmin's pastorale *The Dutch Girl Liza* (tempera). Sketch of a setting for the same pastorale (pencil). *Blue Hydrangeas* (tempera). Set and costume designs for the St. Petersburg House of Interludes' production of *The Scarf of Columbine* after A. Schnitzler's story.

1911 *Portrait of Anfisa Komissarzhevskaya. The Mulatto Girl* (four versions). *Rhododendrons* (tempera). *Still Life with Flowers* (1911, tempera). *Portrait of Liubov Guseva. Pierrot's Supper* (1911 ?, watercolor). *The Death of Pierrot* (watercolor). *Chinese Deity* (watercolor). Curtain and decor designs, plus studies for the K. Nezlobin Theater production in Moscow of Molière's *Le Bourgeois Gentilhomme*.

1912 *Portrait of the Poet Mikhail Kuzmin. Still Life with Vase, Flowers, and Fruit* (tempera). *Tea-*

236. Nikolai Sapunov. Still Life with Vase and Flowers. 1910

237. Nikolai Sapunov. The Merry-go-round

238. Nikolai Sapunov. Still Life with Vase, Flowers, and Fruit. 1912

239. Nikolai Sapunov. Two stage costume designs

Drinking. Sketch (tempera). *Flowers and China.*
Spring. Sketch (tempera). *Spring* (tempera). *Portrait of the Poet Mikhail Kuzmin* (tempera). *Still Life* (gouache). *Portrait of the Poet Valery Briusov* (pencil). *Woman with a Fan* (pencil). *Shrubs* (pencil). Curtain and costume designs for the production of C. Gozzi's *Princess Turandot* at the K. Nezlobin Theater, Moscow.
Sapunov drowned in the Gulf of Finland on June 14 (27), 1912.

240. Nikolai Sapunov. Still Life with Hydrangeas. 1910

241. Nikolai Sapunov. The Embankment in Alexandria. Set design for Shaw's *Caesar and Cleopatra*. 1909

Zinaida Serebryakova

Zinaida Evgenyevna Serebryakova (née Lanceray) was born on December 10 O.S. (22), 1884 on the estate of Neskuchnoye near Kharkov. Her father was a sculptor, her mother Ekaterina (née Benois), sister of the artist Alexander Benois. After her father's death in 1886 she and her brother Evgeny, the future World of Art artist Lanceray, were placed in charge of their maternal grandfather, the architect Nikolai Benois. In 1901–02, she studied under Ilya Repin at Princess Maria Tenisheva's private school, between 1903 and 1905, at the studio of the portrait painter Osip Braz, and in 1905–06 at the Académie de la Grande Chaumière in Paris. Between 1903 and 1906, she traveled to France and Italy. She first exhibited in 1910, co-participating in World of Art shows from 1911 on.

1905 *A Village Girl* (watercolor and India ink).

1908 *Portrait of Boris Serebryakov, the Artist's Husband. Seated Peasant Woman. Orchard in Blossom* (tempera). *Peasant Woman from Kursk Province* (tempera). *The Green of Autumn* (gouache).

1909 *Self-Portrait at Toilette. Young Peasant Woman* (tempera and gouache). *Portrait of a Student* (charcoal and tempera).

1910 *Winter Landscape* (tempera). *Portrait of Maria Solntseva-Lanceray. Portrait of Olga Lanceray. Portrait of Mikhail Benois* (tempera).

1911 *Girl with a Candle: Self-Portrait. Girl Bathing. Portrait of Nadezhda Chulkova. Before the Storm: The Village of Neskuchnoye* (tempera). *Self-Portrait with a Scarf* (tempera). *Portrait of Elena Lanceray. Haystacks* (tempera). *A Young Tatar* (tempera).

1912 *The Bathhouse*, a sketch for the 1913 painting. *Portrait of Ekaterina Lanceray, née Benois, the Artist's Mother. Wetnurse with Child. Peasant* (tempera). *Lukyan the Beggar from the Village of Vesyoloye* (tempera study).

1913 *The Bathhouse. Fields in Neskuchnoye.*

1914 *At Breakfast. Peasants. Two Peasant Girls.* Studies for the 1915 painting *Harvesting. Mountain Landscape* (tempera). *Trees in a Park* (tempera). *Spring in the Crimea* (tempera). *Peasant Woman with a Kvas Pitcher. Peasants at Dinner.*

1915 *Harvesting. Peasant Woman Pulling on Her Boots*, a study for the previous painting. *Portrait of*

Evgeny Lanceray in a Shako (tempera). *Peasant Girl. Fields* (tempera study). *Portrait of Boris Serebryakov, the Artist's Husband* (pencil).

1916 *Siam* (tempera). *India* (tempera). *Turkey* (tempera). *Persia* (tempera). Designs for the decoration of Moscow's Kazan Railway Station. *Young Man in a Blue Jersey. Bleaching Linen*, a study for the 1917 painting. Design of a panel for Moscow's Kazan Railway Station (lead pencil and red chalk). *Two Odalisques* (lead pencil and tempera). *Odalisque* (lead pencil and tempera). *Girls Seated*, a study for the 1917 painting *Bleaching Linen* (lead pencil). Sketches of female figures for the 1917 painting *Bleaching Linen* (lead pencil and India ink).

1917 *Bleaching Linen. Sleeping Peasant Woman. Diana and Actaeon* (tempera study).
Between 1917 and 1919, Serebryakova lived at Neskuchnoye and in Kharkov. In 1920, she moved to Petrograd where she stayed until leaving for Paris in 1924, where she lived for the rest of her life.
Works done between 1918 and 1967 include: *The House of Cards* (1919), *Portrait of the Poet Grigory Petnikov* (1919, red chalk), *Portrait of the Art Historian Sergei Ernst* (1920), *The Attributes of the Arts* (1920–22), *Portrait of Anastasia Notgaft* (1921, pastel), *Blue Ballerinas* (1922), *Ballerina Resting* (1920, pastel), *Herring and Lemon* (1920–22), *Self-Portrait with Daughters* (1921), *Self-Portrait* (1922, pastel), *Little Girls at the Piano* (1922), *Portrait of Katya in a Blue Dress by the Xmas Tree* (1922, pastel), *Portrait of Anna Cherkasova-Benois with Her Son* (1922), *Portrait of the Artist Dmitry Bushen* (1922, pastel), *Portrait of the Dancer Lydia Ivanova* (1922, watercolor and pastel), *Portrait of the Choreographer George Balanchivadze-Balanchine* (1923,

242. Zinaida Serebryakova. Girl with a Candle: Self-Portrait. 1911

243. Zinaida Serebryakova. Harvesting. 1915

244. Zinaida Serebryakova. Village of Neskuchnoye. 1912

245. Zinaida Serebryakova. Self-Potrait at Toilette. 1909

246. Zinaida Serebryakova. The Bathhouse. 1913

pastel), *In the Kitchen* (1923), *Snow Flakes. The "Nutcracker" Ballet* (1923, pastel), *Ballet Dancers in Their Dressing Room* (1923, pastel), *Portrait of the Dancer Maria Dobroliubova* (1922, pastel), *Small Bridge in Gatchina* (1923, pastel), and *The White Lake in Gatchina* (1924, pastel).

During her French period (1924–67), Serebryakova produced primarily landscapes, genre pieces, still lifes, portraits, and studies of models in the media of pastel and tempera.

She died in Paris on September 19, 1967.

247. Zinaida Serebryakova. At Breakfast. 1914

248. Zinaida Serebryakova. House of Cards. 1919

Valentin Serov

Valentin Alexandrovich Serov was born in St. Petersburg on January 7 O.S. (19), 1865. His father, Alexander Nikolayevich Serov, was a well-known composer and music critic, his mother, Valentina Semyonovna (née Bergman), a pianist and civic figure. In 1872–73, he studied under Karl Köpping in Munich. In 1874–75 and in 1878–80, he took lessons from Ilya Repin in Paris and Moscow. From 1880 through 1885, he worked with Pavel Chistyakov both at the St. Petersburg Academy of Arts and in the artist's studio. In 1885, he visited Germany, Holland, and Belgium, and in 1887, Italy. He first exhibited in 1885, co-participating in World of Art shows from 1898 on.

The more significant works completed prior to 1898 include: *Self-Portrait* (1885), *Portrait of Olga Trubnikova* (1885), *The Schiavone Quay in Venice* (1887), *Girl with Peaches* (1887), *Girl in Sunlight* (1887), *Overgrown Pond. Domotkanovo* (1888), *Portrait of Nadezhda Derviz with Her Child* (1888–89), *Portrait of the Italian Singer Angelo Masini* (1890), *Portrait of the Artist Konstantin Korovin* (1891), *Portrait of the Italian Singer Francesco Tamagno* (1891), *Portrait of Isaac Levitan* (1893), *Portrait of Maria Lvova* (1895), *The Coronation* (1896), *Summer. Portrait of Olga Serova* (1895), *October in Domotkanovo* (1895), and *Portrait of Maria Morozova* (1897).

1898 *In Winter* (pastel and gouache). *In the Village. Peasant Woman with a Horse* (pastel). *Self-Portrait* (etching). *October* (etching).

1899 *Children. Sasha and Yura Serov. Portrait of Sophia Botkina. Portrait of Alexander Pushkin* (pencil and watercolor heightened with white). *Portrait of the Composer Alexander Glazunov* (lithograph).

1900 *Portrait of the Emperor Nicholas II. Peter II and Princess Elizaveta Riding to Hounds* (tempera and gouache). *Portrait of Sophia Lukomskaya* (watercolor heightened with white), *Portrait of Isaac Levitan* (pastel). *Model* (pencil, chalk, and red chalk).

1901 *Mika Morozov. Self-Portrait* (watercolor and India ink).

1902 *Young Peter I Riding in the Chase* (tempera). *Portrait of Princess Zinaida Yusupova. Portrait of Mika Morozov. Portrait of the Artist Ilya Ostroukhov. Catherine II Setting Out to Hunt with Falcons* (tempera and gouache). *Portrait of Konstantin Pobedonostsev* (charcoal, crayon, and red chalk). *Portrait of Vera Ziloti* (chalk and charcoal).

1903 *Portrait of Prince Felix Sumarokov-Elston. Portrait of Eudoxia Loseva. The Violinist Eugène Isaÿe* (pencil).

1904 *Portrait of Sergei Diaghilev. Colts at a Watering Place: Domotkanovo. Ballroom of an Old House. Portrait of Genrietta Girshman* (tempera). *Road to Domotkanovo in Winter* (pastel). *Portrait of Cleopatra Obninskaya* (pastel and charcoal). *Madonna* (watercolor).

1905 *Portrait of Maxim Gorky. Portrait of the Actress Maria Yermolova. Horses by the Sea. Bathing the Horse. Model* (tempera). *Portrait of the Poet Konstantin Balmont* (pastel). *Funeral of Baumann* (charcoal, chalk, and gouache). *"Soldiers, heroes everyone, where is all your glory?"* (charcoal and tempera). *Cossacks Dispersing a Demonstration in 1905* (gouache heightened with white). *The Sumy Regiment in 1905* (watercolor, chalk, and pencil). *1905. The Revolt Is Suppressed* (pencil). *Execution. 1905* (watercolor). *Portrait of Fyodor Chaliapin* (charcoal and chalk). *Portrait of the Actress Glikeria Fedotova. Portrait of Pyotr Semyonov-Tien-Shansky* (charcoal, chalk, and crayon). *Portrait of Maria Botkina* (pencil, chalk, and red chalk). *Portrait of Elizaveta Karzinkina* (charcoal heightened with white), *Portrait of Yuri Morozov* (charcoal and red chalk).

1906 *Portrait of Prince Vladimir Golitsyn. Portrait of Elizaveta Karzinkina. Catherine II Driving Out* (pastel and tempera). Cartoon: *1906 Harvest Prospects* (India ink and watercolor heightened with white). *Hunting with Borzoi Hounds in the Eighteenth Century* (pencil and ink).

1907 *Peter the Great* (tempera). *Portrait of Genrietta Girshman* (tempera). *Portrait of the Writer Leonid Andreyev* (watercolor and tempera). *Portrait of the Actors Alexander Lensky and Alexander*

249. Valentin Serov. Portrait of Ivan Morozov. 1910

Yuzhin (tempera). *Portrait of Mikhail Vrubel* (charcoal, red chalk, and chalk). *Portrait of the Pianist Wanda Landowska* (pencil, watercolor, and pastel, heightened with white). Set designs for the St. Petersburg Mariinsky Theater's production of Serov's opera *Judith*.

1908 *Portrait of Dmitry Stasov. Portrait of Evgenia Alafuzova. Portrait of Eudoxia Morozova. Portrait of Maria Akimova. Portrait of Nikolai Poznyakov. The Coachman* (tempera and pastel). *Portrait of Anna Benois* (pastel). *Portrait of the Composer Nikolai Rimsky-Korsakov* (charcoal). *Portrait of the Actor Vasily Kachalov* (pencil). *Portrait of the Actor Ivan Moskvin* (pencil). *Portrait of the Actor and Stage Director Konstantin Stanislavsky* (pencil).

1909 *An Autumn Night. Portrait of Princess Alexandra Liewen. Portrait of Emmanuel Nobel. Anna Pavlova in "Le Sylphides." Poster* (tempera). *The Oprichnik* (tempera). *Portrait of Elena Oliv* (gouache, watercolor, and pastel). *Portrait of Anna Pavlova* (pencil). *Portrait of the Ballerina Tamara Kar-*

savina (pencil). *Parisian Horses* (pencil). *Portrait of Anna Zetlin* (watercolor). *Portrait of the Choreographer Michel Fokine* (red chalk). *Portrait of the Artist Léon Bakst* (India ink and gouache). *Portrait of Alexei Morozov* (gouache, pastel, watercolor, and red chalk, heightened with white). *Parisian Horses. Percherons* (charcoal and chalk). *Peter I*, design for a monument (India ink). *Portrait of Elena Roerich* (pencil).

1910 *The Grand Eagle Cup. The Grand Eagle Cup* (tempera). *Odysseus and Nausicaä* (tempera). *Odysseus and Nausicaä* (tempera and pastel). *Odysseus and Nausicaä* (tempera). *The Rape of Europa* (tempera sketch). *Peter I in Monplaisir* (tempera). *Peter the Great at a Construction Site* (tempera and watercolor). *Portrait of Anna Staal* (tempera). *Portrait of Ivan Morozov* (tempera). *Portrait of Ida Rubinstein* (tempera and charcoal). *Portrait of Margarita Morozova. Portrait of Maria Zetlin* (tempera). *Portrait of Natalia Koussevitzkaya* (tempera). *Portrait of Oscar and Rosa Grusenberg. Portrait of Sergei Muromtsev. Portrait of Vaslav Nijinsky*

241

250. Valentin Serov. Portrait of Ida Rubinstein. 1910

(charcoal and pencil). *Portrait of Isabella Grunberg* (pencil and watercolor). *Portrait of Princess Olga Orlova* (pencil). *Portrait of Princess Olga Orlova* (charcoal, chalk, and gouache). *Portrait of Princess Sophia Olsufyeva* (charcoal, chalk, and gouache). Curtain and curtain design for the Diaghilev Company's production of Rimsky-Korsakov's *Schéhérazade*.

1911 *Portrait of Princess Olga Orlova. Portrait of Vladimir Girshman. Peter I at a Construction Site* (tempera). *Portrait of the Actor Alexei Stakhovich. Portrait of the Actor Alexei Stakhovich* (tempera). *Portrait of Elena Balina. Portrait of Genrietta Girshman* (pastel). *Portrait of Princess Polina Shcherbatova* (unfinished, tempera, charcoal, and pastel). *Portrait of Nadezhda Lamanova* (charcoal, chalk, and red chalk). Illustrations for Krylov's *Fables* (1895–1911; pencil, India ink, etching, watercolor, and charcoal heightened with white). Designs for decorative panels on the themes of Ovid's *Metamorphoses* for the dining room in the Nosovs' residence, Moscow (watercolor, pencil, charcoal, and gouache).
Serov died in Moscow on November 22 (December 5), 1911.

251. Valentin Serov. Portrait of Princess Zinaida Yusupova. 1900–02

252. Valentin Serov. Feast Outside Holophernes' Tent. Set design for Serov's opera *Judith*. 1907

253. Valentin Serov. Portrait of Fyodor Chaliapin. 1905. Sketch

254. Valentin Serov. Portrait of Mika Morozov. 1902

Konstantin Somov

Konstantin Andreyevich Somov was born in St. Petersburg on November 18 O.S. (30), 1869. His father, Andrei Ivanovich Somov, was senior curator at the Hermitage. Konstantin was educated at Karl Mai's gymnasium, where he made the acquaintance of Alexander Benois, Walter Nouvel, and Dmitry Filosofov. In 1884, he started attending Sunday evening classes at the Society for the Encouragement of the Arts. From 1888 till 1897, he studied at the Academy of Arts, where from 1894 he took a course at Ilya Repin's studio. However, in 1897 he dropped out and left for Paris where he frequented various private studios and the Académie Colarossi. In the summer of 1898, he was represented at the Exhibition of Russian and Finnish Artists in St. Petersburg. In 1899, he revisited Paris and traveled to Britain. In 1911 and 1912, he took a cure at Beaulieu, in the South of France, for a sick throat. In 1914, he was made an Academician of the St. Petersburg Academy of Arts. He first exhibited in 1894 and co-participated in World of Art shows from 1899 on.

1897 *Portrait of Andrei Ivanovich Somov, the Artist's Father. In Confidence. Ludmila in Chernomor's Garden* (after Pushkin's poem *Ruslan and Ludmila*). *Pavilion* (watercolor). *In August. Twilight in an Old Park* (gouache and pastel). *Portrait of Anna Somova-Mikhailova, the Artist's Sister* (lead pencil, crayon, and chalk).

1898 *Self-Portrait* (watercolor, pastel, and pencil, heightened with white). *Poets* (watercolor, pastel, and gouache).

1899 *Bathing Girls. An Overgrown Pond. In the Bosquet* (watercolor, gold paint, and varnish). *Portrait of the Poet Alexander Sergeyevich Pushkin* (watercolor heightened with white). *Spring Landscape* (watercolor). *Head of a Girl (Portrait of Elena Vladimirskaya)*. *Study* (watercolor and charcoal). Illustrations and headpiece for Pushkin's *Count Nouline*.

1900 *Lady in Blue. Portrait of the Artist Elizaveta Martynova* (1897–1900). *Island of Love. At the Dacha, or Family Happiness* (1898–1900). *Before Sunset. Summer Landscape. The Concert* (watercolor touched with silver paint).

1901 *Portrait of Anna Ostroumova*. Cover for the *Northern Flowers* almanac.

1902 *Evening* (1900–02). *Martyshkino (near Oranienbaum). Magic* (gouache, gold paint, and watercolor). *Self-Portrait* (lead pencil heightened with white).

1903 *L'Echo du temps passé* (watercolor, gouache, and lead pencil). *Courtesans* (watercolor, gouache, and pastel). *Lady Asleep in a Blue Dress* (gouache and watercolor). *Lady with a Dog* (lead pencil, pen and ink). *Self-Portrait* (watercolor and gouache). *Lady in Pink* (gouache and watercolor).

1904 *Portrait of the Artist Elizaveta Zvantseva* (unfinished). *Bathing* (watercolor). *Portrait of E.P. Ostroumova* (watercolor and gouache). *Fireworks* (gouache). *New and Old Year* calendar (1905) for the Society of St. Eugenia.

1905 *The Lovers* (porcelain).

1906 *Portrait of the Poet Vyacheslav Ivanov* (lead pencil, watercolor, and gouache). *Lady Removing Her Mask* (five copies in porcelain and one in biscuit). *The Lovers* (porcelain, in four copies).

1907 *Harlequin and Death* (watercolor and gouache). *Portrait of the Poet Alexander Blok* (lead pencil, crayon, and gouache). *Portrait of Evgeny Lanceray* (lead pencil and crayon, heightened with white). Title page for Blok's *The Theater*. Frontispiece for Ivanov's *Cor Ardens*. Illustrations for *Das Lesebuch der Marquise*.

1908 *The Ridiculed Kiss. The Rainbow* (watercolor and gouache). Cover for *The Parisienne*.

1909 *Portrait of the Poet Mikhail Kuzmin* (watercolor and gouache). *Self-Portrait* (watercolor and gouache). *Young Woman Asleep* (gouache and

255. Konstantin Somov. Winter. The Skating Rink. 1915

watercolor). Costume designs of Columbine for Anna Pavlova.

1910 *Portrait of Mstislav Dobuzhinsky* (lead pencil and red chalk). *Portrait of the Dancer Nikolai Poznyakov* (lead pencil heightened with white).

1911 *Portrait of Genrietta Girshman. Portrait of Euphemia Nosova. Portrait of S.P. Zvantseva* (lead and colored pencils). *Portrait of Mefody Lukyanov* (lead and colored pencils).

1912 *Love Letter (Young Girl in a Red Dress). Harlequin and Lady* (watercolor and gouache, in two versions).

1913 *Portrait of Margarita Karpova.* Curtain design for Moscow's Free Theater.

1914 *Portrait of Elena Oliv. In the Wood. Portrait of the Singer Deborah Karysheva* (crayons, in two versions). *Portrait of Walter Nouvel* (lead pencil and red chalk). *Marquise and Cupid* (watercolor). *Italian Comedy* (watercolor and gouache). *Allegory of Life and Death* (watercolor).

1915 *Winter. The Skating Rink. The Magic Fairy. Summer Morning. Landscape with a Rainbow. Columbine's Little Tongue* (watercolor and gouache). *Portrait of Genrietta Girshman* (lead pencil and red chalk).

1916 *Portrait of Evgeny Mikhailov. A Youth on His Knees in Front of a Lady in a Lilac Frock with a Rose in Her Hand (The First Love)* (gouache). *Lady in a Blue Burnoose Embraced by a Young Man in a Green Tunic* (watercolor). *Young Woman Seated* (1909–16, watercolor). *Landscape with a Bonfire* (watercolor). *Landscape with a Fire* (watercolor).

1917 *Portrait of Nadezhda Vysotskaya. Evening Shadows* (1900–07). Study for a portrait of Nadezhda Vysotskaya (lead pencil). *Hunter and Peasant Girl in the 18th Century (Village Girl and Rider in the Woods)* (watercolor). Ilustrations and textual arrangement for *Le Livre de la Marquise.*

1918 *Portrait of Mefody Lukyanov. Columbine in Love. Getting Ready to Bathe. Two Bathing Girls.*

256. Konstantin Somov. Young Woman Sleeping. 1922

257. Konstantin Somov. Ploughland. 1900

258. Konstantin Somov. Young Woman. Asleep. 1909

259. Konstantin Somov. Landscape with a Rainbow. 1915

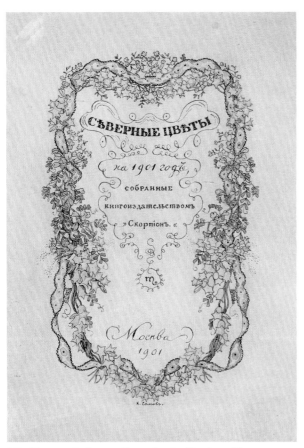

260. Konstantin Somov. Cover for the *Northern Flowers* almanac. 1901

261. Konstantin Somov. A Youth on His Knees in Front of a Lady. 1916

262. Konstantin Somov. Cover design for the fashion magazine *The Parisienne*. 1908

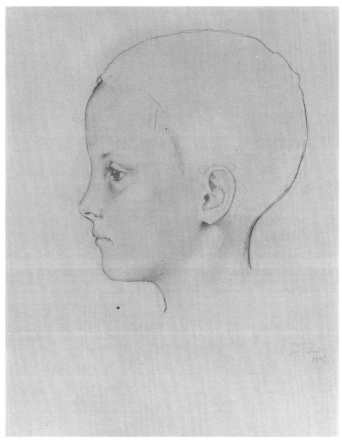

263. Konstantin Somov. Head of the Little Girl Olya. 1896

248

Bluebird (gouache and watercolor). Illustrations for *Le Livre de la Marquise.*

1919 *Lady in a Blue Dress Lying in the Grass. Young 18th-Century Lady in a Park. Lady in an 18th-Century Dress Sleeping in a Room. Summer. Park with Figures and Tubbed Orange-Trees. Landscape with a Rainbow* (watercolor).

1920 *Summer Morning* (version of the 1915 painting). *Lady Asleep. Blue Dress, Yellow Furniture. Harlequin and Lady. Lady in a Yellow Dress Dozing in a Garden* (sketch). *Carnival in Venice (Harlequin and Lady). Italian Comedy. Fireworks in a Park* (watercolor and gouache). *Portrait of Anna Somova-Mikhailova* (lead pencil and red chalk). *Fireworks behind Park Railings. Portrait of Renèe Notgaft* (lead pencil and red chalk, in three versions).

1921 *Landscape with a Rainbow and Bathing Girls (Summer). Portrait of Nadezhda Dobychina* (lead pencil and red chalk). *Self-Portrait* (lead pencil and red chalk). *Portrait of Georgi Nashatyr* (lead pencil and red chalk).

1922 *Harlequin and Lady. Peasant Maiden and Youth in a Moonlit Evening Landscape. Fireworks Display. Portrait of Evgenia Stepanova* (lead pencil).

1923 *Pierrot and Lady. Park. Fireworks. Romantic Ballet in the 1830s. View of the Catherine Canal from the Windows of the Artist's Apartments* (study). *Landscape with a Rainbow, Three Figures,* and *Small Dogs* (five verisons of the 1919 painting). *Nonexistent Porcelain. Still Life with a Chest of Drawers, Vase, Chinaman, and Lilac.*

265. Konstantin Somov. Self-Portrait. 1909

264. Konstantin Somov. Portrait of the Poet Mikhail Kuzmin. 1909

1924 *Portrait of Elena Somova.* Costume designs in 18th-century style for the dancer Tamara Karsavina.

In 1923, Somov went with a group of Petrograd and Moscow artists to the United States to mount an exhibition of Russian visual arts there. Resident in New York in 1924 and 1925, he was befriended by Sergei Rachmaninov and his family. In May 1925, he moved to France where he worked as a painter, graphic artist and illustrator, and miniaturist. He died in Paris on May 6, 1939.

Sergei Sudeikin

Sergei Yurievich Sudeikin was born on March 7 O.S. (19), 1882 into the family of a St. Petersburg official. Between 1897 and 1909, he studied intermittently at the Moscow School of Painting, Sculpture and Architecture and in 1909–10 at the St. Petersburg Academy of Arts. In 1900, he traveled to the Caucasus, presumably in 1904 to Italy, and in 1906 he visited Paris. He first exhibited in 1904 in the Scarlet Rose show and was represented at the Blue Rose exihibition of 1907 and the Wreath show of 1908. He exhibited with World of Art artists in 1907 and 1908, and took part in World of Art shows from 1911 on. In 1905, he worked for the Moscow Art Theater's studio in Povarskaya Street, in 1906, for Vera Komissarzhevskaya's Theater in St. Petersburg, in 1909, for the New Drama Theater there, while between 1910 and 1917 he co-participated in productions of Vsevolod Meyerhold's House of Interludes. Simultaneously he designed productions for the Stray Dog (1912–16) and Comedians' Halt (1916) cabarets.

1903 Illustrations to Maeterlinck's *Death of Tintagiles*.

1904 *Eros. Leda and the Swan. Moon Eros. Bathers. Waterfall.*

1905 Sketch of a *mise en scène* and set designs for Acts 1–3 of Maeterlinck's *Death of Tintagiles* at the theatrical studio in Povarskaya St., Moscow. *The Swings. Duet* (watercolor). *Peacocks* panel and *Picking Flowers* design for the decoration of the 1906 Russian Exposition in Paris. *Night Gala. Pastorale.*

1906 *Festivities. Gondolas. Capriccio. Interior. Pastorale. Ballet Pastorale.* Set and costume designs for Maeterlinck's *Sœur Beatrice* at Vera Komissarzhevskaya's Theater, St. Petersburg. Vignettes and drawings for the *Golden Fleece.*

1907 *Venice. Romantic Landscape* (1907?, tempera). *Columbine. Grape Harvest. Love. Serf Ballet. Evening Landscape. Gavotte. In a Park* (watercolor, gouache, and India ink). *Zephyr and Fawn* (watercolor). *Abduction* (watercolor). Poster for the fancy-dress ball of the Russian Hunters' Club. Frontispiece, vignettes, and drawings for *Vesy* (Scales).

1908 *Winter Skating. Romantic Landscape. At the Seaside. The New Moon. In the Countryside. Evening on an Island. Decorative Motif. The Marquese.*

1909 *Still Life with Porcelain Figurines and Roses. Nothern Poet. Portrait of Olga Glebova-Sudeikina*

as the Muddlehead in Yu. Belyaev's *Play of the Same Name* (India ink and pastel). Set and costume designs for the St. Petersburg New Drama Theater's production of George Bernard Shaw's *Caesar and Cleopatra.* Illustrations for the *Primrose* and *Flowerbed* readers.

1910 *The Ballet. Decorative Landscape. The Merry-go-round.* Set designs for the St. Petersburg New Drama Theater's productioin of O. Dymov's *Spring Madness.* Set and costume designs for the St. Petersburg House of Interludes' production of E. Znosko-Borowsky's *The Transformed Prince.* Curtain design for *Columbine and Punchinello* at the House of Interludes. Drawings for M. Kuzmin's *The Journey of John Fearfax.*

1911 *Saxon Figurines. The Fancy-Dress Ball. Still Life.* Curtain, set, and costume designs for the St. Petersburg Small Drama Theater's production of M. Kuzmin's *Amusements for Virgins.* Curtain design for the same theater's production of Tchaikovsky's *The Swan Lake.*

1912 *Pastorale. In a Café* (1912?, tempera). *Flowers and China* (1912?). *Russians in Paris* (watercolor and India ink). Set and costume designs for the St. Petersburg Russian Drama Theater's production of Jacinte Benavente's *The Seamy Side of Life.*

1913 Curtain design for the Diaghilev Company's production of Florent Schmitt's *La Tragedie de Salome.* Set and costume designs for the St. Petersburg Palace Theater's production of N. Evreinov and L. Urvantsev's *The Runaway.*

266. Sergei Sudeikin. Harlequin's Garden. 1915–16

1914 *Country Hermitage. Shrovetide Characters* series of *lubok* pictures (1914?, watercolor). Set designs for the production of Guy de Maupassant's *M-lle Fifi* at the Theater of the Literature and Art Society, St. Petersburg.

1915 *Petrouchka. The Puppet Theatre. A Sea Idyll. Avenue* (1915?). *The Central Avenue* (1915?). *Pond* (1915?). *Panel on a Venetian Theater Theme. Harlequinade. Park* (51 x 67). *Park* (76.5 x 87). *Shrovetide Fête. Portrait of the Writer Yuri Yurkun* (pastel). Bill announcing the production of Yu. Ozarovsky's comedy *The Giddy Goose's Commands* (tempera and crayons). Set designs for the St. Petersburg Mariinsky Theater's productions of Adam's *Giselle* and Bizet's *L'Arlésienne*, the Moscow Kamerny Theater's production of Beaumarchais' *The Marriage of Figaro* and for Offenbach's *The Tales of Hoffmann* at the S. Zimin Opera House, Moscow. Illustrations for M. Kuzmin's *The Venetian Lunatics.*

1916 *Decorative Landscape. Summer Landscape. Indian Summer. Landscape with Figures* (1916?).

1917 Broadside poster: *Flock Together, Birds of the Air!* (watercolor, gouache, and India ink).

1918 *A Fantastic Scene in the Mountains (Chimera)* (done between 1918 and 1920). *Portrait of Yakov Izrailevich.*

1919 *Don Juan.* Illustrations for V. Kamensky's *The Dugout.*
In 1920 Sudeikin went abroad. Between 1920 and 1922, he lived in France. In 1923, he settled in the United States, from where he made frequent visits to Europe. He worked primarily as a stage designer of operas and ballets by Mozart, Stravinsky, Rakhmaninov, Glazunov, Tcherepnin, Adam, Gershwin, and other composers. He also produced a few easel paintings such as *Russian Idyll, My Life,* and *American Panorama.* He died in New York in 1946.

267. Sergei Sudeikin. Saxon Figurines. 1911

268. Sergei Sudeikin. Park in Front of the Castle. Set design for Tchaikovsky's *The Swan Lake*. 1911

269. Sergei Sudeikin. Still Life with Porcelain Figurines and Roses. 1909

270. Sergei Sudeikin. Costume design for Shaw's *Caesar and Cleopatra*. 1909

271. Sergei Sudeikin. Petrouchka. 1918

Sergei Chekhonin

Sergei Vasilyevich Chekhonin was born in the village of Lykoshino in the vicinity of Tver. In 1896–97, he studied at the Drawing School of the Society for the Encouragement of the Arts, and theareafter till 1900 under Ilya Repin at Princess Maria Tenisheva's private school. In 1904, he worked at the potter's workshop in Abramtsevo. Between 1913 and 1917, he supervised the school of enamel painting and decoration in Rostov-Yaroslavsky. He was represented at World of Art shows from 1911 on.

1905 Drawings and vignettes for *Zritel* (The Spectator) and *Maski* (Masks) magazines.

1906 Covers for N. Morozov's *Revelation in Storm and Gale* and S. Rafalovich's *Don Juan Spurned*. Illustrations for the *Calendar of the Russian Revolution*.

1907 Headpieces and drawings for *The Living Word* reader. Frontispiece for K. Balmont's *The Calls of Antiquity*.

1908 Covers for the collected works of Leo Tolstoy, Dostoyevsky, Victor Hugo, Lope de Vega, Sir Walter Scott, N. Zlatovratsky, and M. Konopnitskaya.

1909 Cover for A. Razin's *The Russian Land's First Toiler*.

1910 Covers for A. Averchenko's *Short Stories* (Vol. 1) and H. Taffi's *The Seven Lights*. Cover for *Severnye zori* (Northern Dawns).

1911 Covers for S. Chorny's *Satires* (Vol. 1), A. Averchenko's *One-Act Plays*, and Ya. Tugendhold's *French Art and Its Representatives*. Flyleaf, title page, initials, and vignettes for Benois' *History of Painting*. Drawings and vignettes for *Satiricon*. Illustrations and vignettes for the *Firebird* anthology.

1912 Covers for S. Chorny's *Satires* (Vol. II), A. Averchenko's *Miniatures and Monologues*, and A. Izmailov's *The Crooked Mirror*. Vignettes for *Apollon*. Drawings and vignettes for *Satiricon*.

1913 Covers for A. Averchenko's *The Devil's Dozen*, D. Tsensor's *Legend of the Daily Grind*, and Voltaire's *Works*. Binding and cover for *Man. His Past and Present*. Frontispiece, initials, vignettes, and cover for F. Uspensky's *History of the Byzantine Empire*. Vignettes for *Apollon*, *Satiricon*, and *New Satiricon*.

1914 Covers for G. Lukomsky's *Architectural Landmarks of Pereslavl-Zalessky, Monuments of Old Architecture in Russia*, and *The Past of Vologda*. Covers for the *Russian Artists* series and A. Averchenko's *Bengal Lights*. Frontispiece and flyleaf for *Modern Russian Graphics* by S. Makovsky and N. Radlov. Title pages for L. Sacchetti's *History of Music* and V. Vereshchagin's *Memories of the Past*.

1915 Cover, title page, and vignette for Pushkin's *Mozart and Salieri*.

1916 *Flowers* (tempera). Cover for *A Wreath for Wrangel*. Cover, title page, frontispiece, and vignette for *Almanac of the Muses*.

1917 Covers for the *Fiction Library* of the Tvorchestvo Publishing House and the *Krasny Krest* (Red Cross) edition of A. Fyodorov's *The Miracle*. Frontispiece for *Apollon*.

1918 Covers for N. Efros' *Nemirovich-Danchenko, Stanislavsky, and Kachalov* and for A. Koiransky's *Dante* and *Yuon*. Cover, title page, vignettes, and illustrations for A. Lunacharsky's drama *Faust and the City*. Cover and frontispiece for *Mysl* (Thought). Cover for *Letuchaya mysh* (The Bat). Design of the *Death to the Oppressors* panel for Petrograd's holiday decoration on November 7, 1918 (watercolor and India ink). Soviet heraldry designs. Plates with inscriptions "The struggle brings forth heroes," and "The mind will not tolerate slavery" (overglaze decoration). Plate with the *Hammer and Sickle* emblem (overglaze decoration).

1919 Covers for A. Lunacharsky's *The Great Revolution*, N. Sukhanov's *Notes about the Revolution*, M. Lermontov's *Collected Works*, N. Nekrasov's *Collected Works*, and A. Ostrovsky's *Collected Works*. Cover, initials, head- and tailpieces for S. Glagol's *Konyonkov*. Covers, frontispieces, initials, and vignettes for *Chekhov's "Three Sisters"*

272. Sergei Chekhonin. Still Life. 1916

273. Sergei Chekhonin. Cover for Izmailov's book
The Crooked Mirror. 1912

274. Sergei Chekhonin. Cover for Tugendhold's book
French Art and Its Representatives. 1911

as *Staged by the Moscow Art Theater* and *Chekhov's
"Cherry Orchard" as Staged by the Moscow Art
Theater.* Decoration for *The Diary of Eugène
Delacroix.* Plates with inscriptions "The job of
science is to serve people" (overglaze decoration),
"Who is not with us is against us" (overglaze
decoration), and "May the slothful belly not swallow
what has been won by the power of working hands"
(overglanze decoration). The *Coral Ribbon* plate
(overglaze decoration with gilding) and plate with the
Hammer and Sickle emblem (overglaze decoration).

1920 Cover and initials for *The Second Congress of
the Communist International.* Drawings, initials,
and tailpieces for the *Museum of the Revolution*
collection. Standard cover for *The Life and Work of
Outstanding People* series. Cover for A. Ostrovsky's
A Profitable Job. Design for the poster *Only Work
and More Work* (India ink). Colophon of the
Communist International Publishing House. Dish
with inscription "The reign of workers and
peasants will never end" (overglaze decoration).

1921 Covers, headpieces, initials, and tailpieces for
Scryabin, Tchaikovsky, Bach, and *Liszt.* Cover and
colophon for *Oktyabr* (October). Cover, frontispiece,
and drawings for N. Evreinov's *What the Theatre
Is.* Plate with inscription "RSFSR" (overglaze
decoration with gilding). Plate with inscription
"From the high peaks of science one can see the
dawn of a new day coming sooner...." (overglaze
decoration with cobalt and gilding). Jubilee plate
"Four years 1917–1921."

275. Sergei Chekhonin. Cover for Lunacharsky's book
Faust and the City, a Drama. 1918

1922 *Portrait of S. Vychegzhanin* (miniature on parchment). *Portrait of P. Neradovsky* (miniature). Book covers for K. Balmont's *The Song of the Working Hammer* and I. Annensky's *The Cypress Casket*. Covers, initials, and headpieces for *Serov, Chopin, Glinka,* and *Mussorgsky*. Cover and title page for the *Fifth Anniversary of the October Revolution*. Decoration for *Profiles of the First-of-March Men*. Plate with inscription "We shall turn the whole world into a blossoming orchard." Plate with inscription "RSFSR" and inscription "Greetings to the 4th Congress – the world leader of the proletariat" (overglaze decoration with cobalt and gilding).

1923 Covers for *The Russian Folk Toy,* Gerhart Hauptmann's *Der Ketzer von Soana* (The Heretic from Soana), A. Fersman's *Three Summers Within the Arctic Circle,* and the *Museum of the Revolution* collection. Cover heading for *Russian Art, No. 1*. Drawings and initial for Anatole France's *Revolt of the Angels*. Cup and saucer *Sheaves* (overglaze decoration). Cup and saucer with inscription "USSR." Bas-relief *Lenin* (biscuit).
Between 1918 and 1923 and between 1925 and 1927, Chekhonin worked as artistic supervisor at the First State Porcelain Factory in Leningrad. From 1925 to 1928, he was active primarily as a book illustrator and decorator of porcelain. From 1928 onward, he lived in France and occasionally visited other countries, working as a book illustrator and stage designer (*The Story-tellers of Novgorod* at the New York Miniatures Theater, 1929). He died on February 22, 1937 in Lörrach (Germany) on his way to Paris.

276. Sergei Chekhonin. Cover for Balmont's book *The Song of the Working Hammer*. 1922

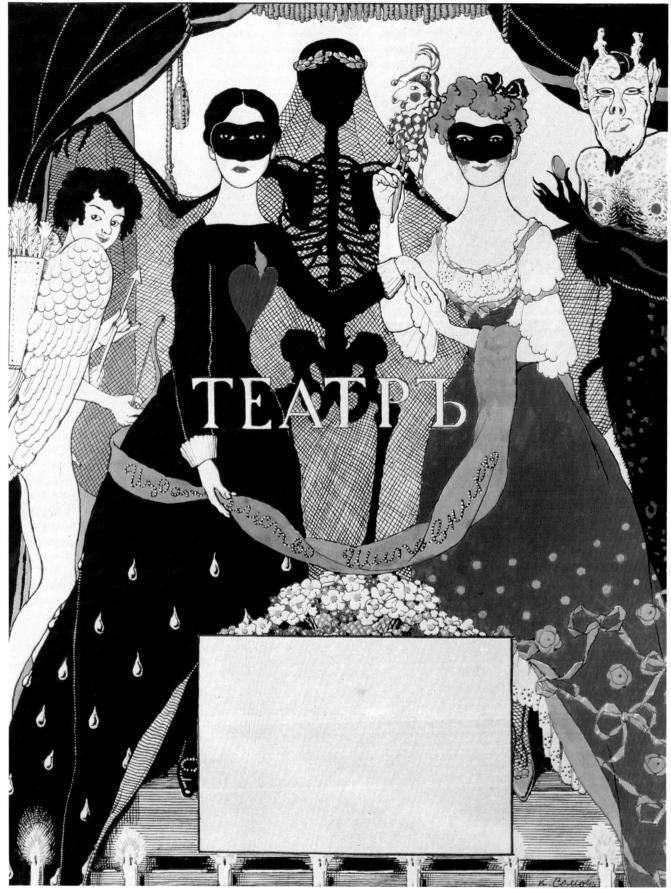

ТЕАТРЪ

277. Konstantin Somov. Title page for Alexander Blok's book *The Theater*. 1907

All World of Art members were strongly attracted to the theater. Much later, in his memoirs, Benois admitted that throughout his life he worshipped the theater, that in his mind the concept of "artistry" was always associated with the concept of "theatricality." The same is true of other World of Art masters who dedicated themselves to stage design and book illustration.

The World of Art group played a preeminent role in twentieth-century stage design, whose significance transcends national boundaries. Indeed, it is of world stature. Implied is not only the extensive acknowledgment throughout Europe of Russian stage designers, but also their direct impact upon scene-painting the world over.

World of Art retrospectivism was most forcefully manifest in the ballets and operas that Diaghilev produced abroad. The imagery of the romanticized past was recreated on the stage, thus enabling each designer to address himself to that chapter of history with which he was most fascinated and familiar.

Vsevolod Petrov

280. Alexander Benois. Italian Comedy: The Indiscreet Punchinello. 1906

SET DESIGNS

278–279. Konstantin Somov. Curtain design for Moscow's Free Theater. 1913

In May and June, the first ballet and operatic performances on the stage of the Théâtre du Châtelet in Paris comprised the first Russian Season. These productions, staged under Diaghilev's overall supervision, were truly Russian in every respect, that is, as concerned the music, the direction, the choreography, and stage design, while all actors, singers, dancers, and musicians were of Russian origin. The spectacular acclaim that this and all subsequent Seasons enjoyed welled up into a triumph for all the inner powers and traditions of Russian culture, let alone the performances as such. In the words of Benois, "Neither Borodin nor Rimsky, neither Chaliapin nor Golovin, neither Roerich nor Diaghilev were the triumphant in Paris; what triumphed was all of Russian culture, the entire originality of Russian art, with its power of conviction, its freshness and immediacy, and its wild force." Moreover, it became clear that the Russian artists themselves were prone to underestimate their own powers and did not realize what sort of an appearance they would present on European stages. "Our Russian 'savage primitiveness,' our simplicity and naivete turned out in Paris – in the most cultured Paris – to be more subtle, more advanced, and sensitive than what was generated locally," Benois recalled later on with acrid sarcasm.

Alexander K

282. Alexander Benois. The Fair. Set design for Stravinsky's *Petrouchka*. 1911

283. Mstislav Dobuzhinsky. The Blue Drawing Room. Set design for Act 1 of Turgenev's *A Month in the Country*. 1909

284. Alexander Golovin. Kremlin Square. Set design for Act 1 of Mussorgsky's *Boris Godunov*. 1911

285. Alexander Benois. Set design for Taneyev's *Cupid's Revenge*. 1900

286. Alexander Golovin. Dr. Vangel's Garden. Set design for Act 1 of Ibsen's *Lady from the Sea*. 1905

287. Alexander Benois. The Blackamoor's Room. Set design for Stravinsky's *Petrouchka*. 1911

288. Nicholas Roerich. In the Monastery. Set design for Maeterlinck's *Sœur Beatrice*. 1914

289. Sergei Sudeikin. Set design for Benavente's *The Seamy Side of Life*. 1912

290. Nikolai Sapunov. The Ball. Set design for Act 2 of Schnitzler's *The Scarf of Columbine*. 1910

292. Sergei Sudeikin. At Olympia's. Set design for Offenbach's *The Tales of Hoffmann*. 1915

293. Mstislav Dobuzhinsky. Set design for de la Halle's pastorale *Le Jeu de Robin et Marion*. 1907

294. Nikolai Sapunov. The Mystic Gathering. Set design for Blok's *Balaganchik*. 1909

295. Alexander Golovin. Don Juan's Dining Room. Set design for Act 4 of Molière's *Don Juan*. 1910

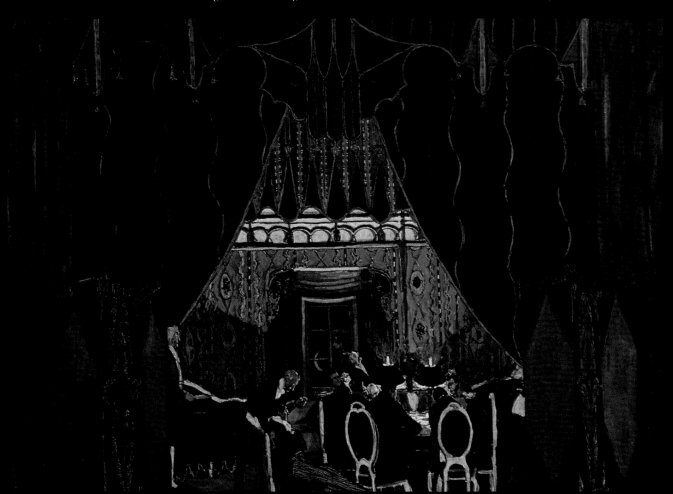

296. Alexander Golovin. The Gambling Room. Set design for Scene 7 of Lermontov's *The Masquerade*. 1917

297. Alexander Golovin. The Commander's Tomb. Set design for Act 3 of Dargomyzhsky's *The Stone Guest*. 1917

298. Alexander Golovin. Set design for the prologue to Rimsky-Korsakov's *Maid of Pskov*. 1901

299. Konstantin Somov. Italian Comedy. 1914

1907

Five Russian historic music recitals at the Paris Opera. Billed were the Overture and First Act of Glinka's opera *Ruslan and Ludmila* and his *Kamarinskaya* dance; scenes from Borodin's opera *Prince Igor*; Pimen's monologue, the Song of Varlaam, and the Second Act of Mussorgsky's opera *Boris Godunov* and also the orchestral introduction, the dance of the Persian girls, and the final act of his opera *The Khovansky Affair* (*Khovanshchina*); the fifth scene from Rimsky-Korsakov's opera *Sadko*, the orchestral suite from his opera *The Tale of Tsar Saltan*, the symphonic tableaux of *The Flight of Vakula* from his opera *Christmas Eve* and *Night on the Three-Headed Mountain* from the opera *Mlada*, and likewise the orchestral introduction and Lel's song from his opera *The Snow Maiden*. Pieces by Balakirev, Glazunov, Cui, Lyadov, Lyapunov, Rachmaninov, Scryabin, Tchaikovsky, and Taneyev were also performed.

May 3–17

Rimsky-Korsakov conducted the symphonic tableau from *Christmas Eve*, Rachmaninov performed his Second Piano Concerto and conducted his *Spring* cantata. Glazunov and Scryabin were also present. Among the participants were the soloists Felia Litvine, Josef Haumann, Dmitry Smirnov, Fyodor Chaliapin, and the conductors Arthur Nikisch, Félix Blumenfeld, and Camille Chevillard.

1908

Mussorgsky's *Boris Godunov* at the Paris Opera. Produced by Alexander Sanin with stage sets by Alexander Golovin (for the Russian scenes) and Alexander Benois (for the

May 6, 8, 11, 13, 18, 20, 22

Polish scenes). Russian costume designs and props by Ivan Bilibin. Konstantin Yuon, Boris Anisfeld and Walter Lockenberg contributed to the execution of the settings, Karl Waltz was responsible for the arrangements, Ulrich Avranek acted as choirmaster. Félix Blumenfeld conducted and the cast included Chaliapin as Boris Godunov, Dmitry Smirnov as the Pretender and Ivan Alchevsky as Shuisky.

1909

May 19

The First *Saison Russe* with its first program at the Théâtre du Châtelet, Paris. Billed on the first night was the one-act ballet, *Le Pavillon d'Armide*, in three scenes to the music of Nikolai Tcherepnin, who conducted. Choreography by Michel Fokine, sets and costumes by Alexander Benois and stage management by Sergei Grigoryev. Though Vera Karalli and Mikhail Mordkin danced respectively Madeleine and Armide and Vicomte de Beaugency at the dress rehearsal on May 18, the chief roles at the opening night were performed by Anna Pavlova and Fokine himself. Other dancers included Vaslav Nijinsky and Georgi Rozai.

Also presented were the *Polovtsian Dances* from Borodin's *Prince Igor* with Sopfia Fedorova, Adolf Bolm, and Elena Smirnova as the chief dancers. Choreography by Fokine, sets and costumes by Nicholas Roerich, and stage management by Grigoryev. Emile Cooper conducted.

Likewise billed was *Le Festin*, a divertissement to the music of Glinka, Glazunov, Mussorg- sky, Rimsky-Korsakov, and Tchaikovsky, with Anna Pavlova, Vaslav Nijinsky, Sophia Fedorova, and Adolf Bolm as the chief dancers. Choreography by Marius Petipa, Fokine, Alexander Gorsky, and Félix Kshessinsky. The sets were by Konstantin Korovin, who, along with Léon Bakst, Ivan Bilibin, and Alexander Benois, also designed the costumes. Stage management was by Grigoryev, and Emile Cooper conducted.

May 24

Rimsky-Korsakov's *Ivan the Terrible (Maid of Pskov)* at the Théâtre du Châtelet, Paris. Produced by Alexander Sanin, with sets by Nicholas Roerich and costumes by Dmitry Stelletsky. The designs had been originally made for an unrealized production, on the Imperial Russian stage, of Alexei Tolstoy's dramatic trilogy, *The Death of Ivan the Terrible*, *The Tsar Boris*, and *The Tsar Fyodor Ioannovich*. Chaliapin appeared in the title role.

June 2

The First *Saison Russe* with its second program at the Théâtre du Châtelet, Paris. Billed were the Overture and First Act from Glinka's *Ruslan and Ludmila*, with Vasily Sharonov and Vladimir Kastorsky as the chief singers. Sets and costumes by Konstantin Korovin; the one-act ballet *Les Sylphides* to the music of Chopin (the second version of *Chopiniana* with the Seventh Valse). Orchestration by Alexander Glazunov and Maurice Keller. Choreography by Fokine, sets and costumes by Alexander Benois, stage management by Grigoryev, with Anna Pavlova, Tamara Karsavina, Alexander Baldin and Vaslav Nijinsky as the chiev dancers and Tcherepnin as conductor; the one-act ballet *Cléopatre*, the revised version of *Nuits d'Egypte* to the music of Arensky, Taneyev, Rimsky-Korsakov, Mussorgsky, Glazunov, and Tcherepnin, who conducted. Sets and costumes by Léon Bakst and stage management by Grigoryev. The choreography was by Fokine, who danced with Ida Rubinstein, Anna Pavlova, Tamara Karsavina, Vera Fokine, Sophia Fedorova, and Vaslav Nijinsky.

1910

May 20

Le Carnaval, a one-act ballet at the Theater des Westens, Berlin, to the music of Schumann. Orchestration by Arensky, Glazunov, Lyadov, Rimsky-Korsakov, and Tcherepnin, who conducted. The libretto was by Bakst, who also designed the sets and costumes, and by Fokine, who was responsible for the choreography. Stage management by Grigoryev. The chief dancers were Tamara Karsavina, Maria Piltz, and Vaslav Nijinsky.

Schéhérazade, a one-act ballet to the music of Rimsky-Korsakov at the Paris Opera. The libretto was by Bakst, who designed the sets and costumes, the choreography by Fokine, and the stage management by Grigoryev. Tcherepnin conducted and Ida Rubinstein, Vaslav Nijinsky, and Alexei Bulgakov were the chief dancers. The ballet had been first performed earlier, on February 10 of the same year at the Pavlova Hall in St. Petersburg.

June 4

Giselle, a ballet in two acts (first performed at the National Academy of Music in Paris, in 1841) to the music of Adam, with the original choreography by Coralli and Perros, revised by Fokine. The book was by Gautier and Saint Georges, assisted by Coralli. Alexander Benois designed the sets and costumes, and Paul Vidal conducted. Stage management by Grigoryev. Tamara Karsavina who danced the title role was partnered by Vaslav Nijinsky.

June 18

300. Michel Fokine. After 1905

L'Oiseau de Feu (The Firebird), a ballet in two scenes, based on a medley of Russian fairy tales to the music of Stravinsky at the Paris Opera. The book and choreography were by Fokine, and the sets and costumes, except for those of the Firebird and the Tsarevna designed by Bakst, were by Alexander Golovin. Gabriel Pierne conducted. Stage management by Grigoryev. Tamara Karsavina, Vera Fokine, Michel Fokine, and Alexei Bulgakov performed the main parts. *Les Orientales*, a medley of dance miniatures, to the music of Glazunov, Sinding, Arensky, Grieg, and Borodin at the Paris Opera. The choreography was by Fokine and the sets and costumes by Konstantin Korovin (except for the costumes that Bakst designed for Vaslav Nijinsky for his performances in Grieg's *Cobold* and Sinding's *Oriental Dance*; these two dances were first staged at the Mariinsky Theater in St. Petersburg on February 11 of the same year). Tcherepnin conducted, Grigoryev was responsible for the stage management. Catherine Geltzer, Tamara Karsavina, Vaslav Nijinsky, Alexander Volinine, and Alexander Orlov performed the main parts.

June 25

301. Anna Pavlova. 1914

302. Scene from *Le Carnaval* (Michel Fokine as Harlequin in the center)

1911

The *Saisons Russes* served to establish over 1911–13 the company that came to be known as the Ballets Russes de Serge Diaghileff.

April 19

Le Spectre de la Rose, a ballet in one scene, to Weber's *Invitation to the Dance* at the Monte Carlo Casino. The book was written by J.-L. Vaudoyer who had been inspired by a poem of Gautier. Choreography by Fokine, sets and costumes by Bakst, and stage management by Grigoryev. Tcherepnin conducted and Tamara Karsavina was partnered by Vaslav Nijinsky.

April 26

Narcisse, a one-act ballet on a mythological theme, at the Monte Carlo Casino, to music by Tcherepnin, who conducted. Choreography by Fokine, sets and costumes by Bakst, and stage management by Grigoryev. Tamara Karsavina, Bronislava Nijinska, and Vaslav Nijinsky were the chief dancers.

June 6

The Underwater Kingdom scene from Rimsky-Korsakov's opera *Sadko* at the Théâtre du Châtelet, Paris. Choreography by Fokine, sets and costumes by Boris Anisfeld, and stage management by Grigoryev. Tcherepnin conducted.

June 13

Petrouchka, a ballet in four scenes at the Théâtre du Châtelet, Paris, to the music of Stravinsky who wrote the book with Alexander Benois. Sets and costumes by Benois. Choreography by Fokine and stage management by Grigoryev. Pierre Monteux conducted and Tamara Karsavina, Vaslav Nijinsky, Alexander Orlov and Enrico Cecchetti were the chief dancers.

November 30

The Swan Lake, an abridged version of Tchaikovsky's ballet in two acts and three scenes at the Royal Covent Garden Theatre, London. The original book by Begitchev and Geltzer, choreography by Marius Petipa, sets and costumes by Konstantin Korovin and Alexander

278

Golovin, and stage management by Grigoryev. Pierre Monteux conducted, and Mathilda Kshessinska was partnered by Vaslav Nijinsky in the chief roles.

1912

Le Dieu Bleu, a one-act ballet to the music of Reynaldo Hahn at the Théâtre du Châtelet, Paris. Jean Cocteau collaborated with Federigo Madrazo on the book which is based on a Hindu legend. Choreography by Fokine, sets and costumes by Bakst, and stage management by Grigoryev. Désire Inghelbrecht conducted and Tamara Karsavina, Vaslav Nijinsky, Margarita Froman, and Lydia Nelidova were the chief dancers.

May 13

Thamar, one-act ballet to music by Balakirev at the Théâtre du Châtelet, Paris. The book, based on a poem by Lermontov, was by Bakst who also designed the sets and costumes. Choreography by Fokine and stage management by Grigoryev. Pierre Monteux conducted and Tamara Karsavina was partnered by Adolf Bolm in the chief roles.

May 20

L'Apres-midi d'un Faune, one-act ballet to music by Debussy at the Théâtre du Châtelet, Paris. Vaslav Nijinsky, who was partnered by Lydia Nelidova in the chief roles, produced the book after Mallarmé's eclogue and choreographed the production. Sets and costumes by Bakst and stage management by Grigoryev. Pierre Monteux conducted.

June 8

Daphnis and Chloë, a one-act ballet in three scenes to music by Ravel at the Théâtre du Châtelet, Paris. Fokine who choreographed the production, wrote the book after a novelette by Longus. Sets and costumes by Bakst. Pierre Monteux conducted, Grigoryev was responsible for the stage management, and Tamara Karsavina danced with Vaslav Nijinsky and Adolf Bolm in the chief roles.

1913

L'Oiseau d'Or (the pas-de-deux of Princess Florine and the Blue Bird from Tchaikovsky's *The Sleeping Beauty*) at the Vienna Opera. Choreography by Marius Petipa,

January

303. Sophia Fedorova in *Cléopâtre*

304. Vaslav Nijinsky in *Les Jeux*

279

305. Scene from *Schéhérazade*

costumes by Bakst, and stage management by Grigoryev. Pierre Monteux conducted and Tamara Karsavina was partnered by Vaslav Nijinsky.

May 15   *Les Jeux*, a ballet to the music of Debussy at the Théâtre des Champs Elysées, Paris. Book and choreography by Vaslav Nijinsky who was partnered by Tamara Karsavina and Ludmila Schollar. Sets and costumes by Bakst and stage management by Grigoryev. Pierre Monteux conducted.

May 22   Mussorgsky's opera *Boris Godunov* at the Théâtre des Champs Elysées. Staged by Alexander Sanin with sets and costumes by Alexander Golovin, except those for the *Scene at the Fountain*, which were designed by Bakst.

May 29   *Le Sacre du Printemps*, a ballet in two acts to music by Stravinsky at the Théâtre des Champs Elysées, Paris. Book by Stravinsky and Nicholas Roerich, choreography by Vaslav Nijinsky, sets and costumes by Roerich, and stage management by Grigoryev. Pierre Monteux conducted and Maria Piltz was the chief dancer.

June 5   Mussorgsky's opera *Khovanshchina*, as abridged by Diaghilev at the Théâtre des Champs Elysées, with Chaliapin in the chief role. The music was orchestrated by Stravinsky and Ravel. Fyodor Fedorovsky designed the sets and costumes, and Emile Cooper conducted. Produced by Alexander Sanin.

June 12   *La Tragedie de Salome*, a ballet based on a poem by Robert d'Humières to music by Florent Schmitt at the Théâtre des Champs Elysées, Paris. Choreography by Boris Romanov, sets and costumes by Sergei Sudeikin, and stage management by Grigoryev. Pierre Monteux conducted and Tamara Karsavina was the chief dancer.

Les Papillons, a one-act ballet to music by Schumann as orchestrated by Tcherepnin at the Casino in Monte Carlo. Mstislav Dobuzhinsky wrote the book and designed the sets. Costumes by Bakst, choreography by Fokine, and stage management by Grigoryev. Pierre Monteux conducted and Tamara Karsavina and Ludmila Schollar were the chief dancers. The first performance had been given in aid of charity at the Mariinsky Theater on September 30, 1912, with sets then designed by Pyotr Lambin.

April 16

Le Légende de Joseph, one-act ballet to the music of Richard Strauss, who conducted at the Paris Opera. Book by Harry Kessler and Hugo Hoffmannsthal, choreography by Fokine, sets by José-Maria Sert, costumes by Bakst, and stage management by Grigoryev. Maria Kuznetsova-Benois, Léonide Massine, and Alexei Bulgakov were the chief dancers.

May 17

Rimsky-Korsakov's opera-ballet *Le Coq d'Or* (The Golden Cockerel) in three scenes at the Paris Opera. The original book that Vladimir Belsky produced on the basis of Pushkin's fairy tale, was re-adapted by Alexander Benois. Sets and costumes by Natalia Goncharova and stage management by Grigoryev. Pierre Monteux conducted, Elisabeth Petrenko and Ivan Alchevsky sang, and Tamara Karsavina, Alexei Bulgakov, and Enrico Cecchetti danced the main roles.

May 24

Stravinsky's opera *Le Rossignol* at the Paris Opera. Staged by Alexander Sanin and Alexander Benois, who likewise designed the sets and costumes. Boris Romanov choreographed the production which was directed by Grigoryev. Pierre Monteux conducted. Stepan Migusov collaborated with the composer on the libretto which is based on Hans Christian Andersen's well-known fairy tale *The Nightingale*.

May 26

Midas, a one-act ballet on a mythological theme to the music of Maximilian Steinberg, at the Paris Opera. Choreography by Fokine, book by Bakst, sets and costumes by Mstislav Dobuzhinsky, and stage management by Grigoryev. Rhené-Baton conducted and Tamara Karsavina, Adolf Bolm, and Margarita Froman were the chief dancers.

June 2

306. Scene from *Schéhérazade*

307. Tamara Karsavina (Firebird) and Michel Fokine (Ivan Tsarevich) in *The Firebird*

308. Scene from *Le Spectre de la Rose*

<table>
<tr><td>*June 7*</td><td>Borodin's *Prince Igor* at the Royal Drury Lane Theater, London, as staged by Alexander Sanin, with sets and costumes by Nicholas Roerich, and Chaliapin in the two roles of Prince Galitsky and Khan Konchak.</td></tr>
<tr><td>*June 26*</td><td>Rimsky-Korsakov's opera *Une Nuit de Mai* at the Royal Drury Lane Theater, London, choreographed by Adolf Bolm with sets and costumes by Fyodor Fedorovsky. Dmitry Smirnov was the chief singer.</td></tr>
</table>

1915

December 20 — *Le Soleil de Nuit*, a ballet based on a medley of Russian pastimes and dances to the music of Rimsky-Korsakov's opera *The Snow Maiden*, at the Geneva Opera. The choreography was by Léonide Massine, who also danced the chief roles with Nikolai Zverev. Mikhail Larionov designed the sets and costumes, Ernest Ansermet conducted, and Grigoryev was responsible for the stage management.

December 28 — *The Enchanted Princess* (the pas-de-deux from Tchaikovsky's *The Sleeping Beauty*) at the Paris Opera. Choreography by Marius Petipa, sets and costumes by Bakst. *Schéhérazade*. Reprise of the ballet premiered during the 1910 *Saison Russe* in Paris. Sets and costumes by Bakst.

1916

August 21 — *Las Meninas*, a pavane to the music of Gabriel Fauré at the Eugenie-Victoria Theater in San Sebastian, Spain. Book by Carlo Sokrate, choreography by Léonide Massine, who with Lydia Sokolova, Olga Khoklova, and Léon Woizikowski danced the main roles. Sert designed the costumes, Ansermet conducted, and Grigoryev was the regisseur.

Kikimora, a ballet to the music of Lyadov, *August 25* based on a Russian fairy tale, at the Eugenie-Victoria Theater in San Sebastian, Spain. Choreography by Léonide Massine, sets and costumes by Mikhail Larionov. Ansermet conducted, Grigoryev was the regisseur, and Maria Chabelska and Stanislas Idzikowski danced the main roles.

A new version of Rimsky-Korsakov's *Sadko*, *August* of which the first performance was given during the 1911 *Saison Russe* in Paris. Choreography by Adolf Bolm, sets and costumes by Natalia Goncharova. Doris Faithfull and Adolf Bolm were the chief dancers.

309. Tamara Karsavina in *Schéhérazade*

Till Eulenspiegel, a ballet to the music of *October 23* Richard Strauss at the Manhattan Opera House, New York. Choreography by Vaslav Nijinsky, who was partnered by Flore Revalles in the main roles and who also wrote the book. Robert Edmond Jones designed the sets and costumes. Anselm Goetz conducted, and Nikolai Kremnev was the regisseur.

1917

New troupe of the Ballets Russes.

Stravinsky's symphonic poem *Fireworks* at *April 12* the Teatro Costanzi, Rome. Diaghilev himself was the regisseur. Giacomo Balla designed the sets and costumes, and Ernest Ansermet conducted.
Les Femmes de Bonne Humeur, a mime-drama after Carlo Goldoni to the music of Domenico Scarlatti as arranged and orchestrated by Vincenzo Tommasini at the Teatro Costanzi, Rome. The choreography was by Léonide Massine, who with Lydia Lopokova, Lubov Tchernicheva, and Enrico Cecchetti danced the chief roles. Bakst designed the sets and costumes, Ernest Ansermet conducted, and Grigoryev was the regisseur.

Les Contes Russes, a ballet suite of Russian *May 11* folk dances and scenes, including *Kikimora* (premiered in 1916), to the music of Lyadov,

310. Léonide Massine (Joseph) in *La Légende de Joseph*

at the Théâtre du Châtelet, Paris. Choreography by Léonide Massine, sets and costumes by Mikhail Larionov in collaboration with Natalia Goncharova. Ernest Ansermet conducted and Grigoryev was the regisseur, with Lubov Tchernicheva, Lydia Sokolova, Léon Woizikowski, and Stanislas Idzikowski dancing the main roles.

May 18   *La Parade*, a one-act ballet to the music of Erik Satie, at the Théâtre du Châtelet, Paris. Book by Jean Cocteau. Choreography by Léonide Massine, who with Lydia Lopokova, Maria Chabelska, and Nikolai Zverev danced the main roles. Picasso designed the sets and costumes, Ernest Ansermet conducted, and Grigoryev was the regisseur.

1918

No premieres.

1919

July 5   *La Boutique Fantasque* (The Fantastic Toyshop), a one-act ballet to the music of Rossini as arranged and orchestrated by Ottorino Respighi, at the Alhambra Theater, London. Choreography by Léonide Massine, who was partnered by Lydia Lopokova in the main roles. André Derain designed the sets and costumes, Henry Delfosse conducted, and Grigoryev was the regisseur.

July 22   *Le Tricorne* (The Three Cornered Hat), a one-act ballet to the music of Manuel de Falla, at the Alhambra Theater, London. Book by Martinez Sierra. Choreography by Léonide Massine, who with Tamara Karsavina and Léon Woizikowski danced the main roles. Picasso designed the sets and costumes, Ernest Ansermet conducted, and Grigoryev was the regisseur.

1920

February 2   *Le Chant du Rossignol*, a one-act ballet adaptation of Stravinsky's opera *The Rossignol* (premiered in 1914) at the Paris Opera. Choreography by Léonide Massine, sets and costumes by Henri Matisse. Ernest Ansermet conducted, and Tamara Karsavina, Lydia Sokolova, and Sergei Grigoryev, who was also the regisseur, danced the main roles.

May 15   *Pulcinella*, a one-act ballet in one scene with singing to the music of Stravinsky based on Pergolesi at the Paris Opera. Choreography by Léonide Massine, who with Tamara Karsavina, Lubov Tchernicheva, Vera Nemchinova, and Stanislas Idzikowski were the chief dancers. Pablo Picasso designed the sets and costumes, Ernest Ansermet conducted, and Grigoryev was the regisseur.

May 27   *Les Astuces Féminines*, an opera-ballet in three scenes with a finale to the music and recitative of Domenico Cimarosa, as orchestrated by Ottorino Respighi, at the Paris Opera. Choreography by Léonide Massine, sets and costumes by José-Maria Sert. Ernest Ansermet conducted and Grigoryev was the regisseur. The cast of singers included Mafalda de Voltri, Romaniza, Aurelio Anglada, and Angelo Masni-Pieralli, and of dancers, Tamara Karsavina, Lubov Tchernicheva, Vera Nemchinova, and Lydia Sokolova.

1921

May 17   *Chout* (The Buffoon), a ballet in six scenes based on Russian folktales to the music and scenario of Sergei Prokofiev, at the Théâtre de la Gaieté-Lyrique, Paris. Choreography by Mikhail Larionov, who also designed the sets and costumes, and Tadeo Slavinski, who was partnered by Lydia Sokolova and Catherine Devillier. Ernest Ansermet conducted and Grigoryev was the regisseur.
Quadro Flamenco, a medley of Andalusian dances arranged by Manuel de Falla, at the Théâtre de la Gaieté-Lyrique, Paris. Sets and costumes by Pablo Picasso. The cast of

311. Scene from *Narcisse*

Spanish dancers included Maria Dalbaicin, La Rubia de Jerrez, La Gabrieleta del Gorrotin, La Lopez, El Tejero, and El Moreno.

November 2

La Belle au Bois Dormant (The Sleeping Beauty), a ballet in four acts after the fairy tales of Charles Perrault to the music of Tchaikovsky, at the Alhambra Theater, London. For this production (the first performance was given much earlier, on January 3, 1890, at the Mariinsky Theater in St. Petersburg), Stravinsky scored several numbers including the Aurora variations, while Nikolai Sergeyev revised Petipa's original choreography. Bronislava Nijinska, who performed one of the title roles, choreographed some of the dances. Other dancers included Olga Spessivtseva, Lydia Lopokova, Carlotta Brianza, Lubov Tchernicheva, Pyotr Vladimirov, Anatole Vilzak, and Stanislas Idzikowski. Bakst designed the sets and costumes, Gregor Fittelberg conducted, and Grigoryev was the regisseur.

312. Scene from *L'Après-midi d'un Faune*

1922

May 18

Le Mariage de la Belle au Bois Dormant, a one-actballet version of the final act of Tchaikovsky's *The Sleeping Beauty* at the Paris Opera. Alexander Benois designed the sets and costumes, Gregor Fittelberg conducted, Grigoryev was the regisseur, and Vera Trefilova was partnered by Pyotr Vladimirov.

Le Renard, a one-act ballet with singing to the music of Stravinsky (who wrote the book), with the French variant by Charles Ferdinand Ramuz, at the Paris Opera. Choreography by Bronislava Nijinska, who was partnered by Stanislas Idzikowski. Mikhail Larionov designed the sets and costumes, Ernest Ansermet conducted, and Grigoryev was the regisseur.

June 3

Stravinsky's opera-bouffe *Mavra* at the Paris Opera with the book by Boris Kochno based on Pushkin's narrative poem *The Little House in Kolomna*. Bronislava Nijinska directed this production, Léopold Survage designed the sets and costumes, and Gregor Fittelberg conducted.

1923

June 13

Les Noces, a medley of dance scenes with singing to the music of Stravinsky who composed the lyrics after folk texts from the collection of Pyotr Kireyevsky, at the Théâtre de la Gaieté-Lyrique, Paris. Choreography by Bronislava Nijinska, sets and costumes by Natalia Goncharova. Ernest Ansermet conducted and Grigoryev acted as regisseur. The cast of singers included N. Smirnova, M. Davydova, and D'Arial, and of dancers, Lubov Tchernicheva, Felia Doubrovskaya and Léon Woizikowski.

1924

January 3

Le Tentations de la Bergère ou l'Amour Vaincu, a one-act ballet to the music of Michel Montéclair as orchestrated by Henri Casadesus, at the Casino in Monte Carlo. Choreography by Bronislava Nijinska, sets and costumes by Juan Gris. Edouard Flament conducted, Grigoryev acted as regisseur, and Vera Nemchinova, Lubov Tchernicheva, Léon Woizikowski, and Anatole Vilzak danced the main roles.

January 6

Les Biches (The House Party), a one-act ballet to the music of Francis Poulenc, at the Casino in Monte Carlo. Choreography by Bronislava Nijinska, who was one of the chief dancers along with Vera Nemchinova, Lubov Tchernicheva, Lydia Sokolova, Anatole Vilzak, and Léon Woizikowski.

January 8

Cimarosiana, a dance suite to the music of Domenico Cimarosa at the Casino in Monte Carlo. Choreography by Léonide Massine, sets and costumes by José-Maria Sert. Edouard Flament conducted, Grigoryev acted as regisseur, and Vera Nemchinova, Lubov Tchernicheva, Lydia Sokolova, Stanislas Idzikowski, Léon Woizikowski, and Anatole Vilzak were the chief dancers.

January 19

Les Fâcheux, a one-act ballet to the music of Georges Auric at the Casino in Monte Carlo. Book by Boris Kochno after Molière, choreography by Bronislava Nijinska, sets and costumes by Georges Braque. Edouard Flament conducted, Grigoryev acted as regisseur, and Lubov Tchernicheva, Anatole Vilzak, and Anton Dolin were the chief dancers.

April 13

Un Nuit sur le Mont Chauve (Night on the Bare Mountain), a choreographic scene to the music of Mussorgsky, at the Casino in Monte Carlo. Choreography by Bronislava Nijinska, sets and costumes by Natalia Goncharova. Edouard Flament conducted, Grigoryev acted as regisseur, and Lydia Sokolova was partnered by Fedorov.

Also presented in Monte Carlo were Gounod's operas *Le Médecin malgré lui*, *La Colombe*, and *Philémon and Baucis* (sets and costumes by Alexander Benois), and Emmanuel Chabrier's opera *Une Education Manquée* (sets and costumes by Juan Gris).

313. Scene from *Hippolytus*

June 20

Le Train Bleu, a one-act ballet to the music of Darius Milhaud, at the Théâtre des Champs Elysées, Paris. Book by Jean Cocteau, choreography by Bronislava Nijinska, who danced together with Lydia Sokolova, Anton Dolin, and Léon Woizikowski. Henri Laurens designed the sets, Gabrielle Chanel the costumes, and Pablo Picasso the curtain. Pierre Monteux conducted and Grigoryev was the regisseur.

In 1925, George Balanchine joined the Ballets Russes as its chief choreographer and dominated this company's last period with his productions, including *Barabau*, *La Pastorale*, *Jack in the Box*, *The Triumph of Neptune*, *La Chatte*, *Apollon Musagete*, *The Gods Go a-Begging*, *Le Bal*, and *Le Fils Prodigue*. He continued to work for Léonide Massine's troupe which produced *Zéphyr et Flore*, *Les Matelots*, *Mercure*, *poses plastiques*, *Le Pas d'Acier*, and *Ode*. Diaghilev's death in 1929 caused the company to break up.

314. Tamara Karsavina and Leonid Leontiev in *Le Carnaval*

287

EXHIBITIONS
CATALOGUE
BIBLIOGRAPHY

Exhibition data are provided in detail whenever possible and are derived from catalogues, periodicals, and other source material of the period.
The exhibitor's country of residence is indicated in accordance with the catalogue of the said exhibition.

1989, January–February

Exhibition of Russian and Finnish Artists (St. Petersburg, Museum of the Stieglitz School).
Russian contributors: Bakst, Benois, Korovin, Levitan, Maliutin, Nesterov, Ryabushkin, Serov, Vasnetsov, and Vrubel.
Finnish contributors: Edelfeldt, Gallen-Kallela, and Jarnefeldt.

1899, January

International World of Art Exhibition of Paintings (St. Petersburg, Museum of the Stieglitz School).
Contributors: Aman-Jean (France), Anquetin (France), Bakst (St. Petersburg), Bartels (Germany), Benois (Russia), Bertson (Belgium), Besnard (France), Blanche (France), Blent (England), Blomstedt (Finland), Böcklin (Switzerland), Boldini (Italy), F. Botkin (Russia), Boutet de Monvel (France), Brangwyn (England), Carrière (France), Cazin (France), Conders (England), Dagnan-Bouveret (France), Degas (France), Dill (Germany), Edelfeldt (Finland), Enckel (Finland), Forain (France), Frédéric (France), Gallen-Kallela (Finland), Golovin (Russia), Hermann (Germany), Jarnefeldt (Finland), Johnston (England), Korovin (Russia), Latouche (France), Lenbach (Germany), Levitan (Moscow), Lhermitte (France), Liebermann (Germany), Maliavin (St. Petersburg), Maliutin (Moscow), Ménard (France), Monet (France), Moreau (France), Nesterov (Kiev), Perepletchikov (Moscow), Polenov (Moscow), Polenova (Russia), Puvis de Chavannes (France), Raffaelli (France), Rivière (France), Renoir (France), Repin (St. Petersburg), Rushchits (St. Petersburg), Serov (Moscow), Shcherbatov (Russia), Simon (Paris), Somov (St. Petersburg), Thaulow (Norway), Trubetskoi (Moscow), Tsionglinsky (Russia), Vasnetsov (Russia), Whistler (England), Yakunchikova (Russia), and Zwann (England).
The exhibition presented 322 pictures as well as objects of jewelry by Lalique (France), vases by Tiffany (USA), glassware by Tiffany, Jacquin, and Emile Gallé (France), Abramtsevo pottery and embroideries after designs by Davydova, Polenova, and others.

1900, January

Second World of Art Exhibition of Paintings (St. Petersburg, Museum of the Stieglitz School).
Contributors: Bakst, Benois, Bilibin, Botkin, Braz, Davydova, Dosekin, Golovin, Golubkina, Kardovsky, Korovin, Kruglikova, Lanceray, Levitan, Maliavin, Maliutin, Nesterov, Ober, Ostroumova, Perepletchikov, Polenova, Purvit, Serov, Somov, Trubetskoi, Tsionglinsky, A. Vasnetsov, V. Vasnetsov, Vrubel, and Yakunchikova.

The exhibition presented 220 pictures, majolica from the Abramtsevo pottery and joinery workshops, and the carpets woven at E. Chokolova's looms in Voronezh Province.

1901, January – February

Third World of Art Exhibition of Paintings (St. Petersburg, Museum of the Academy of Arts).
Contributors: Baksheyev, Bakst, Benois, Bilibin, Braz, Dosekin, Golovin, Golubkina, Korovin, Lanceray, Maliavin, Maliutin, Mamontov, Nesterov, Ober, Okolovich, Ostroumova, Pasternak, Perepletchikov, Purvit, Rushchits, Ryabushkin, Rylov, Serov, Somov, Svetoslavsky, Trubetskoi, Tsionglinsky, A. Vasnetsov, Vinogradov, Vrubel, and Yakunchikova.
The exhibition presented 238 pictures, majolicas from the Abramtsevo potteries, and the embroideries of Yakunchikova and Davydova. Mounted separately was a one-man posthumous show devoted to Isaac Levitan.

1902, March – April

Fourth World of Art Exhibition of Paintings (St. Petersburg, rooms of the Passage Arcade).
Contributors: Bakst, Benois, Bilibin, Botkin, Braz, Grabar, Golovin, K. Korovin, S. Korovin, Kuznetsov, Lanceray, Maliavin, Maliutin, Makovskaya, Mamontov, Ober, Ostroumova, Pasternak, Perepletchikov, Petrovichev, Ryabushkin, Rylov, Sapunov, Serov, Shcherbov, Somov, Svetoslavsky, Trubetskoi, Tsionglinsky, Vinogradov, Vrubel, Walter, Youn, and Yaremich.
In addition to 218 pictures, the exhibition presented glassware from V. Frolov's workshop in St. Petersburg, Abramtsevo majolicas, and objects from the Talashkino workshops. Antique furniture in the rooms was supplied by the A. & M. Mikhankov Brothers, St. Petersburg.

1902, November – December

World of Art Exhibition of Paintings (a review show containing material from several preceding displays; Moscow, Grachov's House).
Contributors: Bakst, Benois, Bilibin, Braz, Golovin, Golubkina, Grabar, K. Korovin, Lanceray, Maliavin, Maliutin, Mamontov, Ober, Ostroumova, Purvit, Petrovichev, Roerich, Rushchits, Sapunov, Serov, Shcherbov, Somov, Trubetskoi, Tsionglinsky, Vrubel, Yakunchikova, Yaremich, and Zhukovsky.
278 pictures presented.

1903, February – March

Fifth World of Art Exhibition of Paintings (St. Petersburg, Society for the Encouragement of Artists).
Contributors: Aladjalov, Arkhipov, Bakst, Benois, Bilibin, Braz, Denisov, Golovin, Grabar, Ivanov, K. Korovin, S. Korovin, Kuznetsov, Lanceray, Lugovskaya, Maliavin, Maliutin, Mamontov, Matveyev, Meshcherin, Ostroumova, Pasternak, Perepletchikov, Petrovichev, Purvit, Roerich, Ryabushkin, Serov, Shcherbov, Somov, Trubetskoi, Tsionglinsky, Vinogradov, Vrubel, Yaremich, and Yuon.
303 pictures presented.

1903, December – 1904, January

First Exhibition of Paintings by the Union of Russian Artists (Moscow, Stroganov School).
Contributors: Bakst, Benois, Bilibin, Braz, Golovin, Grabar, K. Korovin, Lanceray, Maliavin, Maliutin, Roerich, Ryabushkin, Somov, Tarkhov, Trubetskoi, Tsionglinsky, Vrubel, Yaremich, and others.

1904, December – 1905, January

Second Exhibition of Paintings by the Union of Russian Artists (St. Petersburg, Academy of Arts).

Contributors: Bakst, Benois, Bilibin, Braz, Dobuzhinsky, Golovin, Grabar, Korovin, Lanceray, Maliavin, Maliutin, Ostroumova, Serov, Somov, Sudeikin, Tarkhov, Trubetskoi, Tsionglinsky, Vrubel, Yaremich, and others.

1905, February – March

Second Exhibition of Paintings by the Union of Russian Artists (Moscow, *Yakor* Insurance Company).
Contributors: Bakst, Benois, Bilibin, Braz, Dobuzhinsky, Golovin, Grabar, Maliavin, Ostroumova, Serov, Somov, Sudeikin, Tarkhov, Trubetskoi, Tsionglinsky, Vrubel, Yaremich, and others.

1906, February – March

World of Art Exhibition of Paintings (St. Petersburg, Catherine's Hall).
Contributors: Anisfeld, Bakst, Benois, Bilibin, Borisov-Musatov, Dobuzhinsky, Falileyev, Feofilaktov, Golovin, Grabar, Jawlensky, Korovin, Kuznetsov, Lanceray, Larionov, Lindeman, Lokkenberg, Lugovskaya-Diaghileva, Maliavin, N. Milioti, V. Milioti, Noakovsky, Ostroumova-Lebedeva, Rylov, Sabashnikova, Sapunov, Serov, Somov, Ulyanov, Vinogradov, Vrubel, Yuon, and Yaremich.
344 pictures shown

1906, April

Third Exhibition of Paintings by the Union of Russian Artists (Moscow, Stroganov School).
Contributors: Anisfeld, Bakst, Benois, Bilibin, Borisov-Musatov, Braz, Dobuzhinsky, Falileyev, Feofilaktov, Fomin, Golovin, Grabar, Korovin, Kustodiev, Lanceray, Lugovskaya-Diaghileva, Maliavin, N. Milioti, V. Milioti, Ostroumova-Lebedeva, Serov, Shchusev, Somov, Tsionglinsky, Vinogradov, Vrubel, Yaremich, and others.

1906, October – November

Exhibition of Russian Art at the Salon d'Automne in Paris.
Contributors: Bakst, Benois, Bogayevsky, Borisov-Musatov, Dobuzhinsky, Golovin, Grabar, Kustodiev, Kuznetsov, Lanceray, Larionov, Lugovskaya-Diaghileva, Maliavin, Ostroumova-Lebedeva, Roerich, Somov, Sudeikin, Trubetskoi, Vrubel, Yaremich, Yuon, and others.

1907, February – March

Fourth Exhibition of Paintings by the Union of Russian Artists (Moscow, Stroganov School).
Contributors: Anisfeld, Bakst, Benois, Bilibin, Chembers, Dobuzhinsky, Gaush, Grabar, Korovin, Kustodiev, Lugovskaya-Diaghileva, Maliavin, Ostroumova-Lebedeva, Roerich, Serov, Shchusev, Stelletsky, Tarkhov, Tsionglinsky, Vrubel, Yaremich, and others.

1907, December – 1908, November

Fifth Exhibition of Paintings by the Union of Russian Artists (Moscow, Stroganov School).
Contributors: Anisfeld, Bakst, Benois, Bogayevsky, Dobuzhinsky, Feofilaktov, Golovin, Grabar, Korovin, Krymov, Kustodiev, Kuznetsov, Lanceray, Lugovskaya-Diaghileva, Maliutin, N. Milioti, Ostroumova-Lebedeva, Roerich, Sapunov, Serov, Shchusev, Stelletsky, Sudeikin, Tarkhov, Tsionglinsky, Vrubel, Zamirailo, and others.

1908, February – March

Fifth Exhibition of Paintings by the Union of Russian Artists (St. Petersburg, house on the bank of the Moika where Pushkin lived and died).
Contributors: Bakst, Benois, Bilibin, Dobuzhinsky, Feofilaktov, Golovin, Golubkina, Grabar, Krymov, Kustodiev, Lanceray, Lugovskaya-Diaghileva, Maliutin, N. Milioti, Ostroumova-Lebedeva, Sapunov, Serov, Somov, Somova-Mikhailova, Stelletsky, Tarkhov, Tsionglinsky, Vrubel, Yaremich, Zamirailo, and others.

1908, December – 1909, February

Sixth Exhibition of Paintings by the Union of Russian Artists (Moscow, former residence of Prince Golitsyn).
Contributors: Anisfeld, Bakst, Benois, Bilibin, Bogayevsky, Dobuzhinsky, Feofilaktov, Golovin, Golubkina, Grabar, Kustodiev, Lanceray, Lugovskaya-Diaghileva, Maliutin, N. Milioti, Ostroumova-Lebedeva, Sapunov, Serov, Somov, Stelletsky, Sudeikin, Tarkhov, Tsionglinsky, Zamirailo, and others.

1909, February – April

Sixth Exhibition of Paintings by the Union of Russian Artists (St. Petersburg, house on the Moika where Pushkin lived and died).
Contributors: Anisfeld, Bakst, Benois, Bilibin, Bogayevsky, Chekhonin, Chembers, Čiurlionis, Dobuzhinsky, Falileyev, Golovin, Golubkina, Grabar, Korovin, Kruglikova, Krymov, Kustodiev, Larionov, Levitsky, Lugovskaya-Diaghileva, Maliutin, Mitrokhin, Narbut, Ober, Ostroumova-Lebedeva, Petrov-Vodkin, Sapunov, Serov, Shchuko, Somov, Somova-Mikhailova, Stelletsky, Sudeikin, Tarkhov, Tsionglinsky, Utkin, Yakovlev, Yakulov, and others.

1909, December – 1910, February

Seventh Exhibition of Paintings by the Union of Russian Artists (Moscow, premises of the Literary and Art Circle).
Contributors: Anisfeld, Bakst, Benois, Bilibin, Dobuzhinsky, Feofilaktov, Golubkina, Konionkov, Korovin, Krymov, Kustodiev, Lanceray, Lindeman, Lugovskaya-Diaghileva, Maliutin, Ostroumova-Lebedeva, Roerich, Rylov, Serov, Shchusev, Somov, Stelletsky, Tarkhov, Trubetskoi, Tsionglinsky, Vinogradov, Vrubel, Yaremich, Zamirailo, and others.

1910, February – March

Seventh Exhibition of Paintings by the Union of Russian Artists (St. Petersburg, premises of the Armenian Church).
Contributors: Anisfeld, Arapov, Bakst, Benois, Bilibin, Chembers, Chembers-Bilibina, Čiurlionis, Dobuzhinsky, Falileyev, Fomin, Gaush, Golubkina, Korovin, Krymov, Kruglikova, Kustodiev, Kuznetsov, Lanceray, Larionov, Lentulov, Lukomsky, Maliutin, Matveyev, Mitrokhin, Narbut, Ostroumova-Lebedeva, Petrov-Vodkin, Roerich, Rylov, Sapunov, Serebryakova, Serov, Shchusev, Shervashidze, Somov, Somova-Mikhailova, Tsionglinsky, Vrubel, Yakovlev, Yakulov, Yaremich, Zamirailo, and others.

1910, April – May

Seventh Exhibition of Paintings by the Union of Russian Artists (Kiev, Municipal Museum).
Contributors: Anisfeld, Arapov, Bakst, Benois, Chembers, Chembers-Bilibina, Čiurlionis, Dobuzhinsky, Falileyev, Fomin, Golubkina, Grabar, Korovin, Kruglikova, Krymov, Kustodiev, Lindeman, Lukomsky, Maliutin, N. Milioti, Mitrokhin, Ostroumova-Lebedeva, Petrov-Vodkin, Roerich, Rylov, Sapunov, Serov, Shchuko, Shchusev, Shervashidze, Somov, Somova-Mikhailova, Tarkhov, Tsionglinsky, Yakovlev, Yaremich, and others.

1911, January – February

World of Art Exhibition of Paintings (St. Petersburg, premises of the First Corps of Cadets).
Contributors: Anisfeld, Arapov, Benois, Bilibin, Bobrovsky, Bogayevsky, Braz, Brodsky, Charlemagne, Chembers, Čiurlionis, Dobuzhinsky, Falileyev, Falk, Feofilaktov, Fomin, Gaush, Golubkina, Goncharova, Kruglikova, Kustodiev, Kuznetsov, Lanceray, Lentulov, Lindeman, Lokkenberg, Lugovskaya-Diaghileva, Lukomsky, Maliavin, Matveyev, N. Milioti, Mitrokhin, Narbut, Ostroumova-Lebedeva, Raush von Traubenberg, Roerich, Rylov, Sapunov, Serov, Shcherbakov, Somov, Somova-Mikhailova, Sudeikin, Tamanov, Tsionglinsky, Yakulov, Yaremich, Zakharov, and Zamirailo.
301 pictures shown.

1911, February – March

World of Art Exhibition of Paintings (Moscow, premises of the Literary and Art Circle). Contributors: Anisfeld, Arapov, Benois, Bilibin, Bogayevsky, Braz, Brodsky, Chembers, Čiurlionis, Dobuzhinsky, Falileyev, Falk, Feofilaktov, Fomin, Gaush, Golovin, Golubkina, Goncharova, Konchalovsky, Kruglikova, Kustodiev, P. Kuznetsov, V. Kuznetsov, Lentulov, Lindeman, Lokkenberg, Lugovskaya-Diaghileva, Lukomsky, Lvov, Mashkov, Matveyev, N. Milioti, Mitrokhin, Narbut, Ostroumova, Petrov-Vodkin, Raush von Traubenberg, Roerich, Rylov, Sapunov, Saryan, Serebryakova, Serov, Shervashidze, Somov, Somova-Mikhailova, Sudeikin, Tamanov, Tsionglinsky, Ulyanov, Utkin, Yakulov, Yaremich, and Zamirailo.
369 pictures shown.

1911, November – December

World of Art Exhibition of Paintings (Moscow, School of Painting, Sculpture and Architecture).
Contributors: Anisfeld, Arapov, Benois, Bilibin, Bogayevsky, Braz, Chembers-Bilibina, Čiurlionis, Dobuzhinsky, Gaush, Fedotov, Fomin, Gagarin, Goncharova, Kalmakov, Konchalovsky, Kustodiev, P. Kuznetsov, V. Kuznetsov, Lanceray, Larionov, Lentulov, Lermontova, Lindeman, Lugovskaya-Diaghileva, Lukomsky, Mashkov, N. Milioti, Mitrokhin, Morgunov, Narbut, Naumov, O'Connel, Ostroumova-Lebedeva, Petrov-Vodkin, Roerich, Rozhdestvensky, Rubtsov, Sapunov, Saryan, Serebryakova, Serov, Shchuko, Sologub, Somov, Somova-Mikhailova, Stelletsky, Sudeikin, Tamanov, Tarkhov, Tsionglinsky, Ulyanov, Utkin, Westfalen, Yakulov, and Yaremich.

1912, January

World of Art Exhibition of Paintings (St. Petersburg, Lidval House (The Swedish Church).
Contributors: Anisfeld, Arapov, Benois, Bilibin, Bogayevsky, Braz, Chembers-Bilibina, Dobuzhinsky, Fedotov, Fomin, Gagarin, Gaush, Goncharova, Kalmakov, Konchalovsky, Kustodiev, P. Kuznetsov, V. Kuznetsov, Lanceray, Larionov, Lentulov, Lermontova, Lindeman, Lugovskaya-Diaghileva, Lukomsky, Luksh-Makovskaya, Mashkov, N. Milioti, Mitrokhin, Morgunov, Narbut, Naumov, O'Connel, Ostroumova-Lebedeva, Petrov-Vodkin, Roerich, Rozhdestvensky, Rubtsov, Sapunov, Saryan, Serebryakova, Serov, Shchuko, Sologub, Somov, Somova-Mikhailova, Stelletsky, Sudeikin, Tamanov, Tarkhov, Tsionglinsky, Ulyanov, Utkin, Westfalen, Yakulov, and Yaremich. A posthumous one-man show devoted to Mikolajaus Čiurlionis.
451 pictures shown.

1912, November – December

World of Art Exhibition of Paintings (Moscow, School of Painting, Sculpture and Architecture).
Contributors: Anisfeld, Arapov, Benois, Belkin, Bogayevsky, Chembers-Bilibina, Dobuzhinsky, Falileyev, Feofilaktov, Gaush, Grekova, Khrustachov, Kruglikova, L. Kuznetsova, P. Kuznetsov, Latrie, Lukomsky, Matveyev, N. Milioti, Mitrokhin, Narbut, Nakhman, Naumov, Obolenskaya, Ostroumova-Lebedeva, Petrov-Vodkin, Pligen, Roerich, Ryabushinsky, Sapunov, Saryan, Shervashidze, Shitikov, Somov, Somova-Mikhailova, Sudeikin, Tarkhov, Tolstaya, Tsionglinsky, Ulyanov, Utkin, Yakimchenko, Yakovlev, Yakubov, and Zamirailo.
417 pictures shown.

1913, January

World of Art Exhibition of Paintings (St. Petersburg, Lidval House (The Swedish Church).
Contributors: Altman, Anisfeld, Arapov, Belkin, Benois, Bogayevsky, Braz, Burliuk, Chekhonin, Chembers-Bilibina, Dobuzhinsky, Falileyev, Feofilaktov, Fomin, Gaush, Golubkina, Grekova, Gruzenberg, Kalmakov, Karev, Khrustachov, Kliushnikov, Kruglikova, Kustodiev, L. Kuznetsova, P. Kuznetsov, Lanceray, Latrie, Lukomsky, Matveyev,

N. Milioti, Mitrokhin, Mikhailova, Mostova, Narbut, Nakhman, Naumov, Obolenskaya, Ostroumova-Lebedeva, Petrov-Vodkin, Pligen, Roerich, Ryabushinsky, Sapunov, Saryan, Shervashidze, Shitikov, Sologub, Somov, Somova-Mikhailova, Stelletsky, Sudeikin, Tarkhov, Tolstaya, Tsionglinsky, Ulyanov, Utkin, Yakimchenko, Yakovlev, Yakulov, and Zamirailo.

1913

World of Art Exhibition of Paintings (Kiev, Municipal Museum).
Contributors: Altman, Anisfeld, Arapov, Bakst, Belkin, Benois, Bogayevsky, Braz, Chembers-Bilibina, Dobuzhinsky, Falileyev, Fomin, A. Gaush, L. Gaush, Gruzenberg, Karev, Khrustachov, Kliushnikov, Kruglikova, Lanceray, Larionov, Latrie, Lukomsky, Mikhailova, N. Milioti, Mitrokhin, Mostova, Naumov, Ostroumova-Lebedeva, Petrov-Vodkin, Pligen, Roerich, Sapunov, Saryan, Shitikov, Utkin, Yakovlev, and Yakulov.
250 pictures shown.

1913, November – December

World of Art Exhibition of Paintings (St. Petersburg, premises of the Society for the Encouragement of the Arts).
Contributors: Altman, Anisfeld, Belkin, Belogrud, Benois, Bilibin, Blumenfeld, Chekhonin, Dobuzhinsky, Efimov, Fonvizin, Gaush, Grigoryev, Gruzenberg, Ivashintseva, Kalmakov, Khrustachov, Krichinsky, Kruglikova, Kustodiev, Kuznetsov, Lanceray, Latrie, Levitsky, Lindeman, Lukomsky, Matveyev, Mitrokhin, Mostova, Nagubnikov, Obolenskaya, Ostroumova, Lebedeva, Petrov-Vodkin, Remizov, Serebryakova, Shervashidze, Shillingovsky, Shitikov, Sologub, Somov, Somova-Mikhailova, Sorin, Stelletsky, Sudeikin, Tamanov, Tatlin, Utkin, Ukhtomsky, Yakovlev, Yaremich, Zak, and Ziloti.
432 pictures shown.

1913, December – 1914, January

World of Art Exhibition of Paintings (Moscow, premises of the Literary and Art Circle).
Contributors: Altman, Anisfeld, Arapov, Bari, Belkin, Belogrud, Benois, Bilibin, Blumenfeld, Chekhonin, Chernousenko, Dobuzhinsky, Efimov, Favorsky, Feofilaktov, Fonvizin, Fyodorov, A. Gaush, Goncharova, Grigoryev, Gruzenberg, Ivanov, Ivashintseva, Kalinkin, Kalmakov, Kamensky, Kamentseva, Karmin, Khrustachov, Koiransky, Krichinsky, Kruglikova, Kustodiev, Kuznetsov, Lanceray, Larionov, Latrie, Lensky, Levitsky, Liubavina, Lukomsky, Matveyev, Mitrokhin, Mostova, Mozalevsky, Nagubnikov, Nakhman, Nevinsky, Obolenskaya, Ogranovich, Ostroumova-Lebedeva, Pavlov, Sr., Petrov-Vodkin, Popova, Rainova, Remizov, Saryan, Serebryakova, Shervashidze, Shevchenko, Shillingovsky, Shitikov, Simonovich-Efimova, Sologub, Sorin, Stelletsky, Sudeikin, Tarkhov, Tatevosyan, Tatlin, Tolstaya, Ukhtomsky, Ulyanov, Utkin, Yakimchenko, Yakovleva, Yaremich, Yakulov, Zak, Zakharov, and Ziloti.
547 pictures shown.

1915, November

World of Art Exhibition of Studies, Sketches, and Drawings (Petrograd, premises of N. Dobychina's Art Bureau).
Contributors: Anisfeld, Arnstam, Belkin, Benois, Braz, Bruni, Charlemagne, Chekhonin, Chernov, Dobuzhinsky, Dydyshko, Gaush, Gints, Grandi, Grigoryev, Gromov, Gruzenberg, Ivashintseva, Kalmakov, Kruglikova, Kustodiev, Lanceray, Lagorio, Mikhailovskaya, Mitrokhin, Miturich, Narbut, Ober, Ostroumova-Lebedeva, Petrov-Vodkin, Serebryakova, Shmakov, Tretyakova, Tyrsa, Vereisky, Verkhovskaya, Webb, Yakimchenko, Zamirailo, and Zhukovskaya.
326 items shown.

1915, December

World of Art Exhibition of Paintings (Moscow).
Contributors: Alexeyev, Altman, Anisfeld, Arnstam, Belkin, Bilibin, Braz, Bruni, Charle-magne, Chekhonin, Dobuzhinsky, Dydyshko, Feofilaktov, Fyodorov, Grabar, Grigoryev, Gromov, Gruzenberg, Hassenberg, Ivashintseva, Kandaurov, Kolesnikov, Konchalovsky, Kostenko, Kruglikova, Kustodiev, Kuznetsov, Khodasevich, Konstantinov, Kotovich-Borisyak, Lanceray, Lebman, Lindeman, Mashkov, Mikhailovskaya, Mitrokhin, Miturich, Obolenskaya, Ostroumova-Lebedeva, Petrov-Vodkin, Pligen, Nakhman, Saryan, Shma-kov, Shchekatikhina-Pototskaya, Shitikov, Shchusev, Somov, Sudeikin, Tolstaya, Tretya-kova, Tyrsa, Ulyanov, Utkin, Vereisky, Webb, Yakulov, and the sculptors Efimov, Koort, Mezentsev, and Niss-Goldman.
392 items shown.

1916, January

World of Art Exhibition of Paintings (Petrograd, premises of N. Dobychina's Art Bureau).
Contributors: Alexeyev, Altman, Anisfeld, Belkin, Bilibin, Blumenfeld, Boguslavskaya, Chekhonin, Chembers, Dobuzhinsky, Giurjan, Grabar, Grigoryev, Gromov, Kandaurov, Karev, Kholopov, Kolesnikov, Konchalovsky, Kostenko, Kotovich-Borisyak, Kruglikova, Kustodiev, P. Kuznetsov, V. Kuznetsov, Lanceray, Leblanc, Lindeman, Malevannaya-Zaretskaya, Mashkov, Meshchaninov, Mitrokhin, Miturich, Nakhman, Narbut, Nivinsky, Ober, Obolenskaya, O'Connel, Ostroumova-Lebedeva, Petrov-Vodkin, Pligen, Saryan, Serebryakova, Shchekatikhina-Pototskaya, Sheikhel, Shestopalov, Shitikov, Sudeikin, Tolstaya, Ulyanov, Utkin, Volkovsky, Yakovlev, Yasinovsky, Zamirailo, and Zhukov-skaya.
280 pictures shown.

1916, December

World of Art Exhibition of Paintings (Moscow).
Contributors: Alexeyev, Arnstam, Bayev, G. Blumenfeld, N. Blumenfeld, Bobokhova, Boguslavsky, Braz, Chekhonin, Dobuzhinsky, Domogatsky, Falileyev, Feofilaktov, Fyo-dorova-Mashkova, Grekov, Grigoryev, Kachura-Falileyeva, Kalmakov, Karev, Kharybin, Khentov, Khrustachov, Konchalovsky, Konstantinov, Koort, Kotovich-Borisyak, Kran-dievskaya, Kruglikova, Kustodiev, Kuznetsov, Ladyzhenskaya-Shilovskaya, Lagorio, Led-nitskaya, Lermontova, Lindeman, Lissitzky, Lobanov, Martov-Greneberg, Mashkov, Mil-man, Myamlina, Nakhman, Niss-Goldman, Nivinsky, Ober, Obolenskaya, Ostroumova-Lebedeva, Petrov-Vodkin, Polenova, Pozharskaya, Renauld, Rydziunskaya, Shapshal, Shchekatikhina-Pototskaya, Shestopalov, Shitikov, Sofronov, Sorin, Sudeikin, Tolstaya, Ulyanov, Utkin, Voloshin, Wulf, Yakovlev, Yasinovsky, Yastrzhemsky, Yermakov, Zak, Zamirailo, Zelmanova, Zemlyanitsyna, and Zhevakina-Nikolskaya.
365 pictures shown.

1917, February – March

World of Art Exhibition of Paintings (Petrograd).
Contributors: Andrusov, Anisfeld, Arnstam, Bayev, Bilibin, Blokh-Leonora, G. Blumen-feld, N. Blumenfeld, Boguslavskaya, Braz, Brazer, Bushen, Chekhonin, Chupyatov, Dobuzhinsky, Falileyev, Fyodorova-Mashkova, Gaush, Grekov, Grigoryev, Grinberg, Iva-nov, Kachura-Falileyeva, Kandaurov, Karev, Kharybin, Khentov, Konchalovsky, Kotovich-Borisyak, Krashko, Kruglikova, Kustodiev, Lagorio, Lednitskaya, Lermontova, Levitsky, Lindeman, Lissitzky, Lobanov, Lukomsky, Malevannaya-Zaretskaya, Martov-Greneberg, Mashkov, Milman, Mitrokhin, Miturich, Nakhman, Nivinsky, Ober, Obolen-skaya, O'Connel, Ostroumova-Lebedeva, Petrov-Vodkin, Polenova, Pozharskaya, Raush von Traunbenberg, Roerich, Samokhvalov, Shchekatikhina-Pototskaya, Shestopalov, Shi-tikov, Shikhmanova, Shmakov, Shretter, Sokolov, Somov, Somova-Mikhailova, Sorin, Sudeikin, Tolmachevskaya, Tolstaya, Ukhtomsky, Ulyanov, Vereisky, Voinov, Yasinov-

sky, Yastrzhemsky, Yermakov, Zak, Zamirailo, Zhevakina-Nikolskaya, Zhukovskaya, and Ziloti.
403 pictures shown.

1917, December

World of Art Exhibition of Paintings (Moscow).
Contributors: Alexeyev, Arapov, Babichev, Brunov, Chekrygin, Chernousenko, Dobuzhinsky, Domogatsky, Falileyeva, Falk, Fyodorov, Fyodorova-Mashkova, Goldman, Grigoryev, Grishenko, Gumilina, Itkind, Kandaurov, Konchalovsky, Konionkov, Konstantinov, Kotovich-Borisyak, Kruglikova, Kulikov, Kuprin, Kustodiev, Kuznetsov, Labuzhskaya, Lentulov, Levashova, Lissitzky, Mashkov, Milman, Mitrokhin, Nakhman, Obolenskaya, Osmiorkin, Ostroumova-Lebedeva, Ostrov, Polenova, Rozhdestvensky, Savinov, Shchusev, Shevchenko, Shitikov, Smirnov, Sofronov, Sudeikin, Ulyanov, Utkin, Wulf, Yakovlev, Yakulov, Yermakov (Iverm), and Zhegin.
387 pictures shown.

1918, February

World of Art Exhibition of Paintings (Petrograd, Museum of the Academy of Arts).
Contributors: Baranov-Rossinet, Boguslavsky, Bruni, Bursian-Gromova, Bushen, Chekhonin, Cheptsov, Chupyatov, Dobuzhinsky, Dydyshko, Gaush, Geitman, Grigoryev, Gurevich, Ilyin, Iofan, Karev, Kruglikova, Kustodiev, Lanceray, Lebedev, Matveyev, Mitrokhin, Miturich, Petrov-Vodkin, Popov, Ostroumova-Lebedeva, Shikhmanov, Shleifer, Shmakov, Shukhayev, Somova-Mikhailova, Vereisky, and Zamirailo.

1919, April – June

First State General Exhibition of Artworks (Petrograd, Winter Palace).
The works of artists of diverse trends, including those associated with the World of Art, were displayed in 17 rooms.
Contributors: Altman, Belkin, Alexander Benois, Albert Benois, Bilibin, Braz, Bushen, Chagall, Dobuzhinsky, Gaush, Golovin, Grigoryev, Karev, Kruglikova, Kustodiev, Mitrokhin, Ostroumova-Lebedeva, Petrov-Vodkin, Roerich, Shchekatikhina-Pototskaya, Shukhayev, Vereisky, Voinov, Yaremich, and Zamirailo.

1921, June – July

Exhibition of Works by Artist-Members of the House of Arts (Petrograd, House of Arts).
Contributors: Benois, Braz, Shchekatikhina-Pototskaya, and Vereisky.

1921, October – November

World of Art Exhibition of Painting, Sculpture and Architecture (Moscow)
Contributors: Bebutova, Borisov, Chernyshov, Drevin, Falileyev, Falk, Fyodorov, Fyodorova-Mashkova, Fyodorovsky, Gerasimov, Grigoryev, Ivanov, Kandinsky, Kokorin, Kolesnikov, Konchalovsky, Konionkov, Koroliov, A. Korovin, K. Korovin, Krandievskaya, Krymov, Kuprin, Kuznetsov, Lapin, Lazarev, Lentulov, Lobanov, Maliavin, O. Maliutin, S. Maliutin, Mashkov, Monin, Mukhina, Norvet, Osmiorkin, Pestel, Polyakov, Rodionov, Shchusev, Shevchenko, Shemyakin, Shestakov, Sinezubov, Sokolov, Sokolov-Skala, Udaltsova, Ulyanov, Vesnin, Vysheslavsky, A. Yakovlev, B. Yakovlev, V. Yakovlev, Zhegin, and Zholotovsky.
252 pieces displayed.

1922, January

World of Art Exhibition of Paintings (Moscow)
Contributors: Chagall, Drevin, Falk, Fyodorov, Konchalovsky, Konionkov, Koroliov, Korovin, Krymov, Lentulov, Maliavin, S. Maliutin, Mashkov, Osmiorkin, Rozhdestvensky, Sinezubov, and Udaltsova.
151 pictures shown.

1922, May – June

World of Art Exhibition of Paintings (Petrograd, Anichkov Palace).
Contributors: Adamovich, Anenkov, Benois, Braz, Bushen, Chekhonin, Cherkesov, Dobuzhinsky, Domracheva, Fomin, Gaush, Goss, Grabar, Gromov, Ilyin, Karev, Konashevich, Kruglikova, Kustodiev, Lanceray, Lakhovsky, Matveyev, Milashevsky, Mitrokhin, Morozova, Neradovsky, Ostroumova-Lebedeva, Petrov-Vodkin, Radlov, Radlova, Roslavlev, Serebryakova, Shchekatikhina-Pototskaya, Shvede, Smirnova-Ivanova, Somov, Vereisky, Voinov, Westfalen, Zakharov, Zandin, Zamirailo, Zhilin, and Ziloti.
382 pictures shown.

1924, June

Exhibition of World of Art Artists (Leningrad, Anichkov Palace).
Contributors: Abramovich, Belkin, A. Benois, N. Benois, Braz, Bushen, Chekhonin, Dobuzhinsky, Fomin, Golovin, Govorova, Gromov, Ilyin, Karev, Konashevich, Kostenko, Kravchenko, Kruglikova, Lakhovsky, Lanceray, Lvov, Matveyev, Mitrokhin, Morozov, Mostova-Matveyeva, Neradovsky, Ostroumova-Lebedeva, Petrov-Vodkin, Pokrovsky, Psheslavskaya, Radlov, Radlova, Schildknecht, Serebryakova, Shenderova, Shvede, Smirnova-Ivanova, Shiffers-Legrand, Somova-Mikhailova, Ulin, Vereisky, Voinov, Voloshin, Voloshinov, Yaremich, Zandin, and Zamirailo.
351 pieces displayed.

1927, June

Russian Artists of the World of Art Group (Paris).
Contributors: Annenkov, Bilibin, Bushen, Dobuzhinsky, Grigoryev, Korovin, Kustodiev, Milioti, Ostroumova-Lebedeva, Saryan, Shchekatikhina-Potoskaya, Shukhayev, Sorin, and Yakovlev.
137 items shown.

CATALOGUE

LÉON BAKST

8   Portrait of Isaac Levitan. 1899. In: *World of Art*,
No. 6

12   Portrait of Alexander Benois. 1898
Watercolor and pastel on paper mounted on
cardboard. 64.5 x 100.3
Russian Museum, Leningrad

14   Portrait of Walter Nouvel. 1895
Watercolor on paper mounted on cardboard.
57 x 44.2
Russian Museum, Leningrad

16   Portrait of Sergei Diaghilev with His Nurse.
1906
Oil on canvas. 161 x 116
Russian Museum, Leningrad

27   Portrait of Alexander Golovin. 1908
Black chalk on paper. 31.6 x 22
Russian Museum, Leningrad

33   Cover for the *World of Art* (1902, No. 2). 1901

34   Costume design for the Tsarevna in Stravinsky's
ballet *L'Oiseau de Feu* (Diaghilev Company). 1910
Watercolor, pencil, and gold paint.
35.5 x 22
Theater Museum, Leningrad

65   Vase (Self-Portrait). 1906
Gouache and watercolor on paper mounted on
cardboard. 113 x 71.3
Okunev collection, Leningrad

66   Terror Antiquus (decorative panel). 1908
Oil on canvas. 250 x 270
Russian Museum, Leningrad

114   Cover for the journal *Comœdia Illustré*. 1910,
No. 2

128   Costume design for Sophocles' tragedy *Œdipus
at Colonus* (St. Petersburg, Alexandrinsky Theater).
1904
Watercolor and pencil. 28.1 x 44
Bakhrushin Theater Museum, Moscow

136   Costume design for a Bœotian in Tcherepnin's
ballet *Narcisse* (Diaghilev Company). 1911
Watercolor and lead pencil on paper. 40 x 27
Theater Museum, Leningrad

137   Costume design for the Bœotian girls in
Tcherepnin's ballet *Narcisse* (Diaghilev Company).
1911
Watercolor and lead pencil on paper. 40 x 27
Theater Museum, Leningrad

154   Elysium (decorative panel). 1906
Watercolor and gouache on paper mounted on
cardboard. 158 x 140
Tretyakov Gallery, Moscow

155   Frontispiece for Blok's *Snow Mask* volume of
verse. 1907

156   Costume design for Orpheus in an unrealized
production of Roger-Ducasse's ballet
(St. Petersburg, Mariinsky Theater). 1915
Watercolor, gouache, India ink, and silver paint on
paper. 27 x 19.8
Silberstein collection, Moscow

157   Costume design for Florestan in Schumann's
Le Carnaval (Diaghilev Company). 1910
Watercolor on paper. 27.7 x 21.3
Theater Museum, Leningrad

158   Costume design for the dancer Tamara
Karsavina. 1907
Watercolor, India ink, pencil, and gold paint on
paper. 30.8 x 23.3
Russian Museum, Leningrad

159   Costume design for the Blue God in Hahn's
Le Dieu Bleu (Diaghilev Company). 1912
Watercolor, gouache, and gold paint on paper.
25.5 x 17.5
Bakhrushin Theater Museum, Moscow

160   Costume design for Richard Strauss'
Le Légende de Joseph (Diaghilev Company). 1914
Watercolor, pencil, and gold paint. 31.2 x 22.8
Russian Museum, Leningrad

161   The Supper. 1902
Oil on canvas. 150 x 100
Russian Museum, Leningrad

162   Portrait of the Poetess Zinaida Gippius. 1906
Pencil, chalk, and red chalk on paper mounted on
cardboard. 54 x 44
Tretyakov Gallery, Moscow

163   Illustration for Gogol's novella *The Nose*. 1904
Watercolor and gouache on paper. 32 x 34
Tretyakov Gallery, Moscow

ALEXANDER BENOIS

21   Feeding the Fish. From the *Last Walks of Louis
XIV* series. 1897
Watercolor, gouache, and pastel on paper.
47.8 x 62.5
Russian Museum, Leningrad

40   Anteroom of the Grand Palace in Pavlovsk.
1902
Pastel, charcoal, and gouache on cardboard.
31 x 58.4
Tretyakov Gallery, Moscow

51   Frontispiece for Pushkin's *The Bronze
Horseman*. 1905
Watercolor heightened with white on paper.
23.7 x 17.6
Pushkin Museum, Leningrad

57   Oranienbaum. 1901
Watercolor and pencil on paper. 27.7 x 42.5
Russian Museum, Leningrad

58   The King's Walk. 1906
Gouache, pencil, pen and ink on cardboard. 48 x 62
Tretyakov Gallery, Moscow

59   Fantasy on the Theme of Versailles. 1906
Pencil, pen and ink on paper mounted
on cardboard. 49.6 x 67.7
Tretyakov Gallery, Moscow

60   Water Parterre in Versailles. Autumn. 1905
Gouache, watercolor, pen and ink on paper mounted
on cardboard. 47.8 x 65.6
Tretyakov Gallery, Moscow

61   The Bath of the Marquise. 1906
Gouache, pen and ink on cardboard. 51 x 47.5
Tretyakov Gallery, Moscow

63   Parade in the Reign of Paul I. 1907
Gouache on paper. 59.6 x 82
Russian Museum, Leningrad

64   Peter I Walking in the Summer Gardens. 1910
Gouache on canvas. 68.3 x 101.2
Russian Museum, Leningrad

107   Italian Comedy: Billet doux. 1905
Gouache, pen and ink, and pencil on paper mounted
on cardboard. 47.8 x 65.6
Tretyakov Gallery, Moscow

134   Set design for Pushkin's tragedy *The Feast in
Time of Plague* (Moscow Art Theater). 1914
Gouache, charcoal, and pastel on paper. 43.5 x 63.5
Tretyakov Gallery, Moscow

135   Set design for the inn room in Goldoni's
La Locandiera (Moscow Art Theater). 1913
Watercolor on paper
Stanislavsky Memorial Museum, Moscow

148   "Where lonely waters, struggling sought to
reach the sea." Illustration for Pushkin's
The Bronze Horseman. 1916–22
Brush, lead pencil, pen, and India ink
heightened with white. 9.9 x 18.8
Russian Museum, Leningrad

149   "The wide, majestic Neva labors, in granite
clad." Illustration for Pushkin's *The Bronze
Horseman*. 1916–22
Brush, lead pencil, pen, and India ink heightened
with white. 13.2 x 19
Russian Museum, Leningrad

150   "Novembers's breath of autumn cold."
Illustration for Pushkin's *The Bronze Horseman*.
1916–22
Brush, pen, and India ink heightened with white.
13.9 x 18.9
Russian Museum, Leningrad

164   Set design for the seashore in Stravinsky's
Le Rossignol (Diaghilev Company). 1914

Tempera on paper mounted on canvas. 100 x 110.8
Russian Museum, Leningrad

165   The Gambling House. Illustration for
Pushkin's *The Queen of Spades*. 1910
Pushkin Museum, Leningrad

166   Costume design for Truffaldino in Goldoni's
The Servant of Two Masters (Petrograd, Bolshoi
Drama Theater). 1920
Watercolor on paper. 24.5 x 34
Dobychin collection, Leningrad

167   Costume design for the dancing girl in
Stravinsky's *Petrouchka* (Diaghilev Company). 1911
Watercolor and gouache on paper.
35.5 x 22.3
Russian Museum, Leninigrad

168   Costume design for Stravinsky's *Le Rossignol*
(Diaghilev Company). 1914
Watercolor on paper. 47.8 x 30.5
Russian Museum, Leningrad

169   Hermann in the House of the Countess.
Illustration for Pushkin's *The Queen of Spades*.
1905
India ink and watercolor on paper
Pushkin Museum, Leningrad

170   Set design for Scene 2 of Tcherepnin's
Le Pavillon d'Armide (St. Petersburg, Mariinsky
Theater). 1907
Watercolor on paper. 25.2 x 39.9
Russian Museum, Leningrad

171   Venetian Fête in the Sixteenth Century. Set
design for an unrealized production of Debussy's
Les Jeux (Festivities). 1912
Gouache and watercolor on paper mounted on
cardborad. 65.7 x 102
Tretyakov Gallery, Moscow

172   Lake Primel. Brittany. 1905
Watercolor and India ink heightened with white on
paper. 26.5 x 46.5
Brodsky Memorial Museum, Leningrad

173   Frontispiece for *The Theater. A Book About
the New Theater*. St. Petersburg. 1907

280 Italian Comedy: The Indiscreet Punchinello.
1906
Oil on canvas. 68.5 x 101
Russian Museum, Leningrad

282   The Fair. Set design for Stravinsky's
Petrouchka (Diaghilev Company). 1911
Watercolor and gouache heightened with white on
paper. 83.4 x 60
Bolshoi Theater Museum, Moscow

285   Set design for Taneyev's *Cupid's Revenge*
(St. Petersburg, Hermitage Theater). 1900
Watercolor and charcoal on paper. 32.7 x 47.6
Chudnovsky collection, Leningrad

287   The Blackamoor's Room. Set design for
Stravinsky's *Petrouchka* (Diaghilev Company). 1911
Watercolor and gouache on paper. 63 x 48.7
Bolshoi Theater Museum, Moscow

IVAN BILIBIN

39   The Princess in the Tower. Illustration for the
fairy tale *The Little White Duck*. 1902

Watercolor, tempera, and gold paint on paper.
28.5 x 22.5
Goznak Museum, Moscow

118   Chernomor's Gardens. Set design for Scene 1
of Glinka's *Ruslan and Ludmila* (St. Petersburg,
People's House Theater). 1913
Lead pencil on paper. 32 x 52.5
Theater Museum, Leningrad

120   Cover for Pushkin's *Tale of Tsar Saltan*. 1905
Watercolor, tempera and gold paint on paper
mounted on cardboard. 28.4 x 34.6
Russian Museum, Leningrad

121   The Chambers of the Novgorod Fraternity. Set
design for Scene 1 of Rimsky-Korsakov's *Sadko*
(St. Petersburg, People's House Theater). 1913
Lead pencil on paper. 32 x 52.5
Theater Museum, Leningrad

138   Title page for Uspensky's article "Early
Russian Painting (15th–18th) Centuries,"
The Golden Fleece, No. 7–9. 1906
Tempera on paper. 36.5 x 31.8
Russian Museum, Leningrad

174   Dadon's Palace. Set design for Act 1 of
Rimsky-Korsakov's *The Golden Cockerel* (Zimin's
Opera House). 1909
Pushkin Museum, Leningrad

175   Tailpiece for Benois' *Russian School of
Painting*. 1906
Tempera on paper mounted on cardboard.
21.9 x 26.5
Russian Museum, Leningrad

176   Bill: Historical Exhibition of Artworks. 1904
Watercolor, tempera, and gold paint on paper.
63.5 x 43
Russian Museum, Leningrad

177   Program cover for Mussorgsky's *Boris
Godunov*. 1908
Watercolor on paper. 28.4 x 21.7
Russian Museum, Leningrad

MSTISLAV DOBUZHINSKY

43   October Idyll. 1905. In: *Zhupel* (Bugbear),
No. 2

44   Man with Spectacles. Portrait of the Art Critic
and Poet Konstantin Sunnerberg (pen name of
Konstantin Erberg). 1905–06
Charcoal and watercolor heightened with white on
paper mounted on cardboard. 63.3 x 99.6
Tretyakov Gallery, Moscow

46   The City. 1904
Pastel on paper. 40 x 33.5
Gorky Art Museum, Kirov

80   Peter the Great in Holland: Amsterdam, the
Wharf of the East India Company (sketch). 1910
Oil on paper mounted on cardboard. 41 x 52.8
Tretyakov Gallery, Moscow

81   The Provinces in the 1830s. 1907–09
Watercolor and pencil heightened with white on
paper. 60 x 83.5
Russian Museum, Leningrad

82   City Types (City Grimaces). 1908
Watercolor and gouache on paper. 29.2 x 22
Tretyakov Gallery, Moscow

83   Paris. 1914
Red chalk and charcoal on paper. 32.7 x 37.2
Russian Museum, Leningrad

85   Barbershop Window. 1906
Watercolor, gouache, and charcoal on paper.
29.7 x 21.7
Tretyakov Gallery, Moscow

86   A Cottage in St. Petersburg. 1905
Pastel and gouache on paper mounted on cardboard.
37 x 49
Tretyakov Gallery, Moscow

130   Birdhouses, after *Nikolai Stavrogin*, an
adaptation of Dostoyevsky's *The Demons* (Moscow
Art Theater). 1913
Oil on canvas. 87 x 73
Bakhrushin Theater Museum, Moscow

133   The Blue Lounge. Set design for Act 1 of
Turgenev's *A Month in the Country* (Moscow Art
Theater). 1909
Gouache, watercolor, and pencil with silver powder
on paper. 32.4 x 51.5
Tretyakov Gallery, Moscow

140   Sketch-version of the title page for Hans
Christian Andersen's *The Swineherd*. 1917
Watercolor, lead pencil, India ink, pen, and brush
on paper
Russian Museum, Leningrad

144–147   Illustrations for Dostoyevsky's *White
Nights*. 1922

188   Vilna. Noctural Scene. 1910s
Pastel on paper mounted on cardboard. 35.4 x 45.1
Tretyakov Gallery, Moscow

189   Exercises of Army Recruits in the Times of
Nicholas I. 1910
Tempera on cardboard. 61 x 83
Picture Gallery of Armenia, Yerevan

190   Canal in Haarlem. 1910
Watercolor and pencil on paper mounted on
cardboard. 29 x 35.7
Russian Museum, Leningrad

191   Glassmakers' Street in Vilna. 1906
Lead pencil and watercolor heightened with white on
paper. 29.5 x 35.3
Tretyakov Gallery, Moscow

192   Night in St. Petersburg. 1924
Gouache on gray paper mounted on cardboard.
47.5 x 78.5
Tretyakov Gallery, Moscow

193   Scene from the Life of Petrograd in 1920. 1920
Gouache and lead pencil on cardboard. 33.6 x 53
Russian Museum, Leningrad

194   Denmark. A Small Theater. 1912
Gouache and lead pencil on gray paper mounted on
cardboard. 19.4 x 26.3
Pushkin Museum of Fine Arts, Moscow

195   The Kiss. 1916
Lead pencil and red chalk on cardboard. 109 x 76
Okunev collection, Leningrad

196   Curtain design for Lunacharsky's drama
Oliver Cromwell (Moscow, Maly Theater). 1920–21
Watercolor and pencil on paper. 27.4 x 42.4
Maly Theater Museum, Moscow

197   Set design for the prologue to Remizov's
mystery-play *A Devilish Act on a Certain Husband*,

and also *Life's Disputes with Death* (St. Petersburg,
Vera Komissarzhevskaya's Theater). 1907
Gouache and watercolor with bronze and silver
powder. 43 x 53
Bakhrushin Theater Museum, Moscow

198   By Izora's Window. Set design for an
unrealized Moscow Art Theater production of Blok's
The Rose and the Cross. 1916–17
Gouache on gray paper. 32 x 26
Pushkin House (the USSR Academy of Sciences
Institute of Russian Literature), Leningrad

199   The Opening of the Congress. In the album
*The Second Congress of the Communist Interna-
tional.* 1920
Lead pencil on paper. 31.6 x 21.9
Brodsky Memorial Museum, Leningrad

283   The Blue Drawing Room. Set design for Act 1
of Turgenev's *A Month in the Country* (Moscow Art
Theater). 1909
Watercolor, gouache, and pencil on paper mounted
on cardboard. 36.5 x 62
Tretyakov Gallery, Moscow

293   Set design for de la Halle's pastorale *Le Jeu de
Robin et Marion* (St. Petersburg, Antique Theater).
1907
Watercolor heightened with white on paper with
pasted-on strip of gold tinfoil and touched up with
bronze paint. 32.2 x 44.8
Bakhrushin Theater Museum, Moscow

ALEXANDER GOLOVIN

35   Birches. 1908–10
Gouache on cardboard. 68.4 x 78
Tretyakov Gallery, Moscow

36   Kashchei's Kingdom. Set design for Stravinsky's
The Firebird (Diaghilev Company). 1910
Watercolor, gouache, and bronze paint on paper.
82.5 x 102
Tretyakov Gallery, Moscow

111   Self-Portrait. 1912
Tempera on paper. 88.6 x 68.9
Tretyakov Gallery, Moscow

113   Portrait of Fyodor Chaliapin as Holophernes
in Serov's opera *Judith.* 1908
Tempera, gouache, and pastel on canvas. 163 x 212
Tretyakov Gallery, Moscow

115   Portrait of the Stage Director Vsevolod
Meyerhold. 1817
Tempera on panel. 80 x 67
Theater Museum, Leningrad

131   The Ballroom. Set design for Scene 2 of
Lermontov's *The Masquerade* (Petrograd,
Alexandrinsky Theater). 1917
Size paints and gouache touched up with gold
paint on cardboard. 70.5 x 101
Bakhrushin Theater Museum, Moscow

181   Roses and China. 1920s
Gouache on cardboard. 95 x 79.5
Radishchev Art Museum, Saratov

178   Spanish Girl in a Black Shawl. 1908
Tempera, pastel, and charcoal on cardboard.
96.5 x 60.7
Tretyakov Gallery, Moscow

179   Children on the Balcony. Spain
Oil on canvas. 64 x 44
Picture Gallery of Armenia, Yerevan

180   Spanish Woman on the Balcony. 1911
Tempera and pastel on canvas. 141.5 x 88.5
Russian Museum, Leningrad

182   Neskuchny Garden in Moscow. 1920s
Tempera on canvas. 106 x 106
Radischchev Art Museum, Saratov

183   Spanish Girl. 1900s
Gouache and charcoal on cardboard. 89 x 70
Radishchev Art Museum, Saratov

184   Still Life with Flowers
Tempera on cardboard. 84 x 71
Picture Gallery of Armenia, Yerevan

185   The Volga Bank. Set design for Act 1 of
Ostrovsky's drama *The Thunderstorm* (Petrograd,
Alexandrinsky Theater). 1916
Tempera on cardboard. 70 x 104
Bakhrushin Theater Museum, Moscow

186   Careno's Room. Set design for Hamsun's play
At the Gate of the Kingdom (St. Petersburg,
Alexandrinsky Theater). 1908
Gouache heightened with white on paper. 70 x 99
Bakhrushin Theater Museum, Moscow

187   Portrait of Count Vladimir Kankrin, an
Official of the Imperial Theaters. 1909
Tempera and pastel on canvas. 89 x 89
Russian Museum, Leningrad

284   Kremlin Square. Set design for Act 1 of
Mussorgsky's *Boris Godunov* (St. Petersburg,
Mariinsky Theater). 1911
Watercolor and pen and ink on paper. 64.5 x 83
Russian Museum, Leningrad

286   Dr. Vangel's Garden. Set design for Act 1 of
Ibsen's *Lady from the Sea* (St. Petersburg,
Alexandrinsky Theater). 1905
Pastel on cardboard. 56 x 77
Bakhrushin Theater Museum, Moscow

291   Spanish Dance. Set design for Glinka's *Jota of
Aragon* (St. Petersburg, Mariinsky Theater). 1915
Tempera on cardboard. 71 x 84
Russian Museum, Leningrad

295   Don Juan's Dining Room. Set design for Act 4
of Molière's *Don Juan* (St. Petersburg, Mariinsky
Theater). 1910
Tempera on canvas. 80 x 119
Russian Museum, Leningrad

296   The Gambling Room. Set design for Scene 7 of
Lermontov's *The Masquerade* (Petrograd,
Alexandrinsky Theater). 1917
Size paints and gouache touched up with
gold paint. 70.5 x 100
Bakhrushin Theater Museum, Moscow

297   The Commander's Tomb. Ser design for Act 3
of Dargomyzhsky's *The Stone Guest* (Petrograd,
Mariinsky Theater). 1917
Tempera with bronze and silver paint on plywood.
79 x 115
Russian Museum, Leningrad

298   Set design for the prologue to Rimsky-Korsa-
kov's *Maid of Pskov.* 1901
Gouache on cardboard. 54 x 95
Tretyakov Gallery, Moscow

BORIS KUSTODIEV

3   Group Portrait of the World of Art Artists.
Sketch. 1916–20
Oil on canvas. 52 x 89
Russian Museum, Leningrad

89   Moscow Tavern. 1916
Oil on canvas. 99.3 x 129.3
Tretyakov Gallery, Moscow

93   La Belle. 1915
Oil on canvas. 141 x 185
Tretyakov Gallery, Moscow

94   Shrovetide. 1916
Oil on canvas. 89 x 190.5
Russian Museum, Leningrad

95   Shrovetide (Sleigh Riding). 1919
Oil on canvas. 71 x 98
Brodsky Memorial Museum, Leningrad

96   Portrait of Fyodor Chaliapin. 1921
Oil on canvas. 215 x 172
Theater Museum, Leningrad

99   The Fair. 1908
Gouache on paper. 68.2 x 102.5
Tretyakov Gallery, Moscow

201   Merchant Woman at Tea. 1918
Oil on canvas. 120 x 120
Russian Museum, Leningrad

202   Cover for Six Poems by Nikolai
Nekrasov. 1921
Pen and India ink on paper. 15.7 x 10.4
Russian Museum, Leningrad

203   Cover for Ostrovsky's
The Thunderstorm. 1920
Pen and India ink on paper. 21 x 17
Literature Museum, Moscow

204   "In the distance, heavens knows where, a light
twinkled in a watchhouse." Illustration for Gogol's
The Greatcoat. 1905
Charcoal on paper. 20.3 x 32
Russian Museum, Leningrad

205   Merchant Women. 1912
Tempera on cardboard. 81.5 x 108
Museum of Russian Art, Kiev

206   Tula. Sketch for a production of The Flea
after Leskov. 1924.
Oil on plywood. 63 x 76
Literature Museum, Moscow

207   Portrait of Prof. Pyotr Kapitsa and Prof.
Nikolai Semyonov. 1921
Oil on canvas. 71 x 71
Kapitsa collection, Moscow

208   Portrait of the Art Historian
A. Anisimov. 1919
Oil on cardboard. 41.4 x 33
Russian Museum, Leningrad

209   Night Gala on the Neva. 1923
Oil on canvas. 107 x 216
Museum of the Revolution, Moscow

210   The Bolshevik. 1919–20
Oil on canvas. 100 x 140
Tretyakov Gallery, Moscow

EVGENY LANCERAY

37   Medieval poetry in miniatures. Half title for the
World of Art journal. 1904
India ink on paper. 32.5 x 25.7
Russian Museum, Leningrad

50   St. Petersburg. Cover for an edition marking
the city's bicentennial. 1903
India ink on paper. 30.5 x 23.2
Russian Museum, Leningrad

76   Ships in the Times of Peter I. 1911
Tempera on paper. 64 x 86
Tretyakov Gallery, Moscow

77   The Empress Elizaveta Petrovna in Tsarskoye
Selo. 1905
Gouache on paper mounted on cardboard.
43.5 x 62
Tretyakov Gallery, Moscow

141   Road to Tsarskoye Selo in Anna Ioannovna's
time. Headpiece for Benois' Tsarskoye Selo in the
Reign of Empress Elizaveta Petrovna. 1904–12
Watercolor, gouache, lead pencil, and India ink on
paper. 18.1 x 30.5
Tretyakov Gallery, Moscow

142   The taking of the Swedish grange. Headpiece
for Benois' Tsarskoye Selo in the Reign of Empress
Elizaveta Petrovna. 1904–12
Lead pencil and watercolor heightened with white.
23.2 x 25
Tretyakov Gallery, Moscow

143   Hadji Murat coming down the mountain.
Illustration for Leo Tolstoy's Hadji Murat. 1913
Tempera on paper. 46 x 45
Tolstoy Museum, Moscow

211   Cathedral of Our Lady of Kazan in
St. Petersburg. 1897
Watercolor on paper. 60 x 43.5
Russian Museum, Leningrad

212   The Old St. Nicholas Market in St. Petersburg.
1901
Gouache, charcoal, and crayon on cardboard.
44 x 59
Tretyakov Gallery, Moscow

213   Shamil with his lieutenants. Illustration for Leo
Tolstoy's Hadji Murat. 1913
Tempera on paper. 35 x 26
Tolstoy Museum, Moscow

214   Nicholas I. Illustration for Leo Tolstoy's Hadji
Murat. 1914
Watercolor and India ink heightened with white on
paper. 28.6 x 24
Tolstoy Museum, Moscow

DMITRY MITROKHIN

139   Cover for Zamyatin's Provincial Tales.
Petrograd, 1915

215   Cover for Régnier's Seven Portraits.
Petrograd, 1921

216   Cover for Konradi's Among the Paintings of
the Hermitage. Moscow, 1917

217 Cover for Zhukovsky's *The Goblet, a Ballad.* Moscow, 1913

218 Illustration for Hauff's *The Life of Almansore.* Moscow, 1912

219 Cover for Schiller's *Don Carlos.* Moscow, 1919

220 Cover for Rozanov's *Fallen Leaves. The Second and Last Basket.* Petrograd, 1913

ANNA OSTROUMOVA-LEBEDEVA

38 St. Petersburg. The New Holland Arch. 1901
Woodcut

78 The Admiralty Under Snow. 1901
Colored woodcut

79 Amsterdam. The Iron Market. 1913
Oil and tempera on canvas. 67 x 99
Russian Museum, Leningrad

224 St. Petersburg. The Summer Gardens. 1929
Colored woodcut

225 The Biron Palace and Barques. 1916
Colored woodcut

226 The Chain Bridge. 1903
Colored woodcut

227 Venice at Night. 1914
Colored woodcut

228 Petrograd. Red Pillars. 1922
Watercolor on paper. 42.3 x 62.7
Russian Museum, Leningrad

229 Venice. The Grand Canal. 1911
Watercolor on paper. 33 x 46.3
Pushkin Museum of Fine Arts, Moscow

GEORGI NARBUT

221 Illustration for Hans Christian Andersen's tale *The Intrepid Tin Soldier.* 1913
India ink, pen, and collage on paper. 17 x 23
Museum of Ukrainian Art, Kiev

222 Tailpiece for *Teremok. Misgir*
(Moscow, 1910)

223 Illustration for Zhukovsky's tale *How the Mice Buried the Cat.* 1910
Pen and India ink on paper. 26.1 x 20
Museum of Ukrainian Art, Kiev

NICHOLAS ROERICH

18 The Ill-Omened. 1901
Oil on canvas. 103 x 230
Russian Museum, Leningrad

88 Rostov the Great. 1903
Oil on panel. 31.4 x 41
Tretyakov Gallery, Moscow

90 The Slavs on the Dnieper. 1905
Tempera and pastel on cardboard. 67 x 89
Russian Museum, Leningrad

91 The Kiss to Earth. Set design for Stravinsky's *Le Sacre du Printemps* (Diaghilev Company). 1912
Tempera on cardboard. 62 x 94
Russian Museum, Leningrad

92 Tristan's Ship. Set design for Act 1 of Wagner's *Tristan and Isolde* (Moscow, Zimin's Opera House). 1912
Gouache on cardboard. 60 x 90
Bakhrushin Theater Museum, Moscow

132 St. Pantaleon the Healer. 1916
Tempera on canvas. 130 x 178
Tretyakov Gallery, Moscow

230 Guests from Overseas. 1902
Oil on cardboard. 79 x 100
Russian Museum, Leningrad

231 Ancient Life. Sketch. 1904
Tempera on cardboard. 42.5 x 52
Radishchev Art Museum, Saratov

232 The Rocks of Rond. Set design for Ibsen's *Peer Gynt* (Moscow Art Theater). 1912
Tempera on cardboard. 66 x 87
Russian Museum, Leningrad

233 The Idols. Sketch. 1901
Gouache on cardboard. 154.5 x 264.54
Tretyakov Gallery, Moscow

234 The Polovtsy's Camp. Set design for Act 2 of Borodin's *Prince Igor* (Diaghilev Company). 1908
Pastel, charcoal, and gouache on paper mounted on cardboard. 52 x 70.5
Tretyakov Gallery, Moscow

235 Heavenly Battle. Version of the 1909 picture. 1912
Tempera on cardboard. 66 x 95
Russian Museum, Leningrad

288 In the Monastery. Set design for Maeterlinck's *Soeur Beatrice* (Petrograd, Musical Drama Theater). 1914
Tempera on cardboard. 75.5 x 86
Russian Museum, Leningrad

NIKOLAI SAPUNOV

41 The Masked Ball. 1907. Version of the picture of the same year
Oil on canvas. 61 x 86
Museum of Russian Art (Abramyan collection), Yerevan

101 The Merry-go-round. 1908
Tempera and oil on paper. 146 x 193.5
Russian Museum, Leningrad

103 The Green Bull Hotel on the Canal Bank. Set design for Kuzmin's pastorale *The Dutch Girl Liza* (St. Petersburg, House of Interludes). 1910
Tempera on cardboard. 73.5 x 103.5
Tretyakov Gallery, Moscow

104 Tea-Drinking. Sketch. 1912
Tempera on cardboard. 55.8 x 97.8
Tretyakov Gallery, Moscow

105 Spring. 1912
Tempera on cardboard. 69 x 101
Russian Museum, Leningrad

127   The Turkish Ceremony. Set design for Act 4 of
Molière's *Bourgeois Gentilhomme* (Moscow, Nezlobin
Theater)
Tempera on canvas. 86.8 x 133.2
Tretyakov Gallery, Moscow

236   Still Life with Vase and Flowers. 1910
Tempera on canvas. 118 x 114
Tretyakov Gallery, Moscow

237   The Merry-go-round
Tempera on cardboard. 82 x 100.7
Tretyakov Gallery, Moscow

238   Still Life with Vase, Flowers, and Fruit. 1912
Tempera on canvas. 147.2 x 115.8
Tretyakov Gallery, Moscow

239   Two stage costume designs. 1910
Gouache on cardboard. 52 x 44
Brodsky Memorial Museum, Leningrad

240   Still Life with Hydrangeas. 1910
Oil on canvas. 72 x 88.5
Tretyakov Gallery, Moscow

241   The Embankment in Alexandria. Set design for
Shaw's *Caesar and Cleopatra*. 1909
Tempera on canvas. 76 x 103
Russian Museum, Leningrad

290   The Ball. Set design for Act 2 of Schnitzler's
The Scarf of Columbine (St. Petersburg, House of
Interludes, 1910). 1910
Tempera on cardboard. 52 x 70
Picture Gallery of Armenia, Yerevan

294   The Mystic Gathering. Set design for Blok's
Balaganchik (The Fairground Booth) at Vera
Komissarzhevskaya's Theater, St. Petersburg. 1909
Tempera, pen, and charcoal with bronze, gold, and
silver paint. 42 x 84
Tretyakov Gallery, Moscow

ZINAIDA SEREBRYAKOVA

97   Self-Portrait. 1922
Oil on canvas. 69 x 56
Russian Museum, Leningrad

98   Peasants at Dinner. 1914
Oil on canvas. 123.5 x 98
Russian Museum, Leningrad

100   Bleaching Linen. 1917
Oil on canvas. 141.8 x 173.6
Tretyakov Gallery, Moscow

242   Girl with a Candle: Self-Portrait. 1911
Oil on canvas. 72 x 56
Russian Museum, Leningrad

243   Harvesting. 1915
Oil on canvas. 142 x 177
Picture Gallery, Odessa

244   Village of Neskuchnoye. 1912
Watercolor on paper. 40 x 62.3
Russian Museum, Leningrad

245   Self-Portrait at Toilette. 1909
Oil on canvas. 75 x 65
Tretyakov Gallery, Moscow

246   In the Bathhouse. 1913
Oil on canvas. 135 x 174
Russian Museum, Leningrad

247   At Breakfast. 1914
Oil on canvas. 88.5 x 107
Tretyakov Gallery, Moscow

248   House of Cards. 1919
Oil on canvas. 65 x 75.5
Russian Museum, Leningrad

VALENTIN SEROV

5   Portrait of Alexander Pushkin. 1899
Pencil and watercolor heightened with white.
35 x 29.3
Pushkin Museum, Leningrad

6   Children. Sasha and Yura Serov. 1899
Oil on canvas. 71 x 54
Russian Museum, Leningrad

7   Bathing the Horse. 1905
Oil on canvas. 72 x 90
Russian Museum, Leningrad

9   Self-Portrait. 1901
Watercolor and India ink on paper. 49.5 x 36
Art Museum, Odessa

10   First version of a curtain design for Rimsky-
Korsakov's *Schéhérazade* (Diaghilev Company).
1910
Tempera on cardboard. 56 x 72
Russian Museum, Leningrad

22   Peter II and Princess Elizaveta Riding to
Hounds. 1900
Tempera and gouache on paper mounted
on cardboard. 41 x 39
Russian Museum, Leningrad

26   Portrait of Léon Bakst. 1900s
India ink and gouache on paper mounted on
cardboard. 47 x 34
Russian Museum, Leningrad

43   "Soldiers, heroes everyone, where is all your
glory?" 1905
Tempera and charcoal on cardboard. 47.5 x 71.5
Russian Museum, Leningrad

69   Odysseus and Nausicaä. 1910
Tempera on cardboard. 85.5 x 101.5
Tretyakov Gallery, Moscow

70   The Rape of Europa. 1910
Tempera on canvas. 138 x 178
O. Serova collection, Moscow

71   Catherine II Setting Out to Hunt with Falcons.
1902
Tempera and gouache on cardboard. 23 x 40
Russian Museum, Leningrad

74   Peter the Great. 1907
Tempera on cardboard. 68.5 x 88
Tretyakov Gallery, Moscow

116   Portrait of Princess Olga Orlova. 1911
Oil on canvas. 237.5 x 160
Tretyakov Gallery, Moscow

126   Anna Pavlova in *Les Sylphides*. 1909
Tempera on primed canvas. 200 x 175
Russian Museum, Leningrad

249   Portrait of Ivan Morozov. 1910
Tempera on cardboard. 63.5 x 77
Tretyakov Gallery, Moscow

250 Portrait of Ida Rubinstein. 1910
Tempera and charcoal on canvas. 147 x 133
Russian Museum, Leningrad

251 Portrait of Princess Zinaida Yusupova.
1900–02
Oil on canvas. 181.5 x 133
Russian Museum, Leningrad

252 Feast Outside Holophernes' Tent. Set design
for Serov's opera *Judith* (St. Petersburg, Mariinsky
Theater). 1907
Tempera on paper mounted on cardboard. 55 x 73
Russian Museum, Leningrad

253 Portrait of Fyodor Chaliapin. 1905. Sketch
Pencil on paper. 20.3 x 12
Russian Museum, Leningrad

254 Portrait of Mika Morozov. 1902
Oil on canvas. 215.5 x 80.8
Tretyakov Gallery, Moscow

KONSTANTIN SOMOV

15 Self-Portrait. 1898
Watercolor, lead pencil, and pastel heightened with
white on paper mounted on cardboard. 46 x 32.6
Russian Museum, Leningrad

23 Portrait of Ostroumova. 1901
Oil on canvas. 87 x 63
Russian Museum, Leningrad

24 Portrait of Evgeny Lanceray. 1907
Lead pencil and crayons heightened with white on
paper. 49.5 x 34.6
Tretyakov Gallery, Moscow

25 Promenade after Rain. 1896
Watercolor and lead pencil on paper mounted on
cardboard. 36.4 x 73.5
Russian Museum, Leningrad

28 The Ridiculed Kiss. 1908
Oil on canvas. 49 x 58
Russian Museum, Leningrad

32 In the Bosquet. 1898–99
Watercolor, gold paint, and varnish on cardboard.
55.1 x 73.5
Russian Museum, Leningrad

47 Courtesans. 1903
Watercolor, gouache, and pastel on paper.
46.5 x 61.5
Tretyakov Gallery, Moscow

52 Evening. 1900–02
Oil on canvas. 142.3 x 205.3
Tretyakov Gallery, Moscow

53 Fireworks Display. 1922
Oil on canvas. 27 x 31.5
Brodsky Memorial Museum, Leningrad

54 L'Echo du temps passé. 1903
Watercolor, gouache, and lead pencil on paper
mounted on cardboard. 61 x 64
Tretyakov Gallery, Moscow

55 Harlequin and Lady. 1912
Watercolor and gouache on paper mounted on
cardboard. 62.2 x 47.5
Tretyakov Gallery, Moscow

56 Pierrot and Lady. 1910
Gouache on paper. 46 x 35
Picture Gallery, Odessa

84 Portrait of Mstislav Dobuzhinsky. 1910
Lead pencil and red chalk on paper. 44.5 x 31
Tretyakov Gallery, Moscow

112 Lady in Blue. Portrait of the Artist Elizaveta
Martynova. 1897–1900
Oil on canvas. 103 x 103
Tretyakov Gallery, Moscow

117 Portrait of the Poet Alexander Blok. 1907
Lead pencil, crayon, and gouache on paper. 38 x 30
Tretyakov Gallery, Moscow

151 Frontispiece for Ivanov's book *Cor Ardens*.
1907
Watercolor, gouache, pen and ink, and brush on
paper. 28 x 20.2
Tretyakov Gallery, Moscow

153 Harlequin and Death. 1907
Watercolor and gouache on paper. 17 x 12
Tretyakov Gallery, Moscow

255 Winter. The Skating Rink. 1915
Oil on canvas. 49 x 58
Russian Museum, Leningrad

256 Young Woman Sleeping. 1922
Oil on canvas mounted on cardboard. 25.3 x 30.5
(oval)
Brodsky Memorial Museum, Leningrad

257 Ploughland. 1900
Oil on cardboard. 31 x 73
Radishchev Art Museum, Saratov

258 Young Woman Asleep. 1909
Gouache and watercolor on paper mounted on cloth.
30.2 x 41.5
Tretyakov Gallery, Moscow

259 Landscape with a Rainbow. 1915
Oil on canvas mounted on cardboard. 22.4 x 27.3
Valk collection, Leningrad

260 Cover for the *Northern Flowers* almanac. 1901
Watercolor, pen and ink, and brush, heightened
with white. 22 x 15
Tretyakov Gallery, Moscow

261 A Youth on His Knees in Front of a Lady.
1916
Gouache on cardboard. 28.8 x 24.2
Brodsky Memorial Museum, Leningrad

262 Cover design for the fashion magazine
The Parisienne (1908–10). 1908
Pen and India ink on paper. 44.7 x 33.2
Tretyakov Gallery, Moscow

263 Head of the Little Girl Olya. 1896
Lead pencil on paper. 33.5 x 26.6
Tretyakov Gallery, Moscow

264 Portrait of the Poet Mikhail Kuzmin. 1909
Watercolor and gouache on paper mounted on
cardboard. 48.1 x 32.2
Tretyakov Gallery, Moscow

265 Self-Portrait. 1909
Watercolor and gouache on paper. 45.5 x 31
Tretyakov Gallery, Moscow

277 Title page for A. Blok's book *The Theater*.
1907
Watercolor, pen and ink, and brush, heightened
with white. 27.8 x 19
Tretyakov Gallery, Moscow

278–279 Curtain design for Moscow's Free Theater.
1913
Watercolor on paper mounted on cardboard.
75 x 97.7
Bakhrushin Theater Museum, Moscow

281 Colombine's Little Tongue. 1915
Watercolor and gouache on paper mounted on
cardboard. 29.2 x 22.5
Russian Museum, Leningrad

299 Italian Comedy. 1914
Watercolor and gouache on paper. 18.5 x 22
Picture Gallery of Armenia, Yerevan

SERGEI SUDEIKIN

106 Set design for Kuzmin's *Amusements for
Virgins* (St. Petersburg, Maly Drama Theater). 1911
Oil on canvas. 44.5 x 53.5
Museum of Russian Art, Kiev

109 The Ballet. 1910
Oil on canvas. 87 x 99
Russian Museum, Leningrad

110 Park. From the *Summer Gardens Studies*
series. C. 1910
Oil on cardboard. 51 x 67
Russian Museum, Leningrad

226 Harlequin's Garden. 1915–16
Oil on cardboard. 46 x 55
Radishchev Art Museum, Saratov

267 Saxon Figurines. 1911
Oil on canvas. 58 x 71
Russian Museum, Leningrad

268 Park in Front of the Castle. Set design for
Tchaikovsky's *The Swan Lake*. 1911
Oil on canvas. 71 x 90
Russian Museum, Leningrad

269 Still Life with Porcelain Figurines and
Roses. 1909
Oil on canvas mounted on cardboard. 44 x 53.5
Russian Museum, Leningrad

270 Costume design for Shaw's *Caesar and
Cleopatra* (St. Petersburg, New Drama Theater).
1909
Gouache on paper. 32 x 12
Theater Museum, Leningrad

271 Petrouchka. 1915
Watercolor on paper. 48 x 39
Museum of Russian Art (Abramyan collection),
Yerevan

289 Set design for Benavente's *The Seamy Side of
Life* (St. Petersburg, Russian Drama Theater). 1912
Tempera on cardboard. 85 x 99
Picture Gallery of Armenia, Yerevan

292 At Olympia's. Set design for Offenbach's
The Tales of Hoffmann (Moscow, Zimin's Opera
House). 1915
Watercolor and gouache on paper. 54.5 x 73.5
Bakhrushin Theater Museum, Moscow

SERGEI CHEKHONIN

29 Cover for Pushkin's *Mozart and Salieri*.
Petrograd, 1915

122 Frontispiece for the journal *Apollon*. 1917

123 Cover for the journal *Mysl* (Thought). 1918.
No. 1

124 Cover for Averchenko's book *The Bengal
Lights*. Petrograd, 1914

125 Cover for Dante's *Paradise*. Petrograd,
1918

272 Still Life. 1916
Oil on canvas. 59 x 68
Museum of History, Architecture and Art, Pskov

273 Cover for Izmailov's book *The Crooked
Mirror*. St. Petersburg, 1912

274 Cover for Tugendhold's book *French Art and
Its Representatives*, St. Petersburg, 1911

275 Cover for Lunacharsky's book *Faust and the
City, a Drama*. 1918

276 Cover for Balmont's book *The Song of the
Working Hammer*. Moscow–Petrograd, 1922

Inasmuch as hundreds of monographs, art books, essays, and sundry other publications devoted to the World of Art association and its individual members have been put out to date, moreover in various languages besides Russian, the bibliography that follows incorporates only the more significant works. It begins with a list of publications of a general order, and in this connection, it should be noted that though the authorship of the opening item is now disputed by some scholars – for which see. I. Silberstein, V. Samkov. "Speaking of Sergei Diaghilev", in: *Sergei Diaghilev and Russian Art. Essays, Open Letters, Interviews, Correspondence, Contemporaries on Diaghilev*, 2 vols, Moscow, 1982, vol. 1, p. 16 – it is given as its stands. The general bibliography is followed by lists of works devoted to the artists concerned, each arranged in chronological order.

S. Diaghilev, "Slozhnye voprosy. Nash mnimy upadok" (Complex Questions. Our Illusory Decline), *Mir iskusstva*, 1899, No. 1–2

S. Diaghilev, "Poiski krasoty" (In Search of Beauty), *Mir iskusstva*, 1899, No. 3–4

S. Diaghilev, "Pis'mo po adresu I. Repina" (A Letter Addressed to I. Repin), *Mir iskusstva*, 1899, No. 10

I. Repin, "Po adresu Mira iskusstva" (Concerning the World of Art), *Niva*, 1899, No. 15

V. Stasov, "Podvorye prokazhonnykh" (House of Lepers), *Novosti i birzhevaya gazeta*, 1899, February 8. Reprinted in a 3-vol. edition of Stasov's *Selected Works*, vol. 3, Moscow, 1952

"I. Repin Miru iskusstva" (I. Repin Addressing the World of Art), *Mir iskusstva*, 1900, No. 1–2

S. Diaghilev, "Khudozhestvennye kritiki" (Art Critics), *Mir iskusstva*, 1900, No. 7–8

S. Diaghilev, "Vystavki" (Exhibitions), *Mir iskusstva*, 1901, No. 5

A. Benois, *Istoriya zhivopisi v XIX veke. Russkaya zhivopis'* (The History of Painting in the 19th Century. Russian Painting), part 1, St. Petersburg, 1901; Part 2, St. Petersburg, 1902

A. Krainy, Z. Gippius, "O silene iz Mira iskusstva" (The Sylenus from the World of Art), *Novy put'* (New Way), 1903, No. 2

V. Rozanov, "Na vystavke Mira iskusstva" (At the World of Art Show), *Mir iskusstva*, 1903, No. 6

A. Benois, *Russkaya shkola zhivopisi* (The Russian School of Painting), Art book [St. Petersburg], 1904 issue 1–10

A. Benois, "Chemu uchit Akademiya khudozhestv?" (What Does the Academy of Arts Teach?), *Mir iskusstva*, 1904, No. 8–9

A. Benois, "Khudozhestvennye eresi" (Artistic Heresies), *Zolotoye runo*, 1906, No. 2

V. Ivanov, "Predchuvstviya i predvestiya" (Presentiments and Foretokens), *Zolotoye runo*, 1906, No. 4

Salon d'Automne. Exposition de l'art russe, Paris, 1906

K. Sunnerberg, "Vystavka Mira iskusstva" (World of Art Show), *Vesy*, 1906, No. 3–4

A. Lunacharsky, "Vystavka kartin Soyuza russkikh khudozhnikov" (The Union of Russian Artists Exhibition of Paintings), *Vestnik zhizni* (Life Herald), 1907, No. 2

P. Muratov, "Vystavki 'Soyuza' i 'Peredvizhnaya' v Moskve" (Union and Wanderer Shows in Moscow), *Vesy*, 1907, No. 2

A. Rostislavov, "Vystavka Soyuza" (Union Show), *Teatr i iskusstvo*, 1907, No. 2

A. Benois, "Dnevnik khudozhnika" (An Artist's Diary), *Moskovsky yezhenedelnik* (Moscow Weekly), 1908, No. 4

I. Grabar. "Teatr i khudozhniki" (The Theatre and Artists), *Vesy*, 1908, No. 4

S. Makovsky, "Pervye predstavleniya Starinnogo teatra" (The Antique Theater's First Performances), *Starye gody* (Bygone Years), 1908, No. 1

D. Filosofov. "Tozhe Tendentsiya" (Also a Tendency), *Zolotoye runo*, 1908, No. 1

K. Erberg, "Vystavka Soyuza russkikh khudozhnikov" (Union of Russian Artists Show), *Rus*, 1908, March 26

L. Bakst, "Puti klassitsizma v iskusstve" (Classical Trends in Art), *Apollon*, 1909, Nos. 2, 3

A. Benois, "Obzor khudozhestvennoi zhizni" (A Survey of Artistic Life), *Rech* (Discourse), 1909, January 1

A. Benois, "V ozhidanii gimna Apollonu" (Anticipating a Paean to Apollo), *Apollon*, 1909, No. 1

A. Benois, "Khudozhestvennye pis'ma. Eshcho raz o Salone" (Art Letters. Once Again About the Salon), *Rech*, 1909, February 11

A. Benois, "Khudozhestvennye pis'ma. Uchastie khudozhnikov v teatre" (Art Letters. Involvement of Artists in the Theater), *Rech*, 1909, February 25

A. Benois, "Khudozhestvennye pis'ma. Ob otnoshenii k sovremennomu tvorchestvu" (Art Letters. A Contemporary Approach to Creative Work), *Rech*, 1909, March 4

A. Benois, "Khudozhestvennye pis'ma. Russkiye spektakli v Parizhe" (Art Letters. Russian Shows in Paris), *Rech*, 1909, June 16 and 25

M. Voloshin, "Arkhaizm v russkoi zhivopisi: Roerich, Bogayevsky, Bakst" (Archaism in Russian Painting: Roerich, Bogayevsky, Bakst), *Apollon*, 1909, No. 1

L.M. Larionov, "Itoghi Peterburgskogo salona" (Results of the St. Petersburg Salon), *Zolotoye runo*, 1909, No. 2–3

S. Makovsky. "Bilibin," in: *Stranitsy khudozhestvennoi kritiki. Sovremennye russkiye khudozhniki* (Pages of Art Criticism. Contemporary Russian Artists), St. Petersburg. 1909, book 2

S. Makovsky, "Roerich," in: *Ibid*

S. Makovsky, "Retrospektivnye mechtateli" (Retrospective Dreamers), in: *Ibid*

A. Rostislavov, "Khudozhnik v teatre" (The Artist in the Theater), *Zolotoye runo*, 1909, No. 7

L. Bakst, "Otkrytoye pis'mo I.E. Repinu" (Open Letter to I.E. Repin), *Birzhevye vedomosti*, 1910, March 6, evening issue

A. Benois, "Khudozhestvennaya zhizn" (Artistic Life), *Rech*, 1910, January 1

A. Benois, "Khudozhestvennye pis'ma: Vystavka Soyuza III" (Art Letters: 3rd Union Exhibition), *Rech*, 1910, March 13 and 19

A. Benois, "Khudozhestvennye pis'ma. Razyasnenie" (Art Letters. An Explanation), *Rech*, 1910, May 21

A. Benois, "Khudozhestvennye pis'ma. Russkiye spektakli v Parizhe. *Zhar-ptitsa*" (Art Letters. Russian Shows in Paris. *The Firebird*), *Rech*, 1910, July 18

M. Kostylev, "Nash balet v Parizhe" (Our Ballet in Paris), *Apollon*, 1910, No. 5

G. Lukomsky, "Khudozhestvennaya zhizn Moskvy" (Moscow's Artistic Life), *Apollon*, 1910, No. 5

S. Makovsky, "Khudozhestvennye itoghi" (Artistic Results), *Apollon*, 1910, No. 7

S. Makovsky, "Vystavka v redaktsii *Apollona*" (Exhibition on the Premises of *Apollon's* Editorial Office), *Apollon*, 1910, No. 8

P. Muratov, "Peizazh v russkoi zhivopisi 1900–1910gg." (The Landscape in Russian Painting 1900–10), *Apollon*, 1910, No. 4

I. Repin, "Kritikam iskusstva" (To Critics of Art), *Birzhevye vedomosti*, 1910, March 2. Reprinted in *Apollon*, 1910, No. 6, with reply by A. Rostislavov and S. Makovsky under heading "Plachevny vypad" (A Deplorable Attack)

I. Repin, "V adu u Pifona" (In Hell with Python), *Birzhevye vedomosti*, 1910, March 15, evening issue

A. Rostislavov, "Khudozhestvennaya zhizn Peterburga" (St. Petersburg's Artistic Life), *Apollon*, 1910, No. 6

A. Rostislavov, "Stsena i zhivopis'" (Stage and Painting), *Teatr i iskusstvo*, 1910, No. 49

Ya.Tugendhold, "Moskovskiye vystavki" (Moscow Shows), *Apollon*, 1910, No. 10

K. Chukovsky, "Repin and Benois," *Rech*, 1910, April 2

T. Batiushkov, "Po povodu spektaklei Starinnogo teatra" (Concerning Antique Theater Shows), *Studia*, 1911, No. 11

A. Benois, "Khudozhestvennye pis'ma. Pervaya vystavka Mira iskusstva" (Art Letters. The First World of Art Exhibition), *Rech*, 1911, January 7, 14 and 21

A. Benois, "Khudozhestvennye pis'ma. Starinny teatr" (Art Letters. The Antique Theater), *Rech*, 1911, January 16, December 10, 16 and 23

M. Voloshin, "Vystavki Parizha: Pis'ma iz Parizha" (Paris Shows: Letters from Paris), *Moskovskaya gazeta* (Moscow Gazette), 1911, September 28

S. Makovsky, "Vystavka Mira iskusstva" (World of Art Exhibition), *Apollon*, 1911, No. 2

A. Rostislavov, "O postanovkakh Starinnogo teatra" (Concerning the Productions of the Antique Theater), *Teatr i iskusstvo*, 1911, No. 51

V. Svetlov, *Sovremenny balet* (The Modern Ballet), St. Petersburg, 1911

E. Stark, *Starinny Teatr* (The Antique Theater), St. Petersburg, 1911. Reprint: Petrograd, 1911

A. Benois, "Chem mogla by byt' Akademiya Khudozhestv?" (What the Academy of Art Could Really Be?), a paper read at the All-Russia Congress of Artists, *Rech*, 1912, January 6

A. Benois, "Khudozhestvennye pis'ma. Iskusstvo dlya proletariyev" (Art Letters. Art for Proletarians), *Rech*, 1912 March 30

V. Kurbatov, "Gruppa khudozhnikov 'Mir iskusstva.' K vystavke v Kievskom gorodskom muzee" (The World of Art Group. Concerning the Show at the Kiev Municipal Museum), *Iskusstvo* [Kiev], 1912, No. 1–2

V. Kurbatov, "Starinny teatr" (The Antique Theater), *Starye gody*, 1912, No. 1

Essem [S. Makovsky], "Moskva. Vystavka Mira iskusstva" (Moscow. World of Art Exhibition), *Apollon. Russkaya khudozhestvennaya letopis'*, 1922, No. 18–19

Rosstsiy [A.M. Efros], "Vystavka Mira iskusstva" (World of Art Exhibition), *Russkiye vedomosti*, 1912, November 15

A. Benois, "Khudozhestvennye pis'ma. Printsipy Mira iskusstva" (Art Letters. World of Art Principles), *Rech*, 1913, January 11

S. Volkonsky, "Na Manheimskoi teatralnoi vystavke" (At the Mannheim Theater Show), *Apollon*, 1913, No. 3

S. Volkonsky, "Russkiy balet v Parizhe" (The Russian Ballet in Paris), *Apollon*, 1913, No. 6

N. Kostylev, "Nashe iskusstvo v Parizhe. K postanovke *Igr* i *Prazdnika vesny* v teatre Eliseiskikh poley" (Our Art in Paris. Re: Théâtre des Champs Elysées production of *Jeux* and *Le Sacre du Printemps*), *Russkaya molva* (Russian Rumor), 1913, May 24

G. Craig, "Russkiy balet" (Russian Ballet), *Teatr i iskusstvo*, 1913, No. 36

A. Levinson, "Russkiy balet v Parizhe. *Vesna svyashchennaya, Igry*" (The Russian Ballet in Paris. *Le Sacre du Printemps, Joux*), *Rech*, 1913, June 3

A. Levinson, "Ocherki khudozhestvennoi zhizni. Mir iskusstva" (Essays on Artistic Life. The World of Art), *Den'* (Day), 1913, November 12

N. Radlov, "Sovremennaya russkaya grafika i risunok" (Modern Russian Graphics and Drawing), *Apollon*, 1913, No. 7

Rosstsiy [A.M. Efros], "Mir iskusstva" (The World of Art), *Russkiye vedomosti*, 1913, December 22

A. Rostislavov, "Vystavki i khudozhestvennaya zhizn" (Exhibitions and Artistic Life), *Apollon*, 1913, No. 2

V. Dmitriyev, "Po povodu vystavok byvshikh i budushchikh" (Concerning the Past and Future Shows), *Apollon*, 1914, No. 10

A. Levinson, "Balety Nizhinskogo" (Nijinski's Ballets), *Maski*, 1913–14, No. 4

N. Radlov, *Sovremennaya russkaya grafika* (Contemporary Russian Graphics), St. Petersburg, 1914

V. Rozanov, "Na vystavke Mira iskusstva" (At the World of Art Exhibition), in: V. Rozanov, *Sredi khudozhnikov* (Among Artists), St. Petersburg, 1914

A. Efros, "Zhivopis' teatra" (Theater Painting), *Apollon*, 1914, No. 10

V. Dmitriyev, "Protivorechiya Mira iskusstva" (World of Art Contradictions), *Apollon*, 1915, No. 10

Rosstsiy [A.M. Efros], "Mir iskusstva" (The World of Art), *Russkiye vedomosti*, 1915, December 30

A. Benois, "Za Mir iskusstva" (For the World of Art), *Rech*, 1916, February 26

A. Gidoni, "Pis'mo v redaktsiyu. Otvet na statyu A. Benua 'Za Mir iskusstva'" (Letter to the Editor. Reply to A. Benois' Article 'For the World of Art'), *Apollon*, 1916, No. 2

V. Dmitriyev, "Mir iskusstva. Vystavka etiudov, eskizov i risunkov" (World of Art Show of Studies, Sketches, and Drawings), *Apollon*, 1916, No. 9–10

Essem [S. Makovsky], "Zhivopis' i grafika: Na vystavke Mira iskusstva i Soyuza" (Painting and Graphics: At World of Art and Union Show), *Apollon*, 1916, No. 2

A. Levinson, "Russkiye khudozhniki-dekoratory" (Russian Artists-Decorators), *Stolitsa i usad'ba* (Capital and Estate), 1916, No. 57

S. Makovsky, "Po povodu Vystavki sovremennoi russkoi zhivopisi" (Re: Exhibition of Modern Russian Painting), *Apollon*, 1916, No.8

Rosstiy [A.M. Efros], "Mir iskusstva" (The World of Art), *Russkiye vedomosti*, 1916, December 29

Ya. T.d. [Ya.A. Tugendhold], "Pis'mo iz Moskvy" (A Letter from Moscow), *Apollon*, 1916, No. 1

A. Levinson, *Stary i novy balet* (The Old an the New Ballet), Petrograd, 1917

N. Radlov, "O futurizme i Mire iskusstva" (About Futurism and the World of Art), *Apollon*, 1917, No. 1. Reprinted in M. Ioffe, *Nikolai Ernestovich Radlov*, Moscow, 1964

M. Radlov, "Russkaya knizhnaya grafika" (Russian Book Graphics), *Plamya* (The Flame), 1919, No. 59

E. Gollerbach, "Sredi petrogradskikh khudozhnikov" (Among Petrograd Artists), *Novy put'*, Riga, 1921, October 15

W.A. Propert, *The Russian Ballet in Western Europe. 1909–1920*, London, 1921

E. Gollerbach, *Iskusstvo silueta* (The Art of the Silhouette), Moscow, 1922, No. 7

P. Dulsky, *Grafika satiricheskikh zhurnalov 1905–906 godov* (The Graphics of Satirical Magazines of 1905–06), Kazan, 1922

Collection des plus beaux numéros de Comœdia Illustré et des Programmes, consacrés aux Ballets et Galas Russes depuis le début à Paris. 1909–21, Paris, 1922

V. Lobanov, *1905 god v zhivopisi* (1905 in Painting), Moscow, 1922

S. Makovsky, "Na smenu peredvizhnikam" (Replacing the Wanderers), in: *Siluety russkikh khudozhnikov* (Profiles of Russian Artists), Prague, 1922

S. Makovsky, "Stilisty Mira iskusstva" (World of Art Stylists), in: *Ibid*

S. Makovsky, "Vrubel and Roerich", in: *Ibid*

A. Sidorov, *Russkaya grafika za gody revolutsii. 1917–1922* (Russian Graphics During the Years of Revolution. 1917–22), Moscow, 1923

E. Gollerbach, "Gosudarstvenny farforovy zavod i khudozhniki" (The State Porcelain Factory and Artists), *Russkoye iskusstvo*, 1923, No. 2–3

E. Gollerbach, "Gorod grafiki" (City of Graphics), *Spolokhi* (Flashes), 1923, No. 17–18

A. Strelkov, *Mir iskusstva* (The World of Art), Moscow–Petrograd, 1923

Teatralno-dekoratsionnoye iskusstvo v SSSR. 1917–1927 (Stage Design in the USSR. 1917–27). Exhibition catalogue. Collection of articles edited by E. Gollerbach, A. Golovin, and L.Zheverzheyev, Leningrad, 1927

A. Efros, "Mladshiye khudozhniki Khudozhestvennogo teatra" (The Art Theater's Younger Designers), *Iskusstvo*, 1927, No. 1

A. Benois, *Vozniknovenie Mira iskusstva* (The Emergence of the World of Art), Leningrad, 1928

A. Fyodorov-Davydov, *Russkoye iskusstvo promyshlennogo kapitalizma* (Russian Art of the Time of Industrial Capitalism), Moscow, 1929

Ya. Tugendhold, *Iskusstvo Oktyabrskoi epokhi* (Art of the October Epoch), Leningrad, 1930

P. Pertsov, "Mir iskusstva" (The World of Art), in: *Literaturnye vospominaniya* (Literary Reminiscences). *1890–1902*, Moscow–Leningrad, 1933

N. Sokolova, *Mir iskusstva* (The World of Art), Moscow–Leningrad, 1933

N. Sokolova, *Mir iskusstva* (The World of Art), Moscow–Leningrad, 1934

S.W. Beaumont, *Complete Book of Ballets*, London, 1937

V. Bulgakov, A. Yupatov, *Russkoye iskusstvo za rubezhom* (Russian Art Abroad), Prague, 1939

S. Lifar, *Diaghilev, With Diaghilev*, Paris, 1939

B. Brodnyansky, S. Zemtsev, "Stanislavsky i Mir iskusstva" (Stanislavsky and the World of Art), *Iskusstvo i zhizn*, 1940, No. 8

M. Dobuzhinsky, "Krug Mira iskusstva" (The World of Art Circle), *Novy zhurnal* (New Journal), 1943, No. 3, New York

G. Amberg, *Art in Modern Ballet*, New York, 1946

A. Sidorov, *Istoriya oformleniya russkoi knigi* (The History of Russian Book Design and Illustration), Moscow–Leningrad, 1946

V. Stasov, Izbrannoye (Selected Works), 3 vols., Moscow–Leningrad, 1950, vol. 1

S. Makovsky, *Portrety sovremennikov* (Portraits of Contemporaries), New York, 1955

S. Shcherbatov, *Khudozhnik v ushedshei Rossii* (The Artist in Outgone Russia), New York, 1955

A. Kamensky, "O 'zhivopisnosti' i 'stsenichnosti': Zametki s vystavki v TsDRI" (Concerning the 'Pictorial' and the 'Scenic': Notes from an Exhibition at the Central Artworkers' Club), *Teatr*, 1957, No. 9

E.V. Zhuravliova, N.G. Mashkovtsev, "Mir iskusstva" (The World of Art), in: *Istoriya russkogo iskusstva* (The History of Russian Art), Moscow, 1960

C. Gray, *The Great Experiment: Russian Art. 1863–1922*, London, 1962

S. Makovsky, *Na Parnase 'Serebryanogo veka'* (The Parnassus of the 'Silver Age'), Munich, 1962

M. Fokine, *Protiv techeniya. Vospominaniya baletmeistera: Stat'i, pis'ma* (Against the Tide. Recollections of a Choreographer. Articles, Letters), Leningrad–Moscow, 1962

V. Beryozkin, "Khudozhestvenny teatr i Mir iskusstva" (The Art Theater and the World of Art), *Khudozhnik* (Artist), 1963, No. 1

I. Stravinsky, *Khronika moei zhizni* (The Chronicle of My Life), Leningrad, 1963

N.L. Priymak, "Novye dannye o satiricheskikh zhurnalakh 1905 goda *Zhupel i Adskaya pochta*" (New Information on the Satirical Magazines of 1905, *Bugbear* and *Hell's Mail*). In: *Ocherki po russkomu i sovetskomu iskusstvu* (Essays on Russian and Soviet Art), Moscow, 1965

B.V. Asafyev, *Russkaya zhivopis'. Mysli i dumy* (Russian Painting. Ideas and Thoughts), Leningrad–Moscow, 1966

314

E. Lutskaya, "Nasledie segodnya" (The Heritage Today), *Teatr*, 1966, No. 6

N. Roslavleva, *Era of the Russian Ballet*, London, 1966

S. Kaplanova, *Russkaya akvarelnaya zhivopis' kontsa XIX–nachala XX veka* (Turn-of-the-Century Russian Watercolors), Moscow, 1968

R. Kaufman, "Bytovoi zhanr i istoricheskaya zhivopis" (Genre and History Painting), in: *Istoriya russkogo iskusstva* (The History of Russian Art), 13 vols, Moscow, 1968, vol. 1, part 1

N. Lobanov, *Russian Painters and the Stage. Transactions of the Association of Russian-American Scholars in USA*, New York, 1968, vol. 2; 1969, vol. 3; 1972, vol. 6

G.A. Nedoshivin, D.V. Sarabyanov, G.Yu. Sternin, "Vvedenie" (Introduction), in: *Istoriya russkogo iskusstva* (The History of Russian Art), 13 vols., Moscow, 1968, vol. 10

V. Petrov, "Mir iskusstva" (The World of Art), in: *Ibid*, vol. 10, part 1

M.V. Davydova, "Teatralno-dekoratsionnoye iskusstvo" (Stage Design), in: *Ibid*, vol. 10, part 2

M.V. Davydova, "Teatralno-dekoratsionnoye iskusstvo" (Stage Design), in: *Russkaya khudozhestvennaya kultura kontsa XIX – nachala XX veka. 1895–1907* (Russian Artistic Culture. 1895–1907), Moscow, 1969, book 2

N.P. Lapshina, "Mir iskusstva" (The World of Art), in: *Ibid*

V.M. Petrov, A.A. Sidorov, "Zhurnalny risunok v period revolutsii 1905–1907" (Magazine Drawing during the 1905–07 Revolution), in: *Istoriya russkogo iskusstva* (The History of Russian Art), 13 vols., Moscow, 1969, vol. 10, part 2

E. Polyakova, "Stanislavsky – Dobuzhinsky – Benois," in: *Teatralnye stranitsy* (Theatrical Pages), Moscow, 1969

E. Surits, "Russkiye sezony v Parizhe" (The Russian Seasons in Paris), *Teatr*, 1969, No. 11

M. Larionov, *Diaghilev et les Ballets Russes*, Paris, 1970

M.N. Pozharskaya, *Russkoye teatralno-dekoratsionnoye iskusstvo kontsa XIX–nachala XX veka* (Turn-of-the-Century Russian Stage Design), Moscow, 1970

G.Yu. Sternin, *Khudozhestvennaya zhizn Rossii na rubezhe XIX–XX vekov* (Turn-of-the-Century Russian Artistic Life), Moscow, 1970

V. Krasovskaya, *Russkiy baletny teatr nachala XX veka. Khoreografy* (Early 20th-Century Russian Ballet Theater. Choreographers), Leningrad, 1971

M. Wallis. "Mir iskusstwa i jego oddziaywanie," in: *Sztuka XX wieku*, Warsaw, 1971

A. Gusarova, *Mir iskusstva* (The World of Art), Leningrad, 1972

V. Krasovskaya, *Russkiy baletny teatr nachala XX veka. Tantsovshchiki* (Early 20th-Century Russian Ballet Theater. Dancers), Leningrad, 1972

M.N. Mertsalova, *Istoriya kostiuma. Ocherki* (The History of Costume. Essays), Moscow, 1972

Puti razvitiya russkogo iskusstva kontsa XX – nachala XX veka. Zhivopis'. Grafika. Skulptura. Teatralno-dekoratsionnoye iskusstvo (Trends of Development in Turn-of-the-Century Russian Art. Painting. Graphics. Sculpture. Stage Design), Moscow, 1972

L. Haskell, "Russian Drawings in the Victoria and Albert Museum," in: *Oxford Slavonic Papers*, Oxford (new series), 1972, vol. 5

H.H. Hofstätter, *Geschichte der europäischen Jugendstilmalerei*, 1972

Yu. A. Bakhrushin, *Istoriya russkogo baleta* (History of the Russian Ballet), Moscow, 1973

J.E. Bowlt, "Synthesism and Symbolism: the Russian World of Art Movement," in: *Literature and the Plastic Arts*, Edinburg – London, 1973

D. Sarabyanov, *Russkaya zhivopis' nachala XX veka: Novye napravleniya* (Early 20th-Century Russian Painting: New Trends), Leningrad, 1973

M.V. Davydova, *Ocherki istorii russkogo teatralno-dekoratsionnogo iskusstva. XVIII – nachalo XX v.* (Historical Outlines of 18th to Early 20th-Century Russian Stage Design), Moscow, 1974

V.P. Lapshin, *Soyuz russkikh khudozhnikov* (The Union of Russian Artists), Leningrad, 1974

N. MacDonald, *Diaghilev Observed by Critics in England and the U.S. 1911–1929*, New York, 1975

D. Oenslager, *Stage Design. Four Centuries of Scenic Invention*, New York, 1975

Mir iskusstva (The World of Art). An art book with an introduction by V.N. Petrov), Moscow, 1975

V. Beryozkin, "Khudozhnik v sovetskom balete" (Artists in the Soviet Ballet), in: *Sovetsky baletny teatr. 1917–1967* (The Soviet Ballet Theater. 1917–1967), Moscow, 1976

J.E. Bowlt, *Russian Art. 1875–1975. A Collection of Essays*, New York, 1976

A. Gusarova, "Na rubezhe vekov" (At the Turn of the Centuries), *Khudozhnik* (Artist), 1976, No. 8

G.Yu. Sternin, *Khudozhestvennaya zhizn' Rossii nachala XX veka* (Artistic Life ini Early 20th-Century Russia), Moscow, 1976

D. Bablet, *Revolutions in Design of the XXth Century*, Paris–New York, 1977

J. Kennedy, *The "Mir Iskusstva" Group and Russian Art. 1898–1912*, New York, 1977

N.P. Lapshina, *Mir iskusstva: Ocherki istorii i tvorcheskoi praktiki* (The World of Art: Historical Outline and Creative Practice), Moscow, 1977

V.N. Petrov, "Mir iskusstva" (The World of Art), in: *Ocherk i issledovaniya* (Essay and Study), Moscow, 1978

F.Ya. Syrkina, E.M. Kostina, *Russkoye teatralno-dekoratsionnoye iskusstvo* (Russian Stage Design), Moscow, 1978

J.E. Bowlt, *The Silver Age: Russian Art of the Early Twentieth Century and the "World of Art" Group*, Newtonville, 1979

Paris–Moscou. 1900–1930. Centre Georges Pompidou. Catalogue de l'exposition, Paris, 1979

Gosudarstvenny Russkiy muzei. Zhivopis' XVIII – nachala XX veka (The State Russian Museum. Painting in the 18th to the early 20th Century), Leningrad, 1980

D.V. Sarabyanov, "Russkiy variant stilya modern v zhivopisi kontsa XIX – nachala XX veka" (The Russian Version of Art Nouveau in Turn-of-the Century Painting), in: *Russkaya zhivopis' XIX veka sredi evropeiskikh shkol* (19th-Century Russian Painting Among European Schools), Moscow, 1980

Moskva–Parizh. 1900–1930. Katalog (Moscow–Paris. 1900–1930. Exhibition. Catalogue), 2 vols., Moscow, 1981

J.E. Bavet, *Russian Stage Design. Scenic Innovation. 1900–1930* (From the Collection of Mr. and Mrs. Nikita D. Lobanov-Rostovsky), Mississippi Museum of Art, 1982

Gosudarstvennaya Tretyakovskaya galereya: Katalog zhivopisi XVIII – nachala XX veka do 1917 goda (The State Tretyakov Gallery. Castalogue of Painting from the 18th to the Early 20th Century: Up to 1917), Moscow, 1984

R.I. Vlasova, *Russkoye teatralno-dekoratsionnoye iskusstvo nachala XX veka. Iz naslediya peterburgskikh masterov* (Early 20th-Century Russian Stage Design. From the Heritage of the Petersburgian Masters), Leningrad, 1984

LÉON BAKST (1866–1924)

V. Ivanov, "Drevny uzhas: Po povodu kartiny Baksta *Terror Antiquus*" (Bakst's *Terror Antiquus*), in: *Po zviozdam: Stat'i i aforizmy* (Among the Stars: Articles and Aphorisms), St. Petersburg, 1909

L. Bakst, Introduction to the catalogue: *Exhibition of Works by Bakst's and Dobuzhinsky's Pupils (Zvantseva's School)*, St. Petersburg, 1910

A. Benois, "Salon i shkola Baksta" (The Salon and Bakst's School), *Rech*, 1910, April 1

A. Benois, "Khudozhestvennye pis'ma. *Shekherazada*" (Art Letters. *Shéhérazade*), *Rech*, 1910, July 2 and 12

A. Benois, "Khudozhestvennye pis'ma. Novye balety. *Nartsis*" (Art Letters. New Ballets. *Narcisse*), *Rech*, 1911, July 22

V. Svetlov, "Favn" (The Fawn), *Peterburgskaya gazeta*, 1912, May 27

A. Lunacharsky, "Parizhskiye pis'ma. *Elena Spartanskaya*. Baletnaya burya" (Paris Letters. *Helen of Sparta*. Whirlwind Ballet), *Teatr i iskusstvo*, 1912, May 27

Ya. Tugendhold, "Salomeya" (Salome), *Studia*, 1912, No. 38–39

L. Bakst, "Kostium zhenshchiny budushchego: Beseda" (Costume of the Woman of the Future: Interview), *Birzhevye vedomosti*, 1913, March 20

P. Barchan, *Léon Bakst*, Berlin, 1913

L'Art décoratif de Léon Bakst. Essai critique par A. Alexandre. Notes sur les ballets par J. Cocteau, Paris, 1913. Engl. ed.: London, 1913

A. Lunacharsky, "Pisanella" (La Pisanella), *Den'*, 1913, July 15

L. Bakst, "O sovremennom teatre. Nikto v teatre bolshe ne khochet slushat', a khochet slyshat'" (Contemporary Theater. No One in the Theater Wants to Listen Any More – They Want to Hear), *Peterburgskaya gazeta*, 1914, January 21

L. Bakst, "Moda" (Fashion), *Peteburgskaya gazeta*, 1914, February 20

L. Bakst, "Ob iskusstve segodnyashnego dnya" (On Art Today), *Stolitsa i usad'ba*, 1914, No. 8

A. Levinson, *The Story of Bakst's Life*, Berlin, 1922

L. Bakst, *Serov i ya v Gretsii: Dorozhnye zapisi* (With Serov in Greece. Travel Notes), Berlin, 1923

Exposition des œuvres de Léon Bakst, Paris, 1925

M.V. Dobuzhinsky, "O Bakste: Iz moikh vospominaniy" (Bakst as I Remember Him), *Segodnya* (Today), Riga, 1925, January 6

C. Einstein, *Léon Bakst*, Berlin, 1927

Léon Bakst, *Painting and Stage Design. Art and Stage in the 20th Century.* Ed. by Henning and Rischbieter, New York, 1968

S. Spencer, *Léon Bakst*, London, 1973. Reprint: London, 1978

I. Pruzhan, *Lev Samoilovich Bakst*, Leningrad, 1975

N. Borisovskaya, *Lev Bakst*, Moscow, 1979

S. Golynets, *L.S. Bakst. 1866–1924*, Leningrad, 1981

Lev Bakst. An art book, introduced and compiled by I. Pruzhan, Leningrad, 1986

ALEXANDER BENOIS (1870–1960)

A. Lunacharsky, "A. Benua. Istoriya russkoi zhivopisi. Retsenzia" (Review: Benois's History of Russian Painting), *Obrazovaniye* (Education), 1903, No. 2

A. Shervashidze, "Alexander Benois," *Zolotoye runo*, 1906, No. 10

A. Rostislavov, "Neotsenyonny trud. Aleksandr Benua – istorik iskusstva" (Invaluable Effort. Alexander Benois as Art Historian), *Vesy*, 1907, No 7

A. Benois, *Francisco Goya*, St. Petersburg, 1908

S. Gorodetsky, "Po povodu Khudozhestvennykh pisem g-na Benua" (Concerning Mr. Benois's *Art Letters*), *Zolotoye runo*, 1909, No. 11–12

A. Benois, *Tsarskoye Selo v tsarstvovaniye imperatritsy Elizavety Petrovny* (Tsarskoye Selo in the Reign of the Empress Elizaveta Petrovna), St. Petersburg, 1910

A. Benois, *Putevoditel' po kartinnoi galeree Imperatorskogo Ermitazha* (Guide to the Picture Gallery of the Imperial Hermitage), St. Petersburg, s.a.

K. Chukovsky, "Repin and Benois," *Rech*, 1910, April 2

A. Levinson, "O novom balete" (The New Ballet), *Apollon*, 1911, No. 9

S. Yaremich, "Alexander Benois," *Iskusstvo* [Kiev], 1911, No. 4

A. Benois, *Istoriya zhivopisi* (The History of Painting), 3 vols., St. Petersburg, 1912

V. Meyerhold, "Benua-rezhisser" (Benois as Stage Manager), *Liubov k tryom apelsinam* (Love for Three Oranges: Dr. Lapertutto's magazine), Petrograd, 1915, No. 1–3

A. Levinson, "Alexandr Benua v Versale" (Alexander Benois in Versailles), *Iskusstvo*, Petrograd, 1916, No. 3

A. Benois, *Prospectus for a Monograph*. edited by G.K. Lukomsky, Petrograd, 1917

S. Ernst, *Alexander Benois*, Petrograd, 1921

A. Vetrov, *Alexander Benois*, Petrograd, 1921

A. Benois, *Versailles*, Petrograd, 1922

A. Efros, "Apologiya Benua" (An Apology for Benois), *Sredi kollektsionerov* (Among Collectors), 1922, No. 1

A. Efros, "Benois," in: *Profili* (Profiles), Moscow, 1930

A. Benois, *Zhizn' khudozhnika: Vospominaniya* (An Artist's Life. Recollections), 2 vols, New York, 1955

O. Vergani, *Alessandro Benois. Mostra dei Benois: Katalogo*, Como, 1955

S. Lifar, "Alexander Nikolayevich Benois," *Russkaya mysl*, Paris, 1960, February 13 and 16

M.G. Etkind, *Alexander Benois*, Leningrad – Moscow, 1965

Alexandr Benua razmyshliayet.... Stat'i, pis'ma, vyskazyvaniya (Alexander Benois Meditates.... Articles, Letters, Utterances), Moscow, 1968

N. Lapshina, "Alexandr Benua. K 100-letiyu so dnya rozhdeniya" (Alexander Benois' Birth Centenary), *Iskusstvo*, 1970, No. 12

V. Gayevsky, "Prazdniki Aleksandra Benua" (The Galas of Alexander Benois), *Teatr*, 1971, No. 6

I. Gutt, "Khudozhnik, entsiklopedist" (Artist and Encyclopedist), *Khudozhnik*, 1971, No. 9

Alexander Nikolayevich Benois. 1870–1960. Birth Centenary Exhibition. Catalogue, Moscow, 1972

I. Gofman, "O prirode teatralno-dekoratsionnoi zhivopisi Aleksandra Benua" (The Nature of Benois's Scenic Painting), in: *Ocherki po russkomu i sovetskomu iskusstvu. Stat'i. Publikatsii. Khronika* (Essays on Russian and Soviet Art. Articles. Publications. Chronicle), Leningrad, 1974

D. Brownell, *The Nutcracker Ballet from the Designs by Alexandre Benois*, San Francisco, 1977

A.N. Benois, *Moi vospominaniya* (My Recollections), 5 books in 2 vols, Moscow, 1980

IVAN BILIBIN (1876–1942)

L. Kamyshnikov, "I.Ya. Bilibin," in: *Severnye zori* (Northern Dawns), 1909, No. 3

A. Benois, "Khudozhestvennye pis'ma. Postanovka *Orfeya*" (Art Letters. *Orpheus* Production), *Rech*, 1911, December 30

Catalogue d'exposition de Yvan Bilibine sous les auspices des "Amis de l'art," Alexandria, 1924

J.-J. Theraud, "Images de Judee, aquarelles de Bilibine," *L'Illustration*, Paris, 1924, No. 4366

H. Bergasse, "Exposition Y. Bilibine," *Orient Musical*, 1925, January 15

S.E. [Ernst], "I.Ya. Bilibin. K XXV-letiyu khudozhestvennoi deyatelnosti" (Silver Jubilee), *Zhar-ptitsa* [Paris – Berlin], 1926, No 14

V. Šuman, "Yvan Jakovlevič Bilibin," *Dilo* [Prague], book XX, 1927, No. 1

S. Volkonsky, "*Knyaz' Igor* v Teatre Eliseiskikh polei"(*Prince Igor* at the Théâtre des Champs Elysées), *Poslednye novosti* (Late News) [Paris], 1930, November 18

A. Levinson, "*Prince Ygor* de Borodine (Opéra privé de Paris). Les décors et les costumes sont executés d'après les maquettes d'Yvan Bilibine," *L'Illustration*, Paris, 1931, No. 4589

A. Benois, "Bilibin v novoi knizhke" (Bilibin in a New Book), *Posledniye novosti*, Paris, 1932, December 22

A. Benois, "Novaya knizhka Bilibina" (Bilibin's New Book), *Posledniye novosti* [Paris], 1934, January 4

Ivan Yakovlevich Bilibin. 1876–1942. An art book with an introducion by N. Popova, Moscow, 1961

S.V. Golynets, "Knizhnaya grafika I.Ya. Bilibina" (Bilibin's Book Graphics), in: *Kniga: Issledovaniya i materialy* (The Book: Studies and Materials), Moscow, 1968, issue 16

I.Ya. Bilibin: Stat'i. Pis'ma. Vospominaniya o khudozhnike (I.Ya. Bilibin: Articles. Letters. Recollections About the Artist), Leningrad, 1970

G.V. and S.V. Golynets, *Ivan Yakovlevich Bilibin*, Moscow, 1972

Bilibin (1876–1942), Shchekatikhina-Pototskaya (1892–1967). Exhibition Catalogue, Leningrad, 1977

G.E. Klimov, *Poiski pera Zhar-ptitsy: zhizn i tvorchestvo russkogo khudozhnika I.Ya. Bilibina po materialam sobraniya E.P. Klimovoi* (Searching for the Firebird's Feather: The Life and Work of the Russian Artist I.Ya. Bilibin on the Materials of E.P. Klimova's Collection), Moscow, 1981

ALEXANDER GOLOVIN (1863–1930)

S. Makovsky, "A.Ya. Golovin," *Apollon*, 1913, No. 4

V.N. Solovyov, "A.Ya. Golovin kak teatralny master" (Golovin as Theatrical Artist), *Apollon*, 1917, No. 1

E-m S. [Makovsky], "A.Ya. Golovin," *Zhar-ptitsa*, 1923, No. 10

E. Gollerbach, *A.Ya. Golovin. Zhizn i tvorchestvo* (Golovin. Life and Work), Leningrad, 1928

Exhibition of Works by People's Artist A.Ya. Golovin on the 10th Anniversary of His Death. Catalogue. Preface by E. Gollerbach, Leningrad, 1940

A.Ya. Golovin: Vstrechi i vpechatleniya. Vospominaniya o khudozhnike (A.Ya. Golovin: Encounters, Impressions, Reminiscences About the Artist). Edited and commented by E.F. Gollerbach, Leningrad – Moscow, 1940

"Maskarad" Lermontova v teatralnykh eskizakh A.Ya. Golovina (Lermontov's Masquerade in Golovin's Stage Designs). Edited by E. Lanceray, Moscow – Leningrad, 1941

Exhibition of A.Ya. Golovin (1863–1930), People's Artist of the RSFSR. Catalogue, Moscow – Leningrad, 1956

E. Kostina, "A.Ya. Golovin," *Iskusstvo*, 1956, No. 8

Aleksandr Yakovlevich Golovin: Vstrechi i vpechatleniya. Pis'ma. Vospominaniya o Golovine (Alexander Golovin: Encounters, Impressions, Letters, Recollections About the Artist). Compiled and commented by A. Movshenson, with a foreword by F. Syrkin, Leningrad – Moscow, 1960

D.Z. Kogan, *Golovin*, Moscow, 1960

A. Movshenson, *Alexander Yakovlevich Golovin*, Leningrad – Moscow, 1960

I.M. Gofman, "Avtoportrety Golovina" (Golovin's Self-Portraits), *Khudozhnik*, 1968, No. 9

A.I. Bassekhes, *Teatr i zhivopis' Golovina* (Theater and Golovin's Painting), Moscow, 1970

I.M. Gofman, "Portretnoye tvorchestvo A.Ya. Golovina predrevolutsionnykh let. Paradnye portrety" (Golovin's Pre-revolutionary Portraiture. Full-Dress Portraits), in: *Gosudarstvennaya Tretyakovskaya galereya. Voprosy russkogo i sovetskogo iskusstva: Materialy itogovoi nauchnoi konferentsii* (The State Tretyakov Gallery. Aspects of Russian and Soviet Art. Transactions of a Summing-up Conference), Moscow, 1971, issue 2

A.I. Bassekhes, "Golovin i teatr" (Golovin and the Theater), *Teatr*, 1942, No. 2. Reprinted in: A.I. Bassekhes, *Za sorok let* (Over 40 Years), Moscow, 1976

S. Onufrieva, *A. Golovin*, Leningrad, 1977

Alexander Golovin. Introduced and compiled by I. Gofman, Moscow, 1981

I.M. Gofman, *Golovin-portretist* (Golovin as Portrait Painter), Leningrad, 1981

IGOR GRABAR (1871–1960)

A. Lunacharsky, "Igor Grabar. K 40-letiyu khudozhestvennoi deyatelnosti" (Igor Grabar. 40 Years as Artist), *Krasnaya niva* (Red Field), 1929, No. 49

G. Bandalin, "Igor Grabar," *Iskusstvo*, 1936, No. 2

I. Grabar, *Moya zhizn: Avtomonografia* (My Life: Automonograph), Moscow – Leningrad, 1937

Igor Grabar. Jubilee Exhibition Catalogue, Moscow – Leningrad, 1939

V. Lobanov, *Igor Emmanuilovich Grabar*, Moscow – Leningrad, 1945

Igor Emmanuilovich Grabar. An art book introduced by N.G. Mashkovtsev, Moscow, 1962

O. Podobedova, *Igor Emmanuilovich Grabar*, Moscow, 1964

I. Grabar. Pis'ma (Letters). *1891–1917*, Moscow, 1974

I. Grabar. Pis'ma (Letters). *1941–1960*, Moscow, 1983

MSTISLAV DOBUZHINSKY (1875–1957)

B. Gurov, "Khudozhnik goroda" (Artist of the City), *Lebed'* (Swan), 1909, No. 1

B. Gurov, "*Mesyats v derevne* Turgeneva. Dekoratsii" (Sets for Turgenev's *A Month in the Country*), *Utro Rossii* (Morning of Russia), 1909, December 10

P. Muratov, "Dobuzhinsky v Khudozhestvennom teatre" (Dobuzhinsky at the Art Theater), *Utro Rossii*, 1909, December 11

A. Rostislavov, "M.V. Dobuzhinsky," *Iskusstvo* [Kiev], 1910, No. 2–4

A. Benois, "Khudozhestvennye pis'ma" (Art Letters), *Rech*, 1911, January 1, 7 and 14

N.N. Vrangel, "Mstislav Valerianovich Dobuzhinsky," *Apollon*, 1911, No. 2

E. Znosko-Borovsky, "Turgenevskiye p'esy v Moskovskom Khudozhestvennom teatre" (Turgenev's Plays at the Moscow Art Theater), *Russkaya khudozhestvennaya letopis'* (Russian Art Annals), 1912, No. 10

M. Kuzmin, "Andersenovsky Dobuzhinsky" (Andersen's Dobuzhinsky), *Zhizn' iskusstva* (Art's Life), 1919, April 29

E. Gollerbach, "Risunki Dobuzhinskogo" (Dobuzhinsky's Drawings), *Zhizn' iskusstva*, 1919, June 26

N.E. Radlov, "Vystavka M.V. Dobuzhinskogo" (Dobuzhinsky Show), *Zhizn' iskusstva*, 1920, March 30

V.V. Voinov, "Vystavka Doma iskusstv. M.V. Dobuzhinsky" (Dobuzhinsky Show at the House of Arts), *Dom iskusstv*, 1921, No. 2

E. Gollerbach, *Risunki M. Dobuzhinskogo* (Dobuzhinsky's Drawings), Moscow – Petrograd, 1923

M. Dobuzhinsky. Peterburg v 1921 (M. Dobuzhinsky. St. Petersburg in 1921). An album of autolithographs with an introduction by S.P. Yaremich, Petrograd, 1923

S. Makovsky, F. Notgaft, *Grafika Dobuzhinskogo* (Dobuzhinsky's Graphics), Berlin, 1924

G. Lukomsky, "M.V. Dobuzhinsky," *Nakanune* (On the Eve), 1923, December 14

l. Rosenthal, "M.V. Dobuzhinsky," in: *Mastera sovremennoi graviury i grafiki* (Masters of Contemporary Engraving and Graphics), Moscow – Leningrad, 1928

V. Tatarinov, "Grafika V.M. Dobuzhinskogo" (The Graphics of M.V. Dobuzhinsky), *Zhar-ptitsa*, 1925, No. 13

C.W. Beaumont, "Mstislav Dobuzhinsky. Some Recent Designs for Ballet," *The Studio*, 1949, No. 138

A.L. Haskell, "Dobujinsky's Memorial Exhibition," *The Tablet*, London, 1959, March 21

V. Kovarsky, "Dobujinsky – Pictorial Poet of St. Petersburg," *Russian Review*, New York, 1960, No. 19

T. Guryeva, "M.V. Dobuzhinsky. 1875–1957," *Iskusstvo knigi* (Art of the Book), 1956–57, Moscow, 1961, issue 2

A.P. Gusarova, "Knizhnaya grafika M.V. Dobuzhinskogo" (Dobuzhinsky's Book Graphics), in: *Ocherki po russkomu i sovetskomu iskusstvu* (Essays on Russian and Soviet Art), Moscow, 1965

Mstislaw V. Dobujinsky. Plaquette de documentation realisée sous les auspices du Groupe d'amis de l'art de Mstislav V. Dobujinsky, Paris–New York, 1971

G. Chugunov, "Knizhnaya grafika M.V. Dobuzhinskogo. Zarubezhny period: 1925–1957" (Dobuzhinsky's Book Graphics Produced During His Stay Abroad in 1925–57), in: *Kniga. Issledovaniya i materialy* (The Book. Studies and Materials), Moscow, 1972, coll. 24

J.E. Bowlt, "The Early Graphic Work of Mstislav Dobujinsky," in: *Transactions of Russian-American Scholars in U.S.A.*, New York, 1975, vol. 9

Dobuzhinsky Birth Centenary (1875–1975). Exhibition Catalogue. Compiled by A.N. Gusarova et al., Moscow, 1975

E. Polyakova, "Predannost'. K 100-letiyu so dnya rozhdeniya M.V. Dobuzhinskogo" (Devotion. Dobuzhinsky Birth Centenary), *Teatr*, 1975, No. 9

"M. Dobuzhinsky. Iz pisem i dnevnikov" (Excerpts from Letters and Diaries), *Tvorchestvo* (Creative Art), 1976, No. 11

M.V. Dobuzhinsky. Vospominaniya (Recollections). Compiled by R.M., V.M. and V.I. Dobuzhinsky, with a foreword by E. Klimova, New York, 1976

I. Solovyova, "*Mesyats v derevne*. Khudozhestvenny teatr. 1909" (*A Month in the Country* at the Art Theater in 1909), *Teatr*, 1976, No. 7

A. Lupandina, "Dobuzhinsky v teatre" (Dobuzhinsky in the Theater), in: *Sovetskiye khudozhniki teatra i kino '75* (Soviet Stage and Film Designers '75), Moscow, 1977

A. Morov, "M.V. Dobuzhinsky vspominayet...." (Dobuzhinsky Recalls....), in: *Panorama iskusstv '78* (Art Panorama '78), Moscow, 1979

A. Morov, "V Moskovskom Khudozhestvennom: Iz vospominaniy M.V. Dobuzhinskogo" (At the Moscow Art Theater. From Dobuzhinsky's Recollections), *Iskusstvo*, 1979, No. 2

G.I. Chugunov, *Mstislav Valerianovich Dobuzhinsky*, Leningrad, 1984

SERGEI DIAGHILEV (1872–1929)

A. Benois, "Diaghilevskaya vystavka" (Diaghilev's Exhibition), *Posledniye novosti*, 1939, April 8, 15 and 22

S. Lifar, *Serge Diaghilev. His Life. His Work. His Legend*, London, 1940

N. Gontcharova, M. Larionov, P. Vorms, *Les Ballets Russes. Serge Diaghilev et la décoration théâtrale*, Paris, 1955

A. Haskell, W. Nouvel, *Diaghilev. His Artistic and Private Life*, London, 1955

R. Buckle, *In Search of Diaghilev*, London [1955]. Reprint: New York, 1956

M.V. Nesterov, "Odin iz miriskusnikov" (One of the World of Art Members), *Davniye dni* (Long Ago), Moscow, 1959

A.V. Lunacharsky, "Razvlekatel' pozolochennoi tolpy" (Entertainer of the Gilded Crowd), *Vecherniaya Moskva* (Evening Moscow), 1927, July 25. Reprinted in: *O teatre i dramaturgii* (On Theater and Dramaturgy), Moscow, 1958, vol. 2

J. Percival, *The World of Diaghilev*, London, 1974

C. Spencer, *The World of Serge Diaghilev*, London, 1974

Sergei Diaghilev i russkoye iskusstvo: Stat'i, otkrytye pis'ma, intervyu. Perepiska. Sovremenniki o Diaghileve (Sergei Diaghilev and Russian Art: Essays, Open Letters, Interviews. Correspondence. Contemporaries on Diaghilev), 2 vols. compiled, introduced, and commented by I.S. Silberstein, V.A. Samkov et al., Moscow, 1982

BORIS KUSTODIEV (1878–1927)

A. Rostislavov, "B. Kustodiev," *Apollon*, 1910, No. 12

N. Radlov, "Puti k kartine" (Toward the Picture), *Apollon*, 1915, No. 8–9. 1915. Reprinted in: *Ot Repina do Grigoryeva* (From Repin to Grigoryev), Petrograd, 1923

F. Zamyatin, *Rus'. Russkiye tipy B.M. Kustodieva* (Rus. Kustodiev's Russian Types), Petrograd, 1923

A. Bartoshevich, *Kustodiev v teatre* (Kustodiev in the Theater), Leningrad, 1927

I. Grabar, "Boris Mikhailovich Kustodiev," *Krasnaya niva*, 1927, June

E. Gollerbach, *Grafika B.M. Kustodieva* (The Graphics of B.M. Kustodiev), Moscow – Leningrad, 1929

M. Pikulev, *Boris Mikhailovich Kustodiev. 1878–1927*, Moscow, 1951

Kustodiev Exhibition Catalogue, with an introduction by V.P. Knyazeva, Leningrad, 1959

Kustodiev Exhibition Catalogue, with an introduction by T.M. Kovalenskaya, Moscow, 1960

M. Etkind, *Boris Mikhailovich Kustodiev*, Leningrad – Moscow, 1960

V.E. Lebedeva, *Boris Mikhailovich Kustodiev*, Moscow, 1961

T. Savitskaya, *Boris Mikhailovich Kustodiev*, Moscow, 1966

B.M. Kustodiev. Pis'ma. Stat'i, zametki, intervyu. Vstrechi i besedy s Kustodievym (Iz dnevnikov Vs. Voinova). Vospominaniya o khudozhnike (B.M. Kustodiev. Letters, Articles, Notes, Interviews. Encounters and Conversations with Kustodiev: From Vs. Voinov's Diaries. Recollections About the Artist), Leningrad, 1967

V. Lebedeva, *Boris Kustodiev*, Moscow, 1981

Boris Kustodiev. An art book introduced by M.G. Etkind, Moscow, 1982

Boris Kustodiev. Zhivopis'. Risunok. Knizhnaya grafika. Teatralno-dekoratsionnoye iskusstvo (Boris Kustodiev. Painting. Drawing. Book Illustration. Stage Design). Compiled by M.G. Etkind, Leningrad, 1983

EVGENY LANCERAY (1875–1946)

V. Kurbatov, "E.E. Lanceray," *Iskusstvo*, Kiev, 1912, No. 11–12

N. Radlov, "E.E. Lanceray," *Apollon*, 1915, No. 10

A. Rostislavov, "Dekorativny dar E.E. Lansere" (Lanceray's Decorative Talent), *Apollon*, 1915, No. 10

A. Benois, "Lanceray," *Rech*, 1916, March 4

M. Babenchikov, "E.E. Lanceray," *Iskusstvo*, 1935, No. 5

E.E. Lansere. 40 let khudozhestvennoi deyatelnosti (Lanceray. 40 Years as Artist). *Catalogue*, Moscow, 1936

K. Kravchenko, *Evgeny Evgenyevich Lanceray. 1875–1946*, Moscow – Leningrad, 1948

M. Babenchikov, *E.E. Lanceray*, Leningrad, 1949

Evgeny Evgenyevich Lanceray. An art book introduced by N. Shantyko, Moscow, 1952

Lanceray Exhibition Catalogue, with an introduction by N. Mashkovtsev, Moscow, 1961

O.I. Podobedova, *Evgeny Evgenyevich Lanceray. 1875–1946*, Moscow, 1961

Evgeny Evgenyevich Lanceray. An art book with an introduction by O. Podobedova, Moscow, 1964

G. Chakhiryan, "Neizvestnye raboty Lansere" (Unknown Works by Lanceray), *Iskusstvo*, 1969, No. 8

DMITRY MITROKHIN (1883–1973)

A. Mantel, *D. Mitrokhin*. Preface by N. Roerich, Kazan, 1912

V. Voinov, *Knizhnye znaki D.I. Mitrokhina* (The Bookplates of Mitrokhin), Petrograd, 1921

M. Kuzmin, V. Ivanov, *D.I. Mitrokhin*, Moscow, 1922

M. Babenchikov, "Russkiye grafiki. D. Mitrokhin" (Russian Graphic Artists. D. Mitrokhin), *Pechat' i revolutsiya* (Press and Revolution), 1925, book 8

Risunki i graviury D.I. Mitrokhina. 1918–1925 (The Drawings and Engravings of D.I. Mitrokhin. 1918–1925). *Exhibition Catalogue*, Kazan, 1925

K. Tikhonova, *D.I. Mitrokhin. Risunki* (D.I. Mitrokhin. Drawings), Moscow, 1927

M. Babenchikov, "D. Mitrokhin," in: *Mastera sovremennoi graviury i grafiki* (Masters of Contemporary Engraving and Graphics), Moscow – Leningrad, 1928

D.I. Mitrokhin. Graviury reztsom i sukhoi igloi (Engravings in Burin and Dry Point). An art book with an introduction by M.V. Dobroklonsky, Leningrad, 1934

D.I. Mitrokhin. Graviury na dereve (Woodcuts). An art book with an introduction by E.G. Lisenkov, Leningrad, 1934

Yu. Rusakov, *Dmitry Isidorovich Mitrokhin*, Leningrad – Moscow, 1966

Kniga o Mitrokhine (A Book About Mitrokhin). Compiled by L.V. Chaga, Leningrad, 1986

GEORGI NARBUT (1886–1920)

E. Gollerbach, "Grafika Narbuta" (Narbut's Graphics), *Rossiya*, 1922, No. 2

Narbut Exhibition Catalogue, with an introduction by P.I. Neradovsky and A.K. Sokolovsky, Petrograd, 1922

D. Mitrokhin, "Pamyati Narbuta" (Narbut: In Memoriam), *Sredi kollektsionerov*, 1922 No. 9

P. Neradovsky, *G.I. Narbut*, Petrograd, 1922

M. Kuzmin, "Narbut," *Russkoye iskusstvo*, 1923, No. 1

G. Lukomsky, *Egor Narbut. Khudozhnik-grafik* (Egor Narbut, a Graphic Artist), Berlin, 1923

D. Mitrokhin "O Narbute" (About Narbut), *Argonavty*, 1924, No. 1

Pamyati G.I. Narbuta, khudozhnika-grafika i khudozhestvennogo deyatelya (In Memory of G.I. Narbut, Graphic Artist and Art Figure). *Recollections of G.K. Lukomsky, E.F. Gollerbach, and D.I. Mitrokhin*, Berlin, 1923

A.A. Sidorov, "G. Narbut i ego knigi" (Narbut and His Books), *Pechat' i revolutsiya*, 1923, book 5

S. Chekhonin, "Vospominaniya o G.I. Narbute" (Recollections About G.I. Narbut), *Argonavty*, 1923, No. 1

V.K. Okhochinsky, *Knizhnye znaki Georgiya Narbuta* (Georgi Narbut's Bookplates), Leningrad, 1924

E. Gollerbach, *Siluety. G.I. Narbut* (Narbut's Silhouettes), Leningrad, 1926

A.A. Sidorov, "G.I. Narbut," in: *Mastera sovremennoi graviury i grafiki* (Masters of Contemporary Engraving and Graphics), Moscow – Leningrad, 1928

P. Beletsky, *Georgi Ivanovich Narbut*, Kiev, 1959 (in Ukrainian)

P. Beletsky, *Georgi Ivanovich Narbut*, Leningrad, 1986

ANNA OSTROUMOVA-LEBEDEVA (1871–1955)

Exhibition of Woodcuts by A.P. Ostroumova-Lebedeva. Catalogue, with an introduction by N. Romanov, Moscow, 1910

Rosstsiy [A.M. Efros], "A.P. Ostroumova-Lebedeva. Exhibition of Engravings at the Rumyantsev Museum," *Russkiye vedomosti*, 1916, December 8

V.Ya. Adariukov, *A.P. Ostroumova-Lebedeva*, Moscow, 1922

A. Benois, S. Ernst, *Ostroumova-Lebedeva*, Moscow – Petrograd, 1924

Anna Petrovna Ostroumova-Lebedeva. Exhibition Catalogue, with an introduction by P. Kornilov, Kazan, 1928

A.P. Ostroumova-Lebedeva: Avtobiograficheskiye zapiski (Autobiographical Notes), Moscow, 1935, vol. 1; Leningrad – Moscow, 1945, vol. 2; Moscow, 1951, vol. 3. Reprint: Moscow, 1974, 2. vols.

P. Kornilov, *Anna Petrovna Ostroumova-Lebedeva*, Moscow, 1950

Anna Petrovna Ostroumova-Lebedeva. The 80th Birthday. Exhibition Catalogue, Moscow, 1951

N.V. Sinitsyn, *Graviury Ostroumovoi-Lebedevoi* (The Engravings of Ostroumova-Lebedeva), Moscow, 1964

V.A. Suslov, *Anna Petrovna Ostroumova-Lebedeva*, Leningrad, 1967

A.P. Ostroumova-Lebedeva. Graviury na dereve. K 100-letiyu so dnya rozhdeniya (Woodcuts by A.P. Ostroumova-Lebedeva. The Artist's Birth Centenary). Art book, Leningrad, 1971

Peterburg–Leningrad v graviurakh A.P. Ostroumovoi-Lebedevoi (St. Petersburg–Leningrad in Ostroumova-Lebedeva's Engravings). An art book with an introduction by V.A. Suslov and M.I. Flekel, Leningrad, 1973

A.A. Bogdanova, *Anna Petrovna Ostroumova-Lebedeva*, Leningrad, 1976

E.M. Polyakova, *Gorod Ostroumovoi-Lebedevoi* (The City of Ostroumova-Lebedeva), Moscow, 1983

Grafika A.P. Ostroumovoi-Lebedevoi. Graviura i akvarel (A.P. Ostroumova-Lebedeva's Graphic Works. Engravings and Watercolors). An art book compiled and introduced by M.V. Kiseliov, Moscow, 1984

NICHOLAS ROERICH (1874–1947)

S. Makovsky, "N.K. Roerich," *Zolotoye runo*, 1907, No. 4

A. Rostislavov, "Individualizm Roerikha" (Roerich's Individualism), *Zolotoye runo*, 1907, No. 4

N. Belyashevsky, "N.K. Roerich," *V mire iskusstv* (In the World of Art), Kiev, 1908, No. 2–3

A. Benois, "Khudozhestvennye pis'ma. Roerikh na vystavke Salona" (Art Letters. Roerich at the Salon Show), *Rech*, 1909, January 28

A. Benois, "Khudozhestvennye pis'ma. Russkiye spektakli v Parizhe" (Art Letters. Russian Performances in Paris), *Rech*, 1909, June 19

V. Voinov, "Khudozhestvennye pis'ma iz Peterburga" (Art Letters from St. Petersburg), *Studia*, 1911, No. 10

A. Mantel, *N. Roerich*, Kazan, 1912

N.K. Roerich. Sobraniye sochineniy (Collected Works), Moscow, 1914, book 1

A. Digoni, "Tvorchesky put' Roerikha" (Roerich's Creative Career), *Apollon*, 1915, No. 4–5

Roerich. Text by Yu. Baltrushaitis, A. Benois, A. Gidoni, A. Remizov, and S. Yaremich, Petrograd, 1916

A. Rostislavov, "N.K. Roerikh – khudozhestvenny deyatel" (N.K. Roerich as Artist), *Russkaya mysl*, 1916, No. 1

A. Rostislavov, *N.K. Roerich*, Petrograd, 1918

S. Ernst, *N.K. Roerich*, Petrograd, 1918

L. Andreyeva, "Derzhava Roerikha" (Roerich's Realm), *Russkaya zhizn* [Helsingfors], 1919, March

M. Kuzmin, *N. Roerich*, Moscow, 1923

V. Ivanov, *N. Roerikh – khudozhnik i myslitel* (Roerich as Artist and Thinker), Riga, 1937

Exhibition of Works by the Academician of Painting Nicholas Roerich. Catalogue, with an introduction by K. Yuon, Moscow, 1958

N. Dmitriyeva, "Vystavka proizvedeniy N.K. Roerikha" (Roerich Exhibition), *Iskusstvo*, 1958, No. 8

Exhibition of Works by Nicholas Roerich. Catalogue, with an introduction by E. Zhuravliova, Moscow, 1959

Nicholas Konstantinovich Roerich. An art book with an introduction by N. Dmitriyeva, Moscow, 1959

V.P. Knyazeva, *Nicholas Konstantinovich Roerich. 1874–1947*, Leningrad – Moscow, 1963

P. Belikov, "Bibliografiya proizvedeniy N.K. Roerikha" (Bibliography of Roerich's Works), in: *Transactions of Tartu University*, 1968, issue 217

A.D. Aliokhin, *N. Roerich*, Leningrad, 1973

P.P. Belikov, V.P. Knyazeva, *Roerich*, Moscow, 1973 (The *Great Lives* Series)

E.I. Polyakova, Nicholas Roerich, Moscow, 1973 (The *Life in Art* Series)

N.K. Roerich. Iz literaturnogo naslediya: Listy, dnevniki, izbrannye stat'i, pis'ma (From the Literary Legacy: Pages, Diaries, Selected Essays, Letters), Moscow, 1974

N.K. Roerich: Zhizn i tvorchestvo. Sbornik statei (N.K. Roerich: Life and Work. A Collection of Essays), Moscow, 1978

"Perepiska N.K. Roerikha s sovremennikami" (Roerich's Correspondence with Contemporaries), Prepared, introduced, and commented by E. Soini, *Sever*, Petrozavodsk, No. 4

NIKOLAI SAPUNOV (1880–1912)

Posthumous Sapunov Exhibition. Catalogue, Moscow, 1914

N.N. Punin, "N. Sapunov," *Apollon*, 1915, No. 8–9. Reprinted in: *Russkoye i sovetskoye iskusstvo* (Russian and Soviet Art), Moscow, 1976

M. Voloshin, "Pamyati Sapunova" (Sapunov: In Memoriam), in: *To the Memory of N.N. Sapunov*, Petrograd, 1916

F. Komissarzhevsky, "Sapunov-dekorator" (Sapunov as a Decorator), in: *Ibid*

N.N. Punin, "Tri khudozhnika" (Three Artists), in: *Ibid*

V.N. Solovyov, "Vospominaniya o Sapunove" (Recollections About Sapunov), in: *Ibid*

N. Sapunov. Stikhi, vospominaniya, kharakteristiki Valeriya Briusova, M. Kuzmina, P. Potyomkina, F. Komissarzhevskogo, Ya. Tugendholda i A. Efrosa (Verse, Recollections, and Profiles of Valeri Briusov, M. Kuzmin, P. Potyomkin, F. Komissarzhevsky, Ya. Tugendhold, and A. Efros), Moscow, 1916

A. Efros, "Sapunov," in: *Profili* (Profiles), Moscow, 1930

Nikolai Nikolayevich Sapunov (1880–1912). Exhibition Catalogue, with an introduction by E.A. Gunst, Moscow, 1963

M.V. Alpatov, E.A. Gunst, *Nikolai Nikolayevich Sapunov*, Moscow, 1965

ZINAIDA SEREBRYAKOVA (1884–1967)

S. Ernst, *Z.E. Serebryakova*, Petrograd, 1922

Paintings by Z.E. Serebryakova. Exhibition Catalogue, with an introduction by V. Voinov, Leningrad, 1929

N.E. Radlov, *Z.E. Serebryakova*, Moscow, 1929

Exhibition of Works from Museums and Private Collections. Catalogue, with an introduction by A.N. Savinov. Moscow, 1965

E. Dorosh, "Na vystavke Serebryakovoi" (At the Serebryakova Show), *Teatr*, 1965, No. 11

V. Lapshin, "Zinaida Serebryakova," *Iskusstvo*, 1965, No. 11

A.N. Savinov, "Z.E. Serebryakova," in: *Istoriya russkogo iskusstva* (History of Russian Art), 13 vols, Moscow, 1968, vol. 10, part 1

A.N. Savinov, *Zinaida Evgenyevna Serebryakova*, Leningrad, 1973

Zinaida Evgenyevna Serebryakova. Art book, selection and introduction by V. Lapshin, Moscow, 1969

Zinaida Serebryakova. Set of reproductions, Moscow – Leningrad, 1983

VALENTIN SEROV (1865–1911)

V. Briusov, "Valentin Alexandrovich Serov," *Russkaya mysl*, 1911, book 12

Serov Posthumous Exhibition. Catalogue, Moscow, 1914

A. Levinson, *V.A. Serov*, St. Petersburg, 1921

S. Makovsky, "Masterstvo Serova" (Serov's Craftsmanship), *Apollon*, 1912, No. 10

D. Filosofov, "Pamyati Serova" (Serov: in Memoriam), *Staroye i Novoye* (Old and New), Moscow, 1912

V. A. Serov. Solntse Rossii (The Sun of Russia). An art book, St. Petersburg, 1913

I. Grabar, *Valentin Alexandrovich Serov: Zhizn i tvorchestvo* (Valentin Alexandrovich Serov. His Life and Work), Moscow, 1914

V. Dmitriyev, "Oblik Serova" (Serov's Image), *Apollon*, 1914, No. 6–7

M.N. Punin, "V.A. Serov (Po povodu posmertnoi vystavki ego proizvedeniy)" (V.A. Serov. Concerning a Posthumous Exhibition of His Works), *Severnye zapiski* (Northern Notes), 1914, No. 1. Reprinted in *Russkoye i sovetskoye iskusstvo* (Russian and Soviet Art), Moscow, 1976

N. Radlov, *Serov*, St. Petersburg, 1914

N. Radlov, "Tragediya serovskogo tvorchestva: Opyt analiza metodov" (The Tragedy of Serov's Work: Results of the Analysis of His Methods), *Apollon*, 1914, No. 6–7

Rosstsiy [A.M. Efros], "Zametki o Serove. Priroda serovskogo darovaniya" (Comments on Serov. The Nature of Serov's Talent), *Russkiye vedomosti*, 1914, February 18

V. Serova, *The Serovs, Alexander and Valentin*, St. Petersburg, 1914

Valentin Serov, an art book with text by V. Dmitriyev, Petrograd, 1917

S. Ernst, *Serov*, Petrograd, 1921

S. Makovsky, *V. Serov*, Berlin – Paris, 1922

E. Gollerbach, *V. Serov: Zhizn i tvorchestvo* (V. Serov: Life and Work), Petrograd, 1924

B. Ternovetz, *Korovin – Serov*, Moscow, 1925

A.M. Efros, "Serov," in: *Profili* (Profiles), Moscow, 1930

C. Lebedev, *Valentin Serov*, Leningrad – Moscow, 1935

V.A. Serov, Perepiska (Correspondence). *1884–1911,* Leningrad – Moscow, 1937

N. Ulyanov, *Vospominaniya o Serove* (Recollections About Serov), Leningrad – Moscow, 1947

Catalogue Marking the 40th Anniversary of Serov's Death, Moscow, 1953

G.S. Arbuzov, *Serov,* Leningrad – Moscow, 1960

D. Sarabyanov, *Serov,* Leningrad – Moscow, 1961

M. Simonovich-Efimova, *Vospominaniya o Valentine Alexandroviche Serove* (Recollections About Serov), Leningrad, 1964

Serov (1865–1911). Birth Centenary Exhibition Catalogue, Moscow, 1965

I. Grabar, *Valentin Alexandrovich Serov. Zhizn i tvorchestvo. 1885–1911* (Valentin Alexandrovich Serov. His Life and Work. 1885–1911), Moscow, 1965. Reprint: Moscow, 1980

M. Kopshitser, *Valentin Serov,* Moscow, 1967. Reprint: Moscow, 1972

V.S. Serova, *Kak ros moi syn* (How My Son Grew Up), Leningrad, 1968

Valentin Serov v vospominaniyakh, dnevnikakh i perepiske sovremennikov (Valentin Serov in the Reminiscences, Diaries, and Correspondence of Contemporaries), 2 vols., Leningrad, 1972

Valentin Serov, an art book with text by D. Sarabyanov, Leningrad, 1983

KONSTANTIN SOMOV (1869–1939)

A. Benois, "K. Somov," *Mir iskusstva,* 1899, No. 20

Y. Grabar, "Constantin Somoff," *Zeitschrift für bildende Kunst,* 1903, July

O.S. Dymov, "K. Somov," *Zolotoye runo,* 1906, No. 7–9

O. Bie, *Constantin Somoff,* Berlin, 1907

A. Benois, "Khudozhestvennye pis'ma. Somov i Stelletsky" (Art Letters. Somos and Stelletsky), *Rech,* 1909, February 5

A. Benois, "Khudozhestvennye pis'ma" (Art Letters), *Rech,* 1911, January 7

S. Yaremich, "K.A. Somov," *Iskusstvo* [Kiev], 1911, No. 12

V. Dmitriyev, "Konstantin Somov: Opyt istoricheskogo opredeleniya" (Konstantin Somov: An Attempt at a Historical Definition), *Apollon,*1913, No. 9

D. Kuroshev, "Khudozhnik 'radug' i 'potseluyev'" (Artist of 'Rainbows' and 'Kisses'), *Apollon,* 1913, No. 9

S. Ernst, *K.A. Somov,* Petrograd, 1918

M. Kuzmin, "Konstantin Andreyevich Somov," in: *Uslovnosty* (Conventions), Petrograd, 1923

N. Radlov, "K.A. Somov," in: *Ot Repina do Grigoryeva* (From Repin to Grigoryev), Petrograd, 1923

P. Bakchan, "Somoff und sein Erotik," *Kunst und Künstler,* 1914, March

P. Bakchan, "Konstantin Somoff," *Belhagen klassische Monatshefte,* 1924/25, vol. 2

A. Benois, "K. A. Somov," *Posledniye novosti* [Paris], 1939, May 12, 19 and 26

E. Polyakova, "V veke vosemnadtsatom i veke dvadtsatom. Na vystavke rabot K.A. Somova" (In the 18th Century and in the 20th. Somov Exhibition), *Teatr*, 1971, No. 4

Somov Birth Centenary Exhibition. 1970. Catalogue, with an introduction by I.N. Pruzhan, Leningrad, 1971

Konstantin Somov (1869–1934). An art book with an introduction by I.N. Pruzhan, Moscow, 1972

Konstantin Andreyevich Somov. 1869–1939. An art book with an introduction by A.P. Gusarova, Moscow, 1973

Konstantin Andreyevich Somov: Pis'ma. Dnevniki. Suzhdeniya sovremennikov (Konstantin Andreyevich Somov: Letters. Diaries. Comments by Contemporaries). Compiled, introduced, and commented by Yu. N. Podkopayeva and A. N. Sveshnikova, Moscow, 1979

E.V. Zhuravliova, *Konstantin Andreyevich Somov*, Moscow, 1980

SERGEI SUDEIKIN (1884–1946)

S. Makovsky, "S. Sudeikin," *Apollon*, 1911, No. 8

Mantel, "S.Yu. Sudeikin," in: *Zilant sbornik iskusstva* (Zilant Art Anthology), Kazan, 1913

V. Solovyov, "Sergei Yurievich Sudeikin," *Apollon*, 1917, No. 8–10

A. Tolstoy, "Pered kartinami Sudeikina" (Looking at Sudeikin's Pictures), *Zhar-ptitsa*, 1921, No. 1

V. Tatarinov, "Sudeikin v kabare" (Sudeikin in Cabaret), *Zhar-ptitsa*, 1923, No. 12

D. Kogan, *Sergei Yurievich Sudeikin. 1884–1946*, Leningrad, 1974

M. Babenchikov, "Teatr Sergeya Sudeikina. Predisloviye K. Rudnitskogo" (The Theater of Sergei Sudeikin. Preface by K. Rudnitsky), *Dekorativnoye iskusstvo SSSR*, 1975, No. 12

M. Kiseliov, "Zhivopis' S.Yu. Sudeikina: K 100-letiyu so dnya rozhdeniya" (Sudeikin's Painting. The Artist's Birth Centenary), *Iskusstvo*, 1982, No. 2

SERGEI CHEKHONIN (1878–1936)

A. Efros, N. Punin, S. *Chekhonin*, Moscow–Petrograd, 1924

Contents

„Мир искусства"
Объединение русских художников начала XX века

Альбом (на английском языке)

Издательство « Аврора ». Ленинград. 1991
Изд. № 1043. (19-00)
Printed and bound in Finland